The Politics of Abolition R

Originally published in 1974 and the recipient of the Denis Carroll Book Prize at the World Congress of the International Criminology Society in 1978, Thomas Mathiesen's *The Politics of Abolition* is a landmark text in critical criminology. In its examination of Scandinavian penal policy and call for the abolition of prisons, this book was enormously influential across Europe and beyond among criminologists, sociologists and legal scholars as well as advocates of prisoners' rights.

Forty years on and in the context of mass incarceration in many parts of the world, this book remains relevant to a new generation of penal scholars. This new edition includes a new introduction from the author, as well as an afterword that collects contributions from leading criminologists and inmates from Germany, England, Norway and the United States to reflect on the development and current state of the academic literature on penal abolition.

This book will be suitable for academics and students of criminology and sociology, as well as those studying political science. It will also be of great interest to those who read the original book and are looking for new insights into an issue that is still as important and topical today as it was forty years ago.

Thomas Mathiesen earned his Ph.D. in Oslo in 1965 and was a full professor at the University of Oslo from 1972 until 2003. Thomas has been Professor Emeritus since 2003 and has given numerous guest lectures at universities and colleges in Europe, the US and Latin America. Professor Mathiesen was awarded the Denis Carroll Prize in 1978, was given an honorary doctors degree at Lund University in 2003 and was Co-founder of the Norwegian Association of Penal Reform (KROM) in 1968. Thomas is still active in the organization today. Professor Mathiesen has also published a number of books in various languages, including seven books in English, among which are *Silently Silenced* (2004), *Prison on Trial* (3rd ed. 2006) and *Towards a Surveillant Society* (2013).

The Politics of Abolition Revisited

Thomas Mathiesen

Routledge
Taylor & Francis Group

LONDON AND NEW YORK

First published 2015
by Routledge
2 Park Square, Milton Park, Abingdon, Oxfordshire OX14 4RN

Simultaneously published in the USA and Canada
by Routledge
711 Third Avenue, New York, NY 10017

First issued in paperback 2016

Routledge is an imprint of the Taylor & Francis Group, an informa business

British Library Cataloguing in Publication Data

A catalogue record for this book is available from the British Library

Library of Congress Cataloging-in-Publication Data

Mathiesen, Thomas.
  [Politics of abolition]
  The politics of abolition revisited / Thomas Mathiesen.
      pages cm
  Revised edition of the author's The politics of abolition, originally published in 1974.
    Includes bibliographical references.
    1. Prisons—Scandinavia. 2. Prisoners—Scandinavia. 3. Pressure groups—Scandinavia. I. Mathiesen, Thomas. Uferdige. English. 1974. II. Mathiesen, Thomas. Pressgruppe og samfunnsstruktur. English. 1974. III. Title.
    HV9718.M37 2014
    365'.948—dc23
    2014008546

ISBN 13: 978-1-138-68769-1 (pbk)
ISBN 13: 978-1-138-02125-9 (hbk)

Typeset in Times New Roman
by Apex CoVantage, LLC

Contents

Book III. Scholars and prisoners on prisons 247

Images

Contributors

Jane Dullum is a researcher in the Department of Criminology and Sociology of Law at the University of Oslo, Norway. She has done research on prisons, on the decarceration of the mentally ill, on economic crime, restorative justice, topics regarding the rule of law, and miscarriages of justice.

Johannes Feest is Professor Emeritus of Criminal Law and Criminology at the University of Bremen. He has been in correspondence with prisoners in Germany for the last 40 years. His publications include an empirical study of prisoners' litigation and a handbook on German prison law.

Hedda Giertsen is Professor of Criminology in the Department of Criminology and Sociology of Law, University of Oslo. Professor Giertsen has worked on prisons and prison policy, violence, and drug policy and is currently part of a Nordic project on rehabilitation measures for drug users in prison. Her contribution to this book includes notes on abolitionism and prison reform, based on Norwegian experiences.

Yvonne Jewkes is Professor of Criminology in the University of Leicester. She is currently conducting a three-year ESRC-funded study of prison architecture, design and technology in Europe with Dominique Moran, University of Birmingham (prisonspaces.com).

James Kilgore is a Research Scholar at the Center for African Studies at the University of Illinois (Urbana-Champaign). He is the author of three novels: *We Are All Zimbabweans Now*, *Freedom Never Rests* and *Prudence Couldn't Swim*, all of which were drafted during his six and a half years in prison. He writes frequently on issues of criminal justice and the rights of the formerly incarcerated.

Thomas Mathiesen earned his Ph.D. in Oslo in 1965 and was a full professor at the University of Oslo from 1972 until 2003. Thomas has been Professor Emeritus since 2003 and has given numerous guest lectures at universities and colleges in Europe, the US and Latin America. Professor Mathiesen was awarded the Denis Carroll Prize in 1978, was given an honorary doctors degree at Lund University in 2003 and was Co-founder of the Norwegian Association of Penal

Reform (KROM) in 1968. Thomas is still active in the organization today. Professor Mathiesen has also published a number of books in various languages, including seven books in English, among which are *Silently Silenced* (2004), *Prison on Trial* (3rd ed 2006) and *Towards a Surveillant Society* (2013).

Knut Papendorf is a Professor in the Department for Criminology and the Sociology of Law, University of Oslo, Norway. His special research interest is in criminal policy, sociology of law and control politics.

Keramet Reiter is an Assistant Professor in the Department of Criminology, Law & Society and at the School of Law at the University of California, Irvine. In addition to her university teaching, she has taught in high school and college education programs in jails and prisons in Massachusetts, New York, and California. She is currently working on a book project on the history and uses of U.S. supermax prisons, where people are in long-term solitary confinement.

Vincenzo Ruggiero is Professor of Sociology and director of the 'Crime and Conflict Research Centre' at Middlesex University in London. His most recent books are *Penal Abolitionism* (2010), *Corruption and Organised Crime* (2012), *Punishment in Europe* (2013) and *The Crimes of the Economy* (2013).

Preface – 'The Politics of Abolition' 1974

In this book I have collected three series of essays on political action theory. The word 'essay' is used advisedly, in order to indicate that the articles are not meant as finished products. Rather, they are meant as working papers which I – and hopefully others – will follow up later.

For this reason, the connection between the essays is fairly loose, and they may well be read separately. Yet, there is a certain relationship between them: they all discuss aspects of political work geared towards what I call 'abolition' of a repressive social system or a part of such a system.

Part I contains two essays in which these issues are discussed from a general theoretical and methodological point of view. The discussions in these essays are fairly abstract.

Part II contains three related essays which make matters more concrete: they describe and analyse the development of certain Scandinavian pressure groups in the field of criminal policy – KRUM in Sweden, KRIM in Demark and KROM in Norway. Particular emphasis is placed on the Norwegian organization, as an illustrative case.

Part III contains two further essays, the first of which follows up Part II with a detailed description and analysis of prison strikes in Sweden and Norway, and of a series of so-called negotiations between prisoners and prison authorities in Sweden. While Part II describes pressure group organizations outside the prison walls, the first essay in Part III analyses the attempts of the prisoners themselves to organize. The final essay in Part III, which is the concluding essay of the book, returns to some fundamental theoretical aspects of the politics of abolition.

In addition, the book contains a postscript on the development among Swedish prisoners which in part occurred after the main essays were completed. All of the essays are translated [by me] and compiled from two Norwegian books *Det uferdige* ('The Unfinished') and *Pressgruppe og samfunnstruktur* ('Pressure Group and Social Structure') respectively [published in the Norwegian language in 1971 and 1973 by *Pax Publishers* in Norway.]

The essays take a definite stand as regards current penal policy in Scandinavia. They are based on the view that our penal policy to a large extent involves an unreasonable and unjust handling of expelled groups in society – a handling which should in considerable measure be abolished. The major bulk of the essays – all of Part II and the first essay in Part III – are written with a view to transmitting the Scandinavian experiences in trying to reach this long-term goal. In large measure, these particular essays are written with an audience of prisoners – and others who are willing to aid the prisoners' struggle – in mind. It is my hope that our experiences, errors and moderate successes, may be useful to others sharing out aims.

The essays are in large measure based on active personal participation in the political experiences which are described: as chairman and board member of Norwegian KROM from its foundation till today [1973], and as a frequent participant in the activities of Swedish KRUM. Thus, politics and research – which are traditionally kept apart – are here blended. I believe the blending constitutes an important new role for the radical social scientist, and in the essay entitled 'On Action Research' I discuss it in some detail.

Oslo, June 1973
Thomas Mathiesen

Preface – 'The Politics of Abolition Revisited' 2014

The Politics of Abolition was first published in 1974 by Universitetsforlaget in Norway and Martin Robertson Publishers in Great Britain. Martin Robertson has since ceased to exist, and Universitetsforlaget has waived their copyright to the book.

When it appeared 40 years ago, the book created quite a stir among young criminologists and other social scientists of the time. The time, with increased political radicalism (but largely not the violent radicalism of today) in the West in the 1970s, the Cold War and other features, was very different from today.

The Western revolt in 1968 with its aftermath had occurred and radicalized several generations of young people. That radicalism was behind much of the creation of KRUM, KRIM and KROM in Scandinavia and similar pressure groups in Germany and England – even criminals had to have decent lives and human rights. But the sudden (as seen by many of us) fall of the whole Soviet Empire in 1989 onwards, the later downfall of the economy of parts of Europe and the USA, the developments in China which made that country into a world power, the reduction of European radicalism and the advent of modern terrorism, as well as the 'new society' emerging from the Internet and the numberless digital inventions during the beginning of the 2000s – they were all in the future. Indeed, some of these occurrences, such as the sudden fall of the Soviet empire and the fantastic changes following from the advent of the Internet and digitalism, were inconceivable to many back in 1968.

Yet, there are also similarities, especially relevant to the contents of this book. To some extent, things have improved – education of officers in our prisons is more advanced and covers almost all officers (the term 'officer' has military roots, and is actually not used in Scandinavia; the Norwegian 'betjent' is, according to Wikipedia, one who keeps order or provides a service within a territory or an area), teaching facilities for prisoners have improved (at least in Scandinavia), and important reforms took place in the 1970s and 1980s. But to a large extent things have become worse, also in Scandinavia and certainly on a world basis, in particular with the increased repression of poverty-stricken people like that which took place in the times past, and with what is today called *mass incarceration* in Western countries, which brings to mind resemblances with our own brutish past.

I felt that now, in 2014, it might be of some importance for the young and the old to read and contemplate *The Politics of Abolition* anew. I had the book re-published, now under the title *The Politics of Abolition Revisited.*

The original *The Politics of Abolition,* very briefly described in the Preface from 1973, is still the core of the book and is reprinted almost verbatim – I have only added a few very short explanatory footnotes here and there, and resisted the temptation to revise. I decided on the verbatim re-publication several years ago, when I began thinking about a new edition. The verbatim re-publication would, I thought, make us consider (with hind-sight) both errors and successes of the past, why we did things which we decided for, and why we did not do other things which we decided against.

But there are also other and new aspects to the book, which make the title of the present volume – The Politics of Abolition *Revisited* – natural.

Firstly, in the very beginning of the book, I have added a lengthy Introduction to it. Instead of a better word, I have called it 'Book I'. I have not contextualized the story of KROM in the whole sequence of international events briefly listed above – an attempt to do so would have led to a new volume which might go beyond my powers and not a revisited old book. Besides, I think it is also partly the concrete, you might say ethnographic description or account of the movement which is valuable today with respect to comparisons with the present.

The Introduction or Book I, furthermore, contains two parts. *Part I* is called "About KROM – The Starting Point", which mainly relates parts of the story of KROM's (The Norwegian Association of Penal Reform's) history and development after 1974 and after the original book was published until the present, and which is largely written for political activists. *Part II* is entitled "Five Major Theoretical Issues" and discusses five broad problems of strategy which have been with me (and, I believe, with KROM) for a long time, and which are more in line with some peoples' more theoretical interests. The five major theoretical issues are called "A Revisit to 'The Unfinished'", "Long term and short term goals"; "Alternative public space"; "The abolitionist stance"; and "Beyond abolition?". I am sorry that political activism and theoretical interests here are separated. My notion is that they should actually merge.

Then comes the whole old book. Again for the sake of a better word, I have called it 'Book II'. It contains three major Parts, which are listed in the preface to the old volume from 1974. Finally, at the very end of the book, I have added a number of short essays written by other scholars in the field of prisons and by prison inmates. It is called 'Book III'. The essays in Book III largely reflect on various topics in or related to *The Politics of Abolition Revisited.* Some of the writers think that abolition is at least partly a possibility, others think that it is virtually impossible. Some think the theory behind it is theoretically sound and interesting; others, perhaps, in some respects find it unsatisfactory. But all grapple in a constructive way with aspects and problems dealt with in the work as a whole, which is why I have brought them in as important.

Oslo, March 2014
Thomas Mathiesen

Acknowledgements

I wish to thank Norwegian KROM and Swedish KRUM for permission to utilize our common experiences in written form. Furthermore, I wish to thank the delegates of the Swedish prisoners and the delegates of the Swedish prison authorities for permission to sit in as an observer at one of the rounds of so-called negotiations between prisoners and prison authorities in Sweden. Also, I wish to thank the delegates of the Swedish prisoners for permission to utilize observations I made in my role as advisor to their delegation in a later round of negotiations (see Postscript).

Finally, I wish to thank friends and colleagues in Swedish KRUM, Danish KRIM and Norwegian KROM – prisoners, ex-prisoners and non-prisoners – for our co-operation in the endeavor to fight the repressive criminal policy of today's society.

Oslo, June 1973

Thomas Mathiesen

Again, I wish to thank Norwegian KROM, and Swedish KRUM during the period it existed, for permission to utilize our common experiences in written form. I wish to thank the delegates of the Swedish prisoners, back in the early 1970s, for permission to utilize observations I made in my role as advisor to their delegation in a later round of negotiations (see Postscript). I wish to thank friends and colleagues in Swedish KRUM, Danish KRIM, and Norwegian KROM – prisoners, ex-prisoners and non-prisoners – for our co-operation in the endeavor to fight the repressive criminal policy of today's society. Finally, I wish to thank staff members at the Department of Criminology and Sociology of Law at the University of Oslo for inspiration and advice during my work with this book. Particular thanks go to research consultant Per Jørgen Ystehede, who performed important tasks during the initial phase of my work.

I would also like to thank Astrid Renland, Turid Eikvam and Per Jørgen Ystehede for allowing me to use their images in the book.

I acknowledge permissions to publish and, when necessary, to translate:

- From widow Ruth Eriksson an excerpt from the deceased author Jörgen Eriksson's book *Revolt i huvet. Anarkistisk journal* (Revolt in the Head. Anarchist journal), Bonnier 1970 pp. 100–101, here entitled "Organization of the Expelled".
- From *CounterPunch* the essay by James Kilgore: "The Strange Politics of Prisons in America", *CounterPunch*, November 2013 Vol. 20 No. 11, pp. 10–14.
- From *Prisoners on Prisons* (JPP) the article by Thomas Mathiesen: "The Abolitionist Stance", *Prisoners on Prisons* 2008 Vol. 17 No. 2, pp. 58–63.
- From Norwegian *Pax Publishers* the books *Det uferdige* (The Unfinished), Pax Forlag 1971, and *Pressgruppe og samfunnsstruktur* (Pressure Group and Social Structure), Pax Forlag 1973. Universitetsforlaget (The Norwegian Universities Press) has had copyright but has waived their rights to future editions of *The Politics of Abolition* 1974.
- From *KROM – The Norwegian Association for Penal Reform* of Lars' essay "Skrivepulter og moderne fangebehadling" (Desks and Modern Treatment of Prisoners), *KROM-nytt* No. 2/3 1992, pp. 143–148.
- From Norwegian *Pax Publishers* excerpts of Monrad's essay "Femten år for vold" (Fifteen Years for Violence), in Anne Marit Thorsrud (ed.) *Fangeliv* (Prison Life), pp. 19–36.

Every effort has been made to contact copyright-holders. Please advise the publisher of any errors or omissions, and these will be corrected in subsequent editions.

Oslo, March 2014

Thomas Mathiesen

Image 1.1 Professor Thomas Mathiesen 2013. Photo: Astrid Renland

Book I

Introduction: *The Politics of Abolition Revisited*

The present text is written as a fresh introduction to the second edition of my book *The Politics of Abolition*, which first appeared in 1974 in English with the Norwegian Universities Press and Robert Martinson Publishers in the UK. The first edition was a translation and revision of two Norwegian books which appeared in the early 1970s – *Det uferdige* (The Unfinished) with Norwegian Pax Forlag in 1971 and *Pressgruppe og samfunnsstruktur* (Pressure Group and Social Structure) with the same publisher in 1973. The first of the two Norwegian books also appeared in Swedish and Danish, and a combination of the two appeared in English as *The Politics of Abolition*.

For historical reasons, and above all because I believe the original English text contains some important principles which might be lost or made less clear-cut if I were to revise the text now, I have kept the text as it was at the time it was published. Therefore the whole text from *The Politics of Abolition* is kept as it was in 1974. But the present comprehensive Introduction is updated as of 2013 and includes several important amplifications and revisions of the original text. So do the short essays at the end of this book.

Several topics, especially in the US, were not as relevant when the book was published in 1974 as they are today. This especially concerns *gender* and '*race*' in prisons. Today gender is relevant in that the questions of women's rights and related issues come up also in criminological discussions and in prison studies. Carol Smart's classic book from 1976, *Women, Crime and Criminology*, is a case in point (Smart 1976). Women's incarceration rates have increased more quickly than men's during the twenty years after 1980 (Western 2006 p. 15). But the rates for women in Western countries remain low compared to the rates for men, though there are increases due to women's involvement in drug traffic. *Probation Journal* has recently published a study of "'What works' with Women Offenders: The Past 30 years" (*Probation Journal* 2009). About 'race', David Scott tells us that

> Whilst more than 1 in 100 American adults are in prison, the figure is 1 in 50 for Hispanic men and 1 in 20 for black men. The overall penal incarceration rate for men in the USA is 943 per 100,000. When analysed via categorisations of 'race', the rate falls to 487 for white men but rises to 1,261 for Hispanic and Latino men and 3,042 for black men (Lacey, 2011). African Americans make up 13 per cent of the general population but 60 per cent of the US prison population. . . . The centrality of class should not be forgotten here. . . .
>
> (Scott 2013 p. 4)

Scott also reminds us that in other Anglophone countries we can find relevant evidence. In New Zealand in the 1960s the prisoner ADP was around 1,700 and remained relatively stable until the mid 1980s; but from then on the prisoner rate rose from 80 per 100,000 to 126 per 100,000 in 1996, and further to 199 per 100,000 in 2010. Scott goes on to say, "through the lens of 'race', disturbing patterns emerge" (p. 4). For example, Maori men constitute 15 % of the national population but account for 51 % of the male prisoner population.

Moving now to *the first part* of this Introduction, which consists of a revision and amplification of a mimeographed but never published paper called "About KROM. Past – Present – Future" (Mathiesen 1990/2000). It is relatively concrete and descriptive, as a kind of guide to others who wish to learn more about the organization KROM – The Norwegian Association of Penal Reform – which was the starting point for the original book *The Politics of Abolition.*

A second part of this Introduction deals in some detail with five important – you could perhaps say basic – theoretical issues which I have toyed with through the years within the realm of the politics of abolition.

- The first of these theoretical issues is the theory of 'the unfinished', which is central to this book as a whole.
- The second of the theoretical issues concerns the general relationship between major structural change and more detailed improvements of the *status quo*, or, if you like, the relationship between revolution and reform. It is a thorny issue.
- The third issue concerns the development of an 'alternative public space', and is based on remarks I have made several places on alternatives to the television- and Internet-based public arenas of today.
- The fourth issue is contained in a paper I called "The Abolitionist Stance", which is a paper I gave at the conference *Creating a scandal – prison abolition and the policy agenda,* ICOPA XII – International Conference on Penal Abolition, Kings College (Waterloo Campus) 23 July 2008. The paper was subsequently published in several places, first in *Journal of Prisoners on Prisons,* Vol. 17 Number 2, 2008, pp. 58–63, and also presented in a revised form in honour of the late Professor Louk Hulsman at a conference at the University of Padova, Italy, on 25 March 2010. Originally it was a professional communication geared towards two German scholars, Johannnes Feest and Bettina Paul (Feest and Paul 2008 a).
- The fifth issue concerns the question of what comes after the abolition of prisons (or of most, many, some, parts of) prisons. We are certainly not there at the moment, so what I have to say about this will be brief and sketchy.

The *Politics of Abolition* has also been translated into German: Thomas Mathiesen: *Uberwindet die Mauern! Die skandinavische Gefangenenbewegung als Modell politischer Randgruppenarbeit,* translated by Knut Papendorf with an introduction by Karl Schumann, 1 ed. Luchterhand Verlag 1979, 2 ed. AJZ Verlag 1993.

Part I

About KROM – the starting point

The late 1960s

The late 1960s was a turbulent political period.

The United States was in the middle of a long-drawn war in Vietnam. Protests were mounting against the war. The protests reached far beyond the United States, for example to Europe, and to Scandinavia as the northernmost part of our peninsula.

Because of the war, and for other reasons which go beyond the scope of this paper, generalized political protests against established institutional arrangements were mounting in various parts of society, including the universities. This was the time of the student revolts. The protests were, of course, distinctly leftist. Whereas today the Left tries to defend existing welfare state arrangements as best it can, the so-called welfare state was at that time under offensive attack from the Left – for the clientization and marginalization of significant parts of the population. And the prisons were under attack.

This was the context of the development of the Scandinavian prison movements – called KRUM in Sweden (established in 1966), KRIM in Denmark (established in 1967) and KROM in Norway (established in 1968). KRUM was an abbreviation of **Krim**inalvårdens **Hum**anisering, KRIM had to do with **Crime** and KROM – well, it resembled the other two names and was adopted for that reason, but it actually had no specific meaning. Inadvertently this particular point caused some interest among local journalists. There were also similar developments in Finland.

Despite the mounting Cold War and the Soviet colonization of several Eastern European states, the context was one of political enthusiasm and optimistic belief in the future. The Swedish organization ceased to exist towards the end of the 1970s; we will return to the downfall of Swedish KRUM a little later in this Introduction (see also Mathiesen 1992). But Swedish KRUM started it all with a major and most dramatic national meeting in the city of Strömsund in Sweden in 1966, called 'The Parliament of Thieves'. At The Parliament of Thieves, prisoners and ex-prisoners for the first time in Scandinavian (and perhaps in international) history in large numbers and openly told the audience and the press what prison life was like.

I took part in the development of Norwegian KROM, and remember well the optimism. In 1969 I once flew over England and parts of the continent on my way from London to Strasbourg. It was the time when the planes still flew fairly low, so you could see something. And gazing out over the European landscape, I remember I was pondering what I at the time thought was a fact – that I, in my lifetime, would experience a society without prisons, or at least virtually without prisons.

Things developed differently

We know now that things developed differently. The meeting of the so-called European Group for the Study of Deviance and Social Control in Hamburg in 1985 was devoted to the worrying increase in prison figures which then was in the making.

The European Group was at that time 12 years old. It had been founded in Florence back in 1973 – in fact on 11 September of that year, the day when the president of Chile, the socialist Salvador Allende, was murdered during a coup d'état led by the Chilean general Augusto Pinochet. Earlier in 1973 Pinochet had been appointed Commander in Chief of the country by Allende. Now he took over. The news about the assassination of Allende became world news. I and some other Norwegians were at the founding Florence meeting of the Group in 1973. We represented KROM – The Norwegian Association for Penal Reform, only 5 years old at the time and in its early formative years. Within hours there were allegedly 40,000 communists loudly demonstrating in the streets of Florence. I don't know where the press got the figure from; perhaps there were fewer. At any rate they were many, and it all made a profound and lasting impact on the European Group in the making and on the Norwegian participants. Norwegian KROM was radicalized and evolved as a truly political organization; it may have developed differently if it had not been for this world-shaking event.

At the Hamburg meeting in 1985 the prison development was reported to the European Group by Bill Rolston and Mike Thomlinson. A little later their book was published – *The Expansion of European Prison Systems* (Rolston and Thomlinson 1986). To my knowledge it was the first time the worrying prison increase was reported in book form in Europe.

More than worrying

In 1990 the development was more than worrying, and I characterized it then in the following words: "We can look back and ascertain that prisons are thriving more than ever, and that in the Western world prison figures are – with a few exceptions – mounting to unprecedented heights" (Mathiesen 1990). Today, towards the year 2015, this is more the case than ever (Christie 2000; Scott 2013).

There are of course some variations: In 1970 the United States had 166 prisoners per 100,000 inhabitants, at that time the highest of twelve Westernized countries (Australia and New Zealand included). Finland was the second highest, with 113 prisoners per 100,000 inhabitants. All the other countries had fewer than 100 prisoners per 100,000, the lowest being the Netherlands with 21 prisoners per 100,000, Spain being the second lowest with 38 per 100,000 and Norway the third lowest with 44 per 100,000. David Scott has assembled these data in the recently published book *Why Prison?* (Scott 2013). Modes of statistical approaches of course vary, but I believe the general tendency can be trusted.

Today (Scott brings us to 2010) the United States is still by far the leading country, with 748 per 100,000 inhabitants. The figure does not include wives, husbands and children and other relatives of prisoners, who certainly are under the control of the so-called criminal justice system. The United States is now often called a society of 'mass incarceration'. Finland has been going down to 59 prisoners per 100,000 population. Legal changes and a willingness of the criminal justice leadership to go against the high figures are probably responsible. It shows that increase is not automatic and that figures may in fact be reversed. *All other Westernized countries dealt with here* have shown varying degrees of increase (except possibly Germany, which shows relative stability over the years). In 2010, six of the twelve countries had over 100 prisoners per 100,000 population; five of the six had over 133 prisoners per 100,000 inhabitants. Norway had a growth of the inmate population from 44 per 100,000 in 1970 to 73 per 100,000 in 2010. The growth is smaller than in other countries, but we are on the way. Details concerning the development in the twelve countries are shown in Scott's Table 1.1 (p. 3).

Prisons have to do with crime. But the mounting figures in a majority of Westernized countries cannot simply be explained by increasing crime rates. This has been convincingly shown by Nils Christie, who has compared trends in a number of other countries which indicate that other factors are certainly also relevant (Christie 2000). The increase in the twelve countries may be explained by a complex of societal factors, including the anxiety level of society, the criminalization of – and thereby a political standpoint to – new groups of crimes (such as, in my country of Norway, drug-related offences) and certainly the increasing use of longer sentences for important categories (such as, again in my country, drug-related offences).

Interestingly, in several countries such as Great Britain and Norway, the registered crime rate has with some exceptions recently been going *down,* while the prisoner rate has been going *up.* This suggests the possibility that prison sentences have become longer, followed by a slower circulation of prisoners behind the walls – and an increasing prisoner rate. This is at least a hypothesis which could be taken as a point of departure.

Like spitting against the wind?

The explosive development of prison systems throughout the Western world is often taken to signify the uselessness of prison protests and struggles in the West. Is it not like spitting against the wind?

I go strongly against such a signification. Would the conclusion of uselessness of protest and struggle against fascism have been sensible during the major period of fascist growth in the earlier part of the 1900s (or for that matter today)? Would the conclusion of uselessness of protest and struggle against the threat of atomic war have been sensible during the major period of escalation of nuclear arms? The question of the size of prison populations is not a matter of classification of prisoners and simple bureaucratic practices, but a question of values and morality, and values and morality are different in various societies. The Scandinavian countries, which are thought to be exceptional in having low numbers of prisoner per capita (Pratt and Eriksson 2013) have, I think, values and morality which are different from say the United States, which ranks exceptionally high in terms of the number of prisoner per capita. This, at least, is one important factor.

I venture another hypothesis: countries where studies show a high degree of *confidence or trust* in other people and in public institutions are less prone to institute harsh penal measures and long prison sentences. Norway is a "high trust" country (Wollebæk *et al.* 2011, 2012 a, 2012b), and punishment scales are in fact more moderate than in most other Western countries. Central and Eastern European countries rank lower in terms of trust – trust in others, in foreigners, in institutions. The United States ranks lowest in terms of trust (Wollebæk *et al.* 2011, p. 9). It also has the least moderate punishment scales and the highest number of prisoner per capita in the West. To be sure, this may be changing due to a changing world: The EEA (European Economic Area) accord and Schengen agreement in Europe have opened up for freer movements of people between a majority of European states, and therefore also a greater degree of hostility and even fear of foreigners and foreign cultures in, for example, Norway than we have seen so far (about the EEA accord and especially the Schengen agreement, see Mathiesen 2013). But there are many NGOs and other organizations which operate to increase trust. We should nurture the latter, though of course not nurture naiveté.

I think it is important to stress the psychology or definition of the situation saying that when problems are escalating, there is more reason than ever to protest. I believe that the emphasis on such a definition of the situation among those of us who have participated through the years partly explains why Norwegian KROM has survived the 1980s and 1990s, despite the fact that both decades were politically rather dark in Norway and elsewhere. In view of the fact that so many independent non-government political organizations from the late 1960s, on the other hand, have disappeared, KROM's survival actually represents an interesting case. I will touch on other partial explanations for it in later parts of this Introduction.

And maybe, just maybe, we see some signs of a culmination of the curve? Very recent developments in Sweden may be a sign: Swedish prison figures have in fact decreased by 25 % during the past decade. In 2004 Sweden had 5,722 prisoners behind bars. For Sweden this was a top year: by 2013 the number had decreased to 4,377 prisoners. The only category which increased a little during the decade was the category for those with the longest sentences (with 14 years imprisonment or more, or a life sentence). This category had increased from 161 to 266 prisoners through the decade. All other categories had decreased. The decrease was just about evenly distributed between those with short sentences (up to 1 year) and those with longer sentences (more than 1 year, up to 14 years). The decrease was mostly for national Swedes; it applied to a much lesser degree for foreigners. One reason for the decrease seems to be that short-term sentences are supplanted by treatment in the community and various other societal measures. They are cheaper. Also, long-term sentences for drug cases seem to have gone down, perhaps due to signals from the Supreme Court to other courts not to stick automatically to 'sentencing guidelines' in the form of tables showing quantity of drugs, but rather to place an emphasis on other conditions. The conservative government of Sweden may, incidentally, go against this trend, and that may be reflected in election results in 2014. In any case, the number of prisoners has gone significantly down in recent years. To an abolitionist, such information provides a hope for a turning point in terms of trends. It should be noted that the Swedish case has become worldwide news.[1]

Let me now move on to provide a brief history of KROM, a brief account of the organization's activities today, and some remarks on the question of strategies as we are approaching 2015 – which may well differ from those of the earlier decades.

History

As mentioned already, KROM was founded in 1968. Five major ideas, or sets of ideas, guided its early development.

Five sets of ideas

First, there was a pent-up dissatisfaction, and a wish to do something with 'the prison situation', among a number of intellectuals and socially oriented practitioners in Norway, such as social scientists, lawyers, some authors and quite a few social workers. The feeling was that prisons were inhumane, and did not work according to plan.

Second, the notion of involving the grass roots, that is, the prisoners themselves, in political action was central. The prisoners were to be brought into the organization as active participants. In this respect, KROM was a child of its time. The importance of involving the grass roots in political work was generally widespread and strong. But the involvement of prisoners was certainly a novelty, and caused great alarm and major write-ups in the mass media at the time.

Third, there was a strong emphasis on the abolition of prisons. This emphasis was not there in the very beginning. At the very beginning KROM emphasized prison reform with a change towards treatment. But this was, to repeat, 1968, and the treatment ideology in the penal context was moving rapidly towards its end. And KROM changed accordingly, emphasizing abolition instead. This also, I might add, created alarm and sensation in the mass media of the time.

I think it is fair to add also a fourth idea or set of ideas. Those of us who worked in KROM at the time viewed political work as a learning experience and felt that the learning experience was a part of the goal itself. Certainly, more substantial goals were also emphasized, and I will return to them shortly. But the notion of a learning experience as part of the goal was important. For one thing, it made even mistakes and set-backs – of which there were certainly many in the early phase – important and useful. Mistakes and set-backs were not wasted time, but something to scrutinize and use. For another, the notion made us patient. When mistakes and set-backs were not wasted time, it became possible to take the time to go through the mistakes and set-backs. For a third, it made us conceptualize and view political work of this kind as unfinished business. The notion of an unfinished movement became so important that I sat down and wrote a book about it, which became the Norwegian version of *The Unfinished* (see above). Finally, it made it possible for some of us – those of us who were researchers – to define our engagement in the organization as 'action research', and to see it as a part of our research activity during 'working hours'. Let me emphasize that the concept and idea of action research was taken very seriously. We systematized our learning experiences, sifted principles of strategy and tactics from them and published them in article or book form. To some of us, participation in KROM is still action research, in that it provides indispensable documentation of a wide range of practices and policies in penal policy as well as a continual learning experience concerning policy-making.

But these four sets of ideas, though important, could not explain the *advent* of KROM and the other Scandinavian/Nordic prison movements. Though they in an important way explained *inter alia* the anger and consternation, they could not explain why the KROM activity (and especially the Swedish activity, which was the first to occur) *occurred in the first place.* I venture the following explanation, which does not fully explain what happened but at least made the following probable. A fifth and final set of ideas was this: Scandinavia and the Nordic countries in general had, at the time when KROM and the other prison movements suddenly surfaced, gone far in the direction of becoming so-called welfare states. After the end of World War II, in 1945, the so-called welfare states were blossoming in the Scandinavian countries and in other Nordic countries. The typical saying in Sweden, Norway and Denmark was that everybody was being 'taken care of' by the welfare state. Actually, poverty existed, and groups of the population were in acute need of support. But they were hidden or forgotten, at least for a while. Except the prisoners. Though not really true, the prisoners were at the end of the 1960s presumably the only group in drastic need of help. They were seen as such by many of those who worked for them. I remember several occasions on which it was vehemently stated that the prisoners were *left behind* the general development.[2]

One occurrence comes to mind. The Norwegian social democratic Minister of Justice once (in the early 1970s) gave a public talk on the plight and needs of prisoners. The speech was openly and extremely negative and primitive. Prisoners were the scum of the earth. Several people – social democrats – in the audience were outraged, and during the intermission 'the grand old man' of the Labour Party, Einar Gerhardsen, stood up and moved from his table to another table where a well known ex-inmate was sitting, engaging him in a conversation. The grand old man's movement was highly symbolic, and the next morning the news about it was sympathetically carried with pictures and large capital letters in a large liberal newspaper. The times had changed; the welfare state had symbolically landed at the table of a prisoner. The Labour Party won the next election, and one of Norway's most liberal Ministers of Justice ever was installed and stayed in office from 1973 to 1979.

At about the same time, Sweden and Denmark also saw unusually liberal Ministers of Justice. The Swedish Minister of Justice advocated 400 prisoners for Sweden. At the time, Sweden had about 5,000 of them behind walls or fences. The time had come to the prisoners.

Looking back, we know that many new groups in need of help and support (notably the aged, a large group) after a while appeared on the scene, so to speak competing with the prisoners. This dramatically changed the situation.

Activities today

The level of activity in KROM has certainly varied over the years. The late 1960s and good parts of the 1970s were periods of great activity, involving a fairly large number of people. The level of activity in the 1980s was clearly lower. At times, very few people were active. I think this was related to the level of political participation in general in Norwegian society, which probably went down.

But there has always been some activity, which is of crucial importance. There has always been someone who has been doing something. And some people have been active for a very long time. These features, in addition to a certain degree of patience during periods of relative inactivity or latency, have kept a kind of continuity in the organization and helped it survive.

Let me single out some of the activities in KROM today.

Three-day conferences

In the first place, of primary importance are our three-day conferences in penal policy. They take place once a year. Between 1968 and 2013, there have been organized 42 such conferences. Their continuity is important: in the public space concerned with penal policy, the conferences have become an 'institution' – in a positive sense of the word. With a few exceptions, the conferences have also been held at the same place – a particular mountain resort, and in the same month of the year – today in early January (during the early years after summer vacation, in September). This has also helped to 'institutionalize' the conferences, again in a positive sense of the word. The 'Spåtind Conference' as it has been called (during the last couple of years it has been called the 'Storefjell Conference', due to a change of mountain resort) among the interested public, has become a concept.

Image 1.2 KROM panel at the 40th anniversary of the European Group for the Study of Deviance and Social Control held in Oslo, Fall of 2013. Photo: Astrid Renland

At the conferences, general themes of central importance to penal policy are discussed. The conferences have regularly had between 100 and 200 participants; in 2012 it had about 160 participants, in 2013 about 120; in 2014 between 130 and 140. For Norway, these are large figures. The participants come from a very wide range of institutions and professions related to penal policy – social workers, lawyers, criminologists, social scientists, members of various interested organizations as well as people from the Ministry of Justice and the prison system. In the early years the Ministry openly refused to participate, a fact which was severely criticized in the newspapers. Today representatives come as a matter of course. In addition, a fairly large number of prisoners today receive furloughs to participate. Regularly, at least 15 % of the participants are inmates. The debates are hot, and are meant to be hot. The mix of people and professions, and the meeting and clash between top and bottom in the prison system, make the conferences unique in the Norwegian setting, and perhaps internationally. Many participants seem to feel that the conferences 'recharge their critical batteries'. This is an important goal in itself.

Seminars

So much about the large conferences. Second, during the 1970s and 1980s, KROM organized a large number of public meetings, especially in the capital city of Oslo. In the 1970s, in the wake of the turbulent late 1960s, the meetings were very large, regularly with 300–400 participants. We called them 'teach-ins'. During the 1980s the public meetings became smaller, in line with the general political development. In the 1990s we relied more on fairly large evening seminars. Today, we try to organize a seminar each semester, with 20–40 participants, many of whom are inmates on short-term evening leaves. Again, we consider continuity of the seminars important. The seminars will usually be on concrete topics – the situation of foreign prisoners, the situation of mentally disturbed prisoners, drug controls in the prisons, mothers in prison, and so on.

Regularly, people from the Ministry or other relevant authorities are asked to come to present their policy in the particular case, whereupon they are questioned by the inmates and other participants. The authorities present frequently have to defend themselves as best they can, and the sessions have often effectively unmasked the policies of the prison system. Nevertheless, the authorities usually continue to come if they are asked, which – together with their regular (but not inevitable) participation at the large yearly conferences – probably signifies that KROM has acquired a certain status in the area. To refrain from participation would imply a lack of courage.

Newsletter

Third, KROM publishes a newsletter, "KROM-NEWS". We call it a journal. It started coming out in the 1970s, but then disappeared. In the 1990s it was revived, especially by the prisoners who at that time participated in KROM. "KROM-NEWS" published articles by inmates and critical professionals, reports on current concrete issues, book reviews and the like. A main informal guideline for the newsletter or journal was that of unmasking and documenting concrete practices and activities in the prisons – the drug controls which are used, the treatment of foreigners in our prisons, the use of pre-trial detention and so on. In the editorial management, there was close co-operation between inmates and non-inmates. This is an activity in which the contribution of inmates, some of whom are well versed in computer technology and lay-out while at the same time having a fair amount of free time behind the walls, is close to indispensable. Some of them are also extremely good writers.

The newsletter is usually printed in about 1,200 copies, on the simplest possible paper, and distributed free of charge. The newsletter lives on a shoestring budget. Partly for idealistic reasons, a number of interested attorneys have at times advertised their services in the newsletter, which has provided an additional small but important source of income for the newsletter. But without the computer work and lay-out abilities and expertise of the inmates, it would obviously have been impossible to publish it. Their contribution is of crucial importance. But we must confess: since 2007 there has not been published a single issue of the newsletter. We simply have not had the funds necessary for it. But an interesting alternative has come up: articles, book reviews, memos and – above all – consultation papers (opinions on white papers and reports from the government, dispatched for judicial inquiry) are now regularly written and published for and on the net on our home page. During the last year prior to our general assembly in 2013, we published nineteen such consultation papers on our home page. Some were short and hastily written, but several were long and involved, raising intricate issues on prisons. All had a distinctly critical tone. Many consultation papers are produced by state-run organizations and agencies which are not prone to launch a critical stance. Together with some others we introduce a critical voice in the 'choir'.

We are also experimenting with new publication practices. After our conference in 2013, we received five or six well written speeches which easily and fairly quickly could be turned into articles through a certain amount of 'light editing', and which were published on a separate file, thus constituting an issue of an 'Internet journal' on prison policy on the home page. A relatively small number of copies will also be printed on paper for prison inmates, who as a rule do not have access to the Internet. This is one line of experimentation with new publication practices.

Newspaper articles

Fourth, some KROM members try, as often as possible, to write newspaper articles. This is difficult work due to the fundamental changes in the media situation of Norway (as of other countries) which have taken place during the past few decades. Television has expanded enormously in terms of viewing time and, during the past few decades in Norway, in terms of number of channels. As a parallel, television has increasingly become an entertainment business. The American television analyst Neil Postman knew what he was doing when he gave his book on television the title *Amusing Ourselves to Death* (Postman 1985). Large parts of the press, especially the tabloid press, have followed suit. The background for this change, with increasing concentration of capital in a few hands, a changed technology and an increasing market-oriented competition, is extremely interesting, but lies outside the scope of this Introduction. Suffice it to say that news has increasingly become a commodity in the marketplace of mass entertainment.

This has affected the formulation and presentation of news related to penal policy. It has made serious and consistent criticism in the media very difficult, and has opened up for major moral panics around celebrated individual instances of escapes, etc. In turn, this has made it important to establish a public life and debate in the area of penal policy outside the mass media – as KROM tries to do at the yearly conferences and the evening seminars. I will return to this towards the end of this Introduction. Nevertheless, we also consider it important to write articles and have them published. From the start in 1968 until the beginning of the 2000s, KROM has kept newspaper clippings related to KROM's activities and criminal policy in general systematically on file, including all of our own articles. The collection became less systematic as Norway fully entered net-based communication. Articles are now frequently written and communicated on the net. An interesting observation is that when articles become net based rather than paper based, KROM certainly reaches many new readers, but the historical development of the organization becomes more sketchy and less easy to summarize and reflect on. The collection of paper-based clippings constitutes close to sixty very large volumes and is a useful source of information about aspects of criminal and penal policy through more than a quarter of a century. We are looking for alternative sources as articles are becoming more net based.

KROM-inspired books

Several members of KROM write and publish books. Earlier, the organization published its own series with a radical Oslo publisher. The series included volumes on prisoners' experiences of prison, preventive detention, strategies of political action and the like.

Today there is no specific series. Books have appeared covering typical KROM topics. At the organization's 25th anniversary in 1993, a large volume was published, comprising a number of major papers from KROM's early and recent history (Mathiesen and Heli 1993 – unfortunately for English speaking readers, only in Norwegian).

Other books are published by individual researchers as a part of their regular work. It should perhaps be emphasized that these books are not published by or in the name of KROM, but the researchers I have in mind have all for a long time been 'KROM activists', and it is fair to say that the books are in a general way inspired by KROM. Volumes on the fate of a treatment centre in a maximum security prison, the criminality of foreigners (which frequently is exaggerated and reported in a semi-racist fashion in the mass media), the structure and functioning of the police in political contexts, the functioning of the pre-trial detention court (where people are jailed, awaiting trial, for months and at top speed – the average pre-trial detention decision in the Oslo City Court takes about 25–45 minutes), the symbolic system and apparatus of the court system (which is a significant part of the authority structure of the courts) and the like are among the books I have in mind. In addition, a book taking stock of the prison as a mode of punishment was first published in 1986 and has been revised and reprinted several times in several foreign languages (Mathiesen 2006).

These are the main modes of operation in the organization. The list given above suggests that while the prison constitutes the core issue of KROM, the organization is concerned with the area of penal policy as a whole – including the functioning of the courts, the police and so on. The penal policy of the state constitutes an integrated system which must be dealt with as a totality. But it is important to emphasize that KROM's work ties in with concrete issues. It is fair to say that there is a kind of 'pendulum' in KROM, between theoretical concerns based on broad questions of political action, and concrete issues. The pendulum has been there from the start, and is still with us.

Precarious

But it would be wrong not to emphasize that KROM's existence, though it has continued for 45 years, is precarious. Financially, the organization is very poor, as

I have said relying on membership fees and a few small public grants for specific purposes. So far, it has been a matter of principle not to become dependent on larger and permanent public money. This policy may have to be changed in the future. In terms of personnel, the organization relies on people's willingness to use their own free time, outside their work situation. For long periods of time, the organization has been dependent on the contributions of a few dedicated individuals, who have kept things going. The organization has also been dependent on close association with researchers at the Department of Sociology of Law at the University of Oslo (since the 1990s amalgamated with the Department of Criminology). Even minor changes for the worse in these conditions could become a major threat to the organization and its existence, and only the future will tell how the organization will fare.

Strengths

On the other hand, KROM has three strengths which, together with the dedication of a few individuals and the association with an interested university department, probably help explain and promote the organization's continued existence.

Prisoners

First of all, the participation of the prisoners, which in a very significant way places a concrete demand for continuation and action on the organization, is extremely important. I have already said something about the prisoners' participation, and will not repeat that; let me only add that the expectations of the prisoners make it difficult indeed for anyone to close the organization down.

Other recruitment

A second strength is the organization's ability to recruit new activists. This ability is not so much thanks to KROM as it is the merit, if you can call it that, of the context in which KROM exists. There have been two main recruitment sources (other than prisoners): for one thing, professionals who have worked in and left the system – especially teachers and social workers – and who have survived in the sense of keeping their critical spirit alive and undisciplined, have been important. For another, open minded and alert students – in recent years especially law students, and to some extent criminology students, have been recruited. These two sources of recruitment have come naturally to KROM: critical professionals with system experience have as a matter of course oriented themselves towards KROM as the only centre of gravity of a critical kind in penal policy; the law and criminology students have been inspired to participate by university teachers among the older generation of KROM activists. In the context of the law students, a free legal-aid project organized by students, called *Juss Buss,* or "the Law Bus", has recently been a very important channel of recruitment. The organizational structure of the

Law Bus is unusual and interesting. Since the early 1970s, literally thousands of law students have gone through a period of a year or more in the Law Bus. It has a structure which as far as I know has been taken on in several other European countries (and which, interestingly, originated in cities in the US in the 1960s). It has a 'flat' structure and insists on remaining a 'flat' organization, with a minimum of hierarchy. The flat structure, in addition to an 'enrolment policy' consisting of a continual interchange between 'newcomers', 'active participants' and 'reducers', makes lengthy discussions and regular repetitions of policies and values worthwhile and important. This way, a critical spirit seems to have been kept up.

But it should be emphasized that after the 1970s, recruitment through these channels has certainly had its ups and downs. The reason for this, I think, lies in the general change of political climate which began during the 1980s. But it has almost always been possible to recruit at least some new interested participants, who have been able to spend at least some of their time on KROM and who have stayed on at least for a while.

Moral community

A third very important strength of the organization is that a kind of 'moral community' has developed over the years among a core of participants, say among 15–20 people. Most of these people are no longer active on a daily basis, but they are always 'there', in the background. They have a common political history; when they occasionally meet it is almost as if they had never been away from each other, and they may easily be called upon when needed, for example to give papers on criminal and penal policy at our three-day conferences. In dry times in terms of recruitment, the 'moral community' has psychologically been very important in keeping the organization from withering away.

The demise of Swedish KRUM

I have already mentioned that Swedish KRUM, in contrast to Norwegian KROM, did not survive. In the latter part of the 1970s it petered out and disappeared. Why did this happen? In 2004, long after the downfall and disappearance of Swedish KRUM, some old timers in the bygone organization sat down and developed a book containing a series of essays on the KRUM of the past: Monica Adamson *et al.* (eds.): *När botten stack upp* (When the Bottom Surfaced), Gidlunds förlag 2004. I participated with an essay (KRUM – KRIM – KROM), and I am ending this part of my Introduction here with a brief summary of this contribution.

A number of features probably contributed to the downfall of KRUM. First, there was political strife in KRUM. Radical Marxists stood up against liberal socialists. The political climate also changed dramatically in the beginning of the 1980s. But such a change took place in Norway as well, and Norwegian KROM survived.

Second, the mass media changed towards entertainment and sensationalism, whereby important news was quickly forgotten. Public opinion turned more clearly than before against people in our prisons. But these and other developments also took place in Norway, and again, Norwegian KROM survived.

Third, more important was perhaps the structure of Swedish KRUM. It was structured as a mass movement, based on massive prisoner participation and many local chapters throughout the country. In this respect Norwegian KROM was different – it was smaller, with a tighter system, from the beginning less of a mass movement and with fewer local chapters. This possibly contributed to Norwegian KROM's survival and, perhaps paradoxically, to Swedish KRUM's demise and disappearance. Paradoxically, strength became a weakness when the times changed. It was possible to keep the mass activity up during the early times of optimism, but more difficult when the economy – which the many employees in the local chapters had become dependent on – dried out and the employees had to leave.

However, I think there was an overarching fourth factor which also contributed importantly to Swedish KRUM's downfall. This factor consisted, also paradoxically, of the great victory which Swedish KRUM won during the first round of prison strikes, as early as right after 1970. Swedish KRUM did not just send a *signal* to Sweden saying that there was something basically wrong with Swedish prisons. No, after the first major strike, according to some counting about 50 % of the total Swedish population, Swedish KRUM and the prisoners took the authorities by surprise, refused by the thousands to eat and signalled to the country that they had *won over the state.* The authorities in fact agreed to negotiate with them, as if they were down on their knees.

Sending such a message could not be kept up. During the next strike and the strikes that followed, the authorities were prepared; they arrested the strikers who actually became water-strikers rather than food-strikers – a form of strike which after a short time turns extremely dangerous and becomes a serious threat to the prisoners. In fact, Swedish KRUM partly had to collaborate with the authorities to save lives, and basically had to give up the struggle. It was clear to everyone that *the state had won.*

This was, after the great victory in the first round, a terrible disappointment to Swedish KRUM. The first generation in Swedish KRUM could simply not get over it. After thinking that they had won the battle, they had actually lost. At least after discussions and preparation it would have been fairly easy to organize time-limited strikes, which would have meant that the prisoners would go back to order after a short while. They would then have shown that they were the winners – they could (presumably?) go back to order when they wanted to, not when the state wanted to. Swedish KRUM did nothing of the sort, and in the end the organization consequently symbolically lost completely what they had won in the beginning.

The basic structural point was that the prisoners did not have a built-in *contribution* to the prison which they could threaten to withdraw. There were and are some exceptions to this, such as the slave-like labour which prisoners perform in quite a few prisons. Another exception is economies which are so worn down that survival cannot be upheld for any length of time. But even these are not basic contributions; if the prison must, it certainly survives without the prisoners' labour – it doubles up or more in the cells to save money, or gets more money from the state so it can survive. This is (ideal-typically) in stark contrast to the labourers' situation in the factory. The factory is basically dependent on the labourers' contribution for its survival as a factory.

On the basis of my field work for my PhD dissertation (Mathiesen 1965), I pressed this point in several major plenary discussions around 1970 in KRUM, but lost. KRUM and the prisoners kept believing (or pretending) that they had won until most other people understood that they had actually lost. They could have won, or come closer to winning, by organizing time-limited strikes, maybe several time-limited strikes in a row, and so on. They did not do so.

This does not mean, however, that nothing came out of it. Swedish KRUM did humanity a great service in starting a whole development in Northern Europe. They convincingly showed all of the Nordic countries that it had been possible for *the bottom to surface* – to quote the title of the book on KRUM (Adamson *et al.* 2004). In this they were a most significant sign and symbol for many to follow later, when other bottoms in fact surfaced.

Part II

Five major theoretical issues

I move on now to the five major theoretical issues which I promised to attend to in the beginning of this Introduction. Actually, 'theoretical issues' is a misnomer, because 'theory' always involves 'praxis' just as 'praxis' always involves 'theory.' My own experience as an 'activist' has actually taught me this again and again.

A revisit to the 'unfinished'

Through the years the notion or theory of the 'unfinished' has followed me. Time and again I have come back to it and, frankly, been inspired by it. Not that there has been a lack of criticism. On the contrary, there has been a lot of criticism. Much of the criticism has also been inspiring. At one point, a whole book (in Norwegian) was more or less devoted to the theory of the unfinished and a related prison study as I had seen them (Gjerstad 2001). The book's title was *Does Thomas Mathiesen Have a Defence?* (Kan Thomas Mathiesen forsvares?), and was based, ironically, on the first edition of my book *Does Prison Have a Defence?* (Kan fengsel forsvares?, 2. ed. 1995, in English translated as *Prison on Trial*, 3. ed. 2006). It was a scientific-rhetorical study of my book. "The text", the author maintained, "controls its readers' interpretational context by developing a relational work which ties the reader to the text's author, and which gives the text a triadic communication structure with the reader on the same side as the author against a more or less fictitious opponent. The reader, in other words, is not allowed to be a counter-agent". In using metaphors and in the treatment of the adversaries' points of view, "the book makes use of what I call the grip of the monologue" (from a summary on the net,[3] translation by me). The author uses the concept of "rhetoric" in a negative sense. The book led to a very long debate on the Internet and ended, I suppose you could say, with a draw, with points on each side.

Another and more recent critique is that by the Canadian scholar Justin Piché, in a large and – at the time of writing – unpublished article called "The 'Unfinished' as an Abolitionist and State Strategy". It is under review by the Canadian journal *Radical Criminology*. Piché first runs through the theory (which is given in Book II of this volume), the main point being that in contrast to the solid and finished prison walls – built to stand for decades or even centuries – and countless other contrivances and decisions in the criminal so-called justice area (among which the final and finished (after appeals and so on) sentence looms large), he comes to his major point: the theory of the unfinished may be used not only by abolitionists to get rid of their thinking of all of the restrictive and finalizing aspects, but also successfully by the adversary to abolition, the (Canadian) state.

Piché then moves on to a long and clarifying story about the recent developments of criminal justice in Canada. According to him, rather than to develop the unfinished further, the task for abolitionists must be to finish the unfinished – finish the manoeuvring of the state. The recent conservative trend in Canada has been to conceal the projected impacts of their 'tough on crime' policies forecasted by civil servants, and related expenditures. Piché gives numerous examples of this, and, as he says, the paper "explores some of the ways in which this unfinished tendency of the Canadian carceral/penal state has manifested itself" (from the abstract). In endnote 4 he also says that it "should be noted that there are numerous other examples where federal government has advanced initiatives using an unfinished-like approach that could be discussed as well". Concealing the facts and forecasts made is partly planned, partly unplanned. To be sure, there are forces going against this tendency and for transparency. One such force is "public criminology" (Loader and Sparks 2011), which challenges state secrecy that facilitates an expansionary penality. But as a reader, and from experience, I question the drive contained in this counter-force. *If* we by public criminology mean research that resists state manoeuvring and works for transparency, I would not think first of all of public criminology, exposed to grand-scale cooptation as it is at least in my country.

Anyway, the summary question is: is it true that the theory of the unfinished can be used not only by abolitionists but also by state agencies, thus underpinning also a reactionary populist and expansionary penal policy? Does it underpin not only abolition of prisons but also the opposite, an expansion of prisons? Briefly, the following three points:

First, Piché's analysis of Canadian penal policy is interesting and elegant. By postponing or evading facts, by letting forecasts remain vague rather than making them crisp and clear so that it is possible to come to grips with them, Canada has probably entered the popular tendency of expansion in criminal policy. This is noticeable in large parts of the world. This is an achievement on the part of Piché: he bravely faces an explanation of this tendency.

But I don't think it is an achievement he should be particularly proud of. *Second*, through his analysis Piché comes closer to a point of view on criminological/ sociological theory which may be his, and which may contain some truth: theories may be used in different ways, depending on the point of departure and the level of analysis. A theory may on one level be seen and used as a theory of the underdog. On another level it may be used as a theory of governmentality or 'steering' – that is, as a theory of what in Norwegian would be called *styring* performed by agencies of the state, generally a theory of enhancing the goals of those in power.

He tends to find such a double alliance in the theory of the unfinished, which may be used also for enhancing the goals of those in power.

But *third*, we have to keep clearly in mind what the purpose of a theory is. Is the purpose of the theory of the unfinished to use it on various levels? Is the purpose that of developing a general theory such as the one Talcott Parsons envisaged in his great volume on general theory before World War II?[4]

Clearly it is not. If that had been my purpose, it would above all have changed my life completely. I would have done entirely different things than those I do now. I would have been absorbed by entirely different avenues of research, become an entirely different person, away from prisons and poverty, away from crime and deviance. As a consequence I would have written differently. I would have taken the actor's interpretive point of view, which teachers taught me in my young days,[5] but otherwise I would have spent my life on theoretically different levels, perhaps trying to integrate them towards the end. It would perhaps have been valuable, but clearly very different.

I remember the early days, when people cried out to us 'we can't place you people!' 'One day you say one thing, the next day you say the opposite!' The important point was, of course, that neither did we want them to catch us by defining us in *as silent partners* nor by defining us out as *extremists.* We wanted not to be neutralized, we wanted to *define ourselves,* not be defined by others. This, we thought, would keep us alive.

We still think so.

The theory of the unfinished was clearly invented as theory to be used by and for those below. It remains that way.

Long-term and short-term goals

In the early days of KROM, we discussed at great length the relationship between long-term and short-term goals, and emphasized that since the long-term goal was abolition, short-term goals should also have an abolitionist stance, and 'negate' the system rather than be 'positive' and build the system.

The discussion of long-term and short-term goals is still with us. But perhaps we have become less 'purist' in terms of 'negative' rather than 'positive' reforms. Though exceptions do exist, prisons are mostly dehumanizing dungeons. Those who populate them live under the worst possible conditions. Norwegian prisons are generally small relative to prisons in many other countries; some (less than 40 % of our prisons) are halfway open (without walls or other mechanical contrivances to avoid escapes) and treatment is – relative to prisons in many other countries – humane. Prisoners are sluiced to open prisons late in their career behind the walls and after an evaluation. Nevertheless, at least the larger prisons (our largest prison is Oslo Prison, with 392 prisoners or persons on pre-trial detention and 367 staff) are to a considerable extent bureaucratic, rule-oriented and – in the view of many inmates – 'machine-like'. As long as we have prisons, it is important to try to provide a more decent life for prisoners. In this sense, KROM today does work for 'positive' reforms.

And, seen in the long-term perspective, we are not too worried about doing so. In the early days we thought, as I have said, that the 'positive' reforms making prisons more humane also solidified the system. It is doubtful, I think, whether they actually do.

First, the experience of the 1980s and 1990s has shown that prison thrives with or without humanity – and usually, I might add, without it. Other forces than a humane touch in terms of content are decisive for its existence. Therefore, KROM today sees it as important to avoid cell crowding, important to criticize the inhuman living conditions in the so-called bunker (a particular isolation section within a main maximum security prison in Norway), important to provide better health and educational services for prisoners, to work for an expansion of prisoners' rights and so on.

Second, it is even quite possible that within the cultural context of Norway, with a historically exceptional emphasis on welfare state principles for everyone, including the outcasts of society – better health and educational services for prisoners, an expansion of prisoners' rights and so forth – in fact do negate our prisons rather that solidify them. Some of the welfare state principles are impossible, or virtually impossible, to institute fully in any – or almost in any – prison, however benign the prison is, at least if the welfare state ingredients are cutting away at the very fundamentals of prisons. At least some prisons have to have locked doors, and if not walls, at least fences around them. If these features are challenged by welfare state principles, which they certainly may be, the very foundation of the prison structure is challenged. In other words, the concepts of 'negative' and 'positive' reforms receive a new flavour – what was historically positive and thereby solidifying, today involves a critical stance of challenging the very structure of the prison.

This may be taken one step further. Welfare reforms, in other words, may or may not go beyond the possibilities of a prison system. A health reform may follow the guidelines of the prison, and stay within them. We might then call them disciplined reforms. They often end up in very little. But reforms may also go beyond the guidelines of the prison, challenging them. Then you come rather close to what the French sociologist André Gorz called *non-reformist,* as opposed to reformist, reforms. He meant by this that the reforms in fact go beyond the prison, overstepping the functional requirements of the prison.

I took this particular point up in Book II – at the time when I wrote the original *The Politics of Abolition.* At the time I was doubtful or even negative to Gorz' distinction and notion of non-reformist as opposed to reformist reforms, because the former may be coopted. But so may actual 'negative' reforms. I am more open to his way of thinking today. I here bring a quote from my 1974 discussion of Gorz which – hopefully – brings out the favourable associations:

> *André Gorz* represents the view that complete dissociation from short-term reforms is paralysing to a protest movement. He therefore believes that you have to enter on a reform policy. However, he distinguishes between

'reformist' and 'non-reformist' reforms and emphasizes the importance of stressing the latter type. 'Reformist' reforms have goals which are subordinated to the facilities and the presuppositions of a system and a policy presented by the adversary. A 'non-reformist' reform, however, is not geared to whatever is possible within the framework of a given system, but to that which 'should be realizable' in view of human demands and needs. A 'non-reformist' reform, in other words, goes beyond the facilities and presuppositions presented by the adversary's system. Pure wage demands constitute *Gorz's* main example of a 'reformist' reform. Demands concerning the right to decide over working conditions constitute an example of the opposite. According to *Gorz*, in their work for the 'non-reformist' reforms, the labourers must enter into negotiations and compromises with the capitalists. 'This', *Gorz* says, 'can only be shocking to maximalists, whom even Lenin turned against when he maintained that there are good and bad compromises' (p. 51 Norwegian edition). Thus, with *Gorz* the struggle is terminated by a partial victory, but during the struggle the awareness of the labourers has developed, so that one is prepared for new struggles. Thereby, one does not give up one's goals through a compromise, but 'on the contrary . . . approach the goals'.

(p. 51 Norwegian edition)

Still another avenue to the importance of welfare reforms as seen not as a *solidifying* force but as an *emancipatory* force may be found in what Hedda Giertsen in her essay in this volume (see below) calls 'independent reforms', as opposed to 'goal-oriented reforms' (the last concept is mine). She argues, for example, that when education for everyone – taken from Norway's long-standing tradition of maximum emphasis on equality in terms of educational opportunities – simply is taken as a means to make life in prison more livable and inmates more able to tackle life in society when release comes up, well, then increased education is an 'independent reform', as opposed to education as a method to reduce crime after release, which is a 'goal-oriented reform'. She also argues that other welfare reforms and reforms geared towards civil rights of various types may in Norway in principle work as 'independent reforms'. She sees 'independent reforms' as in fact a way out to abolish at least some of the important attributes (the stigma) of prison, and calls on Norway as an international example of a part-way road to 'abolition'.

Put differently, prisoners do not belong to and are not owned by the prisons, but belong to and are owned by the municipality or society in general. This has not only been a growing and informal tradition in social-democratic Norway. It has also been formalized. After a lengthy debate it in fact was adopted as a *principle* in the criminal justice system in 1987. Teachers, medical staff and others were to be employed by municipal authorities, not by the prison system. They were, in other words, to come from the outside. The goal was independence from the prison authorities. This was called the 'importation model', and though it certainly still is debatable and debated,[6] it opened up for the thinking referred to above.

We now have wandered a little around within the realm of long-term and short-term reforms. I will end this discussion by going back to the 'time-honoured'

KROM-approach. The welfare approach in one or several of its varieties may be combined with the 'KROM-approach', the strongly critical, always insistent approach. If welfare reforms involve 'politely' written or polite oral requests followed by equally 'polite' forms of refusals or only partial agreements from decision-makers which let the decision-makers fairly easily have their way – then we are into the realm of what I, as a totality, again would call 'disciplined reforms'. If, on the other hand, we work for welfare reforms in a way which is 'insistent' – which does not give in to the decision-makers' 'polite' refusals or partial agreements but remains persistent, perhaps referring to numerous international agreements and conventions, hammering away in a maximum fashion again and again – then we are in the realm of 'non-disciplined reforms'. The concepts are perhaps not fully usable, but give a direction for thinking. A welfare reform gives *legitimacy*, and a staunchly insistent and non-disciplined form gives *seriousness*. Both are important. We challenge the fundamentals of prisons and may with time win a battle.

A final brief example will illustrate: at KROM's winter conference in January 2014, where isolation in prisons and remand was a main topic for a full day, what appeared to be a long string of student members of the Law Bus were present (there were 30 law and criminology students present out of 130–140 participants). In a row they attacked the authorities in broad and well prepared statements against isolation, arguing actually for a positive reform – relief from isolation, because from isolation follows a long list of damages even from short periods of life without others.

A part of the criticism consisted in attacking the authorities for not providing even basic figures concerning isolation. Finally, at the 2014 conference the assistant director of the Prison Bureau gave in – he agreed and basic figures were produced. They were late – several years in coming. Once they came, he was certainly said to have been brave, but the figures *right away were also criticized.* I believe that when doing this over time, vociferously and again and again, the result will be that isolation will be less prevalent in Norwegian prisons than it is today.

*

Of course, what I have said so far presupposes a welfare system, or at least the rudiments or some historical ideals of a welfare system, to begin with. Norway is high on welfare for everyone, but certainly at least rudiments of a welfare system or rudiments of certain ideals, however lofty or vague, concerning welfare for everyone also do in fact exist in many places. I refer to Europe and North America, and know less about prisons in say Africa and Asia. Even today's prisons in Southern Europe or in large parts of the United States do build on a historical legacy presupposing some welfare ideals in a general sense. Let us look briefly at it.

Greece is, after all, known as 'the cradle of democracy'. This historical legacy is something which is taught in elementary schools all over Europe up till this day. I remember it from my own grade school years. Even full-blown Marxists argue that even if European history and history elsewhere is replete with stories of authoritarian empires definitely not addressing the poverty and problems of the people, Greece is a noteworthy exception (see for example Faulkner 2013 pp. 36–38).

But we are also Roman. *Rome* is perhaps especially interesting. Ancient Rome during the latter part of the first century BC had, as we know, a dictator – Caesar – who was a brilliant military leader but who also distributed large areas of land to poor people and to the *emeriti* ("worn out" soldiers) of his armies. The latter point is less well known. This particular dimension in Caesar is related in detail in Adrian Goldsworthy's monumental biography of the dictator (Goldsworthy 2006). He proposed several acts for distribution of land to the poor in need of help.

The land reform laws of the tribune Publius Servilius Rullus in 63 BC (Goldsworthy 2006 p. 138 on), a little before Caesar reached the top, are perhaps particularly interesting. Immediately after Cicero and Anthony were elected as Consuls (Rome had two rulers at the same time, ruling for one year), 1 January 63 BC, they were confronted by Rullus' radical legal proposal of distributing large land areas to Rome's impoverished population – first the state owned land in Campania. Later Rullus launched a proposal to buy the extra land which was necessary. He also proposed that land in the provinces could be sold to raise the necessary capital. A commission of ten members (*decimvir*) with proprietor-*imperium* for five years was going to keep track of the implementation of the program. According to Goldsworthy, the reform would have improved poor people's situation considerably. Caesar probably supported the proposal, but Cicero was very much against it from the beginning. In a series of speeches to the Senate and at the People's Assembly at the Forum, he went against the proposal. He was critical to similar proposals throughout his life. Many important Senators also went against the proposal. Cicero's rhetorical gifts won the day, and Rullus' land reform was given up (Goldsworthy 2006, p. 140; Rullus' land reform is largely reported by Cicero, p. 141). But land reform, and the distribution of land to offset people's poverty, was clearly a major issue in the Roman Empire of the day.

Michael Parenti has provided us with a much more advanced 'welfare state' program in terms of land reforms (and a much more sympathetic picture of the Roman people) for Rome at the time (Parenti 2003). Parenti relates the story of the assassination of Caesar in a way which is different from the stories related by both historians of the time and later, and later authors. Caesar was not assassinated in order to save the Republic from a dictator, but to save it for the wealthy few:

> Caesar's sin, I shall argue, was not that he was subverting the Roman constitution – which was an unwritten one – but that he was loosening the oligarchy's overbearing grip on it. Worse still, he used state power to effect some limited benefits for small farmers, debtors, and urban proletariat, at the expense of the wealthy few.
>
> (Parenti 2003)

Caesar perhaps carried this with him from his youth. In his younger days he lived in Subura, a relatively poor part of Rome which had less wealthy citizens. Only later, when he became *pontifex maximus,* the highest religious office, and was on his way upwards, did he acquire a grander official mansion at or near the Forum. Even then did he keep his interest in reform.

*

Historically, KROM has been concerned with welfare reforms presented in a way that in fact have challenged the fundamental structure of prisons: early on we used a word which coined a phrase – we argued that given reforms had to be implemented *immediately*. The *principle of immediacy,* which it may be called, slowly but surely made a certain impact – the decision-makers had to hurry. A number of welfare reforms were introduced in this cut-throat fashion – lessening the censure of mail, an increase in furloughs, an increase in visiting possibilities – were presented as *musts* if Norway were to keep up its role as a humanely oriented society. Forced labour for alcoholic vagrants had to be abolished *immediately* and not wait until alternatives where implemented. Also historically we have had ongoing battles and final decisions, over and above penal policy, which point in the same direction. The Norwegian struggle against membership in the European Union is a case in point. Many historical features over the years, which go beyond this Introduction, have made the majority of Norwegians win this struggle, with two major referendums (1972 and 1994) in modern history. The constantly insisting and unqualified NO to EU membership have won the day. The story may be replicated.

There is of course a very long historical road to go between Caesar and say Berlusconi. I only wish to make us remember that Europe and North America do in fact build on certain welfare principles – however lofty and vague, and however often interrupted by long periods to the contrary.

Alternative public space

Thirdly, let me mention in somewhat greater detail one line of action which I touched on above, and which I think is important under today's conditions, especially in view of the mass media situation I sketched earlier.

The key word is, in Norwegian *alternativ offentlighet,* in German *Alternative Offentlichkeit,* in English the much more cumbersome phrase "alternative public space". The point is to contribute to the creation of an alternative public space in penal policy, where argumentation and principled thinking represent the dominant values. I envisage the development of an alternative public space in the area of penal policy as containing three ingredients.

First, liberation from what I would call the absorbent power of the mass media. With the increasing importance of the mass media, and especially of television, many organizations tend to define success, indeed existence, in term of media coverage of what they are doing. Presumably, if your organization and its activities are not given mass media attention, they are worthless and more or less nonexistent. In this sense, we are absorbed into media participation and attention. I believe this is a very dangerous definition of the situation, which we should liberate ourselves from. As I have said, the mass media have developed into a gigantic entertainment business, where we very easily become clowns on a stage. In Western society, it is probably impossible to refrain completely from media participation and, as I have mentioned above, in KROM we do try to participate by writing newspaper articles. But it is certainly possible to say 'no!' to the many talk shows and entertainment-like 'debates' which flood our various television channels, and, most importantly, it is certainly possible not to let the definition of our success and very existence be dependent on the media.

The second ingredient is a restoration of the self-esteem and feeling of worth on the part of the grass roots movements. It is not true that the grass roots movements, emphasizing networks of organization and solidarity at the bottom, have died out. What has happened is that with the development of the mass media which I have mentioned, these movements have lost faith in themselves.

An important example from recent Norwegian history of the actual vitality of grass roots movements: in the early 1990s, thousands of ordinary Norwegians participated in a widespread movement to give refugees from Kosovo-Albania long-term refuge in Norwegian churches throughout the country. The movement ended in a partial victory, in that all of the cases concerning Kosovo-Albanian refugees were to be reviewed again by the Ministry of Justice. The example suggests that grass roots solidarity even with 'distant' groups like refugees did not die out with the Vietnam War.

Third, a restoration of the feeling of responsibility on the part of intellectuals is important. I am thinking of artists, writers, scientists – and certainly social scientists. That responsibility should partly be directed towards a refusal to participate in the mass media show business. Partly it should also be directed towards revitalization of research taking the interests of common people as a point of departure. This point is not new, but goes, of course, several decades back in Western intellectual history. The area is full of conflicts and problems, but they are not unsolvable.

I think we are in a way trying to do some of this in KROM, this strange hybrid of an organization, comprising intellectuals and prisoners with a common cause. The large yearly conferences, repeated again and again over several decades, the smaller seminars going from year to year, the evening meetings where a number of like-minded organizations cooperate, constitute attempts to create a network of opinion and information crossing the formal and informal borders between segments of the relevant administrative and political systems. The point is precisely that of trying to create an alternative public space where argumentation and principled thinking are dominant values, a public space which in the end may compete with the superficial public space of the mass media. The point here is not to institute a principle of immediacy, but rather (or in addition) a *principle of persistence.*

When we, back in the late 1960s, started our yearly conferences, I do not think we saw it this way. At that time, we were greatly preoccupied with getting media attention, and worried if we did not get it. Gradually, the focus shifted.

Our attempt at creating an alternative public space in the area of penal policy, which of course has its set-backs and difficulties, has one advantage over against what goes on in the mass media: it is based on the actual and organized relationships between people. The public space of the mass media is in that sense weak: it is a public space which is unorganized, segmented, splintered into millions of unconnected individuals – this is its truly mass character – and equally segmented into thousands of individual media stars in the media sky. This is the Achilles' heel of the public space of the media, which we try to avoid.

The point, however, is not to create a public sphere which competes with the large and wide-ranging public sphere constituted by the mass media. There are examples of such changes for example in the area of environmental issues. This occurs when the protection of the environment is turned into an activity which is supporting a broad class of people's daily interests. To change public opinion in a similar way in the context of criminal policy seems to be more difficult and long drawn. Towards the end of the 1970s, when the tide of opinion was turning away from being favourable to the prisoners and towards siding with the victims (as if the two were mutually exclusive), it broke the back of Swedish KRUM. Our quest is more modest.

Our quest is that of creating an alternative public sphere not as an alternative to the large mass media of the nation or the world, but an alternative public sphere in terms of criminal policy prisoners, those working in our prisons, social workers in the area of penal policy, judges and defence lawyers, social scientists and so on. This is what Norwegian KROM has done all along. In this it may be said that we have been moderately successful. We have not broken our neck.

Creating a more limited public space, in our case within the parameters of criminal and penal policy, also receives support from the more modern media such as the Internet. The Internet and the modern mass media in general, with millions of participants all over the world, seem to create a confusing and loose public sphere that may sometimes be helpful and sometimes not. There are examples of both possibilities. I have mentioned some examples of the possibility of success earlier. The more or less successful revolts in the Arab countries around the Mediterranean in 2011 to 2014, where technologies of communications related to the Internet certainly were used, are cases in point. Information exchange was planfully used. But unplanned information exchange, for example on Facebook, may also end up in confusing sets of information exchange.

However, within the limits say of criminal policy, information may be sent and exchanged swiftly and with persistent goals, actions may be taken fast because they are easily planned, news about meetings and rallies may be spread to the right people without delay and so on. During the past few years KROM has had many examples of such information exchange to the right people at the right time – see for example the case discussed above of expressing confidence right after the terrorist onslaught in Norway on 22 July 2011. Large-scale "rose demonstrations" were swiftly planned and carried out when based on Facebook communication (Mathiesen 2013 p. 213).

On the other hand, information exchange addressed to a wide ranging and complex public sphere implicating the many large mass media and so on, easily disappears as if in a haze.

The abolitionist stance[7]

In the fourth place, let me make a few more comments on abolitionism, a core ingredient in the KROM standpoint – if not from the beginning (see above), at least from the 1970s on. I have said that the abolitionist principle is far more difficult to carry to success now than before. Conditions which were ripe in the 1970s are not there any more. Is the principle still with us?

I agree with the late criminologist Heinz Steinert who in a preparatory communication designed for *Kriminologisches Journal* stated that some very important abolitionist gains in the area of prisons were made in the 1960s and 1970s (Steinert, in Feest and Paul 2008a). This was indeed a period, as he puts it, of "major historical success" (Feest and Paul 2008a pp. 2–3). I have mentioned some examples from Norway already. In several countries the number of inmates fell significantly and remained lower than earlier for quite some time.

Also, I agree with Heinz Steinert that we don't need to feel desperate or ashamed at the fact that we could not stop the strong wave towards increased punitive populism, media panics and rising prison figures and their societal and political underpinnings, which were increasingly characteristic of the 1980s, 1990s and later. As he says, those of us who belong to the (admittedly vaguely defined) "abolitionist movement" have at least not provided "justifications for the new exclusionary regime" which recently has been on the rise (ibid., p. 3).

But there is also more to be said. What does it mean to be an 'abolitionist'? Concepts such as 'abolitionism' and 'abolitionists' swirl around. Admittedly, I have made them swirl around myself. Why do I call myself an 'abolitionist'?

The classical sociologist Max Weber gave us, if we are willing to accept a parallel, one way of looking at it in his now famous use of so-called ideal types in historical studies. It seems that he conceptualized ideal types by making it clear what an ideal type is not. It is not an average, it is not a hypothesis and so on.

So with 'abolitionism'. An abolitionist, whether a scientist, a teacher or a person practising his/her trade, is not a person who is preoccupied with what I would call system justification. He/she is not a person who is preoccupied with refining the existing.

But it is possible also to define abolitionism in positive terms; not only in terms of what it is not, but also in terms of what it is:

I submit to you: *abolitionism is a stance.* It is the attitude of saying 'no'. This does not mean that the 'no' will be answered affirmatively in practice. A 'no' to prisons will not occur in our time, though it may be a guiding ideal for the future. But as a guiding ideal it easily becomes vague and distanced from concrete political commitment. However, as a stance it is viable and important, and it may be quite concrete. When I wrote the first edition of *The Politics of Abolition* in 1974, and again when I published *Prison on Trial* (Mathiesen 2006), I was certainly pre-occupied with strategies of achieving concrete abolitions. I still am, and even with *small abolitions* which constitute small victories which should be covered in the abolitionist paradigm. This is an important fact which should not be overlooked today. But I was also preoccupied with fostering and developing an abolitionist stance, a constant and deeply critical attitude to prisons and penal systems as human (and inhumane) solutions.

As a stance abolitionism goes beyond the parameters or conditions of existing systems. Systems such as the prison or the penal system are complex, functionally interrelated systems. Therefore, if you criticize one aspect of, say, the prison system, you are immediately confronted with the 'necessity' of that aspect. For example, if you criticize the security regime, you are immediately confronted by the necessity of maintaining the regime in view of, say, public opinion. When something is said to be 'necessary', you should beware: functionally interrelated systems are not inherently conservative, but grow conservative by our succumbing to the parameters of the system. The succumbing to all of the parameters is close to the non-abolitionist stance. The abolitionist stance goes beyond (some of) the parameters. For example, it is possible to say 'sorry, but public opinion is not my concern', or perhaps better, 'public opinion can be changed, or contains other and quite different components' (more about this below).

It is easy to succumb to all of the parameters. Many forces work in this direction. I have outlined some of them in *Silently Silenced* (Mathiesen 2004). These include social pressures at the workplace (you have to cooperate with people; share secrets with them; strike very informal, almost unnoticeable bargains with them; all of which compromise you). Hierarchical disciplinary pressures at the workplace (staying in line) operate in the same direction. Simply fatigue from everyday chores also does so. Imperceptibly, your stance is altered into something more or less different from saying 'no' to given arrangements. To be sure, we cannot, and perhaps should not, have an abolitionist stance to everything in the world. But we should have an abolitionist stance to things highly negative and vital, politically speaking, in our professional lives, and perhaps in our lives as human beings.

Is abolitionism as a stance a movement? There are probably variations nationally and internationally. In Norway I see at least some rudiments of such a movement, indeed despite the dark 1990s and early 2000s. To be sure, prison figures are increasing in a whole range of countries. We all know that. Judging from the media and from superficial opinion polls, there is wide support for the increase. We all know that, also. But there is wide concern and worry, in the professions and among segments of the population, about 'the new exclusionary regime', to use Heinz Steinert's apt term once again. There is also, more specifically, concern and worry about the use of prison, perhaps especially against young delinquents. The concern and worry, and the abolitionist stance, are not so apparent on the surface. The surface is covered by frightening media stories about terrifying murders and rapes, and about people being terrified by the stories. But under the surface layer there are more nuances. We have recent empirical grounds for saying that it may well be a matter of distance and closeness to the crime in question. In any case, Norwegian sociologist of law Leif Petter Olaussen has convincingly shown that representative samples of people clearly underestimate the punishment level of the courts, and – most importantly – *that they are less prone than the courts, in connection with many types of serious crimes* (violence against partner, street violence, rape, kiosk robbery, smuggling of heroin and bank fraud – six types of crime), to give imprisonment as a sentence (Olaussen 2013). This goes for Norway. The same results come out for all of the five Nordic countries (the three Scandinavian countries and Finland and Iceland). A large-scale Danish study, headed by the Danish criminologist Flemming Balvig, was the first of the five (www.advokatsamfundet.dk). Answering a general question about punishment, a representative sample of the population massively wanted stricter punishment, longer sentences – as in all such public opinion studies. When detailed information was given about the six types of serious crime mentioned above, however, the samples became much more nuanced. When videotapes of staged court trials followed by discussion groups took place, people turned far less punitive in terms of prison than the courts.

Though very important, this can hardly be taken as a full-scale proof of the existence of an abolitionist stance, and certainly not of an abolitionist movement in a broad sense. More important is the concern you sense at large meetings with a critical focus, outside the realm of television. Meeting people *as people* rather than during Internet exchanges or via media coverages (which necessarily involve selections which are skewed) is vitally important – especially meetings which forge networks, networks in which people support each other. When I waver, I get support from you, and vice versa. Supportive networks are crucial.

Through the years, and up till the very present, I have attended and participated in organizing a very large number of open meetings on criminal and social policy. The organization KROM (The Norwegian Association for Penal Reform) still exists, and we celebrated our 45th anniversary in 2013. During its 45 years of existence, Norwegian KROM has organized 42 large three-day conferences on penal policy. I have mentioned them and their whereabouts earlier in this Introduction. As we have seen, they are held in a particular mountain resort, giving historical continuity and a sense of belonging. Many generations of professionals and others have been covered by these conferences – altogether thousands of people – prisoners, ex-prisoners, social workers, lawyers, teachers, medical personnel, prison officers, people from the ministries and what have you. As opposed to most meetings of this kind, the conferences are cross-sectional, covering a wide variety of professions and trades. I want to emphasize in particular the mix of academics, prisoners and ex-prisoners. This gives us two advantages: When academics are 'defined out' as coming from the ivory tower, the prisoners are there to alleviate this with their practical experience. When the prisoners are 'defined out' as biased or prejudiced, the academics are there to alleviate this with analyses.

Those who disagree with us are also present: in the 1960s and 1970s, the Prison Department and the political establishment avoided us. Now they feel forced to come. Debates are very heated at these conferences. A main point is the struggle over definition of reality. Traditionally, the authorities have a monopoly on how to define what goes on in the relevant life world. This definition is challenged at the conferences. Cracks in the taken-for-granted definition of the situation, or even full-fledged alternative and competing understandings of what life is like in our prisons and within the penal system, are fostered. Networks are created and maintained.

Other kinds of conferences have for a long time now drawn much larger crowds than first expected. This gives ground for optimism. A one-day public meeting in Stockholm a few years ago on prisons is an example. The organizers expected an audience of one hundred. Four hundred came, and the meeting was a success. And the crowd in fact said 'no!' to some important elements in the development of Swedish prisons. An abolitionist stance surfaced. Another example: during the spring of 2010 three large evening meetings on the criminalization and penalization of drug users were held in Oslo. They had the same general effect – a generalized 'no!' to the very harsh Norwegian penal policy in relation to drugs. Of course, the 'no' did not come as a bolt from the blue. It did not emanate from nothing. Years of struggle on the part of ardent individuals had gone beforehand. Books and articles had been written. But the unified 'no' was vital in creating cracks in traditional penal thinking.[8]

We don't know what kinds of people come to the latter type of meetings. Perhaps they are especially interested. If so, that's all right. Some will perhaps say that meetings of this sort are only dramatized and executed by fossils from the 1960s. I definitely think not – there are too many young people about. An important sense of community, a 'moral community', sometimes appears. Some people have said to me, 'I thought I was alone with my thoughts. But here are many others who view it in the same light!' Isn't this a sign of a movement?

I don't want to idealize this. There are certainly obstacles. One obstacle, again, is television, instigating and 'sucking up' popular meetings, staging their own 'debates' as entertainment events. But we should not think of television and other media as constituting the only public space. I touched on this above, in the section on an alternative public space. Public space is a much more complex phenomenon – there are many alternative public spaces outside the realm of the mass media. Another obstacle is the everyday grind – you grow up, you get married, you get children, you get divorced, you have to go to work to earn a living and you dump down exhausted in front of the TV at the end of the day. But these events, at least some of them, also create vigour and life, and also at least some surplus of energy. A further obstacle is the neo-liberalism and market orientation of our time. But isn't that in part what we are struggling against?

In other words, it is not impossible to nurture an abolitionist stance, a stance of saying no! And in the long run it makes a difference. It may contribute to what I would call turning points. The turning points of the past – the abolition of slavery, the abolition of the death penalty at least in some places, the abolition of the youth prisons in Massachusetts, the abolition of forced labour etc. – should be scrutinized as examples for the future. What fostered them, what caused some of them to return under a different mantle? Turning points probably surface for structural, economic and political reasons. They become 'ripe fruits', to use a Norwegian expression. But people act on and channel them as they surface.

An abolitionist stance of saying no! was certainly a part of past abolitions. It may be so again. All through my professional life I have wondered why *criminologists* are not more vocal in relation to the issue. Listen to this: "The American Society of Criminology is an international organization whose members pursue scholarly, scientific and professional knowledge concerning the measurement, etiology, consequences, prevention, control and treatment of crime and juvenile delinquency. . . . Today, the American Society of Criminology comprises approximately 3.700 members from more than 50 countries. It is the largest professional criminological society in the world. . . . Roughly 60 percent of the membership is made up of university professors . . . ." This is an official statement of the American Society of Criminology. Albeit the largest grouping, there are also others, in other parts of the world. What if this mighty force one day stood up and said a loud 'NO!' to prisons! Would the United States remain a society of mass imprisonment? I think not. Would the number of prisoners in other countries continue to increase? I think not. Would the numbers decrease? I think so.

A wild thought? Most likely. But the times need wild thoughts.

The vital importance of nurturing an abolitionist stance has been my main message in this part of the Introduction. It has also been my message to say that nurturing this stance is not impossible, but certainly possible. We are on the way. *The International Conference on Penal Abolition* as well as *The European Group for the Study of Deviance and Social Control,* are important international participating venues. Louk Hulsman, who died so prematurely in 2009, was in many ways the father of one of them – *The International Conference on Penal Abolition.* There are also others, on the national level. Linking these together, which indeed takes place today, is a crucial task.

But do not let us fool ourselves. It is not done with one stroke. It takes time, and requires hard work. Again Max Weber may be quoted, this time for something he said towards the end of his life in his famous lecture on *Politics as a Calling,* way back in 1919 (Weber 1919/1921). Admittedly, he gave a context for the saying which may make many of us ambivalent today – he talked about leaders and heroes and so on. But the statement itself is highly relevant to the abolitionist stance. I will first read it in German because it sounds so demanding in that language, and then translate it into English: "*Die Politik bedeutet ein starkes langsames Bohren von harten Brettern mit Leidenschaft und Augenmaß zugleich. Es ist ja durchaus richtig, und alle geschichtliche Erfahrung bestätigt es, dass man das Mögliche nicht erreichte, wenn nicht immer wieder in der Welt nach dem Unmöglichen gegriffen worden ware*". And in English: "Politics is like strong, slow drilling in hard boards. It requires passion and an accurate eye at the same time. It is throughout correct, and all historical experience confirms this, that one never reached the possible, if there was not a continuous grasp for the impossible".

Beyond abolition?

Let me end this Introduction by saying a few words about the future – close or distant. What will come beyond abolition?

This question is perhaps not timely. We are in the midst of an upsurge of prisons throughout the world. A question of what will come beyond prisons – when prisons are more or less out of the way – is in this sense premature. Yet, as I said, a few words may be in order.

Several dangers lie ahead. Let me briefly mention two of them.

One is that the medical profession and illness as a concept will take over. The Norwegian sociologist Vilhelm Aubert raised the question of the relationship between crime and illness almost sixty years ago (Aubert 1958). *Illness* pictures the person as a many faceted individual in a holistic way, and the medical profession as a forward-oriented undertaking. What can we do for or with this person in the future? *Crime,* on the other hand, pictures the person as having a very narrow span – the crime itself and perhaps a few ameliorating and aggravating circumstances – and the legal profession is a distinctly past-oriented undertaking. How do we judge this person's past act?

These are of course ideal-type images. But they do contain some truth. In actual legal practice they sometimes collide. Prisons for the criminal beings more or less gone, which we imagine here, would we prefer to have the issues we are concerned with turned over to the medical profession?

The long since gone British author Samuel Butler has given us a clue, in his novel *Erewhon* (Butler 1872). If you read the name Erewhon backwards, it reads 'Nowhere'.[9] 'Erewhon/Nowhere' is a place where a lonely sailor is washed ashore after a shipwreck. It turns out that the people he meets are different from those he is used to. If they commit a crime, they receive medication. If the crime is serious, they are brought to a hospital; they are taken good care of, given treatment, flowers and good food. On the other hand, if they become ill, they receive a punishment; if the illness is serious, like cancer, they are confined and may have to work in the mines.

I don't think I would like to live in Erewhon. I would worry a great deal if something like this became the road. I don't know if I would want men and women who had committed problematic acts to be turned over to the medical profession, with that profession's concern with the whole person and with the person's future in mind. What facts and broad diagnoses tied to him or her would be taken into account, and what would his or her diagnosis concerning the future be like? I would prefer the more simple-minded legal approach, but humanized more often than now by medically oriented men and women.

There is a second danger: the modern technological track. Though I still believe we partly live in an industrial age, we have more than one foot into the digital world. We see clear traces of it in criminal policy. Electronic fetters and a number of other electronic gadgets are used more or less experimentally in a number of places, including Sweden and Norway. In Norway electronic fetters started to be used experimentally in the fall of 2008; the latest data I have found for Norway are from 2010 when they were used in a number of administrative districts.[10] At least in Norway it has so far been used sparingly; if a punishment is to be served by electronic fetters, it must be used only during the last four months of the sentence or the sentence must not be longer than four months. Violence, sexual offences or conditions tied to the home are so far criteria which favour exclusion from the program. But the prison system hopes a larger proportion of inmates wish to serve their sentences with electronic fetters.

In Sweden electronic fetters and other digital or electronic measures *may* be behind a downward trend in the number of prisoners. As I have mentioned, during the last ten years the Swedish prisoner population has in fact decreased by 25%. Let me briefly expand on it in the present context.

I earlier viewed the decrease as a positive sign from the point of view of abolition or prisons (see above), and so it is. But it may also be viewed differently. Registered crime – violence registered with the police, self-reported house burglaries and drug crimes – has not decreased in Sweden during the same period, but has remained stable or has in fact increased.[11] This substantiates the hope that a real prison abolition or at least decrease may be in the making. But admittedly, other factors may be in operation. We are entering a digital phase. Electronic fetters are important in tying the offender to a particular place – the home – more or less converting the home into a prison. The prison system maintains that it saves money,[12] which it certainly does, and makes it possible for some to maintain a job. So does the further advancement of electronic chips on the person. Electronic chips may increasingly be placed on other groups of people – on school children, demented individuals in homes for the aged, patients to ascertain their whereabouts, perhaps several other groups – and again on prisoners, where they may be used rather soon, as a way in which to experiment. Likewise, surveillance of various kinds are being developed and used circumventing prisoners' movements, geographical boundaries may be installed which in various ways limit movements, and the like. In as much as such measures are increasingly used as criminal policy measures, I am not altogether certain that we are facing real prison abolition.

The future is full of dangers. We must be aware of this possibility. One important experience from the past gives us a warning and a glimpse into what must be done – the abolition of forced labour for vagrants and alcoholics in 1970 in Norway (see above). We worked hard for this abolition. Large groups supported us. Finally, a unanimous Parliament voted for abolition. But then the tide turned. The vagrants and the alcoholics came out in the open, in the streets. So far they had been hidden in forced labour camps, but not any more. The danger was imminent: new forced labour measures could be installed. What did we do? We started comprehensive defensive work to consolidate the abolition. An action group among vagrants was established, and worked hard for several years – with success: new forced labour measures were in fact not installed. We won. The abolition of forced labour and the defensive work that followed has until recently[13] had a distinctly civilizing effect on Norwegian criminal and social policy, which lasted for years. It is perhaps the most important victory we ever won.

Similar actions may be necessary in the future. So far and probably for a long time, the abolition of prisons is the foremost task, perhaps mixed with what we already now may see or imagine in the looking glass.

A story at the end

I want to end this story on KROM by bringing us back again from the future to the beginning, to the late 1960s and early 1970s. Something quite important happened then which we were totally unaware of at the time; it only became known in the 1990s. If we had known, it might have made quite a difference. We might have become quite a bit more timid, perhaps scared, possibly stopped as a vocal pressure group. Or we might have ended up with an even more radical spirit.

It is important to recognize that the sudden development of KROM – the Norwegian Association for Penal Reform, was fairly widely considered as a serious *danger sign* in Norwegian society at the time. It was an entirely new association; nothing like it had to my knowledge been heard of before. It had fresh unbureaucratic information on what was going on in our prisons. We argued in a new (and, I think, convincing) way. At the time we were professionally on the top of our field and could compete successfully with almost anyone, certainly the top men in the prison administration. If we forget that, we miss a central point, and it has been with us, albeit more modestly, until this day.

But we basically stayed on the 'side' of Norwegian society. We basically liked (if you can use such a word) the Norwegian state. The Norwegian state had its definite basic shortcomings in the area which concerned us, criminal policy, and we had clear misgivings about it, but we thought that some or many of them could be improved with time. We were, at the time and as a matter of fact not *an enemy of the state.*

And here comes the story. What happened was not known to us at the time of *The Politics of Abolition,* but should be made known now, during a revisit to the book.

This was during the height of the Cold War. Many people were closely followed by the Secret Police. There were rumours and testimonies about this, and finally a parliamentary committee was set down to investigate the matter. And *Stortingets granskingskommisjon for de hemmelige tjenester 1994–1996* (Parliament's Investigative Commission for the Secret Services 1994–1996) found, in fact, that many people – Norwegian citizens, left-oriented people – were closely monitored for years, illegally and secretly, by the Secret Service. It had damaging psychological and other effects on many of those who were followed.

This created an uproar in the Norwegian public sphere and the political establishment. We had been outside of this, had not really thought about it, had gone about our business as usual, but now we started to wonder: had KROM in fact also been monitored by the Secret Police?

Yes, KROM had been monitored. All those who were judged to have been illegally monitored by having their telephones tapped, their letters opened or by being followed step by step, were for a period of time allowed to 'see their files' (and some of them received remuneration). I asked to see my file.

KROM was there. A document dated 5 May 1972, but made known only much later (in 2003), stated about "KROM's board": "KROM's board consists according to reliable source of the following:". The only name mentioned was, however, my name, and it was mentioned as "Chairman: Dr. philos Thomas MATHIESEN". Then came an open space – the names of all of the other members of the board had obviously been deleted because I was the only one who had asked to see my file.

Then followed: "In addition a good many [en del] inmates/prisoners serving sentences who are not referred to by name here".

The report, which was brief, was from our winter conference, in the document entitled "The Spåtind-Conference in the fall of 1971" – our third conference, the heart of KROM. They had been around with us, perhaps they had had wine with us, joked and laughed with us, snapped information from us.

The report contained characterizations: "Statements man to man made under the influence of alcohol in the evening hours ran like this: 'A disgrace that we had to camouflage what we have to do when the real goal is the struggle against EEC [later the EU] as well as the effort during the class war of Norway', and so on; [statements like that] were quite common". The file also included a few other reports concerning *inter alia* my co-operation with and professional visits from behind the Iron Curtain (Poland), and numerous newspaper clippings.

I and KROM were, indeed, officially claimed to be *enemies of the state.* In 1972.

Bibliography of: Introduction to the *Politics of Abolition Revisited*

Adamson, Monica, *et al.* (eds. 2004): *När botten stack upp* (When the Bottom Surfaced). Gidlunds Förlag.

Aubert, Vilhelm (1958): "Legal Justice and Mental Health", *Psychiatry*, Vol. 21 No. 2, pp. 101–13.

Butler, Samuel (1872/1922): *Erewhon: or Over the Range.* London.

Christie, Nils (2000): *Crime Control as Industry.* 3. ed. Routledge.

Einarsen, Kurt Jonny (2010): "Trender i voldskriminaliteten i USA, Sverige og Norge fra 1993–2009" (Trends in Crimes of Violence in USA, Sweden and Norway from 1993–2009), *Samfunnsspeilet* No. 4. published 4 October.

Faulkner, Neil (2013): *A Marxist History of the World from Neanderthals to Neoliberals.* Pluto Press.

Feest, Johannes and Bettina Paul (2008 a): "Zusatzmaterial zum Schwerpunkt 1/2008 des Kriminologishen Journals" (Does Abolitionism Have a Future? Documentation of an Email Exchange among Abolitionists). Universität Hamburg. Fachbereich Sozialwissenschaften.

Feest, Johannes and Bettina Paul (2008 b): "Abolitionismus. Einige Antworten auf oft gestellte Fragen" (Translation: Abolition. Some answers to questions which are often posed), *Kriminologisches Journal*.

Gjerstad, Magne (2001): *Kan Thomas Mathiesen forsvares? En vitenskapsretorisk analyse* (Does Thomas Mathiesen Have a Defence? A Scientific-Rhetorical Analysis). Universitetet i Oslo.

Goldsworthy, Adrian (2006): *Caesar*, Gyldendal Norsk Forlag (Original Caesar. The Life of a Colossus). Weidenfeld & Nicholson 2006; paperback Phoenix 2007.

Kilgore, James (2013): "Are We Really Witnessing the End of Mass Incarceration? The Strange Politics of Prisons in America", *CounterPunch*, November Vol. 20 No. 11, pp. 10–14.

Loader, Ian and Richard Sparks (2011): *Public Criminology*. Routledge.

Mathiesen, Thomas (1971): *Det uferdige* (The Unfinished). Pax Forlag.

Mathiesen, Thomas (1973): *Pressgruppe og samfunnsstruktur* (Pressure Group and Social Structure). Pax Forlag.

Mathiesen, Thomas (1974 a): *The Politics of Abolition. Essays in Political Action Theory.* Universitetsforlaget.

Mathiesen, Thomas (1974 b): "The Prison Movement in Scandinavia", *Crime and Social Justice*, Spring/Summer, pp. 45–50.

Mathiesen, Thomas (1975): *Løsgjengerkrigen* (The Vagrancy War). Sosionomen Forlag.

Mathiesen, Thomas (1990): "About KROM. Past – Present – Future", Mimeographed paper (updated version 2000).

Mathiesen, Thomas (1992): "Om en organisasjons vekst og fall. Noen refleksjoner ved et svensk 25- års jubileum" (On the Rise and Fall of an Organization. Some Reflections at a Swedish 25 Years' Anniversary), *Årsmelding fra Institutt for rettssosiologi*, pp. 62–68.

Mathiesen, Thomas and Arne Heli (eds.1993): *Murer og mennesker. En KROM-bok om fengsel og kriminalpolitikk* (Walls and People. A KROM-book on Prisons and Criminal Policy). Pax Forlag.

Mathiesen, Thomas (1995): *Kan fengsel forsvares?* (Does Prison Have a Defence?). 2nd ed. Pax Forlag.

Mathiesen, Thomas (2004): *Silently Silenced. Essays on the Creation of Acquiescence in Modern Society.* Waterside Press.

Mathiesen, Thomas (2006): *Prison on Trial. A Critical Appraisal.* 3rd ed. Waterside Press (German edition 1989: Gefiingnislogik: Uber alte und neue Rechtfertigungsversuche. AJZ Verlag).

Mathiesen, Thomas (2008): "The Abolitionist Stance", *Journal of Prisoners on Prisons*, Vol. 17 No. 2, pp. 58–63.

Mathiesen, Thomas (2013): *Towards a Surveillant Society. The Rise of Surveillance Systems in Europe.* Waterside Press.

Nadheim with Lerche collaborating www.krad.no/nyhetsarkiv-361-innbrudd-norge-er-best-i-norden

Nordisk Statistik (Nordic Statistics) (2012): Direktoratet for kriminalforsorgen. (Danish Publication).

Öberg, Nils (2013): Article in *Dagens Nyheter*, 11 November. www.advokatsamfundet.dk

Olaussen, Leif Petter (2013): *Hva synes folk om straffenivået? En empirisk undersøkelse.* (What Do People Think of the Punishment Level? An Empirical Study). Novus Publishers.

Olaussen, Leif Petter (2014): "Concordance between Actual Levels of Punishment and Punishments suggested by Lay People – but with less use of Imprisonment." *Bergen Journal and Criminal Justice*, Vol. 2, Issue 1, pp. 69–99.

Parenti, Michael (2003): *The Assassination of Julius Caesar. A People's History of Ancient Rome.* The New Press.

Piché, Justin (2014): "The 'Unfinished' as an Abolitionist and State Strategy". Manuscript under the evaluation of *Radical Criminology.*

Postman, Neil (1985): *Amusing Ourselves to Death.* Viking Penguin.

Pratt, John and Anna Eriksson (2013): *Contrasts in Punishment. An Explanation of Anglophone Excess and Nordic Exceptionalism.* Routledge.

Rolston, Bill and Mike Thomlinson (1986): *The Expansion of European Prison Systems.* Working Papers in European Criminology No. 7 (European Group for the Study of Deviance and Social Control).

Rua, Marte (2012): *Hva gjør fengselsleger? En institusjonell etnografi om isolasjon og helse* (What Do Medical Doctors in Prisons Do? An Institutional Ethnography on Isolation and Health). Department of Criminology and Sociology of Law, University of Oslo, Book Series No. 1.

Scott, David (2013): "Why Prison? Posing the Question". In David Scott (ed. 2013): *Why Prison?* Cambridge University Press.

Smart, Carol (1976): *Women, Crime and Criminology: A Feminist Critique.* Routledge and K. Paul.

Stortingets granskingskommisjon for de hemmelige tjenester 1994–1996 (Parliament's Investigative Commission for the Secret Services 1994–1996).

Weber, Max (lecture 1919/first published 1921, 1958): "Politik als Beruf", *Gesammelte Politische Schriften*, Duncker & Humblot.

Western, Bruce (2006): *Punishment and Inequality in America.* Russell Sage Foundation.

Wollebæk, Dag et al. (2011): *Hva gjør terroren med oss som sivilsamfunn?* (What Does the Terror Do to Us as a Civil Society?). Senter for forskning på sivilsamfunn og frivillig sektor, Oslo/Bergen.

Wollebæk, Dag et al. (2012 a): *Ett år etter 22. juli* (One Year after 22 July). Senter for forskning på sivilsamfunn og frivillig sektor, Oslo/Bergen.

Wollebæk, Dag et al. (2012 b): "Tillit i Norge etter 22 juli" (Confidence in Norway after 22 July). In Helge Skirbekk and Harald Grimen (eds.): *Tillit i Norge* (Confidence in Norway), Res Publica.

Worrall, Anne and Loraine Gelsthorpe (2009): "'What Works' with Women Offenders: The Past 30 years". *Probation Journal. The Journal of Community and Criminal Justice,* Vol. 56 (4), pp. 329–245.

Notes

1. Personal information from Swedish professors of criminology in Stockholm Henrik Tham, 20 December 2013, and Hanns von Hofer, December 2013. For a wider view, contemplating a slight hope also for a few US states, see Kilgore in this volume; Kilgore 2013.
2. I owe this point to a speech by and discussions with the late Swedish author and KRUM activist, journalist in Dagens Nyheter Jörgen Eriksson.
3. DUO, Digital publications at the University of Oslo.
4. See Talcott Parsons, *The Structure of Social Action,* McGraw Hill 1937. I have to confess that *The Structure of Social Action* probably is the best work Parsons ever wrote. Here Parsons integrates sociological theorists, empirical facts and philosophy in an elegant way, approaching a general theory of action in a way which is not surpassed by his later works. For a period of time (actually while visiting Norway) he wrote one book per year.
5. Howard Becker, *Through Values to Social Interpretation,* Duke University Press 1950.

6. See Rua (2012), which delineates the difficulties medical doctors have in being independent from prison authorities. Teachers and medical doctors are in many ways different, also in prisons. Medical doctors have the ability to enter a power game with the prison authorities, and even win the battle. As Rua shows in her book, they may therefore refrain from battle, in order for peace to reign. Teachers do not have the same power, and the authorities in the prison more often let them 'do what they like'. I owe this point to Marte Rua.

7. The following section on "the abolitionist stance" is based on my article "The Abolitionist Stance", *Journal of Prisoners on Prisons*, Vol. 17 No. 2, 2008, pp. 58–63.

8. The three large meetings on drugs were not organized by KROM. Norwegian professor Nils Christie was central among the organizers. A short while later, a government committee proposed several reforms, including the use of heroin as medication for very heavy drug users. In early 2013 the Labour Party Minister of Health advocated the smoking of heroin in 'injection rooms' rather than using heroin for injections.

9. Actually, the *h* and the *w* are wrongly placed. This was, as far as I know, Butler's own invention.

10. Other than to and from work the prisoner must stay at home, and not touch alcohol. http://norwaypost.no/index.php/news/latest-news/24986

11. Violent crimes reported to the police show a downward trend for the US from 1993 to 2009. Norway shows an increase from 1993 to about 2001, after which the increase stopped, went somewhat down and became more or less rectilinear between 2003 and 2009. *Sweden, however, saw a fairly consistent and steep rise all the way from 1993 to 2009.* In 2009 Sweden had the highest rate of violent crimes reported to the police of the three countries. See Einarsen 2010. During the first quarter of 2013, Denmark showed 192 house burglaries per 100,000 inhabitants, Sweden showed 52 per 100,000 and Norway showed 22 house burglaries per 100,000 inhabitants. 'Burglaries' give a sketchy picture because they vary in what they cover, but during the period 2006 to 2012, there was a general increase in all three countries up till 2009. After that, the Norwegian curve decreased markedly until 2011 with a very slight increase between 2011 and 2012, while *the Swedish curve continued its increase until 2011, tapering off very slightly between 2011 and 2012 but not reaching back to the level of 2009.* See Nadheim with Lerche www.krad.no/nyhetsarkiv-361-innbrudd-norge-er-best-i-norden.

    The number of reports on drug crimes provides a very sketchy picture due to great variations in what 'drug crimes' cover. Registration practices may, for example, vary. But at least they *have continually increased in Sweden since 1975.* Between 2000 and 2009 the number of reports was doubled. During this period legislation has become harder and resources for fighting drugs greater (http://sv.wikipedia.org/wiki/Narkotikabrott_i_Sverige).

12. In November 2013 the head of the Prison Department in Sweden (euphemistically called 'The Directorate of Criminal Care') emphasized that the number of prisoners in Sweden is going down and speculated about why (see also above), but surprisingly did not touch on electronic fetters as a possible and partial cause (Öberg 2013).

13. During the summer of 2012, groups of Roma people from Bulgaria and Romania came as beggars to Norway and to many other European countries. The borders were open for long periods at a time due to the European Economic Area accord and the Schengen agreement (see also above). The Norwegian public was enraged, at least as it was reflected in the mass media, and showed its limits to toleration. Restrictions and even criminalization of begging, which by now had been forbidden by the abolition of the remaining parts of the Vagrancy Act, were debated also by the government, which at the time was social democratic. The government vouched for geographic restrictions. But by the summer of 2013, the Roma people became fewer, at least in Norway, and the debate subsided. Nevertheless, the conservative coalition government, now in power after the election in 2013, finally agreed on the prohibition of begging as a municipal choice in 2014, and forced prohibition for all municipalities in the country from 2015.

Book II

The Politics of Abolition (1974)

Part I

The unfinished

The unfinished

1. Introduction

I have gradually acquired the belief that the alternative lies in the unfinished, in the sketch, in what is not yet fully existing. The 'finished alternative' is 'finished' in a double sense of the word.

If it is correct, this view has considerable consequences for political life. It means that any attempt to change the existing order into something completely finished, a fully formed entity, is destined to fail: in the process of finishing lies a return to the by-gone. Note that I am here thinking of change and reversion in terms of structure. The existing order changes in structure while it enters its new form. This was the meaning of the oracles: they provided sketches, not answers, as entrances to the new. This is the meaning of psychotherapy. In the sketches of the oracles and of the therapist to him who asks and to the patient – in the very fact that only sketches are given – lie their alternatives.

Existing order changes in structure *while* it enters the new. The first political question, then, becomes that of how this 'while' should be started, how the sketch should be begun, how it should be mobilized.

The second question, which is politically almost as central, is that of how the sketch may be maintained as a sketch, or at least prolonged in life as a sketch. An enormous political pressure exists in the direction of completing the sketch into a finished drawing, and thereby ending the growth of the product. How can this be avoided, or at least postponed? The answer to this question requires a new understanding of the social forces that work for the process of finishing.

Through both of these questions, *abolition* runs like a red thread. Abolition is the point of departure.

In the following I shall first explain in more detail why the alternative lies in the unfinished. Next, I shall approach the two questions mentioned above: the inception and the maintenance of the unfinished. I will hardly give complete answers to these questions, but I hope to be able to give some suggestions.

2. The unfinished as alternative

The alternative is 'alternative' in so far as it is not based on the premises of the old system, but on its own premises, which at one or more points *contradict* those of the old system. In other words, contradiction is a necessary element in the alternative. It is a matter of contradiction in terms of goals, or in terms of means together with goals.

The alternative is 'alternative' in so far as it *competes* with the old system. An arrangement which does not compete with the old system, an arrangement which is not relevant for the members of the old system as a replacement of the old system, is no alternative. I emphasize that the concept of competition takes, as its point of departure, the subjective standpoint of the satisfied system-member being confronted with an opposition. The political task is that of exposing to such a member the insufficiency of being satisfied with the system. When this is exposed, the opposition competes. This is the case whether the system-members in question are on top or at the bottom of the system. Often those we try to talk to will be at the bottom, because these are considered more mobile for actual political action. The main problem, then, is that of obtaining the combination of *the contradicting and the competing*; the main problem is that of avoiding that your contradiction becomes non-competing and that your competition becomes agreement. The main aim is that of attaining *the competing contradiction*.

*

An opposition may seek to bring a message which is (1) foreign and (2) fully formed. In the subsequent discussion, the fact that a message is 'foreign' will mean that the message in fact does not belong to, is not integrated or woven into, the old system. The opposite of being foreign will subsequently be that of being 'integrated': the message one seeks to bring has in fact already got its defined place, integrated into the old thinking.

The fact that a message is 'fully formed' will subsequently mean that the consequences of the actual carrying-out of the message are clarified, or approximately clarified. The opposite of being fully formed will in the following be 'suggested': the consequences of the actual carrying out of the message are not yet clarified.

The opposition that speaks (1) in a foreign way and (2) in a way that indicates a fully formed message, thus brings a message (a) which does not belong to, is not integrated in, the old system, and (b) which at the same time is clarified in so far as the consequences of its actual practical carrying-out are concerned. The contradiction of this opposition stands in danger of becoming non-competing. Since it is clear – beyond doubt, definite – that the message, when carried out, does not belong to the old system, the satisfied member of the old system may disregard the message as of no importance to himself and his system, as irrelevant, as of no concern to the system. The contradiction of the opposition may be disregarded as permanently 'outside', and thereby be set aside, because it is beyond doubt that the message does not belong to the established system.

The message which is foreign and fully formed thus contains a contradiction, but the contradiction easily becomes non-competing. This analysis, of course, is couched in ideal-typical terms. Some parts of the Marxist- Leninist opposition in today's Scandinavia possibly constitute an example which approaches the ideal type. Let us for a moment take a look at the opposite extreme: the message with a content (1) which in fact is woven into, or integrated in, the old system, but (2) where the content is only suggested, so that the consequences of the actual carrying-out of the message remain unclarified. This message will not so easily be written off as non-competing. Since the question of what the message will lead to is not clarified, the message cannot simply be set aside. But at the same time the message does not contradict the establishment. In fact, it is integrated into, and therefore in accordance with, the premises of the old system. In sum, the message constitutes what may be called a 'competing agreement', a fictitious competition. Do there exist examples which approach such a combination of characteristics?

Perhaps 'the meditating conservative' may give an example approximating to how a message which is integrated and suggested becomes a 'competing agreement' (the concept of competition all the time being defined from the point of view of the satisfied system member). The pipe-smoking, casually philosophizing district attorney in an exclusive interview with the Sunday newspaper may be a case in point. Nothing new is being said, but the old is stated in such a way that the reader is given the impression of interesting depth. Competition takes place – about nothing.

*

Above I have first discussed how a contradiction may become non-competing (because it is fully formed), and afterwards how an agreement may become (fictitiously) competing (because it is only suggested). What we are searching is the alternative, the competing contradiction. The important thing at this point is that neither of the two cases discussed above provides an understanding of the alternative.

Logically there are two other main possibilities.

The first is that of (1) the integrated and (2) fully formed message. The main thing to say about the integrated and fully formed message is that this is a message which brings nothing new. The integrated and fully formed message constitutes what we may call a non-competing agreement. The 'able' student reproducing textbook material from rote learning is probably the core example. This student does not give any hint of an alternative. His examination paper contains no contradiction, and no message experienced as competing. It contains only memorization. The sociologically significant point is that considerable parts of life in our society consist of such reproduction or non-competing agreement, interspersed by a few meditating district attorneys.

The remaining possibility is that of (1) the foreign and (2) suggested message. Here we are faced with a contradiction, and finally at the same time competition. The unclarified nature of the further consequences of the contradiction makes it impossible for the (satisfied) system member to maintain that the contradiction is certainly outside his realm of interest. Contradiction and competition are united – in the alternative.

This is at the same time the definition of 'the unfinished'. To be sure, the foreign and fully formed message is unfinished in the sense that it is outside the established – empirically tested and tried – system, but it is at the same time finished in the sense that its final consequences are clarified. The integrated and suggested message is in fact fully tried out, and thereby finished, even if its consequences are unfinished in the sense of not being set down on paper. The integrated and fully formed message is finished in a double sense of the word: it is in fact fully tried out, and its consequences are even clarified, on paper. The foreign and suggested message, however, is unfinished in the sense that it is not yet tried out *as well as* in the sense that its consequences are not yet clarified. Thus, the alternative constitutes the double negation of the fully formed or finally framed world.

The alternative contradicts the vulgar interpretation of Wittgenstein's closing words in *Tractatus*: 'Wovon man nicht sprechen kann, darüber muss man sehweigen.' The vulgar interpretation of this statement, which I interpret as positivism – the tested and fully formed – in a nutshell, claims (as far as I can understand) that we simply must remain silent unless our message is: (1) foreign and fully formed, (2) integrated and suggested, or (3) integrated and fully formed. But thereby the alternative is also omitted: (1) Either the deviant is rejected as non-competing, (2) or we introduce something which is only fictitiously deviant, or (3) we only repeat what is already established. Wittgenstein's positivistic followers do not allow the fourth possibility: we are not allowed to talk in a foreign and suggestive way; rather than doing so, we must remain silent. However, it is vitally important to insist on the fourth possibility, and in this sense be negative rather than positive; it is vital not to remain silent concerning that which we cannot talk about; it is vital to express the unfinished.

But it is very difficult. I shall return later to the forces we must fight against. First, I shall give some concrete examples of the unfinished, and thereby of the alternative.

Love is an unfinished relationship. In its state of being unfinished, love is boundless. We do not know where it will lead us, we do not know where it will stop; in these ways it is without boundaries. It ceases, is finished, when it is tried out and when its boundaries are clarified and determined – finally drawn. It represents an alternative to 'the existing state of things': to existence in resigned loneliness or in routinized marriage. Resigned loneliness and routinized marriage are not alternatives in relation to each other: contradiction as well as the degree of competition are low, if at all present. (But unfinished loneliness, in which we are *en route* to something through the loneliness, and in which boundaries are not drawn, may certainly be an alternative to – contradicting and competing with – routinized marriage.)

The treatment experiment is an unfinished state while it is being developed. While being developed, it is non-integrated as well as without boundaries; the question of how narrowly the boundaries may be drawn is not determined. The very unfolding of the experiment, the development of the project, is an alternative to the established state of things – for example to hospitals and prisons. In its approximate boundlessness, the experiment contradicts and competes with the established structures. The *content* of the experiment, in the form of concrete 'treatment method', is close to immaterial; the most important thing is the process of development of the project. In line with this, experience shows that as the pioneering period of the treatment experiment ceases, as wondering withers and boundaries are drawn, and as continuation for its own sake becomes the issue, the new experiment is simultaneously incorporated in the establishment. What is strange is that we rarely act in line with this. We rarely view the 'pioneering stage' as life itself; rather we tend to view it as 'only a beginning'.

The third and most encompassing example concerns the notion of the 'alternative society'. Contradiction to and competition with the old society lies in the very unfolding of 'the alternative society'. Contradiction to and competition with the old society lies in the very inception and growth of the new. The unfolding of the new may take place after a revolution, after a war, after a physical catastrophe. The alternative society, then, lies in the very development of the new, not in its completion. Completion, or the process of finishing, implies full take-over, and thereby there is no longer any contradiction. Neither is there competition.

3. The forces pulling away from the unfinished

As I have indicated earlier, the forces which pull away from the unfinished – away from the competing contradiction – are many and strong. We must say something about these forces as a background for our considerations about the inception and maintenance of the unfinished.

Figure 1 schematically presents the material we have covered so far. The Figure is introduced in order to simplify the presentation that follows. The forces that pull away from the unfinished – away from the competing contradiction – move in two directions, as the arrows show.

In the first place, there are forces which finish in such a way that the contradiction becomes non-competing; in such a way that competition is abolished. The vertical arrow shows this movement. Language provides a road to it. The pressure in the direction of finalizing language, the pressure in the direction of

The message is	Foreign	Integrated
Suggested	Competing Contradiction (alternative)	Competing Agreement
Fully formed	Non-competing Contradiction	Non-competing Agreement

Figure 1 The forces pulling away from the unfinished

clarifying what we mean, may lead to a contradiction in this direction. When language is finalized, the answer is given, and the contradiction – though stubbornly maintained as a contradiction – is finished in the sense of becoming fully formed. When fully formed, the foreign language may be rejected, and is rejected, as clearly and definitely of no concern.

But the forces making a contradiction non-competing are, relatively speaking, not so strong. Far stronger are the forces that *abolish* the contradiction, the forces that change the contradiction to an agreement rather than making it non-competing. The horizontal arrow shows this finishing movement. Why are these forces stronger? The main reason is probably that to those working for the new, non-competition seems more dangerous than agreement. First of all: non-competition – when others act as if one's message does not exist – gives little hope of effect. Agreement, on the other hand, gives greater subjective hope. Even if the issue here actually is that of surrender from the side of those who are working for the new, we can fool ourselves into believing that surrender takes place from the receivers' side, and that the receivers agree to the new message.

In the second place, as the concept is used here, non-competition is no relationship. Non-competition therefore seems irrevocable and irreversible. Agreement, on the other hand, is a social relationship, an interhuman interaction. As interaction it is a process, and we therefore easily imagine that our own surrender and agreement may once again be altered into contradiction when this appears necessary. The following sections will hopefully suggest that in reality, this is close to impossible.

Language is important also with regard to the doing away with the contradiction and its change into agreement (rather than the maintenance of the contradiction and its becoming non-competing). To amplify, in a specific and important way, language is related to power. Those in power decide (by and large) what language is to be spoken. The opposition is not in power, and in order for the opposition to ensure that it is defined as a competing party, it must begin to speak the language of those in power. But language not only provides a possibility for transmitting information. It is also active in structuring and defining the problem at hand. The more we use the language of the powerful, the more attuned we become to defining the problems at hand *as the powerful usually do*; in other words, the more integrated we become into the old system. We define the problems at hand in this way in order to persuade the powerful that our contradiction is sensible. But competition is then maintained at the cost of the contradiction itself; the contradiction is abolished and turned into fundamental agreement; the forms which compete are both integrated into the old system, tested out, and finished.

I will give an example. In penal policy there is, from the side of one opposing group, a stress on the use of 'treatment'. To the opposition, the concept of 'treatment' has a professional and specific meaning, and treatment is in itself a goal, though a part of a means-end chain. To make the concept understood and competing, the opposition characteristically translates it into the language of the ruler. For example, the opposition tries to talk of 'influencing', or 'persuading', the 'deviant'. In doing so, however, the opposition has straight away defined the issue as the other party – those in power – usually does. To the other party, the goal is that of creating better 'morals', and the concept of treatment has now been defined in these terms. When the lawyers in the Prison Department have finally understood, those who are out of power – those in opposition – have finally managed to express themselves perfectly in the language of those in power. And at the same time, the contradiction is gone; the problem at hand is defined according to the usual standards of the powerful.

Here competition as well as contradiction will often disappear, because the language of the powerful is also fully formed or finished rather than just suggestive, and in the end we are thus confronted with a non-competing agreement, a nodding, rote-learning candidate. In the following discussion, however, I shall take one thing at a time, by assuming an element of (fictitious) competition between forms which are integrated and not in contradiction.

The general type of competition which I have discussed above is that of 'persuasion'. Representatives of the new message seek, as their point of departure, to 'persuade' the representatives of the old system to replace the old way of stating the problem by a new one. For reasons given above, persuasion must take place in the language of the representatives of the established system, so that agreement about, rather than contradiction to, the tested – finished – way of stating the problem is established.

'Persuasion' is one of three important (perhaps not exhaustive) types of competition. The second type is 'the example'. While 'persuasion' is linguistic, the 'example' is a matter of practice. The representative of the contradiction is challenged to show what his alternative amounts to 'in practice'. If the challenge is not taken up, the contradiction is easily rejected as unable to compete – the vertical movement in our figure becomes relevant. The only chance often is therefore to answer the challenge. But 'in practice' means action based on the premises of the old system. It is the old system which defines what is to be practised, and thereby what is practicable and desirable. To be sure, the 'example' competes, but from the very beginning it competes on the premises of the old system, regarding 'realistic' means as well as 'desirable' ends. Contradiction is abolished; (fictitious) competition takes place between forms which are integrated into the old system.

Again I shall give an example from penal policy. The psychologist who takes up a position as prison governor, in order to 'show' that means and/or goals may be changed, competes from the beginning definitely on the premises definitely on the premises of the established system (with regard to means as well as ends), and he must – in order to be able to perform his duties at all – to a large extent accept the system's definition of 'the realistic' and 'the desirable'.

On the face of it, it seems possible to avoid the grave difficulties attached to 'the example'. It has been maintained that one can enter the old system, work for short-range improvements on the premises of the system, and at the same time maintain the long-range revolutionary goal. Again an example from penal policy: it has been maintained that by establishing democratically elected inmate councils among the prisoners, not only will short-range improvements in general welfare etc. be attained; a means to the final breakdown of the prison system from within will also be reached. What is necessary is constantly to maintain the long-range goal and continually to return to it.

To my knowledge, however, there is no clear example from practice showing that this is feasible – precisely not from practice. The absorption that takes place through such practice is here overlooked. Perhaps such absorption does not necessarily follow, but psychologically it is extremely pressing. From this it follows that one – in practice – departs from the long-range goal. Absorption contains at least three elements. It takes place through *incorporation*: the new is allowed only in a reduced form from the beginning, and concentration on the long-range goal is therefore easily broken down. It takes place through *initiation*: the rebel is initiated into the secrets of the system, and is thereby brought to silence – so to speak through his duties arising from having received privileged communication. Both of these types of absorption may be resisted through stubborn maintenance of the long- range goal. So may the third type, but it is so difficult that it is close to impossible psychologically. The third type of absorption is that of *being held responsible*: as a practitioner, you perform duties on the part of the system for which you are held responsible. The process of being held responsible has consequences for, and guides, your further actions. You cannot avoid your responsibility for having led the development away from the long-range goal.

The third type of competition which is to be discussed here is that of carrying a new message 'into effect'. By 'the carrying into effect' of a new message is meant that you try independently to establish the alternative. The boundaries between 'carrying into effect', on the one hand, and 'persuasion' and 'the example', on the other, are flexible in practice, a fact which – precisely through practice – easily leads to the specific difficulties attached to 'persuasion' and 'the example'. But in principle there is a difference. While 'persuasion' and the 'example' are based on the strategy of *moving into the established system*, the 'carrying into effect' is based on the strategy of *remaining outside the established system*, establishing a new system independently.

'Carrying into effect' consists of two main subtypes: (1) as a non-member of the established system you may try to create the alternative in splendid isolation from the establishment (the hippie society); (2) as a non-member you may try to create the alternative through overthrowing the establishment. Strictly speaking, only the latter type competes with the establishment (if the alternative is isolated, it is outside any relationship with the establishment), but empirically – outside the ideal type – there may also be present an element of competition in the former type. But the competition of the isolated alternative necessarily consists of 'persuasion', with the difficulties which this implies (see above). Thus, only the second subtype of 'carrying into effect' – working for the overthrow – implies a genuinely new type of competition.

The difficulty here is that you are a non-member. You have to be a non- member in order not to become involved in the difficulties of 'persuasion' and the 'example'. But at the same time the danger is great that you no longer compete, and that you thereby follow the vertical arrow, being finished off in that way.

However, empirically this is more complex: as a non-member working for the overthrow of the established order, you may seek to abolish the lack of competition. In other words, this is easier than the opposite, that is, to abolish an established agreement. Here lies the hope for those working for the overthrow of the establishment. You may perform raids into the territory of the establishment, contribute to crises which have a generally alarming effect on members of the establishment (wildcat strikes, for example); you may create cadres which – even if they are in the minority – have ability and strength to perform tasks exposing or unmasking the establishment, and so on. The point is that in contrast to the strategies of 'persuasion' and 'exemplification', you may act 'at the right moment', when the conditions are ripe. Historically, we know that this may be a successful strategy, particularly through the didactic functions of such suggestive actions, and that the established order may be overthrown.

What we also know, however, is that the new order which is established contains elements of the order which one sought to get away from. There is no reason to expect an unproblematical, terminated condition of final abolishment. The overthrow is never terminated in this way, because the new is woven into the old. Perhaps societies like the Chinese and the Albanian will show that this is not necessarily so. Until it is shown, I rely on existing historical examples, which are less optimistic, adding that I do not believe any Chinese or Albanian Marxist/Leninist would claim that their societies have reached any such terminated condition of final abolishment. I shall return to this in later essays.

We have here returned to the process of finishing, a process which may now be discussed in greater depth. I am basing my argument on an interpretation which is in dispute. Any society has certain general needs which must be satisfied. Furthermore, a society has limited ways in which to satisfy these needs, if it is at the same time to exist as a society. The very existence of 'society' is, in other words, in itself structure-forming in a limiting way; it is in itself anti-alternative. The limitations are partly embedded in the society's relations to other societies; other societies which are not changed. But the limitations are also built into the very phenomenon of 'structure'. The new society is therefore – when it is finished as an established order – in fundamental ways like the old society. This is like the new prison which is – when it is finally established – in fundamental ways like the old prison.

What are the general features of structure which are so recurrent? In particular, I have in mind the two dimensions of 'differentiation' and 'integration'. These are quite general processes, and the point is that they appear in combination: a differentiation becomes established, or is ossified, through an integration of the differentiated parts. The two processes have been pointed out in sociology from *Spencer* onwards, and have perhaps particularly been analysed by *Max Weber*. Their concrete forms may vary, one of them being a division of labour coupled with bureaucracy. It seems, for example, that the Soviet Union is faced with these concrete forms of the processes in question, and it might perhaps be said that the problem of the Soviet Union is first of all a 'Weberian' problem. In any case, the critique launched by the Marxist/Leninists against the Soviet Union may be interpreted in this direction.

From this view of the process of finishing, it not only follows that no final condition of terminated abolition can be expected. It also follows that new internal contrasts, inside the new order, do not automatically lead to new contradiction and new abolition. If it had been possible to rely on such an 'automatic' process, at least continually renewed abolition would have been secured. Not even this may be relied on.

The point is, then, to refrain from finishing the new – which means to refrain from terminating the overthrow. This means to *counteract* being pulled in any of the directions shown in Figure 1. Let me repeat, this is not an easy task.

*

The two arrows in Figure 1 have here been treated separately. Before leaving the forces creating a movement away from the unfinished, I shall briefly discuss how the two directions in the Figure may operate in conjunction with each other.

We may take a Norwegian interest organization, KROM, as our point of departure. The policies and practices of KROM will be discussed in detail later; suffice it here to say that the organization works for changes in the penal system beneficial to the prison inmates, KROM contradicts and competes while it is being developed, while it is not yet fully tried out and given its final form. In view of this, it has been correct to keep the relationship between the so-called 'revolutionary' (long-term abolishing) and 'the reformist' elements in KROM's policy open. As long as this relationship is an open one, as long as you have not in a definite way limited yourself to only one of these simplified forms, there is contradiction as well as power of competition in the organization. The premises of the established system are negated, and the receivers of the criticism are unable to rest contented with the view that the contradiction is irrelevant to them. It is symptomatic that the opponents of the organization try to 'place' KROM along the very dimension of 'revolution/reform'. The Norwegian newspaper Verdens Gang has, in line with this, demanded in an editorial that KROM 'must' make a choice between the two lines. In reality, this is the choice between being 'defined out' as irrelevant and 'defined in' as undangerous. And Verdens Gang knows this. Their demand throws light on a fundamental characteristic of that system which at any time is established, and to which Verdens Gang belongs, namely its stress on the terminated or fully formed along the dimension of contradiction. The demand also throws light on a strategy for survival on the part of the established system. The lack of tolerance of ambiguity along the dimension of contradiction, and *insistence on the view that one may only choose between different roads to clarity*, may be said to be one of the characteristics of an 'authoritarian social system'. The point is that any social system which is established, *is also authoritarian in this way*, and that through the choice between defining the adversary out and defining him in, the established social system is using its authoritarian character – together with its power – to place more definitively, and thereby render harmless, organizations which are in the process of unfolding.

In so far as KROM today gives in and takes only the so-called 'revolutionary' stand, to that degree the organization also loses its power of com- petition. The contradiction is experienced as irrelevant. In so far as KROM gives in and takes only the so-called 'reformist' stand, to that degree the organization loses its char- acter of contradicting the establishment. As long as a definitive, either-or choice is not made, and the 'placing' of the organization has not been effected, its unfolding is still in process and the organization contradicts and competes. In so far as the choice is made, it is at least important to qualify the choice by clearly maintaining the right to develop from the chosen standpoint and change it. But, for reasons that have been treated above, such change is not easy, and the first choice is therefore easily the road to being finished. Depending on which choice is being made, the power of competition or the very contradiction is being abolished.

When this happens, the organization should perhaps be dissolved. But if the 'revolutionary' choice has been made, and if the choice has taken time (in other words, if the pressure to choose has been resisted for a while), this is not necessar- ily the case. Possibly, the very development of KROM, and similar organizations, may in the meantime have created a climate in which indeterminateness along the dimension of 'revolution-reform' no longer gives power of competition, and in which the revolutionary standpoint is no longer 'defined out' to the same degree. If so, the organization can only live on through a more 'revolutionary' choice, on the condition of having 'the unfinished' built in at other points.

But the organization can hardly live on if the choice is 'reformist'. As I have suggested, the problem is that this movement is the stronger. Therefore, the deci- sive thing must be to counteract this movement.

*

The preceding paragraphs should enable us to understand the very concept of 'the unfinished' better. The state of the unfinished which we are discussing, and which it is so difficult to maintain, has to do with an unfinished set of goals. It is not enough to have unfinished means only.

However, having unfinished goals does not mean that you do not often have to set up sharply defined short-term goals, or partial goals, *en route*: five-year- plans, or what have you. By the same token, it is of course necessary to plan and co-ordinate the struggle. The point is that you should not make these short-term goals your final ones, but let them remains steps on a road which still is foreign and suggested only – unfinished.

Yet, it should be added that even if it is necessary to have short-term, clearly defined goals with a parallel fighting organization, short-term goals simultaneously mean that the danger of termination – so-called 'consolidation' – is straight away greater. This is one of the most difficult dilemmas, and it will preoccupy us further on.

4. The inception and the maintenance of the unfinished

Imagine that we have aroused an interest in the unfinished among those who have so far been satisfied with their system. How is the unfinished to be started in more practical terms? The question is complex. Let me briefly suggest a few tentative points.

The most general answer is that the inception of the unfinished takes place through *abolishing* the established order. Only the abolishing of what is finished gives the unfinished a chance to appear.

Earlier I have mentioned three examples of the unfinished: love, the treatment experiment, and 'the alternative society'. Love is the relationship in which the state of lovelessness is in the process of being abolished. The treatment experiment is the relationship in which the established institutional structure is in the process of being defeated. The 'alternative society' is the society in which the old social order is being fundamentally changed.

But at this point we may easily fool ourselves. A change through which we leave one order in favour of another *which is waiting*, is no abolishment. It is only a substitution, which certainly may involve differences in detail, and 'improvements' in detail, but which does not involve a change of structure. Structurally, a finalized fully formed new order perpetuates old solutions; our relationship to what is waiting is structurally like our relationship to the old order.

Abolition in other words takes place when we break with the established order and at *the same time* face unbuilt ground. This is to say that the abolition and the very first phase of the unfinished are one and the same. The moment of freedom is that of entering unbuilt ground. Freedom is the anxiety and pleasure involved in entering a field which is unsettled or empty.

But since the abolition and the very first phase of the unfinished are one and the same, the abolition tells us nothing about how the unfinished is set in motion, and we have actually not answered the question we raised. What is it that triggers abolition or the first phase of the unfinished?

The abolition, and by that token the unfinished, is at least not triggered through continual reforms improving the prevailing order. That is, through reforms improving the prevailing order, the main structure is maintained; the changes are in detail only. I have already discussed the psychological mechanisms impeding one's maintenance of the long-range goal of change when reforms improving the prevailing order are being carried out. Let me add at this point: actually, reforms of an improving kind may, through the very adjustment and legitimation of the prevailing order, postpone the abolition and the unfinished. Work for such reforms may thus in fact strengthen and integrate the prevailing order.

The abolition, and thereby the transition to the unfinished, is triggered through making those who are implicated conscious of the fact that one is necessarily faced with *a dilemma*; through the conscious experience of in fact having to choose between a continuation of the prevailing order (possibly with minor changes) and a transition to something which is unknown. Such a conscious experience is no sufficient condition for the inception of the abolition and the unfinished, but it is certainly a necessary one. It implies that veiled, unprincipled reliance on combinations, which deceives you into continuing the old structure, must be unveiled, and the choice between the horns of the dilemma must be clearly presented. In part, this means that we use one of the weapons characteristic of the prevailing system: this time we demand that the representatives of the system must make a clear choice. But here the similarity ends. The horns of the dilemma are not two different ways to the maintenance of the status quo (revolution that is 'defined out' and reform that is 'defined in'). The horns of the dilemma are the road to the status quo (reform without consequences) and the road away from the status quo (effective abolition). Thus, the issue is not a choice between roads to finalized clarity, but between finalized clarity and the unfinished. The choice points out tolerance of ambiguity as the counterpart to the status quo. Let me repeat: the consciousness of this dilemma is a necessary, but not a sufficient, condition for the breaking-away and for the inception of the unfinished.

I shall not discuss all of the concrete ways in which to induce such consciousness. At any rate, the consciousness of this dilemma and of the fact that we must choose between the status quo and abolition, creates a sense of liberation which gives abolition and the unfinished its full meaning.

For example, such a consciousness was established in Norway in connection with the changes in the so-called Vagrancy Act during the spring of 1970.[1] In its bill during the spring of 1969, the Ministry of justice recommended a few mitigating changes in the Vagrancy Act's provisions concerning forced labour and criminalization of public drunkenness. The Ministry simultaneously recommended that a committee be established to review the possibilities of more general abolishment of the provisions in question. The committee in question was set up in August 1969. In its bill, the Ministry of justice departed somewhat from the original recommendations of the advisory penal committee, but the structure of the system was maintained.

However, the opponents of the Vagrancy Act used the fall of 1969 to clarify the *dilemma* we were faced by, and the fact that by choosing the policy of the Ministry of Justice *the old structure would actually be chosen anew*. It was necessary to clarify that nothing but an *abolishment* of the prevailing order would lead to another distribution of resources (development of 'alternatives') for 'the clients'. A new distribution of resources would not appear 'of its own accord'; the abolishment could not wait until 'alternatives were established', because real alternatives would then never be established; the abolishment was necessary in order to press forth new solutions.

During the spring of 1970, important repeals were made in the Vagrancy Act: criminalization of public drunkenness was repealed as well as the system of forced labour – this *without* waiting for ready-made (finished) alternatives. Shortly after, the country entered a period of intensive redistribution of resources to vagrant alcoholics. Also, the vagrant alcoholics had become more visible and had thereby entered in to a relationship to the remainder of society. Among other things, others had become more conscious of the poverty of the country's poor. Shortly after the changes in the Act we were *in* one of the possible alternatives: the development of new resources.

*

However, how long will the alternative – the unfolding of the unfinished – last? This is not an easy question to answer. The problem is general. The core of it is this: a prevailing system has boundaries by which it is protected against influence from the outside. These are the boundaries one wishes to abolish, precisely because they maintain the prevailing system. But when the boundaries are erased – which was the goal in the first place – we have simultaneously opened the way for influence from other systems of an unwanted character, influence which the prevailing system, with its old boundaries, actually kept outside. This is not only a problem in connection with the Vagrancy Act's relationship to the policy of control in general. (The policy of control in general may be expected to invade the liberated field and lead to new forms of control.) It is also a problem in connection with the control policy's relationship to social policy in general; with the social policy's relationship to general politics within a society; with general politics as it is related to the international system, and so on. Originally, the change in the Vagrancy Act was not a matter of sheer positive reform, because the boundaries between the system which was abolished and other systems were abolished. But the change may become (has perhaps already become) a matter of sheer reform, precisely because the clear boundaries in question were abolished. This may be called the paradox of abolition. As indicated already, the same point is crucial in a more general revolution in a society. In an international perspective – because the old system borders are abolished – such a revolution may in turn become an integrated reform. I view this as one of the most fundamental reasons why the unfinished has such difficulties in remaining an unfinished process.

What is the answer to this? One answer, of course, lies in total abolition, simultaneous abolition on all relevant system levels. But as we know, this is not an easily performed task. And after such a total abolition, the unfinished process of development will not continue forever. Such a process does not continue 'of its own accord'. I am basing this view on the argument sketched earlier. The process will stagnate as problems are being solved, and system boundaries will be crystalized anew.

If *the problem* lies in the paradox of abolition, the answer to the problem is also embedded in the paradox of abolition. Let me repeat: the problematical aspect lies in the fact that the abolition of boundaries in itself leads new and more encompassing boundary-creating systems into the liberated field. The answer to the problem lies in the fact that this opens a possibility for a new abolishment, and thereby for a renewed unfinished process. Without new boundaries to abolish, new abolitions, and thereby renewed existence of the uncompleted, would be unthinkable. The answer, in other words, lies in the very opposition between the abolishing and the system-building forces, and in the continual abolition, rebuilding, re-abolition, on continually new levels. The point is a continually rotating transition to the uncompleted. I experience this as the process of life itself.

If this is the answer, it will be granted that the answer is not easily carried out in social structures. But in my view this is where the hope lies – for social structures too. At this point I shall only mention one difficulty related to a traditional policy of reform, which you do not have to encounter here. I believe it is to a large extent possible to avoid the psychological strings – mentioned earlier – which are tied to the standard policy of reform. These strings exist in so far as the revolutionary goal is only a very long-range goal believed to be obtainable through a series of reforms adding improvements to the prevailing order. It is through this process of adding improvement that we deviate from the long-range goal. These ties may be avoided if the abolition of existing orders is not just the encompassing and long-range goal, but *also all the time the goal which is close at hand, if necessary within a very restricted part of the total field.* In other words, it is decisive that the work for the abolition, and thereby for the unfinished – the alternative – is not only seen as long-range, *but that it takes place always, as directly and concretely as possible.* The abolition must be quite close as an immediate and constant objective within the field we have chosen to work in. At any time, we must work concretely, not with reforms of improvement as links in a long-range policy of abolition, but with *concrete, direct, and down-to-earth partial abolitions as links in the long-range policy.* A stubborn maintenance of such an immediate objective in everyday life is absolutely essential if we are to avoid the above-mentioned psychological ties.

And even then it is certainly difficult.

On action research

The concept of 'action research' has increasingly been employed in Norwegian sociological debate. 'Action research' constitutes an attempt to solve one of the dilemmas of sociology: the dilemma between the disclosure of new knowledge and practical action. In action research there lies a possibility of building a bridge between these two aspects. In this essay I shall investigate this possibility more closely.

1. 'Traditional' research

To obtain any disclosure of information from social systems implies that you expose the system to 'stimuli'. The questionnaire is a 'stimulus' which people are exposed to. So is participant observation. The various types of 'stimuli' lea d to the disclosure of more or less differing sets of information from the system in question, In other words, 'the response' of the system members to 'research stim-uli' will vary with the type of 'stimulus'. But regardless of the type of 'stimulus' used, and regardless of the kind of information that is 'stimulated', the informa-tion in question is traditionally brought back to a sociological theory – a theory which constituted the point of departure for the hypotheses or problems which were to be investigated. 'Sociological theory' does not necessarily constitute a theory in the formal sense – often it consists simply of interwoven 'thoughts' or ideas. But in any case, the information is collected for 'thinking'; this is where our loyalty lies; it is *theory* which is supposed to be refined and improved through the gathering of information.

Furthermore, it is assumed that the refined theory will, through new hypoth-eses, lead to a new and refined disclosure of information, in a feed-back process with theory. In this way, research is in principle an *unfinished* process: theory is improved by information, whereupon the gathering of information is improved, whereupon the theory in turn is improved, and so on. It is this character of being in principle unfinished that may give vitality to research. In this respect, research perhaps resembles art, and is very unlike a series of other activities in society – in the world of labour and leisure – which are not in principle unfinished.

The problem of traditional research is, however, that its character of being in principle unfinished tends in practice to be set aside. What happens is that theory becomes a closed system. The reasons are – as far as I can understand – of an 'irrelevant' psychological kind rather than a matter of principle. Theories are psychologically binding. The result of a combination of one set of variables must – we feel – stand in a logical relationship to the result of a combination of other variables. A logically coherent system is created, tied to a continually greater sense of loyalty. This, at least, is the way things may go – only the best of us manage to avoid it, and very few of us seem to be as good as that. The obligating, logical system becomes increasingly completed, to an increasing extent information fits into boxes, and research becomes continually less unfinished and simultaneously less vital. This corresponds to the finishing of a book: loose ends are tied up; various parts are re-written in order to relate logically to each other; the book is finally a coherent system. And at this point it may no longer be touched, because if it is, the relationships are easily totally disturbed. This is often also the fate of sociological theory.

2. Action research

Since all research involves an influencing of the system which is being investigated, and since all information which is disclosed constitutes a 'response' to such influence, all research may be said to be 'action research'. Seen in this light, what varies is simply the way in which you influence the system, and the concrete information which is thereby gathered.

Here, however, I want to delimit 'action research' through some additional criteria.

In the first place, I limit 'action research' to that gathering of information in which the action stimulating information *first of all* constitutes an attempt to realize given practical or political values. In other words, the disclosure of information as well as practical or political values constitute objectives for the action, but the latter are decisive for the content of the action. Thus, action research constitutes a conscious attempt to combine activities which researchers have traditionally tried to keep separate, a combination which has often been met by cries of anger. In this respect, action research is a follow-up of an insight which became commonplace a few years ago, namely that research – at least in its consequences – cannot be value-free.

In action research we try to combine the disclosure of information with a conscious attempt to realize given practical or political values – the latter values being primary. But note that an element of – a consciousness about – systematic gathering of information must also be present if we are to talk of action *research*, and not just of 'action'. I grant, however, that the borderline between 'systematic' and 'unsystematic' gathering of information is unclear.

Secondly, I limit 'action research' to the gathering of information in which the new information is, first of all, related back to the action itself, in an attempt to improve and refine the action, and not first of all related back to a general socio-logical theory. *In other words, the loyalty is towards the action, and not towards the theory.* The assumption is that the information which is related back to the action improves the action, which in turn leads to a new disclosure of informa-tion, and so on. In this way, the action takes the place of the theory, in a feed-back process with the gathering of information.

A practical relief project, in which the living conditions of a group are improved, and where you at the same time follow the project systematically in order to improve the next round of relief work, may be called action research. Political pressure group activity, in which your goal is to change the general conditions for a group, and where you at the same time follow the activity systematically in order to refine and improve the next round of political work, may be called action research. The difference between practical and political action is unclear, but this is of less importance at this point. *What is important here, is the feed-back process from practical/political activity, through a systematic gathering of infor-mation, back to the practical/ political activity.* This feed-back process makes action research different from 'traditional' research, in which a feed-back process takes place from a non-practical/political, theoretically oriented influencing of the system, through the gathering of information, to a sociological theory – often a theory of a deductive kind.

In contrast to what we might think, action research does not provide a solution to the moral relationship of research to society. The researcher must still make moral choices. Certain types of advertising research in private industry constitute action research; for example, the advertising campaign which is followed up by a gathering of information concerning the effects of the campaign – with a view to improving the campaign. Certain types of radical political pressure-group activi-ties constitute action research: those in which the participants try to describe the activity and the establishment's reception of it – with a view to improving the next round of pressure-group activity. Both of these forms are 'action research', but politically they are very far apart, and the researcher/actor must make his choice of values. Action research, in other words, is not in itself morally right or proper.

It follows from the preceding paragraph that neither does action research neces-sarily oppose the established or prevailing order. In practice, projects involving action research will often be of an oppositional kind, at least in certain phases, because the social scientist is often at the outset doubtful or critical of his society, but this characteristic does not follow necessarily from action research. Again, the researcher/actor must make a choice in the light of his view of society.

It might be argued that the moral choices, or evaluations, which easily remain unexposed in 'traditional research', are clearly exposed to the researcher in an action research setting. This, however, is not necessarily the case. To amplify, the established system responds to influence not only by giving information. The 'stimulus-response' terminology used above is naturally an over-simplification: the system also responds by trying to neutralize influences which are threaten-ing. The system often does so by trying to integrate or absorb the researcher/

actor into the system. Such a response may be made to influences stemming from 'traditional' research as well as from action research. It may take many concrete forms – from an apparent openness in attitude to the establishing of new posts and distribution of medals of honour – which I will not deal with in detail here. The point I want to emphasize is that the researcher operating within an action-research setting stands – after having made his first moral choices or evaluations – in danger of feeling that the moral issue is then 'over', and that he has clarified his role as being a man on the 'right side'. In reality, however, this role is not secured once and for all, but is relative to the attempts coming from the system at integrating the researcher and his findings. Even a revolutionary effort may in this way, if the researcher is unaware of the problem, be transformed into a mildly reform-oriented activity supporting the establishment, Also action research – perhaps particularly action research – constitutes a continual moral activity, in which moral choices must continually be made. In this way, action research is simply a part of life, and not different from life. So is also the very model of action research. Practical action followed by a disclosure of information, and in turn by a feed-back return to practical action, is also the process of every-day life, and the way in which action and knowledge are combined in every-day life. What the action researcher is doing, then, is so to speak to begin all over again as an ordinary human being. This is precisely the way in which the transition from a 'traditional' sociological project to an action research activity is experienced. The transition gives a strong sense of freedom – freedom from the old loyalty to the logically coherent construction of sets of variables, a construction which to an ever greater degree was terminated and closed. During the transition the road ahead is open. The important point here is that through the transition, the unfinished process is once again initiated. This time it is the practical/political action that is refined by the information which is disclosed, through which the action once again is improved, and so on. This is not just a formal statement of the matter. I have experienced it myself. I can mention the organization KROM as an example. KROM was started with a view to changing penal policy in Norway. It is not necessary to describe the objective more closely here (it will be discussed at length in Part II); the point is that the goal of the organization was purely political. However, for those of us who worked in the organization, it soon became clear that a systematization of our experiences might be useful. I started to keep a diary of the work we were doing, and to write a personal commentary on what was happening. I believe this was useful for our political work. For example, in the diary and the commentary I forced myself to be as honest as I possibly could be, something you are certainly not always forced to be in politics alone. Thus, the dishonesty characteristic of politics did not have a chance to accumulate to the extent that it otherwise would, a fact from which I believe our action benefited on a long-term basis. Our policy acquired a certain asceticism; we acquired strength to avoid the temptation to utilize short routes and white lies; we acquired strength to act in accordance with basic principles, at least to a somewhat greater extent than we would have done otherwise. This is action research.

When we started writing down our experiences, I thought of publishing something about them in standard sociological form – over and above what I am writing in this book. Gradually I understood that this would be a difficult thing to do, for reasons of discretion as well as for other reasons. Gradually, however, I also became conscious of the fact that such a publication would be less vital. The important thing was that the disclosure of information contributed to an improvement of the action itself. Gradually, my loyalty swung more clearly over from theory to the action itself. The political action became the essential activity; if anything were to be written later – if anything is to be written later – it must be done in order to improve the political action. I became a more genuine action researcher.

3. Theory and action research

However, what I should like to arrive at in this essay, is to emphasize how even action research may become finished.

Again I will take a personal experience as my point of departure. As mentioned above, the transition from a 'traditional' sociological activity to an action-oriented effort provides great freedom. The road ahead is open. The problem, however, is that when you are finally well settled in the new field, a lack of freedom and a form of enclosure may again appear. As an actionist, you may begin with a 'do as you like' approach. There are no limits to your possibilities for action. The limits, however, come through the very reactions of the environment (that is, of the established system) to your action. In part, you make choices which – in their consequences – further limit your possibilities of choice, because the consequences constitute 'cross-roads' created by the environment. But in part the environment more actively sets up dilemmas which you are forced to choose between, and which therefore lead to limitations on your further actions. An example: from the beginning, KROM's position on the scale of 'revolution-reform' was unfinished. The environment – the prison system and especially parts of the mass media – exerted pressure to place the organization in one, and just one, of the two categories. As described in the essay on 'The Unfinished', the attempts at placing us at the same time constituted attempts at defining us. As exclusively 'revolutionary' we would be 'defined out' as irrelevant; as exclusively 'reformist' we would be 'defined in' as undangerous. Regardless of which choice was made, it would constitute a neutralization, The creation of such dilemmas, dilemmas through which you cannot maintain a short-term and a long-term objective, but where you must make a choice between the two and exclude one, may quickly reduce the actionist to silence, or at least strongly limit his freedom of speech and action, if the actionist chooses the 'reformist side', any reference to something radical or 'revolutionary' is later picked up by powerful adversaries as something illegitimate and inadmissible. If he chooses the 'revolutionary side', it suddenly becomes 'illicit' for him to adopt changes which are near-at-hand, pressing and wanted, and he is separated from those he wishes to work for.

The issue may be stated in more precise terms. A choice between 'revolution' and 'reform' constitutes a hopeless dilemma. You therefore look for a road which may lead around the choice, and which may maintain the state of the unfinished on this dimension. The road leading around the choice goes through a gradual totalization on the part of the 'clients': you let the group in question (workers, prisoners) take as their point of departure reforms which are close to them and which will change their concrete situation, from which you totalize – through 'didactic' activity – to continually larger and more encompassing fields. The group learns to 'see' – to an increasing degree – the further connections. Through the dissatisfaction which the group feels towards the reforms which are carried into effect, through the feeling that the victory soon wanes, the actionist is given an opportunity to show the continually more encompassing causal connections, and the need for a continually more total protest.

The process of totalization involves a number of problems which I will not deal with here, but possibly later. What I want to get at here is that by forcing the actionist to make the choice between 'revolution' and 'reform', the established forces participate in severing the opportunities for the kind of totalization discussed here. The choice, once made, means that you have once and for all taken an explicit either – or stand at the level of totalization: either you work directly for the total change, or you only work for limited change. Totalization, which means the transition from the limited to the total, is the very transition which then becomes illegitimate, inadmissible, and easily exposed to attacks which appear convincing to others. This is only one example of the dangerous 'finishing' of an action. But did we not say that the disclosure of information, in a feed-back process with the action, was to trigger the unfinished? Yes, but this does not mean that the process is automatically maintained. The external forces which I have discussed here – the reactions to the action – exert pressure on the process of action research. Even if the information gathered works back with a vitalizing effect on the action, the delimiting forces from elsewhere may be so strong that the disclosure of information is not enough to keep the wheel in motion.

Another way of putting this is to point out that not even the process of action research exists in a vacuum, but in a context. The context consists of the reactions which the environment makes to the action – reactions which in the program of action research are studied with a view to improving the action – but which do not work back on the action only through the 'research filter', but also directly. The direct repercussions constitute forced dilemmas which, when the choices are made, put strong limitations on further action, and thereby on further research.

Through such a finishing of the action, the action research may in other words also be finished.

As you see, I am here assuming that the unfinished and freedom are related. The unfinished is at the same time freedom. To me, freedom in research means having an opportunity to support the cause I believe is right. If freedom meant something else, for example a separation from causes and interests in society, it would in reality involve a form of lack of freedom and a limitation on action. When an action, and thereby the action research, is finished, freedom is limited, in this very sense of the word: the action is limited or brought to silence. And – this is what I want to get at – at the same time you get the feeling that you have lost something through the transition to action research. Actually, this is a false feeling, because the traditional research was completed when you left it. What has happened is that against the background of the experiences with action research, 'new light' has been thrown on traditional research, traditional research has become new. What gave new life when you left the old research was the movement towards action research; when you are in the middle of action research the transition is over and the built-in process of incompletion is halted for reasons spelled out above.

But the process may be maintained through a movement towards the old type of research, which then is *new*. The chief result, then, must be an oscillation *between* theory and action research. In a way, the result is quite trivial. There will always exist a 'theoretical' framework for an action, a framework which you do not liberate yourself from, cannot liberate yourself from. And it is a standard recipe in social research that 'theory' and 'data' must be related. What I am getting at here, however, is something more. What the social scientist must be made conscious of, is the very movement, back and forth, without the goal being reached; the necessity of all the time hurrying away from what you are doing towards the other side. When the action researcher has finished moving away from traditional research, action research is also finished, and vice versa. The point, then, is always to turn before it is too late. In this process lies freedom, also freedom to support your cause.

This means that you never finish anything. But this is precisely the point. Concretely it means that the movement from theory to action gives release, and thereby insight and freedom of action, up to a certain point, and that the movement from action to theory gives release, and thereby insight and freedom of action, up to a certain point.

I have to add a closing remark about the problem of movement between theory and action. To the individual, this movement in other words provides an opportunity for action as well as withdrawal. For him, the task is all the time to develop out of, or unwind, the ties attached to action as well as to withdrawal. Such must have been the situation during the first years of psychoanalytic theory and practice. By continually developing out of these ties, the individual is free to take his standpoint and support the interests he thinks should be supported, including the interests of small or large groups in society.

Such a movement is foreign to traditional research institutes. It is also foreign to traditional politics. In the former case, resistance to the movement occurs, inter alia, because it is believed that the freedom of the researcher will be limited from the outside. There may be something in this, but if so, this must be fought, because the alternative is limitations from the inside, through one-sided theoretical withdrawal. In the latter case, resistance occurs because it is believed that through such a movement, realistic political activity will be side-tracked. There is something in this, too, but the answer is that realistic political activity should be side-tracked, because it is limited and tied. The bases for resistance which have been mentioned here, are among the many which contribute to the maintenance of a relationship between research and politics through which both activities are exposed to internal binding, internal strangulation. The conscious breaking-down of the boundary between them may possibly create the foundation for research and politics being more of a liberated common field for all the people; research being liberated by politics, and politics by research.

At least, this may be an ideal goal.

Part II

Pressure group and social structure

III

Background

1. Introduction

During the latter half of the 1960s a new type of political interest organization developed in the Scandinavian countries. These interest organizations had as their short-term objective the improvement of the situation of prison inmates, and as their long-term goal the substitution of other forms of reaction and other measures for imprisonment in general. At the time of writing – spring 1973 – the organizations are still quite active, even if they have now in part changed character. Their growth and development tell us a good deal about the place of interest organizations in the social structure, and about the reactions of the social structure to such organizations. In this Part, I shall analyse some aspects of the development of these Scandinavian organizations,

First, however, I must say a few words about my own relationship to these organizations. I took a personal part in establishing one of them – the Norwegian one – and from its foundation in 1968 till the spring of 1973 I was chairman of that organization. At the time of writing, I am a member of its board. A good deal of my working time has been spent on activities connected with the organization. This has been possible because I have had a fairly free position as a social scientist – first as research supervisor at the Institute for Social Research in Oslo, and later as a professor at the University of Oslo. It has also been possible because I have gradually tried to combine my activity in the interest organization with a research effort, regarding the political activity as a type of 'action research'. The concept of 'action research', and its relationship to 'traditional research' and to 'politics', has been discussed in Chapter II above.

A consequence of my particular connection with the Norwegian organization is that I will give a more detailed description of the development of this association than of the development of the other Scandinavian sister organizations, simply because I am best acquainted with the Norwegian development. However, I will also utilize material from the other organizations – especially the Swedish one.

A main objective of the Scandinavian organizations has been to establish political contact with the prisoners, so as to include them in political work for the improvement of their situation. This collaboration between people with a political interest and the prisoners – political contact across the prison walls between radical outsiders and the inmates – apparently presents a threatening aspect to the prison authorities. In varying degrees the authorities in the Scandinavian countries have tried to prevent such contact. The Norwegian authorities have been particularly active in this respect. A main objective of the present account will be that of analysing why such contact is regarded as threatening to the establishment. I will try to show that the lines of development in the Norwegian organization have gone from a 'co-operation model' to a 'conflict model' in relation to the authorities, and that political contact between such an organization and the prisoners 'disturbs' or 'threatens' major social functions of imprisonment.

2. The first organization: Swedish KRUM

The first Scandinavian organization was founded in Sweden in the fall of 1966, and was a product of the so-called 'Parliament of Thieves' in Strömsund. The 'Parliament of Thieves' was a large meeting, discussing penal and correctional policy, at which a number of ex-inmates, together with lawyers, psychiatrists, social workers and sociologists, expressed themselves on the political issues involved. For the first time in Scandinavia, ex-inmates publicly announced their view of prison conditions and the treatment of prisoners.

The criticism of prison conditions expressed at the 'Parliament of Thieves' was severe, and the Swedish organization which was founded became a national one, under the name of Riksforbundet för Kriminalvårdens Humanisering ('The National Swedish Association for Penal Reform') – abbreviated as KRUM. At the time of writing the organization has about 1,200 members (including prisoners or ex-prisoners), distributed among fifteen local chapters (active in varying degrees) in Sweden. The national board of the association has membership from the various local chapters, and the national organization has offices in Stockholm.

From the beginning, one of the main objectives of KRUM has been to have past and present inmates co-operate with non-inmates for the changing of penal conditions. In some prisons the association has to some extent been allowed to engage in study-group activity with the inmates. At an early stage the organization was rather strongly characterized by the emphasis it put on concrete social aid to inmates. Thus, for a considerable period the rule was that every KRUM-person should on some occasion meet a released inmate at the gates of the prison and try to take care of him and help him during his re-entry into society. At the same time, KRUM early stressed the importance of 'treatment' of prisoners – psychological and psychiatric treatment, individual treatment and group treatment. It was claimed that the idea of treatment had never been carried out in Swedish penal institutions, and that it ought now to be carried into effect. In other words, the activity of the association was critical, but at the same time humanitarian and treatment-oriented.

The humanitarian activity and the treatment-oriented criticism confronted KRUM with some problems which were only clarified at a much later point in time.

*

The early humanitarian activity in KRUM gave the participants in the organization an important contact with the practical realities of so-called correctional and penal practice. At the same time this activity was attended by a vacillating attitude towards the political task. Should KRUM engage in concrete humanitarian work, or should the organization primarily concern itself with questions of criminal *policy*?[2] The members wished to do the latter, but to a large extent the former became the usual practice. The political and the humanitarian are in fact activities which are not easy to combine. In the first place, people who work in voluntary organizations are generally short of time and resources. The humanitarian work therefore competes directly with the political activity. In the second place, one is easily 'absorbed' by humanitarian work. Partly because the humanitarian work forces one to make politically unsound short-term choices, and partly because the concentration on the individual case easily leads to a fading away of the problems of principle involved, the critique of the system which one wants to change or do away with is weakened. In the initial stages, therefore, the vacillating interest in criminal policy constituted a problem for KRUM: the organization stood in danger of being diverted from its objective of filling in a political vacuum. Later – and especially from 1970 onwards – the commitment to questions of penal and 'correctional' policy was strengthened and clarified. This clarification was probably related to a growing scepticism as regards the notion of treatment in the penal setting, a scepticism which will be briefly described below.

*

The treatment orientation in KRUM led to standpoints which, if they had been carried out, would to some extent have increased rather than decreased legal insecurity in the field of penal law. Important representatives of the organization at one point suggested that while lawyers and the courts ought to decide on *the question of guilt* in criminal cases, the *choice and duration of the measures to be applied* ought to be decided by social scientists, psychologists, and psychiatrists. In practice such a proposal would undoubtedly only have increased legal insecurity in the prison system. The proposal was never carried into effect, but the general treatment orientation in KRUM probably to some degree influenced Swedish 'correctional' policy.

However, around 1970 the participants in KRUM gained a deeper understanding of the issues of legal security associated with the treatment ideology in the penal system, and the activities of the organization became more clearly 'defensive': instead of working for treatment alternatives, the participants geared their activities to the problem of avoiding the establishment of new systems of control – hidden for example under the treatment philosophy. A clear example of this change in orientation may be found in the publication *Autopsy of a Dead Committee Report*, published in 1972. The authors – Stig Edling and Göran Elwin – had both for a period been members of KRUM's national board. In the book they present a clear criticism of the plans launched in the so-called Committee for Institutional Treatment in the Correctional System, plans to increase the treatment orientation in penal institutions. For example, in Chapter 6 the authors discuss the consequences of the committee's proposal to abolish isolation as a means of punishment. They point out that an abolition of isolation as punishment does not imply an abolition of isolation, and that after the abolition of isolation as punishment, isolation may be carried out under conditions characterized by an even smaller degree of legal security.

Autopsy of a Dead Committee Report constitutes a distinct example of a 'neo-classicist' approach to penal law.

*

A third dimension in the development of KRUM, which is related to the two to which I have already referred, must also be mentioned. As a parallel to the development from an emphasis on humanitarian work and treatment to a stressing of issues of penal and correctional policy and legal security, there has also occurred a development from an emphasis on criminal policy narrowly defined to a greater stress on political principles of a general kind.

Again around 1970 two groups within the organization to some degree conflicted with each other – one group having a more narrow interest in penal and correctional policy, and the other being more strongly oriented towards general political principles of a socialist kind. At that time the conflict remained unresolved. At the organization's annual meeting in the spring of 1970 the topic was brought up, with speakers from the two main groups taking part, but the ensuing discussion was surprisingly brief. However, the topic was reintroduced on several later occasions, and a tentative conclusion was reached in a new statement of objectives and principles adopted at an extraordinary general meeting in March 1971. The development of the organization may be seen by comparing KRUM's statement of objectives from 1967 with its statement of objectives from 1971. In 1967 a KRUM-pamphlet said that:

> The National Swedish Association for Penal Reform (KRUM) will attend to the interests of those who are punished, and ease their re-adjustment to society. KRUM works for a radical reform of the correctional system and the treatment of prisoners. Legislation and treatment of criminals ought to be liberated from punitive thinking. The present system of institutions ought to be abolished, and incarceration reduced to a minimum. Offenders who have social handicaps ought to be met by a social policy which is liberated from moralization and authoritarian thinking.

The general meeting in March 1971 adopted the following statement of objectives:

> KRUM wishes to analyse and fight the class society, which through its unequal distribution of power and opportunity contributes to the creation

of groups which are socially, economically, and culturally expelled. KRUM is working to abolish imprisonment and other types of forced incarceration within the correctional system, child and youth welfare, mental health care, alcohol care, narcotics care, handicap care, etc.

The new formulation differs in several respects from the old one. In the first place, fighting the 'class society' has now been added as an important independent goal. Secondly, this goal is placed ahead of the goal related more directly to criminal policy. In the third place, the risk of changing criminal policy is now only one of several similar tasks within the general area of social policy.

The organization, however, still works independently of political parties, and its concrete activities have not altered much since the political change in objectives.

Let me add that the annual meeting which adopted the new statement of objectives included at least one lively debate. A small fraction in the association viewed the addition concerning the combating of the class structure as an unfortunate phrase of a general political kind. Some felt that the statement about abolition of imprisonment ought at least to be placed ahead of the statement concerning abolition of the class structure. These viewpoints, however, were not followed up – the majority felt that the issues involved had been discussed thoroughly enough for one and a half years – and the new statement of objectives (in part formulated at the meeting) was finally adopted.

3. The Danish and the Finnish associations

The parallel associations in the other Scandinavian countries were established with KRUM's first years as a background; that is, with an emphasis on a treatment-oriented criticism, humanitarian aid, and neutrality in terms of general political issues as major guide lines.

Danish KRIM – Foreningen for Human Kriminalpolitik ('The Association for a Humane Criminal Policy') – was founded during the spring of 1967, while two Finnish organizations, 'The November Movement' and KRIM – Foreningen for fångar ('The Association of Prisoners') – were established during 1967/68. The two Finnish associations quickly became quite different in character. The November Movement became a strongly critical politically oriented pressure group, while Finnish KRIM became much more of a humanitarian organization. As a parallel to this difference in character, a difference in the organizations' relationship to the inmates could also be discerned: while the November Movement only to a small extent became a prisoners' organization, Finnish KRIM grew strong roots and enlisted a wide membership among the prisoners. And there was a third difference. While the November Movement ceased to exist in 1971 (formally the organization still exists but all its activities have ceased), Finnish KRIM is still active – with study groups in the prisons, cultural programs for the prisoners, and other humanitarian activities. Possibly there is a connection between these factors. The purely political organization fills a blank space on the political map, but finds it difficult to reach the grass-roots, and ceases to exist when the first generation of activists moves on to other activities. The purely humanitarian organization does reach the grass-roots, and does not cease to exist, but on the other hand finds it difficult to fill any blank space on any political map. The dilemma is the same as that met by Swedish KRUM, and we shall meet it again below – in our discussion of the Norwegian organization.

KROM – 'The Norwegian Association for Penal Reform' – was founded in the spring of 1968. At the time of writing, the association has approximately 1,500 members, about half of whom are inmates or ex-inmates (the country has about 2,000 prison inmates at any one time).[3] The organization has a board of 11 members (five of whom are ex-inmates), and several active committees working in specialized areas. The organization has had local chapters in the two largest cities outside Oslo. Below I shall discuss the development of the Norwegian organization in detail, beginning with the initial phase of the organization, because the initial period contained the seed of important later characteristics in the organization's relationship to prisons and society.

IV

First phase: co-operation or conflict?

I. The idea is conceived

The idea of founding a Norwegian association for the 'reform' (in one sense or another) of prisons and the criminal justice system came from Sweden, and was conceived in Norway during the fall of 1967. Early that fall the question of establishing an organization was discussed at a meeting arranged by a Norwegian author, and among those invited were a number of criminologists, lawyers, practitioners from the prison service, etc. As far as I know no prison inmates or ex-inmates had been invited. The meeting led to a conflict between two groups – a wing containing among others a few authors, and a wing including practitioners from the prison service. The 'authors' wing' was clearly more critical of the prison system and penal and correctional policy than the 'practitioners' wing'. A criminologist who was present tried to negotiate between the two groups, and the meeting ended with the establishment of a 'working committee', consisting of representatives from both wings. The task of the 'working committee' was to secure the foundation of an 'association for humane penal and correctional policy'.

Through the fall the 'working committee' held a few meetings. However, the committee all the time contained the seeds of internal conflict. Independently of the 'working committee', still another group interested in establishing an organization was now formed. This group consisted mainly of sociologists, lawyers, and other academics. The participants were previously well acquainted with each other, and the group probably had greater internal solidarity than the 'working committee'. Some of the participants in the new group had been present at the first discussion meeting early that fall and one of them was also a participant in the 'working committee'. Neither group had prison inmates or ex-inmates as participants. The 'academic group' had a few meetings through the fall. The participants discussed their relationship to the 'working committee', and especially the question whether one might establish an organization independently of the 'working committee'. The participants hesitated to do so, feeling that this might later lead to a conflict with the 'working committee', a conflict from which only the opponents of the organization would gain. The 'working committee' remained similarly silent, and as a whole, then, the splintering into groups had a postponing effect on the founding of the organization.

However, towards the end of November 1967 a further development took place. The secretary of the 'working committee' had summoned a meeting of the committee in order to discuss a proposal for the drafting of statutes for an association. The proposal was characterized by great emphasis on humanitarian aid. The tasks of influencing public opinion and working for changes in criminal policy were also included in the proposed statement of objectives. But humanitarian work – in the form of 'contact with prisons and security institutions in order to give the inmates aid and support', assistance to enable 'the released to lead a non-criminal life in society', and 'aid and support which contributes to and secures a just treatment of fellow human beings' – was a central feature. The 'academic group' had, in contrast to this, placed little emphasis on such work at its meetings. The 'working committee' had also planned to discuss the composition of the organization's board, a council for the organization, etc.

However, the proposed meeting of the committee never took place. On the appointed day the chairman of the Swedish organization KRUM was to give a talk to the law students' association in Oslo, so the 'working committee' cancelled their meeting in order to hear this talk, and for the first time participants in the 'academic group' and the 'working committee' met in a common discussion. The members of the 'academic group' participated rather actively in the discussion; they primarily stressed the need for future work aimed at influencing criminal policy – and not humanitarian work – and on the following day one of them participated in a radio program – with the Swedish chairman – discussing the need for a 'reform organization'. The foundation of an association could now hardly take place without the participation of the 'academics'.

The new situation led to a new postponement of the founding of the organization, which eventually took place 27 May 1968. A joint meeting between the 'working committee' and the 'academic group' was held some time before the actual founding, at which a representative of the 'working committee' proposed to 'get the organization going'. The 'academic group' was by now sufficiently influential to make it natural for the 'working committee' to suggest that one of the 'academicians' might give the introductory speech at the inaugural meeting. Once again the chairman of KRUM was invited to give an additional lecture, and the final invitation to the founding meeting was formulated by the 'academic group'. The group named the organization 'Norwegian Association for Penal Reform'. In the invitation there was an exclusive stress on tasks concerning penal and correctional *policy*. Two general main objectives were formulated:

1   'In the long run to change general thinking concerning punishment, and to replace the prison system by up-to-date and adequate measures'.
2   'In the short run to tear down all walls which are not strictly speaking necessary: to humanize the various forms of imprisonment, and to soften the suffering which society inflicts on its prisoners'.

A number of concrete working tasks were specified, but humanitarian aid was not mentioned. As we shall see, however, the conflict between the concern for penal and correctional policy on the one hand and humanitarian considerations on the other was not terminated.

The name of the organization was abbreviated as KROM – actually a nonsense word, but a word which was analogous to Swedish KRUM (an actual abbreviation). The invitation to the inaugural meeting was sent to 480 individuals – social scientists, lawyers, doctors, and other academicians – and to 35 public and private institutions and organizations. The participants from the 'working committee' and the 'academic group' co-operated in setting up a proposal for an interim board for the organization, consisting of a lawyer with prior practice from the Prison Department, a prison minister, a university lecturer in criminology, a social worker from the Probation Service, a psychiatrist with experience from prisons, a law student, and a sociologist with research experience from prisons. (The sociologist – the present author – made the introductory speech at the founding meeting.) It was decided to keep three places open on the board, to be filled later through appointment by the board. One or two of the latter were to come from the prisoners' ranks. In other words, the board which was proposed was distinctly 'academic' in terms of background. Several had experience from prisons, but the prisoners themselves played an insignificant role. In the invitation to the meeting, participation of the prisoners was mentioned, but only in a general way. After the statement of main objectives (see above), a sentence explained that 'KROM is an association open to everyone – inside and outside prisons – who will co-operate towards these goals'. As a final item in a long list of concrete tasks it was stated that one would endeavor to 'enlist as many inmates as possible in the association, thereby having the experience of the prisoners themselves represented in the work for reform'.

Thus, at this juncture inmates' participation was wanted, but this was stated as a goal rather than as *a point of departure*. As we shall see, owing to the reactions of the prison system the work for this goal proved to be long and arduous.

At the founding meeting the proposed board was elected, and 164 persons became members of the association. However, during the days immediately preceding the meeting certain things started to happen in the milieu in which the initiative was to be launched – things which were to have a rather decisive effect on the early activity of the organization.

During the week-end before the founding meeting, the law students' association in Oslo arranged a seminar on penal and correctional policy, which ended by raising the question whether a KROM was needed in Norway. The participants in the closing panel discussion – the sociologist from the planned interim board, the chairman of the Swedish KRUM, a social worker from the Probation Service, and a law professor, all answered 'yes' to the question. The seminar nevertheless constituted the very first confrontation between the organization which was to be established and the prison system. Prior to the seminar, the sociologist from the proposed interim board had telephoned the Director of Prisons, whom he knew through his research work, to ask him whether the prison administration would like to be represented at the seminar. He stressed that this was a seminar arranged by future lawyers, and that the prison administration could send as many representatives as they wanted. The Director sharply rejected the invitation, simply stating that it would not be in the interest of the prison service to be represented at a meeting discussing the foundation of an association opposing the prison system. In spite of this abrupt refusal, the sociologist called again and stressed that the new association wanted 'co-operation' and 'dialogue' with the authorities, and that he still hoped the authorities would accept the invitation. No positive reply was given to this, and the authorities were not represented. A prison governor was present, but he stressed that he was there as a private person.

A while before, the sociologist had had long talks with the governors of two important penal institutions, in order to tell them about the establishment of the organization and to emphasize the wish for 'co-operation' and 'dialogue' on the part of the organization. Both governors, who were previously acquainted with the sociologist, were negative to the initiative, one of them stressed that if this reform organization had arrived ten or fifteen years earlier he would have understood it, because at that time there was a need for reform. But now the development was going in the right direction, with satisfactory training of prison officers and so on. He further stressed that the association might later be taken over by unknown fanatics, and the prison system would be left with the responsibility for the consequences of this among the inmates in the prisons.

In other words, the reactions of the authorities to the new initiative were very negative, despite the fact that the representatives of the association – rather naively – proclaimed their wish for 'co-operation' and 'dialogue'. Also from other parts of the environment there now came reactions to the founding of the organization – first of all from the press. An interview with the sociologist on the planned interim board a few days before the founding meeting was given front-page headlines in a prominent evening paper: 'Property Criminals Out of Prisons – New Association calls for Insurance and Compensation'. The compensation was intended for the victims, and was to come from government sources. The organization's long-range goal, 'to replace the prison system by up-to-date and adequate measures' (see above), was actually mentioned quite cautiously by the sociologist, at a late stage of the interview, but it was nevertheless given considerable – and somewhat scandalous – publicity through the above-mentioned headlines. We knew in advance that the journalist in question was sceptical of our activities, but we had nevertheless contacted the newspaper because it was important to make our initiative known. On the day of the founding meeting the same journalist interviewed an insurance agent who stated that the idea of abolishing imprisonment for theft, etc. was a 'completely far-fetched idea'. Despite the fact that the long-range goal had been stated very cautiously to the press, this was what the paper emphasized. For a long time afterwards, this interview was referred to as unfortunate – even by adherents of the organization. For the first time we discovered what we were later to experience very often: that the press – and the mass media in general – constitute a 'mine field'. Depending on the personal attitude of the journalist, the immediate need for news on the part of the newspaper, etc., 'explosions' may suddenly take place – explosions which appear to be beyond one's understanding or control. Let me add that the 'explosion' described above, certainly had a feed-back effect on the attitude of the authorities, making that attitude still more negative. Through the interview, the suspicions of the authorities appeared to be confirmed.

In short, this initial period in the life of the organization was critical and acute. This was to be expected, but we did not fully understand it at the time. We built on the shoulders of others, the Swedes, but these shoulders were already torn by a conflict between a treatment/humanitarian stance and a generalized political stance. Various groups with interests in what was happening appeared on the scene – amongst others the 'the working committee' and 'the academic group' – a certain measure of struggle over power between these groups took place, in which 'the academics' tended to win the struggle (equipped as they – we – were with professional know-how and argumentative ability), various kinds of meetings were held, the press turned out to be somewhat of a mine field, the prison authorities unexpectedly went against us and did not want our services.

Had we known all of this in advance, we might not have lived through the opening phase. What kept us alive and consolidated, was the overarching fact that we were 'children of our time': the 1968 revolt in Europe and elsewhere, which imbued us with a staunch optimism and belief in the future. I remember well people, our people, coming back from France that spring, with shining eyes filled with enthusiasm at what was happening. I believe this was among the most important and general historical facts leading us through the first difficult phase.

And this was not the end of our first difficulties at that: we had not yet heard a word from the prisoners – the people we were going to work for.

2. Movement among the prisoners: the group of nine

The founding of the new association thus quickly created unexpected and uncontrollable reactions in important parts of the organization's environment – especially among the authorities and in the press. But there were reactions in other parts of the environment as well – and especially from the ranks of the prisoners. Two days after the founding of KROM a letter was sent to the organization from nine inmates in Botsfengslet – the country's main prison at that time.

> The undersigned are a group of inmates at Botsfengslet who have noted with interest and pleasure that KROM has also been established in Norway.
>
> In this connection we should like to know whether one or more of the present inmates may be represented on the interim board.
>
> Furthermore, we ask KROM to take steps to contact the authorities at Botsfengslet, and to appeal to them not to create obstacles to positive co-operation. We are looking forward to hearing from you as soon as possible.

Here finally was a positive reaction from a part of the organization's environment. The letter was discussed at the first meeting of the newly elected interim board, a week after the founding of the organization. Some of the board members had not met each other before, some had met each other only just before the inaugural meeting, and common attitudes and goals were diffuse and indeterminate. We did not know how to handle this first incident, which had come more or less as a surprise (of course, we ought to have expected such an occurrence, but at the time we nevertheless experienced it as unexpected). We only had a strong feeling that the incident was important, and that it might be very important for our future relationship to the inmates.

The board decided to ask the group at Botsfengslet to suggest two representatives from Botsfengslet – eligible for furloughs or leaves – for the interim board. Eligibility for furloughs or leaves was stressed because this alone could enable the representatives to participate in the work of the board. We also decided to mention, as an assumption on our part, that the representatives suggested should be 'as representative as possible of the views and opinions prevalent among the inmates', and that we – in line with the wishes of the inmates – would then 'contact the authorities at Botsfengslet in order to work out a way so that the inmates' representatives can participate in board meetings' (quotations from our letter, sent the day after the board meeting). At the same time we decided – rather naively – to subscribe to the institution's newspaper, and to submit to it an article about the founding of KROM. In addition, at this first board meeting we decided to add two ex-inmates to the board. Our work for establishing contact with the grass roots had begun.

However, as already mentioned, that work was to prove long and arduous. We were successful in adding two ex-inmates to the board, but this was of course the least problematical part of the task.

Our application for a subscription to the prison newspaper was directed to *the editor of the newspaper*. It was quickly answered – by *the governor of the prison*. He wrote that 'The ABC-paper [the name of the prison newspaper] is an entirely internal institution newspaper intended only for inmates in Botsfengslet. Subscription to the newspaper is not permitted. Earlier copies may not be lent out. The ABC-paper is at present not being produced'. We knew, however, that the newspaper was given to a number of outside individuals and organizations, and we wrote another letter to the governor asking him to reconsider his decision. We never received a reply.

The handling of our proposed article about KROM took a somewhat longer time. First, we learnt informally and indirectly that the prison authorities had 'disliked' the content of the article we had submitted. Later, a re-written article was sent. Its form was very neutral and descriptive. It was rejected – by the governor.

However, the most important matter was, of course, that of our contact with the group of nine at Botsfengslet. The prisoners' reply to our letter was considerably delayed by the prison censorship. In the letter the representative of the prisoners stressed – quite correctly – that inmates eligible for furloughs or leaves might well be unrepresentative of the prisoners, since they were in practice chosen on the basis of the criteria of the institution. The group of nine had therefore elected two inmate representatives *independently* of eligibility for furloughs and leaves. The group had asked the prison authorities for an opportunity to meet in the prison. Their request had been rejected. The group felt that KROM's goals were far from clear. The group could not, of course, know that KROM had tried in vain to submit an account of the organization's goals to the prison newspaper. The prisoners again asked KROM to contact the prison authorities in order to bring about satisfactory working conditions for inmates with an interest in KROM. In other words, they asked for help.

As I have said before, the interim board lacked experience, all of this had happened suddenly, and we were doubtful as to how the problem should be approached. On the one hand, it was clear that 'eligibility for furloughs or leaves' did not constitute a good basis for representation, for the reason mentioned by the inmates. On the other hand, such eligibility provided the only realistic possibility of having inmates participating in board meetings. We considered the possibility of applying to have board meetings at Botsfengslet – if we were allowed to hold board meetings there, the authorities could hardly refuse participation of inmates not eligible for furloughs or leaves. At the same time, it now seemed as if the group of nine had chosen two representatives from *among the members of the group*, and not from all inmates in the institution. We were not certain as to how democratic the election had been and how the election would affect our relationship with other inmates.

We know very little about what happened inside the prison during this period; perhaps information about this may later be supplied by the inmates themselves. What we do know is that the authorities of the prison did not, to put it mildly, open the way for KROM-activities among the inmates. Naïvely we had believed that they might perhaps do so. The fact that the group of nine chose representatives from the group itself is not at all surprising in the light of the system within which inmates must live and act. The system is such that the prison authorities have considerable power over important privileges – such as release on parole, furloughs, etc. Therefore, the authorities may easily play the inmates off against each other. Consequently inmates often feel that few fellow prisoners are to be trusted. The group of nine probably felt in this way.

In KROM we now decided to contact the prison governor (since the group of nine had asked us to do so), and to do this before sending our next answer to the group of nine. The sociologist on the interim board – who had by now been elected chairman of the interim board – telephoned the governor to make an appointment. The governor thought it was 'a good idea' to have a meeting, in order to 'clarify what the rules should be like'. When saying so he clearly meant that the authorities – in this case himself – were to clarify the rules to the association. The 'clarification' of the rules took place at a meeting between three representatives of the interim board and the governor together with two of his associates.

By the time the meeting took place, the interim board had received a long and dramatic letter from the group of nine, in which we were told that the group was now in deep internal conflict. Several inmates wrote individual letters giving us the same information. One of the main reasons for the internal conflict was that several members of the group themselves actually viewed an election within the group as undemocratic. They emphasized general elections. If the prison authorities had opened the way for more general elections, or for easier contact between prisoners and KROM so that we could have clarified misunderstandings, the conflict could probably have been avoided. The authorities, however, did nothing of the kind. It was not in the interest of the prison.

The meeting between the representatives of the interim board and the prison authorities took place in the office of the prison governor – the first and last meeting of this kind between prison authorities and KROM. From the inmates' letters it had appeared that the question of our contact with the prisoners was now an urgent one, and the representatives of the interim board asked whether it might be possible to meet some of the participants in the group of nine. The request was rejected. The prison governor referred, inter alia, to prison rules about privileged communication. The representatives of the interim board wondered whether it might be possible to have general elections in the institution. This, it was stated, would not be possible. The representatives then asked whether it might at least be possible to have a somewhat better arrangement for forwarding inmates' mail to KROM. They suggested a KROM-mailbox in the prison, from which the organization could fetch mail at regular intervals – after the standard censorship of mail had taken place. The KROM people believed that the inmates might in this way be able to express their views more informally. This was rejected rather condescendingly: such an arrangement would not work, and the inmates would not like it because they preferred to be quite formal when writing to outsiders. The governor in addition stressed that the conflicts which KROM had created among the inmates were actually dangerous. An example was mentioned of two inmates who had started to fight with pairs of scissors. The fact that the reaction of the inmates was to a great extent related to the life situation of the prisoners in the totalitarian prison system was not mentioned. Neither was the fact that the actual conflict partly resulted from the personal relationship between the two inmates (the last point became known later, through are leased member of the group of nine). The governor criticized the organization for writing to him through different board members. He felt that all letters should go through the chairman (the application for a subscription to the prison newspaper and the article about KROM to the paper had been sent by other board members). In other words, we were briskly required to adhere to the prison authorities' own bureaucratic structure and style. The KROM people intimated that board meetings might perhaps take place in the institution – reasons of security would then not prevent any inmate from participating. This left the governor at a loss for a reply – apparently, he had not thought of this possibility. Finally, the representatives of KROM presented a draft of a mimeographed one and a half page letter addressed to the inmates – a neutral and cautious letter giving information about the organization – which the association wished to send to all inmates in the institution. In this way the KROM people hoped to be able to give a minimum of information to everyone, thereby preventing rumours and unrest. The governor could not decide on this question – the association had to apply to the Prison Department. If the Department said 'yes', the local censorship would let the letter pass. And there the conversation ended. Shortly after, the association sent an application to the Prison Department, asking for permission to send the mimeographed letter to the inmates. This was the only result of the meeting.

I shall return to this application. In view of the letters from the inmates concerning the conflicts in the group of nine and the need for general elections, the board now wrote to the inmates supporting such elections. But we had to emphasize that the task of working for general elections would be a long-term one. This was quite apparent in the light of the conversation we had had with the prison governor. Yet, despite the difficulties, we still counted on being able to accomplish more through one or another form of 'co-operation' with the authorities. We were therefore very cautious in describing our meeting with the governor. To the prisoners we wrote that 'We have had a conversation with governor N.N. about the question [of elections], and we have gained the impression that our labour for this right will not be easy, but KROM will view the task as a very important one'. We even sent a copy of the letter to the governor (as we had also done in the case of earlier letters to the prisoners) – as a matter of politeness only, because we were well aware that the governor himself censored our mail. As far as we know the group of nine then died out, five or six weeks after the founding of our organization.

In short, in connection with the founding of KROM, rather dramatic reactions occurred in the environment of the organization: extremely negative reactions from the authorities, rather negative reactions from the press, and group processes as well as conflicts among the inmates. In other words, during the initial phase, the environment surrounding the organization was – to put it mildly – turbulent, and though we were not at the time fully conscious of it, much of our work consisted in soothing the turmoil in the environment which we had created. We did not wish for a 'calm' environment, but we did wish to time our influencing of the environment according to own plans. So far, the environment had reacted without our having control over the when-and-how of the reactions, and without our understanding very much of why they occurred. I shall return later to my present notions as to why the reactions took place.

3. The great silence

And then there was silence.

A few letters and some new membership registrations were received – and the membership increased somewhat – but the visible activity in the organization's environment tapered down to almost nothing. In the first place, the association heard nothing from the prison authorities concerning the application to send a mimeographed letter about the organization to the prisoners. And in the mass media only a few trickles of news concerning the association appeared during the next few months. From the prisoners we only received a few individual letters. As it was now summer, the external silence could partly be blamed on vacation time. But the board members could not simply hold the time of the year fully responsible. Several of us felt strongly that the silence was of an ominous kind, but we had some difficulty in expressing more precisely our sense of foreboding. Partly we felt this as a calm before the storm, and partly as a deadly silence which could lead the organization to oblivion. In any case, we experienced ourselves as weak in relation to the environment.

The board of the organization was an interim board, and its task was to arrange for the final organizing of the association. In view of this, we had appointed several committees: a committee responsible for recruiting members, and a committee preparing a draft of the final statutes for the organization. We had also worked actively with a series of other organizational matters – the question of the economy of the association, the presentation of the association in various journals, the question of printing pamphlets and posters for the organization, etc. However, even during the first turbulence in the environment we had had an unclear feeling that if we were only to work with matters of this kind, we should easily lose the initiative completely and become nothing but an object of the whims of our environment. A member of the association not on the board had then emphasized to us that we had to cut through the organizational preparations and start to act politically – the implication being that only in this way could we count on not just being a victim of the environment. The advice was taken seriously. As the news about the conflict in the group of nine reached us, the chairman sent a letter to the other board members in which he stressed the need to 'do something' in terms of criminal policy. The letter was also motivated by the conflict in the group of nine. The chairman indicated that the organization would be ill advised to devote all its time to penetrating the institution through the group of nine.

Active concentration on concrete political tasks became all the more relevant as the great silence grew over us. Such concentration was necessary in order to break through the silence. Various concrete tasks relevant to criminal policy were discussed, and the board began to concentrate heavily on its first important political job in the realm of penal practice: that of trying to make the regulations concerning furloughs, censorship of mail, and visits in the prison system more liberal. These issues were chosen because we counted on the prisoners viewing them as important, because we reckoned with agreement on them within the association, and because we knew that reforms in this direction were fairly easily obtainable. The prison authorities themselves had begun to prepare certain changes, and activity from our side might accelerate the development. We chose to present our views on these issues in the form of a lengthy memorandum to the prison authorities. In addition, a briefer memorandum concerning the future practice in prisons of the pending Law of Public Administration was prepared (the two memoranda were later referred to as the first two 'reform papers' of the association), a public meeting concerning the 'detention center system' was planned for the fall, etc.

But work with memoranda and plans of this kind took time. In the meanwhile the external silence continued. No answer was received from the Prison Department concerning our application for sending in the mimeographed letter, despite reminders by us. The only reaction was a telephone call from a secretary asking us to send the Department a photostat copy of our application – our original letter had been mislaid. The fact that the bureaucracy had nevertheless admitted a bureaucratic failure cheered us up for a brief period of time, but did not solve any problem. In the mass media silence also continued. Members of the association began to ask us questions – friendly but problematical questions – about how things were going. We took it that these inquiries revealed a general concern: What had happened to the association?

The persistent silence caused us to exercise our imaginations, and our actions to a large extent resembled a fumbling in the dark. From diary notes made during this period it nevertheless appears that we followed certain general guidelines in our actions – without always being fully conscious of them at the time.

In the first place, we continued to stress the need for 'co-operation and dialogue' with the authorities. We viewed this as the path which would lead us to accomplish something in regard to prison reform. This stressing of the co-operative line manifested itself in a number of ways, and a few brief examples will be given here.

At this time – while our application concerning the dispatch of a general mimeographed letter to the inmates was before the Prison Department – we were not very active in inviting prisoners to become members. Only to a small degree did we send material to them, because we counted on the authorities experiencing such activity as unwillingness to co-operate. One line in a letter to some inmates who had written to us – 'We hope to see you as a member of our association' – presented problems to the author of the letter. Even by taking such a cautious initiative he had at that time a feeling of deviating from the 'line of co-operation'. I have previously mentioned that out of courtesy copies of all our letters to the prisoners were always sent to the prison governor. Together with such copies we once sent a long letter to the governor of Botsfengslet, explaining that the letters to the inmates were 'sent in order to counteract misunderstanding, at least among those inmates who have written to us, concerning the fact that permission to send general information about membership etc. has not yet been received . . . We have not yet received an answer [from the Prison Department], and we do not know when the decision of the Prison Department will be in hand. We would prefer not to have interested inmates misunderstand the work of the association because of this'. We also wrote: 'As we have mentioned earlier, we are seriously interested in finding a way of co-operating with the prison authorities regarding inmates' membership etc. We therefore hope that you find our way of handling the matter correct, and that the letters we have formulated are satisfactory also from your point of view'. No answer from the governor was ever received. Long before – when the application to the Prison Department was sent – we had sent a long account of the goals and activities of the association to the governors of the six largest penal institutions in the country, stressing, inter alia, that the interim board 'will seek to establish a kind of activity in the association which is both objective and constructive. In this connection we are looking forward to co-operation with the prison authorities in the future'. The account sent to the governors was accompanied by a copy of the general letter which we were applying to have distributed among the inmates, and the account concluded with the following words:

> The Norwegian Association for Penal Reform considers it very important that inmates get an opportunity to become members of our association. We view membership as a significant way of engaging the inmates in a co-operative relationship concerning important matters. It is also important that the information which the letter [to the inmates] gives about the association reaches the individual inmates. We are therefore looking forward to co-operating with you concerning this matter.

We never received any reply from the governors. Despite this, we optimistically continued to pursue 'co-operation' in every way.

The co-operative line also prevailed in the above-mentioned memorandum concerning furloughs, censorship of mail, and visits, which the association was now preparing. We carefully saw to it that we did not use expressions which might offend the authorities who were to receive the memorandum. By way of introduction, we wrote, inter alia, that as 'we have written in earlier letters to you, KROM wishes to follow an objective and constructive line in its work for reforms in the criminal justice system and the penal service . . . We are aware of the fact that the Prison Department itself is working for reforms in the prison system. We feel, however, that it is expedient . . . that proposals for changes also come from a detached organization such as our own'. We wrote this in order not to 'hurt' the Prison Department by implying that the department was not working for reforms. Still by way of introduction, the memorandum continued: 'We respectfully ask for your reaction to our proposals. If you find it difficult to carry out our proposals immediately, we should like to know if you still agree with them in principle. In this way it will be possible for our association to co-ordinate its activities with those of the Prison Department, thus contributing to a more rapid solution to problems which both parties are concerned with'. We wrote this in order to emphasize our wish to co-operate, and in order – this time – politely to secure an answer from the authorities. We had now discovered that the authorities had a tendency to refrain from answering our communications. In our discussions concerning these and other formulations – discussions which in part took place over the telephone – some of the board members felt that we were being a little too cautious. However, the cautious line prevailed. In order to avoid provocation, the memorandum was not sent to the press, but as a typed letter in the mail to the Prison Department. The memorandum consisted of eight single-spaced pages, and contained a long series of concrete proposals for reforms. It was mailed on 27 August 1968.

Two weeks later the Prison Department replied. The reply as a whole read as follows:

> Receipt is acknowledged of your letter of 27 August 1968, in which you, on behalf of KROM, set forth proposals for changes in the existing prison regulations concerning the inmates' contact with the outside world through furloughs, exchange of letters, and visits.
>
> In this connection you are hereby informed that the Prison Department is at all times attentive to the question of changes in regulations, and that questions of change are constantly under review. Changes are being considered in the field mentioned in your letter as well.

The authorities wished to point out that any reforms in this sphere would come quite independently of KROM's activity. The answer could hardly have been briefer. To complete the story one must add that the Prison Department announced some changes in the prison regulations in October of that year; concerning, among other things, furloughs, the censorship of mail, and visits. In the association we received congratulations from some of our supporters. The Prison Department, however, stressed in the newspaper reports that the authorities had been working on these matters for a very long time, thus implying that not even the timing of the changes was in any way influenced by the activities of KROM.

Let me add that our 'wish to co-operate' with the authorities introduced a certain remoteness into our relations with the prisoners. Some of us felt that the organization ought to be slightly cautious in developing a co-operative relationship with the prisoners, because such co-operation apparently irritated the authorities. Obviously, caution in this respect was dangerous to us. It led to certain negative reactions from inmates in the mass media.

Parallel to the stress on 'co-operation' or 'dialogue' with the authorities, the association put *in the second place* a rather extreme emphasis on 'honesty' towards the authorities. Thus, we placed great stress on avoiding 'round-about ways' to reach short-term goals or advantages; round-about ways which the authorities later could refer to as deceit on the part of the association. This manifested itself in a number of concrete ways through the decisions made by the board. As an example it may be mentioned that we once decided, in an over-cautious way, to refrain from giving information about KROM to an inmate through a prison officer who was sympathetic to us. The inmate was thinking of preparing an internal radio program about the organization.

However, what we did not see so clearly at the time was the fact that the 'demand for honesty' could conflict with the wish to co-operate, in the sense that honesty could lead to statements and actions which the authorities might dislike. Without being very conscious of the process at the time, we were – because of our wish to co-operate – *in the third place* led to adopt a certain 'duplicity' in relation to the authorities. To a considerable extent we toned down our real views on the prison service and the criminal justice system, in order to avoid 'offending' our counter-part. An example of this may be mentioned from our work with a memorandum on the democratization of prison institutions. The memorandum was never sent to the authorities because, among other reasons, we were uncertain as to what 'democracy in prisons' actually was to imply, but our work with the memorandum nevertheless illustrates the point about duplicity. While working on the draft, the author found it natural to describe the prison system as 'totalitarian'. At the same time he sensed quite clearly that such an expression would 'offend' those authorities who might be expected to contribute to a democratization of the institutions. The word 'totalitar-ian' was therefore deleted and replaced by expressions such as 'undemocratic' and 'not democratic'. This type of 'duplicity' in relation to the authorities also led us to a parallel duplicity in our relationship with the inmates. In order to keep up a consist-ent front it was necessary to tone down our views in relation to the inmates as well. Letters to the inmates at this time represented a constant source of conflict. On the one hand, we wanted to write what we actually felt – at the same time we knew that the mail was censored, and that if we wrote what we felt we might thereby irritate those authorities with whom we were so terribly eager to co-operate. Some of us were during this period constantly worried over the problem of honesty/duplicity. As a rule, we chose – because of our wish to co-operate – to be honest or false depending on what we felt might soothe the irritation of the authorities.

In the fourth place, during this period we involved ourselves in a strange 'reli-ance on' or 'use of' the prison authorities' own regulations, regulations which we were opposing in principle. This 'reliance on' regulations which we in principle viewed as doubtful was also related to our wish to co-operate. Let me explain by way of an example. As indicated above, we were hesitant in recruiting prisoner members through individual letters while waiting for the Prison Department's reply to our application concerning a mimeographed letter to all inmates in the prisons. However, as I have also indicated, it was at times impossible to refrain from writing cautious sentences such as 'we hope to see you as a member of our association'. In connection with sentences of this kind we took comfort from the fact that the prison authorities exercised censorship of mail, and that if the authorities were later to attack us for not having 'waited' for the answer from the Department, we could refer to the fact that the individual letters had been accepted by the prison censorship. Without being conscious of it, we thus went a long way towards accepting prison regulations as premises for our action.

Fifthly, and lastly, in our external moves concerning criminal policy we went far towards accepting the wish of the environment not to have the association and its particular views emphasized, but rather to emphasize quite general questions relating to criminal policy. For example, when we contacted a particular mass medium to discuss a possible presentation of our views, the representative of the mass medium in question emphasized that they did not want any presentation of KROM, but possibly of certain topics within the area of penal and correctional policy. At the time we readily accepted this. In connection with a lecture given by KROM's chairman to the Norwegian Association of Criminalists (whose mem-bers are judges, district attorneys, prison administrators, and representatives of similar professions), it was emphasized by the Criminalists' Association that their intention was not to take KROM as a point of departure for discussion. Their intention, they said, was not to place their association at the disposal of another organization, and KROM's chairman was asked to discuss in a general way results and conclusions from prison research as well as 'realistic' prison reforms. In other words, the well-established organization wanted a lecture on the terms of the prison system, and nothing about KROM. The chairman agreed to this, feeling that he could accomplish more as a private person than as chairman of KROM. Again, the emphasis on co-operation was evident.

These were some of the more important features of our thinking while the great silence prevailed. Through emphasis on co-operation, honesty towards the authorities, duplicity in order to appease the authorities, reliance on the authorities' own regulations, and a tendency to refrain from emphasizing the association itself, we were – without being particularly conscious of it – far along the road towards being integrated into or absorbed by the system we were trying to change. (By 'integration' or 'absorption' is meant that an organization changes its course of action in such a way that its activities mainly take place on conditions provided by the opposite party, and according to principles accepted by the opposite party.) Some members of the board did not always share the views schematically outlined here, and pointed out that we ought not to give in too much to the authorities. They were right, but their view did not have a decisive effect on our early thinking.

A brief excerpt from my diary from this period summarizes some of the points discussed above – and shows how close we were to being absorbed:

> If we are to accomplish anything at all, it is important not to create distur-
> bance, but at the same time – in order to live – it is important to do some-
> thing in relation to the external world. And it struck me that perhaps I ought
> actually to change this interview with X (a weekly journal) and to stress less
> clearly this business of our applying to the Prison Department for permission
> to send a general letter to the inmates . . . Perhaps I am going too far in endan-
> gering the reputation of the department and making it very difficult for them,
> and in creating the very unrest they are afraid of – and that we in view of this
> will be unable to accomplish anything. Perhaps it will even prolong the life of
> the present system of furloughs, etc. In a sense all of these problems present
> themselves simultaneously in a very pointed form which is quite strange.

If the authorities had at that time invited us to enter into a 'co-operative relationship' – for example non-committal 'discussions' of questions of reform, KROM would most likely have accepted the invitation and been absorbed.

4. Towards a clarification

However, no such invitation was ever received.

The reasons for this are unknown, but we may speculate about the matter. In the first place, the prison authorities probably hoped that KROM could be handled by maintaining silence. In the second place, the authorities were probably largely unaware of how far the organization had gone in the direction of accepting the authorities' 'conditions for co-operation'. In other words, the authorities were probably not aware of how easily they could have neutralized us. There were some exceptions: an official in the Ministry of justice later made the point that if he had been in charge, he would have seen to it that all prison governors became members of KROM – after becoming members they could easily have taken over. But by and large, the authorities were hardly conscious of the possibility of neutralization – perhaps precisely because they communicated so poorly with us, but probably also because the bureaucracy lacks a sociological understanding of the problematic position of new counter-organizations. Bureaucracy is preoccupied with maintaining a *calm* environment. The goal of 'calmness' is important because the bureaucracy is frequently exposed to criticism. It is also important as an end in itself. Even friendly initiatives from the bureaucracy towards new counter-organizations imply a brief period of unrest, and even if such unrest would scarcely be dangerous to the long-term policy of the bureaucracy, representatives of bureaucratic organizations also try to avoid creating unrest of this kind, because unrest is in itself viewed as an evil. Instead, potential unrest is met by silence.

Our experience from these first few months in the life of KROM leads us to a few tentative conclusions concerning strategies which established institutions employ against new counter-organizations. The first – and most dangerous – strategy is that of absorption. Generally, in the early life of a counter-organization the organizational structure is weak, goals are diffusely formulated, and few concrete issues have yet been taken up. During this first phase the counter-organization strongly needs signs of success, and a quick 'offer of support' – or at least an 'open attentive attitude' – on the part of the institution which the organization is trying to change is very easily taken as such a sign. Later it is dangerous for the counter-organization to act in ways which may be criticized by those who have provided support – such criticism gives the impression of an incorrect development – and absorption therefore easily becomes a fact. Especially during the first phase of a counter-organization (but also later) it is therefore *extremely important for the organization to be on the alert for such support and absorption, and to view them as a bad sign.*

Another main strategy which may be employed by the establishment during the initial phase of a counter-organization is the one which the Norwegian prison authorities utilized in this instance – withdrawal and silence. You refuse to be represented at conferences, you do not answer external communications unless you absolutely have to – and if you have to, you answer in as brief and non-committal a way as possible. This strategy is less dangerous to the organization in question because it does not irrevocably lead to its death as a counter-organization; it gives the organization a chance to survive as a counter-organization. From the point of view of the new counter-organization, withdrawal and silence are therefore preferable to support and absorption. Yet, withdrawal and silence are dangerous enough, because during the initial phase it is difficult to take the more long-range perspective which I am here relying on in retrospect. During the initial phase, withdrawal and silence are experienced as extremely problematical. It seems as if nobody reacts to what you are doing, apparently you make no impression whatsoever on the establishment, apparently the other party is quite independent of what you are doing.

In a situation in which you, in addition, want to become the ally of and to aid a third party (in this case the prisoners), the withdrawal and silence of the rulers is particularly problematical: to those you wish to aid (the prisoners), silence on the part of the rulers easily appears as if the counter-organization makes no impression on, and in no way influences, those in power. Most likely, this experience is more pronounced the more powerless the third party is in relation to those in power. The more powerless the third party is, the more its members probably look for signs of such effectiveness on the part of the counter-organization. As is well known, the prisoners are to a considerable extent powerless in their situation, and the silence of the authorities was therefore especially troublesome.

*

The strategy of withdrawal and silence was, then, very trying. But let me repeat, the strategy of co-operation would have been even more dangerous.

The withdrawal and silence at least gave us *time to reflect* on our situation. During the great silence, this reflection gradually hardened us somewhat in relation to the authorities. While the silence lasted we gradually became a little more tempted to fight than to co-operate. A few of the factors which contributed to this development in our thinking may be briefly mentioned.

In the first place, there were people on the board of the organization who did not share the 'co-operative point of view'. Even if these were not in the majority to begin with, they did colour our discussions, and they constantly reminded the majority of the dangers of being 'too weak' in relation to the authorities. Since no offer of co-operation was received (if it had been received, the various groups within the board might have been played off against each other), this point of view gradually acquired more adherence also among those who were willing to co-operate.

Secondly, among the board members – also among those who at this time adhered to the 'co-operative line' – there did exist an understanding of the dangers of absorption facing professional people working within the prison system itself. We were well acquainted with instances in the literature showing how psychiatrists, psychologists, and social workers working in prison institutions are neutralized. It is true that knowledge of this literature would at this time hardly have been enough to make us withstand an invitation to 'co-operate' with the authorities. At the time, we did not clearly understand the similarities between our own potential position and the position of those working in the system. We viewed ourselves as being more on the outside. (True enough, we were more on the outside, but the general dangers of absorption were still present in the same way.) Also, we had earlier gone very far in stressing our own wish to 'co-operate' – which suggests that the most effective strategy on the part of the establishment against a new counter-organization is perhaps that of *combining* the strategies of silence and co-operation: an initial phase of silence, provoking promises of co-operation from the counter-organization, followed by an opening for a 'dialogue' with the counter-organization. Our knowledge of the literature did, however, lead to increased *reflection* on the silence of the authorities, and to a dawning – at that time vague – understanding that actually, we were fortunate in not receiving any invitation from the authorities; fortunate because we would have been unable to withstand it; fortunate because the authorities would have won several points if had we in any way tried to withstand it. In retrospect it seems to me that this understanding in turn made us feel – through reflection – that silence and withdrawal were perhaps not quite so dangerous after all, and that they perhaps in a way protected us against something worse.

In the third place, the prison system did not manage to maintain complete silence. Indirectly – through others – we gradually received fragments of information indicating that the authorities were not perhaps so impervious to our efforts after all. Through a prison officer we learnt that a letter to us from an inmate had been stopped by the assistant governor with the justification – given to the prisoner – that KROM was recognized neither by the Prison Department nor by the institution. If KROM represented no threat whatsoever from the point of view of the authorities, they would most likely not have worried so much over a single letter, we thought. We gradually understood that the question of the prison authorities' participation in public discussions with KROM was discussed on the top level in the Ministry of justice, and that the authorities tried to postpone such discussions in the mass media as long as possible. These pieces of information gave us the impression that the authorities – behind their silent front – were very conscious of our presence and that they even felt that they were under pressure from us.

A fourth set of factors gradually persuading us to fight back is related to certain topics which were discussed on the board of the organization during the silence. As mentioned already, a sub-committee preparing a draft of the final statutes of the organization had begun its work, with a view to formulating a proposal which could be discussed at the coming organizing meeting in the association. The work on the statutes led to lengthy discussions of principle concerning KROM's more precise goals, and the outcome of these discussions was of direct importance for the issues being treated here. In particular, two series of board-meeting discussions were important and will be described in some detail.

*

The first round of discussions focused on *the relationship between penal and correctional policy on the one hand and humanitarian work on the other.* The sub-committee's first draft of statutes contained a number of provisions about activities concerning penal and correctional policy. However, in one sentence having to do with the methods to be used by KROM, it was also mentioned that

KROM 'will initiate practical projects giving aid to the individual inmate'. The members of the sub-committee explained to the rest of the board that the sentence had been added because such activity ought somehow to be included. A board member opened the discussion by strongly maintaining that this sentence ought absolutely not to be included. The initiation of practical aid projects was in her opinion the responsibility of other, 'public', institutions and organizations – probation offices etc. – and KROM's task should be that of supporting and criticizing such activity rather than being directly involved in it. This general principle concerning humanitarian work was not quite understood by the other board members straight away. Another board member supported the first speaker, but on a different and more practical level. He referred to the many difficulties which members of Swedish KRUM had encountered in their humanitarian work, adding that it would be dangerous to promise the prisoners more than could be performed. The first speaker now also relied on this view, and recounted how on a trip to Goteborg she had passed by a door displaying a KRUM-sign and had gone in – only to discover that their humanitarian work was a complete failure, even according to those present in the KRUM-office. In the discussion that followed, a clear difference of opinion now developed concerning this question. Other board members maintained that the prisoners would remain uninterested in joining the organization if the sentence concerning practical aid projects was not included. The first speaker replied to this that, according to her opinion, this implied an underestimation of the inmates, and that the prisoners would very likely be interested in broader and more general issues. Her implication was that KROM's task ought to be that of freeing the inmates from the habit of viewing themselves through the eyes of the oppressor – as unpolitical and inarticulate. The board member who had supported the first speaker did so again, and argued that the organization was perhaps confronted by a conflict between being a political 'reform organization', and being a more practically oriented 'prison union'. After a lengthy discussion in which various attempts were made to find compromise formulations, the question was postponed till a later meeting. At the next board meeting the discussion of the topic was introduced by the board member who had previously supported the first speaker. He now concretely proposed to delete the sentence as a whole. For the first time one of the ex-inmates now expressed himself on the matter. He forcefully maintained that the sentence must definitely be included. People could not be denied the possibility of taking part in practical projects, and if there were to be any room for ex-inmates in the organization, it had to be related to practical work of this kind. Both ex-inmates on the board had previously maintained that it would just be foolish to have too many ex-inmates participating in the work concerning penal and correctional policy – according to the two of them, ex-inmates were not quick enough to grasp the issues and would just create difficulties. The inmates' view on humanitarian work received support from other board members. It was maintained that humanitarian work had to be included in one way or another if the organization were not to be just 'an academic club'. The wing more exclusively concerned with issues of criminal policy again maintained that the ex-prisoners underestimated themselves concerning political work, that practical aid projects were not proper tasks for this organization, and that KROM's task was to support and criticize public measures and projects while it was the task of the authorities – with their resources – to perform the actual practical work. An ex-inmate replied to the last argument that he found it extremely difficult to ask for something at the probation office. He implied that KROM for this reason had to initiate some kind of aid to people released on parole. Again he was supported by other board members, who added that if this association were to develop into something more than an organization concentrated in the capital city, the organization had to let people participate in practical projects for inmates. The rejoinder was that if the sentence concerning practical aid projects was included in the statutes one would only remedy the housewives' 'need to help', and not the prisoners' 'need for help'. The counter to this was that the motives of the housewives might be just as good or bad as our own. If we were to question other people's motives for wanting to help, we might just as well begin to question our own motives for wanting to work politically. From the wing oriented more exclusively towards penal and correctional policy a compromise was finally suggested: instead of saying that KROM 'will initiate practical projects giving aid to the individual inmate', the sentence 'may also seek to organize practical projects for law-breakers' was suggested. This sentence, which was adopted at the organizing general meeting, did not explicitly state that the aid should be given to the individual inmate; it refrained from using the word 'aid' (a word which the most strongly politically oriented board members had viewed as condescending), and – most importantly – the sentence did not make the organizing of practical projects obligatory for the association; it just provided an opportunity for it.

The discussions concerning the relationship between criminal policy and humanitarian work probably had a clarifying influence on us. The choice of mainly emphasizing issues of policy rather than humanitarian aid had actually been made before: from the very beginning there had been wide agreement on' the notion that the organization simply did not have the resources to take up the cases of the individual inmates. Through the board discussions, however, the issue was now considered as a matter of principle, and from this angle as well we arrived at a political answer. Humanitarian aid was not to be obligatory, and was therefore mainly to be a task for institutions of a public kind. By implication, we began to view humanitarian aid as a way of deviating from our actual goal: that of making public institutions possessing the necessary resources do a better job.

The general standpoint discussed above had consequences for us – consequences which we hardly anticipated fully at the time, but which appeared little by little. One of them will be pointed out here. The standpoint was among the factors that strengthened us in relation to the authorities during the persistent silence. If the authorities had 'offered co-operation' when the silence finally ended, we would probably still have accepted the offer, and become integrated. But towards the end of the period of silence, we were nevertheless much more willing to fight, partly owing to the clarifying discussion of principle concerning our goal. We had clarified that we were not to be a kind humanitarian organization, but rather a political one. *And politics means fighting.*

The other series of board discussions concerning statutes, which became important in strengthening our wish to fight, *concerned the question of alternatives to imprisonment.* As already mentioned, the association had from the beginning the long-range objective to 'replace the prison system by up-to-date and adequate measures' (see above). But what measures?

'Treatment' was, of course, the solution in vogue at the time. Even in the first – above-mentioned – major newspaper interview with the sociologist who became the chairman of the interim board, 'treatment' had been mentioned as an alternative. In reply to a question from the reporter whether the new association would 'simply throw the prisons on the scrap-heap', the chairman, inter alia, answered: 'If so, it must be said to be a very long-range objective. We view it as unrealistic to liquidate the prisons "overnight". But we wish to work for alternative treatment offers, for release homes, for therapy, for protected industry, and for treatment of criminals in freedom.' 'Treatment' and 'therapy' were, in other words, stressed. The concepts were employed rather imprecisely, and with a certain reserve. The representative who was interviewed was acquainted with a number of the depressing follow-up studies of 'treatment experiments' with offenders, and with the view that it might therefore be sensible to place greater emphasis on justice than on 'treatment'. Despite this, the concept of 'treatment' was, so to speak, employed as a way out.

The concept of 'treatment' reappeared in full strength in the discussions concerning the statutes. The committee preparing the statutes had formulated a proposal for a statement of objectives as follows:

KROM is an association which is neutral in terms of party politics and religion, and which will work for a humanization and an increase in the treatment efficiency of society's measures towards offenders.

a. On a short-term basis we wish to change the conditions within the existing prison system, including the various special institutions, in such a way that the incarceration which is employed leads to the least possible damage to the individual inmate. We will seek to attain this by, among other things, increasing the inmates' facilities for contact with the surrounding world, and by developing psychological/psychiatric treatment measures.

b. On a long-term basis we will work for a thorough-going change of the present system of measures towards offenders, and to the largest possible extent replace institutional treatment by various treatment measures in the community.

The proposal became the subject of great discussion on the board. The sociologist on the board experienced the concrete reference to 'psychological/psychiatric treatment measures' as problematical. Somewhat vaguely, he felt that a reference specifically to these alternative measures would quickly tie the organization to standpoints which would, after a while, become obsolete. He expressed this view in the discussion by maintaining that the whole of the last sentence in clause (a) in the proposal ought to be deleted. Those who in the discussion of criminal policy versus humanitarian work had advocated a purely political line, now mustered in support of this view. To this onslaught the defence was made that the statutes had to say something about what we were to work for – the statutes could not be 'empty paragraphs'. The assailants, however, maintained that the statutes ought to be general, and contain brief, and forceful sentences, not specified alternatives. A proposal for making the goals more concrete in a parallel 'work program', which could continually be revised, was met with enthusiasm by everybody, but the group which felt that the statutes ought to contain something about psychological/ psychiatric treatment, still maintained that people would study the statutes – and not the work program – most closely when seeking what the organization stood for. Those who felt that the statutes ought to be brief and general maintained, on the other hand, that the work program should be studied more closely. Finally, one of the latter proposed that the board had better think the issue over for a period of time. The other side, however, maintained that time was now running out, and that it was necessary to find a formulation. That evening, therefore, the board went through the proposal as a whole, changing a number of smaller points, and reaching a temporary agreement concerning a majority of rules. However, the great decision on principle concerning the issue of 'treatment' remained open, giving the 'treatment sceptics' time to think.

During the days following the board meeting, one of them formulated a new proposal for a statement of general aims. He had now also become sceptical towards the concepts of 'humanization' and 'increase in the treatment efficiency' as parts of the general statement (see above). The concept of 'humanization' could easily lead to, or imply, that the framework – the prison institution – was accepted, and 'increase in the treatment efficiency' could imply that the interests of the established society – and not those of the prisoners – were emphasized. Particularly through the latter formulation, the organization might be side-tracked from being an interest organization for the inmates. He therefore replaced these concepts by 'worthy of human beings' and 'expedient' – concepts which he felt that the organization would be less tied by. Furthermore, he deleted the sentence concerning 'psychological/psychiatric treatment measures', and introduced a few other minor changes.

The formulation of general aims was discussed anew at the next board meeting. A non-board member of the sub-committee preparing the statutes was present during the meeting. By way of introduction, he maintained that it might be an idea to prepare 'soft' statutes – that is, statutes which the authorities might easily accept – and he proposed that one might, for example, use the word 'humane' rather than 'worthy of human beings' – a more acceptable wording to the authorities. This point of view, however, was rejected by a joint board. The irritation with the contemptuous silence of the authorities had now begun to harden. The suggestion of 'soft' statutes was probably of importance for the further development. Our protest against it made us conscious of the danger of submitting toe much to the demands of the authorities, thus probably swinging some who had earlier taken the treatment-optimistic view over to the other side. This change was probably partly responsible for carrying through the more 'anti-treatment oriented' view. For the first (and almost the last) time, a round of formal voting took place in a board which before and after this was strongly characterized by a 'seminar form'. After a series of votes, the following statement of objectives was adopted with small majorities – as the proposal of the board to the general organizing meeting:

> KROM – Norwegian Association for Penal Reform – is, in terms of party politics and religion, a neutral association. The association will work for measures towards offenders which are more worthy of human beings and more expedient. The organization will:
>
> a. On a short-term basis work for reforms in the administration of criminal law and the prison system which may reduce damaging effects of incarceration, and which may make the incarceration less burdensome for the inmate.
> b. On a long-term basis work for thorough-going changes in the present system of measures, trying as much as possible to replace incarceration by other measures and treatment methods in the community.
> c. Serve as a mouthpiece for present and past inmates, with a view to promoting their general rights and claims in a constructive way.

With one change, this proposal was later adopted by the organizing meeting. The change consisted of calling the organization 'independent' rather than 'neutral' in terms of party politics and religion. With the exception of the general expression 'treatment methods in the community', the treatment-optimistic perspective had disappeared from the statutes.

The treatment perspective was still included in the 'work program' which the board prepared, and which was later adopted by the organizing meeting. This first work program of the organization included four main items: I. The situation of the inmates, II. The situation of prison personnel. III. The system of penal measures in general, and IV. Other issues. The item concerning 'the situation of the inmates' included: 1) the inmates' contact with the surrounding world (rules concerning furloughs, censorship of mail, visits, etc.), 2) the relationship of the prison administration to the inmates (its impersonal character, etc.), and 3) democratization of the penal institution. 'The situation of prison personnel' included the headings: 1) strengthening the treatment offers, 2) the isolated situation of the treatment staff, and 3) the situation of other staff members. 'The system of penal measures in general' and 'other issues' included the headings: 1) juvenile offenders, 2) preventive detention, 3) forced labour, 4) measures and treatment methods in the community, 5) the publication of research findings, 6) influencing public opinion, and 7) the strengthening of KROM's organization. The treatment perspective – again in a somewhat vague sense of the word, but with stress on individualized psychiatric/ psychological treatment – saturated the program. For example, under the item of 'strengthening the treatment efforts' it was stated that 'the treatment staff in penal institutions are extremely scarce . . . KROM will work for an increase of this staff group. A strengthening of the psychiatric/psychological service, however, presupposes more than just an increase in the number of positions. The organizational structure of a penal institution very easily leads to a total neutralization of the possibilities and offers of the treatment staff. KROM will therefore also work for a change of this organizational structure, in order that the treatment staff may really contribute something to their clients'. In other words, we believed that the prison structure could be changed in such a way. Under the item concerning 'the isolated situation of the treatment staff' it was, inter alia, stated that in 'connection with its work for intensifying the treatment offers, KROM will work for an improved integration between the treatment staff and the rest of the treatment milieu . . .'. Under the item concerning 'the situation of other staff members', the position of correctional officers and work supervisors was discussed, and emphasis was placed on 'work for making this group of staff members better prepared for co-operation with the psychiatric/ psychological group in the institution'. Under the item 'juvenile offenders' it was stated, inter alia, that the organization wanted to 'work for the introduction of various types of treatment, on an experimental basis . . .' and so on.

But in spite of this stress on the 'treatment alternative' in the work program, its omission from the actual statutes was of great importance. For one thing, the work program was meant to be more changeable, so that it was later easier to alter it. More importantly, the intensive discussions on the board concerning the relationship between treatment goals and statutes had an independent and considerable significance. These discussions were responsible for a hardening of our attitude towards the authorities during the persistent silence. Through the discussions of principles concerning the 'treatment alternative', we clarified to ourselves that we were not necessarily willing to support the more 'acceptable' alternatives to imprisonment, of which 'treatment' was one, but – if necessary – willing to insist on more 'unacceptable' solutions. The question of which solution remained open, but we were, at least in principle, prepared to adopt a more negative attitude towards the authorities.

*

The board's discussions of general principles underlying the statutes were concluded at a board meeting 3 ½ months after the association was founded. On the day after the meeting, the reply to our application concerning the mimeographed letter to the inmates came from the Prison Department.

The silence was finally broken.

5. At the cross-roads

We had arrived at a cross-road. Let me repeat, the board's disposition was still such that if the answer from the Prison Department had been favourable, the 'co-operative line' would probably still have been followed with integration as a possible result. But at the same time we had also become considerably hardened in our attitude to the authorities, in the sense that we would not give up if the answer was negative. And it was as negative as it could be, thereby preparing the ground for the continued development of a 'fighting line' rather than a 'co-operative line'.

In our application, we had, inter alia, informed the prison authorities that we were interested in having inmates as members, and in their taking an active part in co-operation with the association. The Prison Department's reply was brief. In addition to repeating the main content of our application and informing us 'that one generally does not oppose inmates' seeking or maintaining membership in associations or organizations' (by what right could 'one' 'oppose' this?), the Prison Department answered that 'with regard to co-operation of the kind you are mentioning [between the prisoners and KROM], the Prison Department doubts whether this may be reconciled with the principles and rules relating to the carrying-out of penal measures in a prison institution. It therefore appears inappropriate that the prison system or its staff members should assist in such a distribution of letters to inmates as you are asking for'.

The answer was discussed at an emergency board meeting a few days later. We tried to interpret the answer from several points of view. We discussed whether we ought to contact the press, or the Ombudsman, about it. We were reluctant to do either. We were not certain that the press would support us, and were fairly certain that the Ombudsman would view the answer of the Prison Department as within the framework of current regulations. We discussed whether an oral contact with the Prison Department might be useful, but rejected it; most likely, little more would emerge from that. We finally decided that we would send the letter which had now been banned for inmates in general, to those inmates who had personally written to us – inmates to whom we therefore could write individually. In an additional note to these inmates – carefully read by our legal advisors – we described what had happened, stating quite explicitly that we felt it unreasonable that other inmates were denied a minimum of information about KROM.

The mail to these inmates was not stopped by the institution – not surprisingly, because such a step would have been illegal. However, it was greatly delayed because it was sent to the Prison Department for censorship. At the board meeting at which the reply of the Prison Department had been discussed, a board member had also reported that one of the lectures given at the founding meeting of KROM, and the informational letter in question, had been distributed by the board member in the waiting-room of a probation office, but that it had been confiscated by those in charge. In short, it was quite clear that when we approached the so-called 'clientele' with points of view concerning criminal policy, a reaction took place, no matter how cautious our approaches and views were. It was as if we here almost automatically released a kind of allergic counter-reaction.

But we did not at the time understand why.

*

The later development substantiates the view that almost any political approach to the 'clients' was met by sharp counter-reactions and by attempts to interrupt our communication with the 'clients'.

The refusal to send the general informational letter to the inmates was taken up in the press before the formal organizing meeting of the association. A large social-democratic morning paper contacted the association for an interview, and it then seemed unnatural to conceal what had happened while waiting for the meeting (originally, we had planned to do this). Our application to send the informational letter to the inmates was presented in the paper as one of our attempts to contribute to a democratization of the life of the prisoners. Since we now at last found ourselves interviewed by a friendly newspaper, we took the opportunity to reveal other things which had happened. The refusal to print an article about KROM in Botsfengslet's institutional newspaper had arrived by this time, and the prison authorities had also said 'no' to being represented at a Scandinavian conference on correctional and penal policy which KROM was to arrange in Sweden together with its fellow organizations. In reply to a long invitation, which included the statement that we had 'the pleasure of inviting you to participate with three representatives from the prison system', the Prison Department had simply answered that they 'had to announce that the prison system would not be represented at the planned conference in Uddevalla during the period 25–27 October 1968'. This news was given considerable space, over four columns, with the headlines 'BOTSFENGSLET'S institutional paper closed to KROM'; 'The Prison Department will not take part in conference on correctional and penal policy'.

The conference in question was covered by two morning papers from Oslo, and was positively reviewed in both. One of the papers was a right-wing conservative paper, and the positive review there was undoubtedly due to the special views of the journalist. But the journalist's articles were at least given very good space in the paper. A conservative evening paper in Oslo, which was not represented at the meeting, also supported the 'new ideas'. In an editorial this paper wrote, inter alia, that 'There is no doubt that the treatment of offenders in general lags behind, linked to a view which ought to be obsolete, and that the attempts which are being made to lead those who have been punished back to society, have given very small results. New and apparently radical ideas therefore definitely deserve to be discussed seriously'. The paper concluded that '. . . here a tremendous amount remains undone. Hardly in any field are we so far behind as in the treatment of offenders'. This was not a bad press coverage. To be sure, the paper also added a warning: it was doubtful whether it was wise to push the matter to such an extreme as, in the paper's opinion, 'the most zealous reformists' did. In addition, it was pointed out that 'when the participants at the conference in Uddevalla day-dreamed about a Scandinavian prisoners' strike – to be sure, only for one day – this is hardly the right way in which to create publicity for the reform movement which has now been organized in associations with the strange names of KRIM, KRUM, and KROM'. On the last evening of the conference, the possibility of a strike had been referred to in a highly informal setting, and on the next day a Swedish participant had given the news to a Danish news agency. All the organizations had later disclaimed the forming of any 'plan' in the press. At that time, we viewed the possibility of a prisoners' strike as dangerous in relation to public opinion, a fact which the above-mentioned editorial certainly confirmed. But over and above this, the attitude in the editorial was – to repeat – by and large positive. In general, it seemed as if we had made a step forward in relation to the press, even if letters to the editor about 'these false humanists' had also been given space in the same evening paper.

Why was the reaction relatively positive? The very first press reaction – in connection with the founding meeting – had been negative, and the reactions from the authorities to our wish for contact with the prisoners had been negative. The positive reception now was related to several factors – as previously stated, the attitude of particular journalists was one important element – but what I should like to emphasize here is that at the Uddevalla meeting we actually placed little emphasis on *political* contact with the prisoners. The lecturers were mainly 'experts' who talked about matters other than a political exchange between the organizations and the prisoners. Among other things, we talked a great deal about 'treatment', and 'treatment' is acceptable even to conservatives. When we did discuss political contact with the prisoners (as in connection with the possibility of a prisoners' strike), the negative reactions were apparent. However, we rarely talked about such contact.

But the positive reaction did not last long. In November 1968 – a little more than five months after the foundation of the association – the organizing general meeting was held, at which a permanent board was elected (consisting, with two exceptions, of the same members as the interim board). The interim board presented a comprehensive report on what it had achieved since the foundation. The above-mentioned reform papers, the fall meeting on 'detention centres', the conference in Uddevalla, plans concerning the publication of books, etc., were discussed – and the final treatment of the interim board's proposal for a work program (summarized above) had to wait till a meeting in December. In the meantime, the storm broke loose in the press.

The gathering point for the storm was a question put to the Minister of justice in Parliament. The questioner – a representative of the Socialist People's Party – brought up the three confrontations which the association so far had had with the authorities: the stopping of the informational letter to inmates, the refusal to print our article in Botsfengslet's institutional paper, and the refusal of the authorities to participate at the Uddevalla meeting. The form of the question, which had some influence on the further chain of events, went like this:

> Will the Minister of justice say that it is an expression of the general atti-
> tude of the prison authorities towards the Norwegian Association for Penal
> Reform when the prison system is unwilling to help with the distribution of
> an invitation to membership among the inmates, refuses to send representa-
> tives to a conference concerning criminal policy which the association par-
> ticipates in organizing, and refuses to give space to an informational article
> concerning the association in an internal institutional paper?

The association had taken some *preparatory steps* before the question was answered – we had for instance, sent the final statutes of the association to the Ministry of justice. Indirectly, we had earlier learnt that the Ministry of justice, when communicating with the mass media, usually referred to the fact that the association was not finally established, so that the authorities were in the dark as to what it stood for. We tried to prevent such a dilatory answer by sending the recently adopted statutes to the Ministry.

Our worry about a dilatory non-committal answer was unnecessary. The Min-ister's answer was forthright and negative. By way of introduction, the Minister briefly recapitulated the paragraphs in the statutes concerning the inmates' par-ticipation in board activities in KROM. She pointed out that according to 'the statutes of the Norwegian Association for Penal Reform, it is the objective of the association to work as "a pressure group towards authorities and political agen-cies" in the field of criminal policy', and continued by saying that it 'is apparently the objective of the association to utilize inmates in the institutions of the prison system as a link in such a pressure group'. The expression 'utilize' carried over-tones of 'exploit'. Over and above this, the Minister concentrated on one of the three issues mentioned in the question put to her: the refusal to help distribute the informational letter to the prisoners. She supported the refusal (the authorities had 'found it inappropriate that the prison system should actively contribute to bringing about membership, and that it would not be defensible to permit inmates to engage in such active membership as the association proposes'), with the fol-lowing justification:

> When the Norwegian Association for Penal Reform seeks to have inmates
> participate in a pressure group against the authorities, and wants to organ-
> ize co-operation between the association and inmates in the way which has
> been mentioned, it seeks to influence the inmates independently of, and partly
> in conflict with, the authorities' own influence. This may contribute to an

undermining of the confidence in the ruling authorities, and it may inhibit and damage the execution of punishment. Furthermore, it may contribute to increasing the dissatisfaction and other negative feelings which are naturally associated with a sentence for a crime and the incarceration following it. Among inmates who join the association, expectations which cannot be fulfilled may also be created. Neither can one disregard that such an activity may lead to difficulties in terms of order.

It could hardly have been much worse. The only 'positive' thing which the Minister had said was that the prison system 'has not prevented inmates who wanted it from joining as members of the association, or from corresponding with the association according to the standard rules for correspondence with inmates'.

To repeat, a storm broke loose in the press after this, in a negative direction for us.[4] The conservative evening paper which had just previously expressed itself positively in an editorial, now wrote (again editorially) that 'the association will not be taken seriously, if it continues as it has done up till now. It seems to be of the utmost importance for it to carry out propaganda and organizational activity *inside* the prison walls, and to display an activity which makes the difficult work of the prison authorities even more difficult . . . Work for penal reforms must be performed outside the walls, and we believe that it will be neither appropriate nor expedient to organize the prisoners as a protest group'. The conservative morning paper which had featured a positive review of the Uddevalla meeting, now published an editorial very negative in tone, under the title 'Beyond all reason'. This editorial concluded, inter alia, that 'to work for reforms in our prison system is something which law-abiding citizens are entitled to do, from their proper position outside the prison walls – everything is turned upside down if we begin to include the criminals themselves while they are still atoning for their deeds'. A press release on the Minister's reply was featured in a number of other papers, under headlines like: 'The prisoners should not be preoccupied with penal reforms', 'Not defensible to permit the prisoners active membership', 'Not defensible to let inmates participate actively'. Some papers also stressed in their headlines that 'Prisoners are not prevented from becoming members!' – the only positive thing the Minister had said – but the negative view on the prisoners' more active organizational participation naturally constituted the main content of the headlines.

These editorials and the new statements were answered by the association in several long articles. A part of the newspaper debate concerned a misunderstanding which in itself is interesting. The questioner in Parliament had, inter alia, asked why the prison authorities 'refused to send representatives to a conference concerning criminal policy which the association participated in organizing'. The question concerned the refusal of the prison authorities to send their own representatives to participate at Uddevalla.

In several papers, however, the issue was understood to mean that the prison system had refused to give inmate representatives leave to attend the meeting. The very thought of inmates being given permission to go to a conference on criminal policy created violent resentment in the press. The above-mentioned conservative evening paper wrote editorially that 'We have reached a complete farce, when the authorities are criticized for not giving furloughs to prisoners for participating in conferences arranged by the association . . . [The] Minister of Justice gave a clear answer to these provocations in Parliament yesterday'. The above-mentioned conservative morning paper wrote that 'to demand that the criminals, during the serving of the punishment which their crimes have brought on them, are to be given furloughs in order to participate in a conference which is to discuss reforms in the prison system, is, we think, pretty far off the track . . . And the Minister of Justice also gave a clear and concise answer, which undoubtedly is representative of the general feeling of justice in this country'. The misunderstanding was pointed out by the association in both papers – but in the latter paper the association's letter writer added 'Personally, I do not think it would be so unreasonable if some inmates were given furlough to participate in a conference concerning prison reforms'. The addition made the paper again react violently in an editorial. Under the warning tide 'They are criminals', it was stated, inter alia, that the letter writer's 'own views concerning the reasonableness of giving criminal prisoners furloughs to participate in conferences concerning the prison system, show, however, that there is good reason to sound an alarm here. It simply seems to be forgotten that we are dealing with criminals. . . .' Typically enough, the misunderstanding was very difficult to eradicate – it was introduced again in a television program a few days later, in which the association presented itself for the first time in this medium. An informational television program had been planned for a while, but in view of the sudden outbreak of interest concerning the matter, the program was changed to a news program. The prison authorities were invited by TV to participate with two representatives, but they refused to attend. TV finally chose two newspaper men to meet KROM's chairman and an ex-inmate on the board. One of the journalists had conducted the introductory newspaper interview with the chairman in connection with the founding of the association. As has been stated, his attitude was negative, and he now stressed among other things that – in his opinion – it was entirely unreasonable to invite inmates to conferences. From KROM's side it was pointed out that the invitation had not gone to inmates, but to employees in the prison system. The journalist still did not get the point, and carried on with renewed criticism. When he finally grasped the point, the program was nearly over. The association scored a few points by the journalist's obvious misunderstanding. After the program the headlines in one paper quipped 'Do the prisons keep pace? Editor XX and journalist NN do not'; in another there was a report stating that 'NN made a fool of himself to the TV viewers', But the main reaction was still negative. A radio program reviewing statements made by inmates at the Uddevalla conference also led to certain negative reactions. In the above-mentioned conservative morning paper, which had been represented at the conference, the discussion continued with a series of articles, especially concerning the topic mentioned here: the question of a contact relating to correctional and penal policy between KROM and the prisoners.

6. The social functions of imprisonment

In this way, the question of a political contact with the prisoners crystallized as the main topic and the main question as early as during the first nine months of KROM's existence. As long as the association did not raise this issue, as long as it remained a traditional academic group trying alone to influence the authorities, society remained rather indifferent. When the association raised the issue, when it tried to enter a 'horizontal', political relationship with the inmates, society – the authorities, public opinion, and in part the press – reacted angrily and deeply provoked.

Why the strong and provoked reaction to such contact? I interpret the strong resistance as follows. 'Horizontal' contact between the prisoners and an outside political organization touches and 'disturbs' important aspects of the social functions of imprisonment in our society. 'Disturbance' of the social functions of imprisonment is met by considerable resistance, because it indirectly 'disturbs' some main features of the social structure.

Firstly, political contact between prisoners and an outside organization like KROM disturbs *the expurgatory function* of imprisonment. In our society, 'productivity' is to a considerable and increasing degree geared to activity in the labour market. At the same time, our social structure probably increasingly creates groups which are 'unproductive' according to this criterion, A social structure which does so must rid itself of its unproductive elements, partly because their presence creates inefficiency in the system of production – it 'throws sand into the machinery' – and partly because the 'unproductive' brutally remind us of the fact that our productive system is not so successful after all. A society may get rid of its 'unproductive' elements in many ways. One way is to criminalize their activities and punish them by imprisoning them. This may be done towards a sub-category of the unproductive. In this perspective, the rulers of the prison system are merely the executives of the expurgatory system in society. KROM, on the other hand, tries to expose the ideological superstructure of the prisons, unmasking the real expurgatory function of the system. Concretely, contact between KROM and the prisoners implies that the wall between society and the 'unproductive' has been breached, and that the 'unproductive' indirectly come within the field of vision of the society which wants to get rid of them. Against this background, the provoked reaction on the part of people in the prison system, and their allies, becomes understandable.

Secondly, political contact between the prisoners and KROM disturbs *the power-draining function* of imprisonment. We shall return to this function in detail in Part III below; suffice it here to say that the prisoners, who are fundamentally powerless in relation to their rulers when confined and isolated in the prison, receive added strength and power of opposition, when allied with more powerful forces in the outside society. Contact between KROM and the prisoners thus implies added power of opposition on the part of the prisoners. Again the provoked reaction on the pan of representatives of the prison system, and their allies, becomes understandable. Not only is the purging of society disturbed; those who were earlier quietly expurgated now even become articulate in their protest, through alliance with more powerful outsiders.

Thirdly, contact between the prisoners and KROM disturbs *the diverting function* of imprisonment. In our society, acts dangerous to fellow human beings are increasingly being committed. Largely, however, these acts are committed by individuals and classes with considerable power in society. Pollution, exploitation of labourers in a manner dangerous to their health, production forms which ruin the life standard of the working class, and so on, are acts for which the most powerful members of society are in the last analysis responsible. However, punishment – in our age, imprisonment – is largely used against petty thieves and other relatively harmless individuals. For one thing, penal law first of all criminalizes their acts: furthermore, they have fewer possibilities of avoiding registration and sanctions. Thereby, imprisonment has the function of diverting the attention from the really dangerous acts committed by those in power: This diverting function is well supported by the press and other mass media; by presenting the prisoners as much more dangerous than they really are, the mass media constitute a selective filter between those who are imprisoned and public opinion. Contact between KROM and the prisoners provides a point of departure for exposing who are imprisoned, and who are not. Information about this, to the public, thus disturbs the diverting function. The information makes it clear that the really dangerous are by and large not imprisoned. Again, the provoked reaction of the rulers to contact between KROM and the prisoners becomes understandable.

Finally, political contact between the prisoners and KROM disturbs the *symbolic function* of imprisonment. The symbolic function of imprisonment is closely related to its diverting function, but a difference may be discerned. When someone is imprisoned, a process of stigmatization takes place. Those who are imprisoned are stigmatized as black. Thereby the rest of us, outside, may define ourselves as white. We may regard ourselves as all the better, more correct, more harmless. Contact between KROM and the prisoners implies a blurring of the demarcation line between black and white. For one thing, such contact leads to an exposing of the prisoner which shows that his acts are nevertheless not so much blacker than ours. Furthermore the contact entails that the prisoners organize themselves to fight for their interests, and such organization indicates that they are not so different from the rest of us after all. In this way, the contact threatens all those who would like to remain white.

*

In brief, then, the negative reaction to contact between KROM and the prisoners probably means that KROM, through its attempts to seek contact, has touched and disturbed significant social functions of imprisonment. This conclusion, how-ever, raises a further question: Would society – the authorities, the press and the public – have reacted to any kind of contact with the prisoners involving political issues? Or were special features of KROM's political form and activity especially provoking?

As their point of departure, the authorities would probably have reacted adversely to almost any approach from the outside which did not completely accept the rules and sovereignty of the authorities. Our own experience suggests this. Most likely, parts of the mass media would, as their point of departure, have done the same. Despite this, I assume that certain important special features of KROM's general development made the reaction remain strongly adverse. If these features in KROM's general development had not been present, the envi-ronment of the association would probably have calmed down, also with regard to the question of contact with the prisoners. It should be added that, of course, such a calming down is no goal for a pressure group.

What, then, had such an increasingly provocative effect? Some of the factors have actually been alluded to in our brief discussion of the social functions of imprisonment, In the first place, we here return to the two main questions which were discussed so carefully at the board meetings in the early days of the asso-ciation: the question whether we were to engage in humanitarian work or purely political activity, and the question of treatment as an alternative in contrast to a more open approach to the issue of alternatives. Let me repeat, certain provisional choices were made as regards these questions as early as at these board meetings. The provisional choices which were made – the 'political line' and the 'open approach' respectively – were developed further as time went on, and undoubt-edly contributed to the fact that KROM remained a provocative body.

Secondly, three further lines of development, which in large measure followed from the first two main tendencies, contributed to KROM's remaining a pro-vocative organization. We may call these lines of development the development towards a 'defensive' criminal policy, the development towards an 'exposing' criminal policy, and the development towards a policy in which genuinely 'vol-untary' help is stressed. We shall return later to more detailed definitions of these concepts. When we have discussed all the lines of development in some detail, we will be able to understand better why KROM, through its attempts to contact the prisoners, has disturbed significant social functions of imprisonment, and why those in power consequently have tried so hard to prevent such contact.

V

Second phase: from conformity to challenge

1. Towards a purely political line

The story of the development towards a purely political line is rather brief.

As we have seen, the purely political line had prevailed at the early board meetings in the association. But the formulation in the statutes – 'KROM may also seek to organize practical measures for offenders' – made the following-up of this line dependent on the interest of those who took the initiative in the association. To be sure, the association was committed, through its statutes, to work for a new policy towards prisoners. The paragraph relating to practical measures also stated that 'Through direct communication and actions KROM will operate as a pressure group towards authorities and political agencies in respect to criminal policy, and, through information and persuasion of public opinion, will bring about a change in public thinking concerning punishment'. Despite this, the main emphasis might clearly in practice be placed on practical aid projects. 'Pulls' as well as 'pressures' exist in this direction.

'The pulls' in the direction of practical aid projects – which were not insignificant during the first years of the association's existence – had several sources. In the first place, we are here confronted with a group of people who in a series of ways are characterized by poverty and lack of resources; a group which is treated very unfairly by public institutions. In itself, this makes humanitarian work very relevant. Secondly, political work – including political work in the field of so-called correctional and penal practice – is a long-range activity. Concrete results of what you are doing may rarely be seen on a short-term basis. The need to 'see' results is great, pulling in the direction of individualized humanitarian work. Thirdly, and more subtly, humanitarian work constitutes a way in which to 'appear protesting' towards the establishment. By performing humanitarian work, you maintain a kind of 'criticism' against the establishment which does not challenge the premises and rules of the establishment. You may be interested in 'appearing to protest' in this way, in order to be shielded in several directions – towards groups expecting protest as well as towards the establishment,

Let me emphasize here that humanitarian work is important in a society like ours. My point is that humanitarian work performed by an organization like

KROM would have pulled the association away from the blank space which otherwise would not be filled: that of criminal *policy*. In an area where public criticism and the will to bring about changes is only intermittent and unsystematic, a concentration on humanitarian activity would have meant that the structure which overshadows the prisoners would again have been left unassailed. In addition, whatever humanitarian work KROM might have carried out would – for reasons of time and money – have been trifling compared to the need, while work in the area of correctional and penal policy could – because such work is organized differently – be much more comprehensive.

The 'pressure' in the direction of engaging in humanitarian rather than political work came from three sides.

In the first place, it came from external individuals and organizations, who – during the early days of the association – contacted the association with suggestions, for example, of building after-care homes under the auspices of the association. This pressure was the easiest to handle. More difficult was a second pressure, from inmates in the prisons. The association early established a legal committee, working on general issues in criminal policy. To the prisoners, however, it appeared natural to ask for free legal aid from the committee members. Through the years we received a number of inquiries from prisoners concerning personal legal aid. Some of these requests were forwarded by us to institutions giving free legal aid – where this was possible. Over and above this, we had to answer that we could not undertake to give individual aid. We put a great deal of work into our replies to such requests, because we knew that the answers might be communicated to other prisoners. It is our impression that our reasoning was understood and accepted by the prisoners. However, contact was almost always through writing, and therefore of a remote kind, and the understanding which was created probably quickly disappeared with the turn-over in the institutions. Close contact with the prisoners could have created continual understanding, but such close contact was not permitted.

And even with close contact, emphasis on the political perspective could only be maintained through continual discussion. As indicated earlier, the ex-inmates brought with them an abundance of concrete experience from prisons and penal practice, an experience which became entirely indispensable to the association in view of the closed character of the prisons. Without the experience of the ex-inmates, KROM's work would simply have been made impossible. At the same time some of the ex-inmates were, for obvious reasons, preoccupied with humanitarian efforts. On one occasion a work group in KROM – in which some ex-inmates participated – had made plans to prepare a memorandum stating that KROM ought to establish a probation house for prisoners. The memorandum was never written, but the plan shows the pull from ex-inmates in the direction of the concretely humanitarian. On another occasion some ex-inmates prepared a plan for a contact centre in KROM, to be manned by ex-inmates *themselves*, catering for recently released inmates. The ex-inmates who were preoccupied with this had several group meetings concerning the matter, and presented their plan to the board. The group wished to place the contact centre under KROM's authority, and to have KROM as a 'shield' against the environment. The plan, which everyone found very interesting, provided an occasion for a renewed discussion of principle concerning the relationship between criminal policy and humanitarian work in the organization. Among other things, we discussed at great length how such a contact centre, under the authority of the association, might lead KROM to compromise relations with the authorities – a compromise which could be binding and dangerous. A contact centre would among other things presuppose special 'contact' with the institutions from which prisoners are released, and such contact could easily bind KROM in its political work, or lead to various parts of KROM – the humanitarian and the political parts – being played off against each other by the adversaries of the association. To amplify, in order to initiate and maintain co-operation with the authorities concerning contact with released prisoners, we could easily have been subjected to pressure to stifle our criticism of the system. And if we had continued our criticism, the authorities would easily have been able to play us off against the prisoners by obstructing contact with inmates to be released. We see here a rather clear example of the contradiction which exists between 'humanitarian' and 'political' work, and of how humanitarian organizations are made dependent on the established system, thereby becoming partly or wholly paralysed from a political point of view. On the basis of these main considerations we agreed that the contact centre was to be placed outside KROM, so that KROM could continue to devote itself to the political aspects.

In view of this decision, the ex-inmates felt that their enterprise needed another 'shield' instead of KROM, and approached some of the authorities – a prison governor, a district attorney, and a couple of business men, concerning the matter. These authorities, however, imposed various conditions on the enterprise, and it was therefore delayed, so that at the time of writing it has not been realized.[5]

I cannot get away from the feeling that the ex-inmates here fell between two stools, and that we others in KROM were perhaps at fault in not advocating inclusion of the effort in the association. On the other hand, an inclusion would, as suggested above, have meant compromise relations which undoubtedly could have damaged our joint political activity. The conflict is difficult.

The third side from which there was pressure in the direction of humanitarian work was from the authorities and their closest allies – conservative newspapers and newspaper men. From their point of view, KROM neglected its real duty by not taking up humanitarian tasks. An employee in the Prison Department expressed it this way in a newspaper: 'And when the convicted are released, KROM has nothing to offer. During the course of their stay in prison, the inmates ought to have contact with those with whom it is of importance to have contact – in connection with resocialization. The Red Cross and the Salvation Army, which also speak for the inmates, perform much valuable work here'. The implication was that conservative organizations like the Salvation Army do more valuable work than KROM. Stronger accusations were also levied from time to time; KROM was presented as an organization so political that it was uninterested in the welfare of the inmates.

Such accusations sting, and as previously indicated, they constitute a pressure in the direction of engaging in humanitarian work. This is probably also partly why the accusations are put forward by the authorities. If KROM engaged in humanitarian work, the association would no longer challenge the foundations of the established system, but would rather act in conformity with these conditions. This leads us to the conclusion to this section.

If KROM had developed in the direction of a humanitarian organization, society – the authorities as well as parts of the press and the public – would probably have reacted differently to any residue of political work still pursued by the organization. Such a residue would probably have been accepted, at least after a while, because it would to a large extent have been undisturbing and harmless, owing to the demands accruing from humanitarian activity. As it was, however, KROM to an increasing degree represented a rather purely political line. This meant that the organization permitted itself freedom in relation to important postulates and expectations on the part of those in power. This constitutes an important part of the background for understanding the persistent resistance and reaction of the authorities to contact of a political kind between KROM and the prisoners.

But of course, the way in which freedom to formulate a policy was used, the content of our policy, was equally important. We now turn to the question of content.

2. Towards a policy of abolition

The second line of development, which contributed to the background of the authorities' reaction to contact between KROM and the prisoners, is a development towards an 'open' approach to the general question of alternatives to existing arrangements in penal and criminal law,

We have already seen how the 'treatment alternative' to imprisonment was taken out of the actual statutes early in the life of the association. As we have seen, this had an important effect in hardening our general attitude towards our silent adversaries. But as mentioned before, the 'treatment alternative' to imprisonment nevertheless remained central in the early work program of the association. And even if we could refer to our 'open' statutes, the early work program meant that we in actual practice still went far in accepting the postulates and conditions of the existing penal system. The 'treatment alternative' in the work program meant acceptance, as the goal of our activity, of the protection of society against crime – despite the fact that our point of departure had been that of changing the system of control in a direction ameliorating conditions for those exposed to the system. The 'treatment alternative' made us veer towards the other objective – that is, towards the objective of the power holders and the authorities rather than the interests of the prisoners. Such a change of direction is not part and parcel of the 'nature' of treatment, and is not built into treatment seen in isolation from its environment – that is, in isolation from the imprisonment which treatment is to be a step away from. The change of direction occurs, however, precisely when 'treatment' *is seen as an alternative to imprisonment, and it takes place in connection with all specified 'alternatives' to imprisonment.*

In more detail: in order to be an 'alternative', or something 'to take the place of' the original, a proposed new arrangement must satisfy the same objective as the arrangement you wish to get away from – and if possible, in a more effective way. If the proposed new arrangement does not satisfy the same objective, it is rejected as not being a real 'alternative'. The objective of imprisonment is – in the widest sense – to protect society against crime. Since this is the objective of imprisonment, any new arrangement must, in order to be accepted as an 'alternative', as 'something to take the place of imprisonment, also have the protection of society against crime as its objective. Stated differently: in order to be accepted as an 'alternative', a new arrangement must combat crime in a more effective way. Effective combating of the acts which in a society are defined as 'criminal' need, obviously, not coincide with the interests of those who are exposed to that society's system of control and sanctions.

In this way, the demand for 'alternatives', which is often raised by supporters of established arrangements when these arrangements are criticized, may be understood more clearly. By demanding 'alternatives' before a change in the established order is implemented, it is made certain that the framework for discussion becomes the question of attaining whatever objective the established order already has. In this way, the demand for 'alternatives' has a conserving effect: the demand contributes to the maintenance of the establishment's objective, so that – if anything – only the means to reach the old objective are changed. In itself, this is a crucial limitation on the change which may be carried out.

However, the demand has a further conserving effect. Not only does it limit any change to a change of means; it also limits very strongly the choice between various means. To amplify, usually the general objective of an arrangement consists of a larger or smaller number of partial goals. For example, the general objective of imprisonment-protection of society against crime – consists of the partial goals of custody, individual prevention, and general prevention, and these partial goals in turn consist of further partial goals. If an alternative method is proposed to achieve the general objective of the 'protection of society against crime' (for example an alternative which at least to a somewhat greater degree takes the interests of the offenders into consideration), this proposal may immediately be met by a demand to the effect that the new arrangement must, in order to be accepted as an 'alternative', also satisfy one or more of the partial goals – for example custody, individual prevention, and/or general prevention. Thereby, not only are you cut off from working for a change of objectives; in practice you are also limited in your work for variations in means. The more specific the goal is made, the closer you come, in terms of means, to the old arrangement – which you originally intended to abandon. For example, the goal of custody may only be achieved through some form of deprivation of liberty. If you add a measure of deterrence, etc., your proposal of new methods comes suspiciously close to the old structure – the prison – which you were intending to get away from. Let me add that if you at some point or another in the chain say 'stop' to the adversary's specification of partial goals – if you, for example, state that 'this business of incarceration is something I will not go along with, this is not my goal', the immediate rejoinder is that you are not presenting any 'alternative' to imprisonment.

The spokesmen for the established order who demand 'alternatives' in this way in practice represent a strongly conservative attitude. To a large extent, the demand for alternatives is probably a conscious strategy on the part of these spokesmen. The conserving function of the demand for alternatives may be seen in a number of political fields – not only in the sphere of correctional and penal policy. The function may, for example, be observed in connection with the question of European economic/political co-operation. Norwegian entry into the European Economic Community[6] would have constituted a continuation and further consolidation of the main features of the established system and of the social structure which we have to-day. Adherents of Norwegian entry – for example, conservative newspapers – at intervals and with capital letters demanded 'alternatives' from the opponents of Norwegian entry. The demand forced a number of opponents on the defensive; they, for example, proposed 'free trade agreements' etc. as alternatives, thereby giving the adherents of full membership a good hand. The adherents could then make a point of the fact that a free trade agreement largely pursued the goals of the E.E.C., but in a less satisfactory way. This forced their opponents to offer further specifications of a 'free trade agreement' which were extremely close to full membership in the E.E.C. What started as a clear no became, among these opponents, almost a yes.

The demand for 'alternatives' was tactically a very wise move from the point of view of the adherents of the E.E.C. – as it is wise from a conservative point of view in discussing criminal policy. In the first place, the presentation of the demand was probably among the factors responsible for reducing the no-majority which was the result of the referendum. Secondly – and at least equally important – the answers which were given to the demand are binding for the future. The ranks of the opponents became widely committed to working for a very extensive agreement with the E.E.C., and the boundary to membership may easily be blurred. In general terms, the following may be said. If the demand for alternatives is not answered, if the opponents of an arrangement put forward a no; and emphasize a set of basic values different from those adhered to by the supporters of the arrangement, the opponents may easily be rejected as 'unrealistic' and 'irresponsible'. When emphasis is placed on completely different values, they may with great force be described partly as unattainable on a short-term basis ('unrealistic'), and partly as uncertain with regard to further consequences ('irresponsible' – you know what you have, but not what you may get). Values other than the established ones *must* necessarily – simply because they are other than the established ones – be long-term and uncertain. *The opponent of the prevailing order is therefore presented with the choice between specifying alternatives – and thereby coming very close to the prevailing order in what he suggests – or emphasizing completely different values – and thereby being rejected as irresponsible and unrealistic.* The choice is difficult, and many choose the former solution.

It is, however, the more dangerous solution, for reasons given above. Despite the difficulties connected with it, the latter solution must be the right one if you, initially, either disagree with one or more of the goals of the prevailing order, or give priority to goals which are in conflict with the prevailing ones. If you do not, in one of these ways, disagree with regard to goals, the question is a different one. But if you disagree, the right thing must be to stand on your no, and on the other values, and seek to communicate the values to groups in society which may participate in fighting for them. The ridicule and pressure which you are then exposed to is of course great: ridicule and pressure are means of obstructing the communication of values to potential allies. And not only is the ridicule and the pressure there – the accusations of 'undermining' society, 'political extremism', etc., are also strong, because the new values necessarily presuppose – if they are to be put into effect – comprehensive changes over and above the specific political area (for example, the area of correctional and penal policy) which constituted your point of departure, In other words, the choice easily becomes one between specifying 'alternatives' which in reality are very close to the prevailing order, and facing attempts from the establishment at 'defining you out' through accusations such as those mentioned above. Both horns of the dilemma are effective weapons in the hands of the establishment. The latter, however, is the less dangerous to the opposition, assuming that the channels for communication of the new values to potential allies are not completely blocked.

*

Confronted with the choice between, on the one hand, specifying 'alternatives' which in reality are very close to the prevailing order, and, on the other hand, the possibility of being 'defined out' through the many accusations attendant upon reliance on new values, KROM stressed the 'alternative solution' in the early work program. A part of KROM's struggle through the years therefore consisted in liberating itself more fully from the 'alternative side' of the choice, and transforming the independence implicit in the statutes into actual political practice. This struggle went through several steps, which will briefly be sketched below.

The first step coincided with the resistance towards the projected *detention centre* in Norway. The detention centre – adopted in the Juvenile Offenders Act of 1965, but at the time of writing not put into effect – was planned as a 60-day 'short-term measure' for young offenders without a strongly criminal background. The detention was to take place in a closed institution, under strict supervision, 'moderately demanding labour' and discipline. The plan was based on the British detention centre model, providing a 'link' between the child welfare system and standard penal measures. The detention centres were to be placed under the authority of the Prison Department.

Several years before the founding of KROM, in connection with the introduction of the Act itself, protests against the plans had appeared from social scientists. A lengthy memorandum concerning the plans had been prepared by a work group consisting of sociologists and treatment personnel. A later member of the board of KROM had participated in the work group. In the memorandum the authors had, inter alia, referred to alternative treatment measures such as the Highfields project in the United States. The memorandum had been addressed to the Legal Committee in Parliament, and the work group had also had a meeting concerning the matter with the Committee. The group emphasized its goodwill by not bringing the memorandum to the attention of the newspapers. Perhaps in part because of this, the memorandum had no short-term effect on the result – detention centres were adopted in the Act – but on a long-term basis it gave ammunition for further resistance against the idea.

The question of detention centres became one of KROM's first important issues. As early as before the organizing general meeting in the fall of 1968, the association arranged – as mentioned earlier – a meeting concerning young offenders and imprisonment, at which the detention centre question was a central one. The chairman of KROM's interim board participated in a panel at the meeting, and emphasized among other things that the planned detention centre ought to become an 'observational centre'. His idea was that the scarce treatment resources of the prison system ought to be gathered in one place – in the new institutions – which then might 'constitute the first criminal/psychiatric milieu in the prison system. Thereby the prison system will get something which it really needs, a professionally well-founded treatment staff' (from a newspaper review of the meeting). The chairman had thereby gone a long way towards the alternative thinking which was discussed above. An 'observational centre' of the kind he was sketching would retain so many features of the prison that the difference would be small.

The chairman followed the idea up in a lecture given to the Norwegian Criminalists' Association later that fall – in which he criticized the detention centre and asked for a treatment experiment instead. The lecture was reviewed in a prominent evening paper. The journalist in question was conservative and negatively inclined towards KROM, and his review is interesting. He stressed – and placed a main emphasis on – the obviously weak point in the chairman's lecture: the chairman's clear rapprochement with the established order through his stress on a treatment alternative. By way of introduction the journalist stated, inter alia, that 'a rather moderate version of Dr. T. M. yesterday gave a lecture in the Criminalists' Association . . . At least, several of the speakers in the following discussion remarked that they had expected considerably stronger medicine. T. M. stated in the lecture that he would not advocate revolutions within the prison system, but would restrict himself to asking for one whole-hearted, really concentrated and new experiment in the treatment of juvenile offenders: a treatment institution for a limited and selected clientele, in which all scientific capacity was used in the rehabilitation'. The journalist quoted the chairman in the following words (fairly correctly): 'I propose the abandonment of the plan of a detention centre in Nannestad – an institution which actually may become dangerous for certain types of criminals. And that we instead construct an entirely new institution with a total treatment system'.

The further discussion at this meeting also illustrates the dangers inherent in getting involved in specified 'alternatives' of this kind. Not only did the chairman, through his proposal, in practice to a considerable extent accept the prison system – a fact which was used against him in the newspaper review – but in the discussion representatives of the prison system also emphasized how such a treatment institution must – in order to be 'realistic' in relation to the objectives of the prison system – come very close to the prison system in terms of structure. A prison governor stated (from the same article, rather correctly reviewed): 'We worked with optimism as well as enthusiasm [in my youth prison], but the therapy stopped by itself, – first of all because the inmates themselves would only unwillingly be confronted with their weaknesses . . . It appears that the unstable clientele you have to deal with in practice had better have a firmer structure. In fact, they prefer it themselves. Custody must be the solid platform, – and then the treatment experiments must be performed on the basis of this platform. You can give the inmates better support then, than in a system which is so loose that it ends in chaos'. The quotation is saturated with politically relevant material. For one thing, reference is made to the inmates' apparent support of a prison-like structure, We shall, however, return to the importance of this later. Here I shall emphasize how the governor turned the proposed 'alternative' into being almost a regular youth prison, based on the traditional main objective of the prison: security and custody. At this meeting, the chairman did not clearly say no to this objective, fearing that he might immediately be labelled too far-reaching and Utopian.

The third main drive against the detention centre came in the form of a reform paper from the association in February 1969. Somewhat later, the paper was published in a professional law journal, thereby receiving double attention in the newspapers. By this time the association had received new ammunition. In England – the native country of the detention centre – scepticism had begun to appear concerning the system of detention centres. A white paper from the Home Office in 1968 had proposed a gradual abolition of detention centres for young offenders under 17. Rather accidentally, the association had become acquainted with the contents of the white paper through a Norwegian Supreme Court judge, and naturally made more of it than the authorities (we did become acquainted with the white paper before the meeting in the Criminalists' Association, but, interestingly, not then as an important factor). It constituted a main point in the reform paper. In addition, the board of the association had now begun to develop a certain scepticism towards the 'treatment alternative', which had been emphasized so optimistically at the outset. This scepticism was among other thing a more long-term effect of the discussions of the organizational statutes mentioned earlier. For these reasons, the content of the reform paper was rather different from the early lectures concerning this matter. Treatment alternatives were, to be sure, discussed over four (of altogether 16) pages – we discussed the Highfields system, the Community Treatment Project, the New Careers experiment in California, and 'the more traditional psychiatric/psychological endeavours', as four alternatives to detention centres. But the discussion had a more careful and less optimistic form than earlier. It was emphasized that the projects 'do not give completely secure results with regard to recidivism to crime; so far we do not know enough about the treatment of criminals to expect this'. Secondly, the more directly critical – negating – material received a very significant place, and British experience was referred to in this connection. The chairman of the association at this time participated in a research project under the auspices of the Council of Europe, a fact which led him into contact with Englishmen who had detailed knowledge of the discussion on detention centres in England. Twice he went to London to produce written and oral material, which could be used in further newspaper articles concerning the matter throughout the summer of that year.

The final result of the action came during the late fall of 1969. A member of Parliament had posed the following question to the Minister of Justice: 'Is the Ministry of justice willing to look again at the regulations in the Juvenile Offenders Act of 1965 concerning detention centres before the planned building at Nannestad is begun, in view of the criticism which has lately been raised in Great Britain as well as in Norway against punitive measures of this kind for young offenders?' Considerable suspense was attached to the reply. A good deal of prestige was now associated with the issue, and one might expect that the prison authorities, who were responsible for planning the institution, would advise the Minister of Justice to retain the detention centre plans. In KROM we were also anxious about the result because the same Minister of justice had, a year earlier, expressed herself so negatively on KROM in Parliament (see above). Apparently against the advice of the Prison Department, the Minister of Justice held – as one newspaper expressed it – 'a funeral feast for the detention centre'. In her reply, she said, inter alia:

> I am, however, aware of the fact that there may be varying opinions concerning the question of introducing such a new measure into our penal system, and I am not without understanding of the doubt which therefore may be present.
>
> I am prepared to take up for consideration whether the development which has taken place since the Act was adopted, in Great Britain and elsewhere, may give cause for looking more closely at the legal regulations concerning detention centres.

The reply was a diplomatic phrasing of a clear repudiation of the detention centre plan, based in particular on the development in the country of origin. In the departmental estimates for the budget of 1971 the consequence of this was apparent, in so far as it was stated that the planning of the detention centre would 'be suspended'.

We learnt much from our struggle against the detention centre. In the first place, we became considerably more sceptical about specifying 'alternatives' which might be acceptable from the point of view of the authorities. Secondly, it had proved possible to have an implemented plan (some money had already been granted) *abolished* without 'alternatives', geared more or less to the same function, being introduced at the same time.

Further preoccupation with and articulation of these points of view was occasioned by another struggle, which became vital to the association, and which was already developing.

*

This was the struggle against *forced labour* in Norway. Forced labour was introduced in the Act relating to Vagrancy, Begging, and Drunkenness of 1900, abbreviated as the 'Vagrancy Act'. According to the 'forced labour rule' in 'the Act, a person who regularly abused alcohol, and who had repeatedly appeared intoxicated in public, could be subjected to forced labour. This generally meant induction into Oppstad labour camp, actually a rigorous prison. In practice, the rule was employed against alcoholic vagrants from the bottom layer of the working class, and was thus a clear example of a class law. A little before the rule was finally repealed, the time spent in forced labour was half a year for first offenders, and about one year for recidivists, The rule led some alcoholics to spend over 20 years of their lives in forced labour. A socio-psychological analysis of the inmates in the most important forced labour camp, from 1959, showed that the forced labourers were frequently very sick, physically and psychologically broken down, with needs which could not under any circumstances be satisfied in a prison system. The same Act also criminalized 'evident intoxication in public places', and punished those who, while intoxicated, 'disturb general peace and order or legal traffic' etc. It is unnecessary to discuss here the details in the legal background of these regulations. The point is that the struggle against forced labour was simultaneously a struggle against these forms of criminalizing alcoholism and its consequences.

The struggle against forced labour became relevant to KROM at one of the very first board meetings in the association, during 'the great silence'. As early as in 1964, the Ministry of Justice's Advisory Council on Penal Issues had published a lengthy recommendation on the matter, in which they had recommended a new Act – but notably an Act which in practice maintained forced labour and criminalization of public drunkenness in almost the same form. The recommendation of the Advisory Council had not, however, yet led to any bill concerning the issue. In KROM's board we now decided to establish an 'Advisory Council' in KROM – consisting of lawyers – which was to deal with matters 'as for example the "Oppstad issue"' (from the board meeting protocol). KROM's 'Advisory Council' later took the name 'KROM's Legal Committee', and during its first period it came to concentrate rather heavily on the 'Oppstad issue'.

The first serious move on KROM's part against the Vagrancy Act came during the spring of 1969 – a year after the founding of the organization, and not long after the reform paper on detention centres. That spring the association took part in arranging a large teach-in on the Vagrancy Act. Before this, strong criticism had for a long time been levelled against the Vagrancy Act, especially by professional people in sociology and social medicine. In the earlier criticism, one point had been central: forced labour was originally introduced against alcoholics on the more or less explicit ground that it constituted a form of 'treatment' from which the 'clients' could benefit. It had been pointed out that the 'treatment idea' had in reality become a wedge for stronger control and more coercion towards the 'clients' (*Nils Christie: Forced Labour and the Use of Alcohol*, Oslo: University Press, 1960). This criticism against forced labour had strengthened our general scepticism towards 'treatment' as an alternative solution. At the teach-in, which was extensively covered in the press and by the Norwegian Broadcasting Corporation (the meeting coincided with publication of the first of a series of KROM books, which created a sensation in the press, and which will be referred to in Part III below), the particular criticism mentioned here was central, and a clear demand was raised to the effect that forced labour *must be abolished*.

Representatives of the prosecuting authorities, the police, and the treatment system for alcoholics participated at the teach-in. The authorities were not exactly enthusiastic about forced labour, but they stressed rather strongly that before an abolition could take place, one had to have alternatives – one had to have something else instead.

Never before has the conserving function of the demand for alternatives in criminal policy been clearer. It was rather obvious that as long as forced labour, and criminalization of public drunkenness, remained, decent facilities for alcoholics would not be created. The establishment is its own best defence. It saps resources, paralyses other initiatives, and inhibits other developments by the very fact that it exists. Thus, by demanding the implementation of alternatives *before* an abolition of the prevailing system, the conservative forces demanded something which could not materialize, or which at least would materialize only extremely slowly, and be very similar to what already existed.

In practice, the further struggle against forced labour focused on this question – whether one should 'cut out' and abolish forced labour, or whether one should 'wait for the alternatives'. At the teach-in, KROM with great clarity emphasized abolition. But on a couple of other occasions during the further development we wavered – maturation and training in the ability to see through the adversary's strategy to ok time. The process is instructive, and therefore merits some space.

The first wavering came a short while after the large teach-in. A week after the meeting a bill concerning the Vagrancy Act was approved by the Cabinet. The bill departed from the recommendation of the Advisory Council: instead of proposing a new Act, the bill proposed to maintain the old one with a few adjustments (there were proposals for the reduction of the upper limit in forced labour to 12 months, for the repeal of imprisonment for public drunkenness, and for power to detain those arrested for drunkenness in sick wards as an alternative to regular prison arrest, etc.). The reason why the bill did not follow the recommendation of the Advisory Council, and why it did not propose a new Act, was that the authorities wanted 'closer investigation of the possibilities for a complete or partial abolition of the Drunkenness Act'. In the light of this, the authorities would 'very soon appoint a broadly composed committee to investigate these issues'. The committee was not only to 'examine the legal aspects of the questions, but also look at what practical measures a repeal of the Drunkenness Act would necessitate'.

The bill was very wisely formulated from a conservative standpoint. In the first place, certain liberalizing adjustments were introduced to please the critics. Secondly, the appointment of a committee was proposed – and the work of such a committee would clearly have a postponing effect. Thirdly – and most importantly in this connection – this committee was given as its mandate, inter alia, to examine the question of alternatives to forced labour. This appears in the last sentence quoted above ('... what practical measures a repeal ... would necessitate'), and still more clearly from the more detailed formulation of the mandate. Here it was stated, inter alia, – and note the hypothetical form – that the committee to be appointed should 'examine whether it is conceivable that it will under existing conditions be possible to abolish the use of forced labour towards this clientele. The committee must also examine what alternative measures would eventually be necessary, especially in the care of alcoholics and the general social care, if the use of punitive measures were to be reduced or abolished. An examination of these questions will take time, and in the event of a change it will take even longer to bring about the actual conditions for a possible new system ... The complex of issues is in general very comprehensive, and it seems to necessitate a coordinated examination, not only of medical, sociopolitical, punitive, legal-administrative, and other legal aspects, but also of the practical and economic questions which must be solved. It will call for a development and timing plan for institutions and the recruitment of qualified personnel to the institutions, The various measures which are needed, must also be examined in relation to other social tasks' (Bill No. 54, 1968/69, p. 51).

There was, in other words, almost no end to the difficulties. By including the question of alternatives in the mandate, it was made certain: 1) that 'alternatives' would be viewed as necessary before an abolition, 2) that the abolition could be pushed very far into the future – because the construction of alternatives would be, as indicated, very time-consuming, and 3) that – if and when forced labour finally was abolished – 'other' arrangements taking care of the main function of forced labour – control and purgation of the city – would have been secured.

Towards this bill KROM wavered in its attitude. The wavering appears first of all from the correspondence of the association with inmates in Oppstad labour camp. To a prisoner who had written to KROM concerning his view on forced labour, the chairman of the association replied:

> I thought you might be interested to learn that the government bill concerning the Vagrancy Act went through Cabinet yesterday ... I have been informed that it at least contained two hopeful points: In the first place the bill does not follow the Advisory Council's proposal to introduce a new Act on alcohol use ... I view this as an advantage, because it will be more difficult to have a new Act in this field repealed later. Secondly, I understand that the bill advises the appointment of a broadly composed committee which is to take

up the question of complete de-criminalization in this field . . . The last point is, of course, the most important one. But obviously, it is then important that the committee, which will probably be appointed after Parliament's sanction of the bill, will be fast working, so that new long years do not go by. This will be the next thing we must work for.

In other words, the association was not so far from accepting the establishment of a committee, and thereby the need for an examination and specification of alternatives. The same appears in the initial work on the matter in KROM's Legal Committee. As has been stated, our committee had been appointed more or less with this issue as its mandate. A month after the bill was presented, the committee wrote a brief two-page report, intended for the parliamentary legal committee, in which it was emphasized that forced labour etc. had to be abolished, and that 'Parliament may and should abolish the system of forced labour at once, without any new examination', but in which it was further alternatively emphasized that 'If, however, Parliament does not find it possible to repeal §§ 16/18 in the Vagrancy Act at once, KROM will emphasize the extreme significance of an examination taking place quickly . . . If Parliament finds that there is a need for a new committee examination, KROM will ask Parliament to decide that the committee is to be appointed at once, and that it is to give its report within one year . . .'. Privately KROM's committee informed the board that the primary standpoint had been included more or less as a bargaining measure, that the alternative standpoint was the only realistic one, and that it was actually difficult to say much negating the idea of a committee examination.

There was, however, discussion about the matter in KROM's Legal Committee. One member felt that this implied going too far in the Ministry's direction, that the issue had now been 'examined' for years, that forced labour etc. *could* be abolished at once, and that this ought to be KROM's standpoint. Throughout the spring this led to intensive discussions in the committee and on the board, where a clearer standpoint in favour of abolition began to harden. The brief memorandum quoted above was never sent to Parliament.

But nothing else was sent to Parliament, either. The reason was that the Parliament did not discuss the bill that spring. In the parliamentary legal committee some representatives were doubtful about the Ministry's solution. They were, however, not numerous enough to present a committee proposal with a different content, so that a postponement was their only possible step. So the postponement inevitably took place.

This gave KROM a respite during the summer. This summer, the standpoint stressing abolition was definitively decided on as 'KROM's point of view. The most important provisions in the Vagrancy Act could and ought to be abolished *at once*. During a hectic weekend the association's Legal Committee completed a very comprehensive memorandum concerning this, which became KROM's fifth reform paper, addressed to Parliament's legal committee. In the memorandum, KROM's committee discussed in detail the arguments favouring maintenance of forced labour etc., showing how the various arguments through the years had been abandoned by representatives of the existing system (for example, forced labour as a treatment measure and forced labour as a part of general prevention in society), as well as how the Ministry in its new bill had even abandoned the argument concerning public order (the bill referred to the fact that more malignant crime is often followed by milder measures than forced labour), and how the Ministry's final argument the view that forced labour could have a beneficial effect on the inmates' physical health – was quite untenable. It was emphasized that *alternatives were not necessary to abolish forced labour*:

> To be sure, it is essential that an inquiry be instituted to seek better solutions for the care of alcoholics. But Oppstad forced labour camp does not under any circumstances give any such help to its clients as may defend a maintenance of the prison while waiting for new institutions. And neither as a means of public order nor as protection does society need Oppstad . . . For years our forced labour system has survived all weighty objections. There is every reason to fear that the system will continue to be a cushion – an obstacle to active and creative reform activity in an area which cries out for radical changes, not for new inquiries.

The reform paper was dated 4 August 1969, and sent a few days earlier to all the main newspapers in the capital city, to radio and television, and to the Norwegian Press Bureau. The paper was given news coverage in the social-democratic capital city paper, editorial treatment in several other large Oslo papers, and a comprehensive review on television. A press release concerning the paper was given considerable space in a number of newspapers throughout the country. A general editorial article was printed in a number of Labour Party papers outside the capital city. Party politics had begun to enter the issue. The main theme in the headlines was that forced labour 'Ought to be Abolished Without New Inquiry'.

The reform paper had a short-term effect which probably was not insignificant. On the day of its release, the government appointed the committee which had been referred to in its bill that spring. The appointment of the committee, which under other circumstances undoubtedly would have received coverage in the press, causing a delaying effect, was now more or less drowned in the demand for *immediate abolition.*

The reform paper probably also had a long-term effect, though it must be emphasized that the opinion against forced labour manifested itself from many quarters, so that the pressure for a repeal was broad, In September 1969 a Parliamentary election took place, and a new legal committee in Parliament was appointed. The Ministry presented its bill again, with almost identical content, but the air had by now been let out of the Ministry's balloon. The proposal for an examination by a committee was at this juncture long since outdistanced by our much more radical move.

It should be stressed that articulate public opinion at this time was for abolition of forced labour. If the general opinion had not been for it, the more far-reaching standpoint would perhaps have been defined as dangerous and unrealistic. This, however, did not happen.

The rest of the story is fairly brief. From now on, KROM maintained the standpoint stressing abolition. A board member in KROM became secretary for the parliamentary legal committee in its work on the issue. The parliamentary committee made two journeys – one to Finland (where the criminalization of public drunkenness had already been abolished) and one to Oppstad forced labour camp. As far as is known, both journeys were important in convincing the committee members that forced labour and criminalization of public drunkenness ought and could be abolished without a waiting period. Prior to the visit to the labour camp, KROM had had frequent contact by letter with several inmates there. These inmates had gradually become rather conscious of the significance of immediate abolition of forced labour (earlier inmates had written to us saying that they thought the time spent in forced labour ought to be shortened – the idea of abolition was outside the frame of reference with which they had been presented in their institutional existence). The inmates took some members of the parliamentary committee aside when the latter arrived at the institution, and had lengthy talks with them. The internal negotiations in the parliamentary committee are only to a small degree known, but it is clear that the Labour Party view – immediate abolition of forced labour and decriminalization of public drunkenness – became, after lengthy negotiations, a unanimous view on the part of the committee. It is not improbable that KROM's activity outside Parliament had an influence on this development. Members of the association – not least among the inmates at Oppstad – frequently wrote articles on the matter in the press. Perhaps it was also important that the other matters which KROM dealt with at the time – the issue of the detention centres as well as matters to which I shall return below – also created continual discussion in the newspapers. In this way, a broad and general pressure was placed on the legal system, which probably had an effect on the weakest point of the system – which was now the Vagrancy Act. An article supporting Oppstad in a conservative magazine, bearing the title 'A Prison Guard speaks up: A Cow is more Useful than a Psychologist' (the work at Oppstad to a large degree consisted of outdoor labour on a farm), at this time created indignation rather than sympathy with the criminal justice system. Several inmates answered the officer in question in the press, and in addition asked KROM to file a complaint with the Professional Council of the Press. KROM complained and won the complaint, thus creating even more discussion of the issue.

In March 1970 the association arranged a teach-in on the Vagrancy Act in Trondheim. This was immediately prior to the publication of the proposal of the parliamentary committee, and the speakers consisted of a Labour Party representative from the parliamentary committee, a district attorney, a representative of KROM's legal committee, KROM's chairman, and an ex-inmate from the forced labour camp. For the last time, the demand for alternatives was presented in defence of the established order, by the district attorney: '[I believe] that it is not appropriate that we without further ado abolish the Vagrancy Act or the labour camp at Oppstad; we must have an alternative, something to place in its stead' (quotation from a newspaper review). But the matter was now clear. A week later the proposal of the parliamentary committee was published, unanimously recommending abolition of forced labour and decriminalization of public drunkenness. The committee also recommended giving the Ministry of justice a respite until July 1971 for carrying the repeal into effect. The respite was criticized by KROM – we regarded it as too long. During the parliamentary debate on the issue, the Minister of Justice emphasized that since the regulations were now to be repealed, it was natural to repeal them at once, and the repeal was carried into effect on 1 July 1970. In advance, the number of forced labourers at Oppstad had gradually been reduced.

Let me add that those who had maintained that an abolition would press forth a sociopolitical initiative which would otherwise not have come, turned out to be right on a short-term basis. Immediately following the decision in Parliament, the Ministry of Social Affairs appointed a committee to examine what should now be done in the social sector, The committee gave its first – preliminary – report after six weeks, and two days before the repeal was carried into effect. It proposed the building of so-called protection homes, sick wards, and 'detoxification stations' to meet the most acute needs during the first winter, A month later, the municipality of Oslo issued an action plan following the main guidelines of the committee, an action plan which KROM supported. This development would hardly have taken place without the changes in the Vagrancy Act.

But by now public opinion favouring the vagrants was past its peak. As an ominous sign of what was to come, the following editorial comment appeared in a conservative morning paper during the course of that summer:

> The abolition of the Vagrancy Act was a gigantic error – an unstated invitation to all kinds of rabble and mob: You just drink, fellows, there is nothing wrong in that . . . The result is, naturally – this all sensible people could predict – that drunkenness and street disorder flourish in the city of Oslo as never before . . . Pollution is being discussed these days – but what about this disgusting pollution of highways, byways, and parks . . . Of course, it may be said that vagrants and habitual drunkards are not among the most dangerous criminals. But at least they are shameful stains on society – they contaminate it, making it disgusting. Get them away from the surface!

We shall return later to what followed after this.

*

In this way the 'open' policy – whereby you work for abolishing measures of control which you view as unnecessary rather than for 'alternatives' with the same function as the old measures – was fully acknowledged in KROM during the struggle against forced labour. The same line was followed by the organization in all later significant issues of criminal policy. They may be mentioned rather briefly here.

In the first place, the line was followed in the endeavour to have an important so-called 'protectional school' for boys of school age closed down. The school was under the authority of the Child Welfare Board, and was placed on an island far out in the Oslo-fjord. In the publication *Security in Norway*, published by the Ministry of Social Affairs (Oslo: University Press, 1967), it was said about the 'school' that 'particular emphasis is here placed on work training and preparatory vocational training, and supplementary school education is given. For boys of school age education is sought to be adjusted to the individual pupil's qualifications'. People with experience from the 'school' knew that the reality was different, and a struggle to do away with the quartering of children and young persons on an isolated island had begun long before KROM was started. KROM participated with newspaper articles. The school was abolished in 1970.

Furthermore, the stress on abolition was followed in the struggle against the systems of youth prison, security, and remand. In Norway, these are three important penal measures, and KROM's work to have them abolished has been rather comprehensive, including teach-ins, books, reform papers, a long series of newspaper articles, etc. It is not necessary to discuss the measures in detail here. The main point is that KROM has emphasized that the youth prison system (a particularly long, indeterminate incarceration of young offenders – first of all in closed prison units) as well as the security system (a series of measures – among them institutional detention – used in relation to possible or probable future criminal acts by so-called 'abnormal' offenders) may very well be abolished. Regular imprisonment, which we already have, is a lesser evil (among other things shorter and determinate) than these systems, and sufficient for fulfilling society's protectional need. Furthermore, the association has advocated that the system of remand, which is widely used in Norway (in 1970 5,584 arrests in remand were made; 1,740 of these concerned children and youths under 21), must be drastically reduced. Here, then, we have not advocated full abolition, but a development in the direction of abolition.

At the time of writing, the work to attain these goals is not completed[7]. The experiences from the struggle against forced labour are being repeated. An important part of the work consists in clarifying the view that 'alternatives' – other arrangements with the same function – are by and large a repetition of the old system. And again we see how the demand for alternatives conserves. In a parliamentary debate on the youth prison system in February 1972, when a Parliament member had asked the Minister of Justice 'What experiences does the Ministry have with the Juvenile Offenders Act of 1965, and what reactions and measures of a supplementary and alternative character may be thought of as applicable towards young offenders?' (the Parliament member in question had received some written material from KROM, and had had a discussion with three of us, concerning, inter alia, the question of alternatives being discussed here), the Minister replied, inter alia, 'The questioner, who towards the end of his statement himself tries to suggest alternatives to the use of prison – which we are always on the lookout for when it comes to young offenders – concludes with the alternative of examining and stimulating new measures. But we rarely hear anything about concrete alternatives'. The questioner had briefly referred to some treatment alternatives from Holland, the United States, and Switzerland – including one implying very lengthy incarceration – and the Minister of justice tried to entice him on further. In the discussion itself, the Minister of Justice – from the Labour Party – received solid support from the most important spokesman of the conservatives, who stated, inter alia, 'I feel that today's questioner somewhat one-sidedly joined the row of critics who seem to be more preoccupied with tearing down than with suggesting constructive alternatives. To the small extent that alternatives are at all indicated, these do not seem to point ahead, but rather back towards a view which was abandoned generations ago.'

The systems of youth prison, security, and remand have an important characteristic in common. According to the ideology, youth prison is to constitute treatment and training, security is to be a particular protection of society combined with treatment, and remand is in the main 'only' to be an aid in police investigation. KROM's work against these masked forms of punishment (the exposure of them had begun earlier – see particularly Christie 1962) made us even more conscious of the dangers inherent in proposing 'alternatives' to the systems which we were struggling against. In a way, youth prison, security, and partly remand have constituted the system's own attempts to find 'alternatives' to imprisonment – in a treatment direction, The fact that the attempts in practice turned out to be particularly hard forms of punishment, under other and nicer names, contributed to hardening us in our line towards abolition.

*

In practice, then, KROM developed into a typical 'no-organization'. It is not easy to be a 'no-organization' in a society which is distinctively 'positivistic'; in a society where being 'positive' rather than negative, 'constructive' rather than destructive, 'supportive' rather than negating, constitute central values – values which support a development of the establishment in the establishment's own direction. In line with this, the criticism against KROM has been hard, precisely for being negative and destructive, and for not wanting to advance 'constructive alternatives'. Let me add that the pressure in the direction of specifying 'alternatives' has come not only from those in power or their representatives, but also – at least informally and by way of suggestion – from some prisoners. To the prisoner the prison – or the prison-like existence – from time to time becomes the only 'solution' to his issues. He is not provided with other offers and possibilities by the authorities confronting him. The authorities are interested in maintaining such a limited perspective, because it makes also the prisoner's attitude 'conservative'. The thought of abolishing (parts of) the prison system – without other, similar arrangements in its place – appears ominous from this perspective. As in connection with the line of development towards purely political activities, the pressure on KROM comes in other words from both sides within the prison system.

But of course, the pressure applied by those in power is clearly the stronger. This leads us to the conclusion to this section. If KROM had not developed in a 'no-direction', but rather in 'yes-direction' in which 'constructive' alternatives with great resemblance to the establishment's system had been proposed, society – the authorities, the press as well as the public – would probably have reacted differently to the policies of the association. Our criminal policy would much more easily have been accepted, because it would have been an extension of the criminal policy of the authorities. Thereby, contact concerning criminal policy between KROM and the prisoners would probably also gradually have appeared as considerably more acceptable to the rulers. As it was, however, KROM developed in a distinct 'no-direction'. This meant that the organization permitted itself to remain independent in relation to certain important postulates and expectations from the rulers' – the authorities' – side. If KROM were to be given access to the prisoners, this would at least as a beginning take place on this basis. This constitutes still another important part of the background for understanding the rulers' persistent resistance to political contact between KROM and the prisoners.

3. Towards a defensive policy

The third line of development, which is part of the background for the reaction of the authorities against contact concerning criminal policy taking place between KROM and the prisoners, is the development in the direction of what may be called a 'defensive' criminal policy.

The 'defensive' policy consists, briefly stated, in working to prevent new systems of the kind you are opposing from being established. The 'defensive' policy is thus distinct from the 'abolition' policy. The 'abolition' line comprises working to do away with already *established systems* which you oppose. Yet, there is a natural connection between the two lines: after a struggle for abolition has succeeded, or as a parallel to such a struggle, forces will assert themselves to create similar arrangements, with the same functions, in other parts of the social structure. This is the point at which the 'defensive' policy is implemented. However, the 'defensive' policy may also be relevant without a prior or parallel abolition.

I shall give two examples of how the defensive policy developed in KROM in connection with the abolishing changes that we worked for. Through the coupling of an abolishing and a defensive policy, we also became more aware of the connections between various parts of the criminal policy, and between criminal policy and aspects of the general political system.

*

In the first place, the need for a defensive policy became apparent after the termination of the struggle against the detention centre. I mentioned above that in the budgetary proposals of the Ministry of justice for 1971, it was stated that the planning of the detention centre would 'be suspended'. The complete sentences in question, however, read like this: 'Since the need for a closed section in the youth prison has gradually become pressing, the Ministry has found that it should give priority to this rather than to Maura detention centre. The planning of the detention centre will accordingly be suspended' (Parliamentary Bill No. 1, 1970/71, p. 25). Elsewhere in the same bill (p. 24) the following was stated concerning the need for a new closed youth prison: 'The pressing need for an appropriate – and more up-to-date – closed unit for juvenile offenders has led the Ministry to accelerate this project, and to give it priority ahead of projects which have earlier been given a high ranking. In the present situation, this project will be given priority ahead of other prison projects for juvenile offenders'. The youth prison receives a some-what different group of offenders – somewhat older and with a somewhat more serious criminal record – than the detention centre was planned for. In practice, however, there was reason to count on the groups being rather similar.

As a continuation of the line of abolition towards the detention centre, there-fore, a defensive line against the plan for a new closed youth prison (originally planned for 96 inmates at the cost of 18 million Norwegian kroner) was adopted. The defensive line against the new youth prison was also a parallel to the demand for abolition of one of the most unacceptable closed units in the existing youth prison. The discussion of this issue in part concentrated on the question whether a new youth prison was needed, and in part on the possible content of such a 'new' prison.

The *need* for such a prison has been emphasized by many of KROM's oppo-nents, even by some who have been more or less against the plan for a detention centre and the special measure of an indeterminate youth prison. The governor of the youth prison, who opposes the indeterminate youth prison measure as such, had this to say in a comprehensive newspaper discussion following the teach-in which KROM had arranged on the issue, in the early summer of 1971: 'I believe that we need a new prison for juveniles, and as I have earlier stated and written, I assume that determinate sentences would be preferable. They would among other things lead to a far better utilization of the open unit at Berg'. From other legal authorities, the governor has received strong support for his view concerning the need for a new prison. He has received less support for his view concerning the youth prison measure itself.

The possible *content* of a new youth prison has also been emphasized by the prison authorities. It has been emphasized that a new youth prison will be 'up-to-date' – whatever that means – and that it will, among other things, provide facili-ties for the education and training of inmates. We shall return to the reference to education and training in a later context. Suffice it here to say that in trying to prevent a new youth prison, KROM has urged that: 1) such a prison is unneces-sary, and 2) its content will not really be new at all. Both arguments are typically defensive, and necessary in the wake of – or as parallels to – abolishing changes.

*

The other example of how the need for a defensive policy appears after an aboli-tion has taken place is taken from our struggle against the Vagrancy Act.

As we have seen, the significant change in the Vagrancy Act was carried into effect on 1 July 1970. As early as at the time of the parliamentary debate concerning the matter, months before the repeal was carried out, a demand had been raised (among others from the head of the national system for the care of alcoholics) for a closed treatment institution instead. (Actually, the demand was old, but now it received renewed strength.) KROM argued against the demand in the newspapers by showing that if it was implemented, it would actually re-introduce the system of forced labour through the back door.

However, the demand that something must be 'done' more or less clearly in the direction of ensuring a purgation of the cities as regards alcoholics appeared in full strength immediately before the repeal was carried into effect. Under large headlines warning 'Danger of Deterioration in Oslo when the Vagrancy Act is Changed', a conservative morning paper stated that 'Senior District Attorney E. fears "invasion" of alcohol abusers'. The district attorney expressed himself more moderately than many who came later. He maintained, however, that the authorities had already noticed that 'an increasing number of alcohol abusers assemble in the capital city'. And the problems would increase, he argued. He was critical towards the repeal, which had not yet been carried into effect: '[We do not] have anything to put instead of the old measures of incarceration or threat of incarceration. Former attorney general AA once said: "When you are out there rowing in the stream, you mustn't throw away your oars because they are too short". We must not throw overboard the system of measures which we have before we have something else and better'. Furthermore, the district attorney stated, the repeal would harm the alcoholics themselves: 'I am seriously worried on behalf of these people. I am afraid that they, as individuals, must stand at the very rear end of the line when society's social cake is to be divided . . . The other groups cannot very well be set aside at the expense of the vagrant clientele!' These two views – that the repeal had come too early, thus flooding the city with alcoholics, and that the repeal harmed the alcoholics themselves – later became the main arguments for a re-introduction of measures with an expurgatory function.

KROM answered the contentions of the district attorney. We argued that his thinking was static, and maintained that his arguments called for a full-scale development in social policy rather than new types of coercion. However, the tide had now really turned, and it was not at all easy to stem it. Argument No. 1 mentioned above was used first. Still before the repeal was carried into effect, another large conservative newspaper in the capital city claimed, in large headlines over five columns, that 'The Vagrants "Conquer" the Parks – Drunkenness and Garbage Follow Them', ' "The Booze" More Dominating IN THE CITY! the Chief of Police Asserts', 'Worthy Ideals in a Quagmire', and so on. KROM tried to stem the tide with articles and statements – after each main newspaper story we systematically tried to answer by pointing out that the repeal was necessary in order to force through the sociopolitical measures which might solve the problems. In this way we tried to channel the development away from new coercive measures, and into a track which could lead to a real improvement for the alcoholics. But it was far from simple. It is not easy to say how large the increase in the number of 'drunkards' (expressions which earlier had been stamped as unethical by the Professional Council of the Press were now used without restraint in a number of newspapers) actually was in the capital city. It is certain, however, that the alcoholics were more visible, and this was provoking. The summer was warm and dry, and this did not make things better for those who did not like the sight of the alcoholics. As mentioned earlier, the repeal in fact undoubtedly led to a strengthening of the sociopolitical effort – including among other things a sensible short-term action plan for the capital city early in the fall – but the demand (expressed more or less explicitly) for new types of forced incarceration was nevertheless marked.

The winter of 1970/71 was cold, and argument No. 2 was introduced: the repeal had presumably been harmful to the alcoholics themselves. People who were earlier placed at Oppstad or in the prisons now died in the streets, it was claimed. Those who had advocated the change in the Vagrancy Act – including members of Parliament – were stamped as the most inhumane of all. No causal connection between the repeal and mortality among the alcoholics has been demonstrated – over-mortality has always been great in this group – but the argument was nevertheless used, and it stung. Our answer – that the repeal was necessary in order to initiate a sociopolitical initiative, and that the problem should be solved by rapid building of decent living quarters and other voluntary measures rather than by coercion – was partly drowned in the accusations. In addition, it was claimed that force simply *had* to be used against some individuals in order to save them. Our answer to this contention was that the voluntary measures had to be maximized before the need for force could be determined, that voluntary measures were only to a small degree established, and that if a re-introduction of forcible measures now became the starting point, this would therefore be a completely wrong beginning. Our arguments were presented at a meeting in the so-called 'Temperance Department', where KROM was called in with a number of others to give its view on the need for coercion – a view which proved to be a rather isolated one.

The spring came, and with it warmer weather. The alcoholics again appeared from their hiding places, the apparent interest in their welfare disappeared, and argument No. 1 again became predominant. In large headlines, the country's largest paper – a conservative capital city paper with a reputation for impartiality and balance – now maintained: 'Drunkenness Beyond All Reason: The Coolers [short-term jails for intoxicated people] Completely Overcrowded'; 'Oslo: Sanctuary for Vagrants – Those who Can't Crawl Are Brought In'. KROM answered, and tried to stem the tide with the old arguments. The same paper still thought (in an editorial) that 'The drunkards contaminate Oslo and are a true plague for the large majority of the inhabitants of this city. This is a "pollution" which is just as bad as many of the other forms of pollution with which we are so preoccupied these days'. Shortly after, the conservative paper was followed by the country's largest social democratic paper, stating on its front page and partly over four columns that 'The Oslo Police ask for Overalls – The Uniforms are Messed Up – Drunkenness in Oslo gets out of Hand'. In a news story in the same paper a few days later it was claimed in the headlines that '"I am Drinking Red Biddy like I Drink Blood" – Indifferent Vagrants with Little Reaction to Sinister Death Lists from Last Year'. The social-democratic paper stated by way of introduction: 'The two vagrants just shrug their shoulders. Eighty of their friends have died during the last year. Unrestrained drinking broke them down. They miss their friends, but it does not worry them that they may meet the same fate. As long as they have enough to drink for today, they do not have to think of what will happen tomorrow', In the commentaries consideration for the city's image was coupled with consideration for the alcoholics in a way which was bound to lead the readers to demand new measures of coercion. Some later articles in the same paper, more 'friendly' towards the alcoholics, did not make up for this in terms of coverage. The conservative and the social-democratic press had joined forces. A demand for new forcible measures – partly in the shape of new legal provisions, and partly new closed institutions – was extremely close that spring. So far, however, the demand has not been fulfilled. Why? Three factors probably contributed.

In the first place, the country's 'temperance director', who was also chairman of the fast-working committee appointed by the Minister of Social Affairs to examine the question of measures for vagrant alcoholics, came out in favour of KROM's standpoint. Under the headline 'Dangerous to Call for Coercion in the Care of Alcoholics – The Voluntary System of Aid must First Be Developed', he stated to a liberal evening paper that 'It is extremely dangerous to call for force as the central measure in the care of alcoholics when the situation is difficult, as it is now. Then our attention is distracted from the fact that it is necessary to invest enormously in the voluntary social aid system'. This probably dampened the demand for coercion on a short-term basis.

Secondly, it is probably important that the committee of which the temperance director was chairman, arrived at a moderate tentative conclusion with regard to the question of force. In March 1972, the committee concluded – in a report to which I shall return below – that there was no need for new legal provisions for forced incarceration. What was needed legally was already available, including brief periods of forced incarceration of individuals whose lives were directly threatened. This issue had been debated at a meeting arranged by the Health Directorate in the fall of 1971. There, it had been maintained that a new legal basis was needed for such brief incarceration of narcotics and alcoholics. Three or four KROM representatives present had opposed this strongly, feeling that new regulations could easily become much more comprehensive than planned. They had maintained that the necessary legal provisions already existed – a typically defensive standpoint. Pressed by the adversary, one KROM representative had claimed that he believed the legal department in the Ministry of Justice would support this view. The question was sent to the legal department for examination, and the viewpoint did in fact receive support. In the light of this, it was difficult for the committee examining the whole complex to come to any other conclusion than that the necessary legal provisions already existed. In its report in March 1972, the same committee simultaneously postponed the question of building a new closed institution for the care of alcoholics. As indicated already, this question had been raised at the time of the change in the Vagrancy Act.[8]

However, a third reason why unconcealed measures of force have so far not been introduced must be added, and this reason gives less ground for hope. In the report which was issued in March 1972, a large-scale development of so-called 'protection homes' for vagrant alcoholics was also proposed. The building of altogether 2,200 places in 'protection homes' and 'protected living quarters' was proposed, at an estimated cost of altogether 180 million Norwegian kroner, over a ten-year period. The proposal is seemingly progressive. However, in practice – and whether or not this has been the conscious intention of the committee – 'protection homes' will easily become new settlements on the periphery of society, in 'ghettos' more or less exclusively reserved for the vagrants. Furthermore, settlement there will – again in practice – easily develop a forced character. Even if settling in a protection home is formally to be voluntary, the lack of other regular types of living quarters creates compulsion: you have little else to choose from. Thus, the proposal for a large-scale development of 'protection homes' was in practice a masked proposal for new institutions based on force. Thereby, the proposal probably had a 'soothing' effect on the press and the public; the cry for unconcealed force was somewhat dampened – at least for the time being. Whether something was won by changing to a proposal for more concealed force, is, however, more than doubtful.

KROM's defensive policy has continued towards this new and more concealed possibility of force as well, Precisely because the force is concealed, the work is more difficult. A brief summary may give an idea of the complexities involved in defensive work towards concealed force.

An action group for vagrants was formed just before the New Year 1972. The initiative was taken by some KROM members working in the municipal social care for the homeless and some vagrants, Their standpoint was that the vagrants themselves now had to become participants in political activity. KROM had little access to contact with the prisoners – a fact which I shall return to in detail later – and the association therefore strongly supported the initiative. Here we could at least have contact with those we had managed to bring out of the prisons – the earlier forced labourers.

The action group led a rather chaotic life during its first months. A number of meetings were held, but the participants to a large degree consisted either of people who had little experience with the problems of the vagrants, or of vagrants themselves – and the latter group undeniably had a tendency to disrupt the meetings. A street demonstration, to call attention to the situation of the vagrants, was considered but given up, partly because the support among the vagrants was small and partly because such an action might have a boomerang effect. Instead, a more limited campaign for signatures from those living in the hostels for vagrants was initiated, with the objective of getting new and better offices for the particular department having to do with this group. The signatures were handed over to the municipal deputy mayor of finance, under a certain press coverage. With regard to the question of new offices, the action group had a certain hope that this demand might be fulfilled – a fact which was viewed as important in giving necessary strength and optimism to the participating vagrants. New offices were in fact provided (but hardly gave the vagrants better treatment).

On the basis of this result, the action group now proceeded to a much firmer and more active approach. For a while, the group operated in an advisory capacity for a film team making a film about life in the hostels – it was shown on television and followed by a panel discussion in which one of the members of the action group participated. Somewhat before the television program, however, the above-mentioned report proposing the construction of 'protection homes' was published. The action group was now prepared to deal with this (the report had been expected for some time) and prepared a memorandum in which it advised against 'one-sided development' of protection homes. The memorandum was addressed to the Minister of Social Affairs and was covered by the press.

Roughly at the same time the action group initiated two other projects. On the day of a second showing of the TV film on the hostels, the group set up three stands in the capital city, handing out 20,000 leaflets about the film. The action was covered by several newspapers and by television, Two days later a delegation of vagrants living in the hostels presented a statement about the hostels to the city's deputy mayor of social affairs. (Again a street demonstration was first considered, but the group agreed that a large delegation would be more effective than a small demonstration). The statement, which stressed that the vagrants living in the hostels now wanted to get out of the hostels and into 'housing fit for human beings', was signed by about 600 vagrants. About twenty vagrants participated in the delegation itself, together with other members of the action group. An articulate, active vagrant – with many years experience of forced labour – now had a leading role in the action group. On the day of the presentation of the statement to the deputy mayor of social affairs, an important evening paper published a comprehensive interview with him, in which he equated the 'protection homes' with the old system of forced labour. Not all vagrants in the action group shared this view: several maintained that the protection homes which had already been built constituted an improvement. They had, however, little but the worst – that is, forced labour – to compare with. Thereby, the difference between forced labour and the protection homes seemed great. The leading vagrant took a broader view. He included *regular housing* – which other people had – in his frame of reference. To him, therefore, the difference between forced labour and the protection home was small – the protection home was actually a concealed type of force. Together with others in the action group, he tried to communicate this broader frame of reference to the vagrants in general.

The results of these actions are not yet in sight.[9] I have referred to the activities of the action group through its first half year of 1972 in some detail in order to give an impression of some of the difficulties involved in defensive work against concealed force. *In the first place*, the concealed force must be exposed, so that those who might participate in a protest can see what it is all about. A general way in which to expose concealed force – which was utilized here – is to widen the frame of reference for evaluation of the proposed reform. One of the means of the rulers is to produce support for their reform from the oppressed themselves. They produce such support by failing to give the oppressed a broader frame of comparison for the reform. Thereby a measure of agreement between the rulers and the oppressed is established, which the rulers may in turn refer to. The work of the action group in part consisted of breaking through this, and in widening the frame of reference. *Secondly*, when concealed force has been exposed, the defensive work must be intensified in order that the force is not to become a reality. The intensification may take place in several ways – and one of them is to work simultaneously for an abolition in a closely related area. By doing so, the proposed new system, which you fear, more easily appears as unreasonable and 'already out of date'. The action group utilized this technique. While working defensively against new protection homes, the group also worked for abolition of the existing – thoroughly unsatisfactory – hostels. By working against the existing hostels, the protection homes – the 'new hostels' – were made to appear as a doubly unreasonable backward step. This coordination of defensive and abolition work was hardly fully intended, but functioned this way in practice. At the same time, of course, the abolition work against the hostels was of very great value in itself.

But let me repeat, the results of these actions are not yet in sight. A reversal may very well come about. The defensive work following an abolishing reform is long-range and arduous.

*

Above I have given two examples of the need for defensive work after successful actions for abolition. At the same time I have tried to exemplify how the coordination of abolishing and defensive policies makes the actor more aware of the connections between various parts of the political field. Unless you counteract it, an abolition of one part of the control structure may lead to a new development with the same functions elsewhere. The new development (which is generally promoted with greater strength the more important the functions of the original arrangement are) may even be more dangerous than the old arrangement, because the old functions may be masked by a nicer-looking ideology. Therefore, the defensive work is at least as important as the initial abolishing activity.

Before closing this section, I should repeat that defensive work may also be relevant without a prior or parallel abolition. Thus, it will be relevant in periods when the general development moves in a wrong direction – and, as is well known, these periods may be long. Through the years, KROM has been engaged in several defensive projects of this kind. The most important has been the work to prevent a proposed new penal procedure Act from being adopted. The proposed Act opens the way for greater police control, and, in general, more 'law and order', and KROM has here worked defensively through the publication of a reform-paper, newspaper articles, etc.

*

We may now return to our point of departure, If KROM had not followed up the work for abolition with intensive parallel defensive work – if, in other words, we had let new control measures appear unopposed under other names – the authorities, the press, and the public would probably more easily have accepted the policies of the association. This would have been the case to an even greater extent if we had also omitted other defensive activities, of the kind just mentioned. Under these circumstances, contact concerning correctional and penal policy between KROM and the prisoners would probably also have appeared considerably more acceptable. The defensive policy again implied that we tried to remain uncommitted to important demands from the rulers. This constitutes a further important part of the background for understanding the rulers' persistent resistance to political contact between KROM and the prisoners.

4. Towards an exposing policy

The fourth line of development in KROM which will be mentioned here, and which is part of the background for the reaction of the authorities against contact between KROM and the prisoners, is a gradual development in the direction of what may be called an 'exposing' policy. Increasingly KROM has viewed it as its task to unmask the ideologies and the myths which the punitive system relies on – ideologies and myths concerning effective protection of society, individual prevention, and general prevention – so that real interests and actual conditions may be revealed. This has increasingly been viewed as a necessary – but not a sufficient – condition for the abolition of unnecessary and dangerous measures of control.

We have already discussed several sequences of events which simultaneously give examples of KROM's exposing work. A comprehensive exemplification of this line of development should therefore not be necessary. I limit myself to recounting briefly one main example.

The example is taken from the struggle against the youth prison system – and shows how the exposing activity is a part of the work for abolition. Towards the spring of 1971 the youth prison system had come far towards being 'empty' in terms of ideological content. Several books – written by the governor of the institution – were published, in which everyone could see for himself that the training given in the institution was minimal, the 'treatment' content even smaller, and recidivism sky-high. In the spring of 1971 KROM arranged the above-mentioned teach-in on the youth prison system, where we, in a reform-paper, published a series of mimeographed directives to the prisoners from the inspector of one of the closed units – directives which rather clearly unmasked the attitude and tone in the unit. A part of one of the directives may be quoted by way of example:

> . . . Furthermore you are informed that the inmates who meet in council meetings are to have their shoelaces tied. The governor is especially on the watch for this, and it is regarded as a great minus for the individual inmate if he has not tied his shoelaces properly.

A more serious example may be found in the treatment of a very sick boy who had swallowed metal objects:

> To U207 N.N.
>
> Excerpt from council meeting protocol from the Council Meeting at the Oslo unit of the Youth Prison 31 August 1970:
>
> At the Council Meeting the following case was reviewed and decision made:
>
> *Disciplinary case:* Has eaten nails and spoon, stolen a sand bag.
>
> *Decision:* U 207 NN is warned against food containing surplus iron, such as nails etc. He is kept in single room [that is, he is given isolation] for the present pursuant to section 53.2 in the prison regulations, and he is denied access to the canteen [the prison store, where tobacco, coffee, etc. may be bought] for the present pursuant to section 36.1.3.

The inmate in question was clearly in need of treatment very different from isolation and restrictions on tobacco, etc. No defence was delivered for the directives, and the system was in fact glaringly exposed.

Before the teach-in, however, two full-time teachers were employed in the youth prison unit in question. A few weeks before the meeting, the Department of Education in the municipality of Oslo had taken over responsibility for the educational system. The educational activity was referred to at the teach-in by the defenders of the system, but not yet as a major feature, because it was so new. But a short while later it was referred to in considerably more detail, in a grand and long-lasting attempt by the system to get back on its feet.

Under the title 'Youth Prison – A Uriah's Post' the governor of the institution – who had earlier published books including critical comments on the institution – now published a lengthy article in an important evening paper in the capital city. The article contained a defence of the institution. The governor's main point of view was that working in this institution was really a 'thankless task'. A representative of KROM answered with an equivalent article, in which he, inter alia, again published the directives mentioned above, and in which he asked the governor whether he could show anything on the positive side for the institution. Between the two articles, a well-known lawyer had published a lengthy article in another newspaper, in which he too supported abolition of the youth prison system and the closing down of the particular unit referred to. Other activities in correctional and penal policy – among other things the repercussions of a prison strike described in Part III below – created a rather intense political atmosphere,[10] which did not favour the penal system. The leaders of the institution had to find a good defence for the institution, and they found it in the educational system. Under the tide 'Dangerous Youth Prison?' the governor replied: 'Let me first of all mention the comprehensive system of education which is being carried out with the aid of impressive support from the Department of Education in Oslo. At the present time, a silent pedagogical revolution is taking place in the Oslo unit – an activity which has been planned for a long time . . .' Almost simultaneously, the inspector of the particular unit in question wrote that his unit was 'in startling development in the direction of being governed according to the most modern principles of special education . . .' The inspector ended his article as follows: 'When KROM attacks the Oslo unit of the youth prison to such an extent, KROM ought to keep abreast of the situation as it is today in the youth prison. When you are shooting rabbits you have to aim at where one is jumping, not at the place where it was sitting several months ago'.[11]

At the time, KROM's participant in the debate was away, so that his reply was delayed. The delay was fortunate. Under the tide 'Pillows in the Concrete Walls', the two teachers in the unit in question now unexpectedly published a strongly critical article on the educational system, in which they wrote, inter alia, that they would 'advise most severely against using the educational system as a reason for maintaining the youth prison as a punitive measure. What we do as teachers is only to try to counteract the harmful effects following from the long imprisonment. We are pillows in the concrete walls. The fact that the education is so ineffective, and this goes for all subjects, has several causes'. The most important cause in their opinion was the prison framework for the educational activities. The teachers disagreed with KROM concerning the need for immediate abolition of the most important closed unit, but agreed with the organization concerning the youth prison sentence in general, and KROM could therefore refer to the teachers' own statement in a later article. The governor, however, thought that the admission of failure was premature – 'let competent authorities from the Department of Education in Oslo and from the youth prison [the teachers themselves, then, were not included say what they think in a year from now'. KROM replied once again, believing that the educational ideology would in the future mask the reality of the prison without the education becoming real, and that the education therefore would only legitimize, and thereby maintain, the youth prison system. 'It is praiseworthy', the representative of the organization wrote, 'that an attempt is made to initiate education, but as I have indicated before, it is now really high time that we learnt the lesson of history, and that we do not permit yet another educational system to delay for an indeterminate period the highly necessary changes in the youth prison system'.

But a delay followed. In the fall of 1971 two new full-time teachers were appointed, together with a number of part-time teachers, and the educational experiment continued. At a large meeting that fall KROM uttered another warning and maintained – in a press interview – that if the teachers were to remain in the institution they would be incorporated in the system, and utilized as a legitimation of the system. At first, the new teachers disagreed with this, but changed their view in the light of their experiences in the institution. After a long development during which the prison authorities clearly attempted to incorporate or absorb the teachers (one of the teachers was given a sharp admonition for having published an article critical towards the prison; directives for the teachers were issued by the prison; the prisoners were given wages according to school attendance, and had as an alternative to remain in their cells – so that the voluntary character of the education program became an illusion; etc.), the teachers found it necessary to resign from their position. Their resignation was extensively covered by a Labour Party newspaper in the spring of 1972, about one year after the previous round of discussions on the youth prison system. The governor and the inspector of the institution published an answer in the newspaper, this time maintaining, inter alia, that the education 'in the youth prison has to a considerable extent been characterized by poker, bingo, table tennis, and Chinese checkers. I have not seen a single boy come from or go to the schoolroom with an exercise book – or even seen a boy in the prison write a lesson! [the inspector]'. The teachers in turn answered these challenges. An important evening paper published an editorial supporting the teachers; a university lecturer on education wrote a supportive article in the same paper, and KROM gathered signatures from a sizeable group of teachers, inserting an advertisement supporting the prison teachers in their resignation, The social-democratic youth organization also supported the prison teachers, stating that the organization would 'urge the Oslo Educational Board to find an arrangement securing the independent position of the teachers, and making it possible for them to work according to defensible principles of education, so that the education in the prison is not arranged according to obsolete and authoritarian guidelines. If it is not possible to make such an arrangement, AUF in Oslo believes that education in the closed unit of the youth prison cannot be desirable – and that it is accordingly not defensible to place youth of school age here'. The prison teachers themselves had suggested to some members of the Municipal Educational Board that positions for teachers had to be placed outside the institution, and that the prisoners had rather to be brought out to the teachers than the teachers in to the prisoners. Thereby the teachers hoped that the educational system could not so easily be used as a legitimation of imprisonment for youth, while they also avoided sacrificing the boys' need for education on the altar of system critique – something which the authorities accused the teachers as well as KROM of doing.

The preliminary end of the development was that new positions *inside* the prison were nevertheless advertized – the 'constructive' forces were strong – and the two posts were filled. In the press, the governor emphasized that 'The Oslo Department of Education will also in all probability stress the appointment of teachers who consider education in the prison possible'. With a view towards this, he looked forward to an 'intensified co-operation between the Department of Education and the prison administration'. Actually, this meant that a serious attempt would now be made to find teachers who could be incorporated. In this, the prison was not successful. In the fall of 1972, the two prior teachers published a book – in the KROM series – on their experiences in the prison. The book created a new round of heated discussion, and one of the two new teachers now added an appendix to the book, in which she stated explicitly that the conditions and issues in the prison were exactly as before.

But the struggle is not over.[12] The responsible politicians are on the lookout, and if they find teachers who are willing to subordinate themselves, the youth prison system may continue for a considerable period of time. A conservative member of Parliament spoke for many when he stated (in a parliamentary debate on the youth prison system) that 'For my part, I cannot let go the treatment idea, and this will be the result if we place these young people among older criminals in our regular district prisons [that is, if we abolish the youth prison system]. In my view, to abandon the treatment idea will be a statement of bankruptcy . . .'

Here lies the significance of the exposing or unmasking policy which the above-mentioned sequence of events illustrates. Let me repeat: By unmasking the ideology and the myths with which the penal system disguises itself – for example through political work of the kind described here – a necessary basis for the abolition of unnecessary and dangerous systems of control is created. The example illustrates the struggle involved in such a work of exposure. The system continually tries to adopt new disguises. We must continually try to unveil them.

*

Let me add that KROM has also increasingly come to regard the system's refusals to accept inquiries, applications, complaints, etc. from the association and the prisoners as such exposing material. In Part III we shall discuss some of these refusals in more detail; suffice it here to say that by us they were increasingly utilized to show the authoritarian way in which the prison system functions. In this way, lost battles were turned to our advantage. For example, we increasingly came to view refusals to grant applications concerning contact between prisoners and outsiders interested in correctional and penal policy in this light.

The development on the part of the organization in the direction of an exposing policy also constitutes a part of the background for the negative attitude of the authorities towards contact between KROM and the prisoners. I repeat that our development in this direction was gradual, and originally to a large extent the result of the negative initial attitude on the part of the authorities towards KROM. If the authorities had received and accepted the invitation for co-operation from KROM discussed earlier, it would have been more difficult to 'expose' the authorities, because they would then have seemed less authoritarian, and because KROM would have been more closely bound by the authorities – more incorporated. As it was, KROM in the end had to try to turn the lack of willingness to cooperate on the part of the authorities against the system, and to use it to show how authoritarian the system actually is.

As a parallel to the gradual development in the direction of an emphasis on exposing or unmasking the actual functioning of the punitive system, a gradual elaboration of the means of doing so took place. To begin with, the unmasking by and large was brought about from the outside – by KROM itself – among other methods through the publication of the various refusals of the authorities to permit contact between the prisoners and organizations outside, Gradually, however, emphasis was also placed on unmasking the functioning of the system from the *inside*. This was taken up in its full significance at a large meeting in the fall of 1971. The background is of a certain interest, because it shows that the choice of means which at the outset may be rather arbitrary, may be confirmed later on because the rulers show unexpected and open anxiety over the means.

At the meeting, where the above-mentioned situation on the part of the teachers in the youth prison was discussed, KROM was criticized for 'maximizing a crisis' – that is, for recommending professional people like teachers and psychologists to leave the prison system in order to let the system remain without ideological defence lines. Central people in KROM had, true enough, earlier considered this, on the basis of the view that such professionals will in any case be unable to do anything useful for the prisoners. The viewpoint is difficult, however, because professionals might, of course, be able to do *something* of use, even when incorporated, and at the meeting KROM therefore took a middle course. Professionals, we said, can and should enter the system if they simultaneously commit themselves to continually emphasizing to the external world how narrow are the limits which the prison places on their activities and, to supplying revelatory material to the public. Only then, we said, may the professionals avoid being used by the representatives of the system to 'legitimize' or justify the further existence of the system. We did not urge anything illegal, only externally addressed criticism to which the representatives of the system could not raise any legal objection. Between ourselves, some of us had little faith in this strategy. We viewed it as very probable that the professionals would quickly be incorporated in the system, and thus become unable to bring out exposing material. The view was maintained, however, because we did not wish to sacrifice the short-term interests of the prisoners on the altar of general system-abolition. It appeared, however, that the view created great commotion and anxiety among the authorities and in the conservative papers; so great a commotion that we understood we had touched upon something essential.

What we had touched on was, of course, the question of internal loyalty in the prison system. The prison system has few rewards for its employees. The work is in part poorly paid, the prestige associated with the work is very low, and the tasks are not tempting. To an even greater degree than in many other branches of administration, internal solidarity in the system must therefore be based on personal *loyalty to* – and *obedient submission towards* – the system and the superiors. Accordingly, superiors also place great emphasis on personal loyalty. In the prison system, the definition of disloyalty is not limited to actions at variance with the regulations; it also covers the whole spectrum of actions which – independently of the regulations – may harm or 'hurt' the system, or individuals in it. Fully legal but critical newspaper articles for example fall within the spectrum. By urging employees in the system to commit themselves to providing the public with disclosive material (as for example the teachers in the youth prison actually did), we attacked the very foundation of internal solidarity in the system. Well knowing that the system has little else to fall back on should loyalty break down, the system representatives – and with them the conservative press – reacted strongly and anxiously against our urging.

5. Towards the principle of voluntariness

The fifth and last line of development in KROM which will be mentioned here is a gradual development in the direction of a policy with a strong emphasis on measures of a voluntary kind for those who are today exposed to coercive means. This line of development may be discussed briefly, because it has been touched on several times already – for example in connection with our discussion of the vagrant alcoholics and of children and young persons in prison.

The main point is this. As indicated in earlier sections, we in KROM have to an increasing degree viewed it as our task to abolish and prevent various forms of coercion in society – in the form of imprisonment or under other names. At the same time we are also aware of the fact that the groups in question have a marked need for a considerable supply of resources – economic and other material resources, decent living quarters, etc. – and for a considerable opening of new opportunities for living. Increasingly, we have worked for the view that such a supply of resources, and such an opening of new opportunities in life (for example an increase in housing facilities for vagrant alcoholics, discussed above) must – if it is not to be converted into new coercion with the same functions as the old deprivation of liberty – take place on a genuinely voluntary basis. Increasingly, representatives of the association have emphasized that such new resources etc. are also largely accepted by the receivers if they are genuinely voluntary.

Against this it has been argued (for example in connection with the discussion of the vagrant's situation) that there must exist possibilities of coercion against some individuals, in order to save lives and to protect the life and health of others. Our counter-argument to this view is (as mentioned above) that all the emphasis must at present be placed on the development of voluntary offers. Only when they are developed to a maximum, will it be possible to ascertain to what extent coercion is in fact necessary – again for example towards vagrant alcoholics or young persons. By beginning the development on the coercive side – for example through a closed institution for alcoholics, or a new youth prison – the pressure on the authorities is eased so that voluntary measures are not realized.

Furthermore, we have increasingly maintained that if coercion nevertheless is used, it must at least be used openly and under the control of the courts. On this basis the association has, for example, emphasized a clear division of labour in the so-called 'care for offenders at liberty'. The offers of resources – which should be increased – must, as I have said before, be genuinely voluntary, and to the extent that society is still thought to require measures of control, the control must be performed openly, and by agencies other than the ones offering help.

The stress on genuinely voluntary measures has largely developed as a parallel to the defensive work discussed above. As was the case in connection with the defensive work: if KROM had let new measures of control appear unopposed, for example under other names, – if we, in other words, had not emphasized genuine voluntariness as an absolutely necessary condition for rehabilitation – the authorities as well as the conservative press would probably have found it easier to accept the policies of the association. We should then to a lesser extent have been free in relation to traditional methods and guidelines in this field.

6. Conclusions

To summarize, KROM's development may be characterized as a development in the direction of a line rather exclusively emphasizing criminal policy, coupled with stress on abolishing changes, systematic defensive and exposing political work to support the abolitions, and emphasis on genuinely voluntary measures. The five lines of development finally (in the spring of 1972) crystallized into a new work program for the association, which departed strongly from the original program. To be sure, the main lines are at times departed from – in practice we are probably unable to stick strictly to them – but the main emphasis is nevertheless on them. This is also the case for many of the smaller reforms on the work program: abolition of controls on visits, abolition of collective punishment, abolition of censorship of mail and manuscripts, and so on. These concrete abolishing reforms were accorded a central position in the program – partly a result of an initiative from the ex-inmates at the board meetings, and partly of a letter smuggled out to the general meeting from the prisoners in the country's main prison.

The present discussion may now be tied to the concluding remarks made in Chapter IV. By emphasizing the above-mentioned lines of development, KROM has continued to disturb the social functions of imprisonment. By questioning the policy of the authorities, by staunchly stressing abolition of their measures of control, by clearly saying that new measures of a similar kind are not to be allowed under new names, and by unmasking the ideological ways in which the authorities defend their measures, KROM has continued to disturb the expurgatory, power-draining, diverting, and symbolic functions of imprisonment. Those who are removed from society are to be brought back into it; those who are made powerless through confinement are to be given power through outside alliance; those who are used in diverting our attention from society's real threats are to be presented as they truly are: very unthreatening individuals; and – by the same token – those whose presumed blackness is used to symbolize our own presumed whiteness may no longer be exploited in this way. The secrets of the prison are to be exposed; for those we have sent away are to be among us.

For these reasons, the prison authorities have persistently denied KROM political contact with the prisoners. In Part III below, the concrete denials will be discussed in detail. Suffice it here to say that the extent to which the rulers in a society deny a political organization access to its prisoners may be taken as an index of the extent to which that organization truly threatens the social functions of imprisonment. Paradoxically, therefore, great openness on the part of the rulers towards an outside demand for contact with the prisoners may be taken as a sign that the outsider is performing his political work poorly, and that he is actually being absorbed by the establishment. Similarly, attempts on the part of the rulers to strangle the contact which the outsider demands, signifies that his aim is correct. The strangulation implies that the outsider is touching on the social functions of imprisonment, and thereby the connections of the prison to the social structure. When in touch with these functions and connections, he may *expose* them to others in the society. He may say to those others: 'Here you may see for yourself how imprisonment functions in your society'. By doing this, he may in turn give material to political groups and organizations which are also willing to work for the cause of the prisoners. Only by doing this, only by thus performing a politico-didactic task, does he perform a task which – in however long a time-perspective – really may change the prisoners' situation.

One final question: Will KROM remain a threatening force?

It is hard to say. The danger of being transformed into a non-threatening, pleasant appendix to the criminal justice system is ever-present. A main source of the danger may – perhaps paradoxically – be found in the relationship to the inmates. On KROM's present work program certain short-term reforms of a non-abolishing kind are also mentioned as important. Increase of prisoners' wages is only one of them, KROM must necessarily view it as its task to work for all real improvements for prisoners – including those which do not abolish and unmask. This does not constitute a problem if continual interpretation of short-term improvements takes place in a perspective of abolition: if, in other words, the very limited character of the gains won through short-term improvements is transformed, through constant political discussion and maturation, to an understanding and a force working for abolitions of a continually more encompassing kind. It is the tragedy of political life in general that this political discussion and maturation, and the ensuing transformation, is so often barred. Firstly, important conserving forces inherent in the established order in question operate to prevent the transformation, thus leaving the ruled satisfied with minor improvements. Secondly, bureaucratization and ensuing separation between the elite and the 'grass roots' on the side of the protestants easily bar the transformation. The development of the labour movement illustrates both sets of forces. The problems are equally great on the prison scene. Here the authorities' effective prevention of communication between KROM and the prisoners may quickly create an ambiguity between short-term improvements and abolitions. KROM must live with this ambiguity; among other things we must take the prisoners' needs as our point of departure if we want to co-operate with them; only the rulers will gain by representing KROM as uninterested in the needs of the prisoners, thereby separating KROM from the prisoners. But though we must live with the ambiguity, the ambiguity is difficult. It implies that the work involved in determining the general guidelines discussed in this essay never ends. We are always in danger of sliding back into the non-abolishing, the non-defensive, etc. Concerning the future, it is perhaps doubtful whether we will in fact manage to avoid incorporation in the establishment. Possibly, the most important 'result' of our political struggle will be the extended knowledge we have acquired concerning the difficulties of remaining unincorporated.

If so, our most important job will be that of communicating this knowledge – communicating our errors – to political groups coming after us.

Part III

Organization among the expelled

VI

Organization among the expelled

Now others are coming. Of fewer words. Who have long been forced to eat their own misery and swallow it as bitter dregs. They have nothing to lose. They know how much arrogance and humiliation are contained in the extravagant welfare attitude of the authorities. So now they mean business.

They come from juvenile correctional institutions and prisons, from youth hostels and hostels for vagrants, from condemned houses and slums, from mental hospitals, old people's homes, and institutions for alcoholics, from establishments for handicapped people and for the psychologically damaged, from depopulated areas and Lapp towns, from ghettos for gypsies and immigrants . . .

At Kungsgatan in Stockholm they form an enormous parade, which not even the total police force of the city can withstand. The wild horde of psychopaths and habitual criminals (affective, rootless, irresponsible, deceitful, enemies of society) make their way in the first row with bayonets, crowbars, and sawn-off guns. Behind them the deformed and disfigured bang their way ahead in wheel chairs and with crutches. Their weapon is obscene self-abandonment, slanting bodies and blind faces are offered without reserve to the swords and clubs of the police – a lump of plasma made of silent suffering, which after each blow of a club immediately returns to its terrible shape. And when the handicapped are threatened with being massacred by police on horse-back, a staggering crowd of vagrants launch an attack with injection needles and old beer bottles. The street whores pull out large knives and prepare to come out of the whole affair with a cock as a souvenir. The gypsies sneak around stealing horses from under the police officers. The mental patients, the unaccountable, those not responsible for their acts, scuttle back and forth and confuse law and order, spitting, scratching, tearing, biting. And the Lapps? Well, they force their last herd of reindeer into an enormous traffic jam at Sture-plan . . . This is the way it will look when the 'minorities' take power. When the myth of Social Solidarity finally breaks down and lets a dawning speck of light in the land.

> In row after row they march up to Hötorget with their black banners and posters.
> In the first row: EXISTENCE and IDENTITY.

In the second row: EQUALITY and SOLIDARITY.
In the third row: FREEDOM.

Excerpt from Jörgen Eriksson's book *Revolt i huvet. Anarkistisk journal* (Revolt in the Head. Anarchic Journal), Stockholm: Albert Bonniers Publishers, 1970.

Organization from below is considered a rational answer to coercion from above. The labour movement has given this answer to coercion from factory owners and factory administrators. University students have partly given the same answer. In our time the answer is also beginning to come from groups like prisoners, handicapped people, and others who are expelled. Here I wish to discuss some aspects of the situation of groups which are expelled. However, I will also deal with issues of a more general kind concerning organization from below.

1. Diversionary ideologies

The fundamental idea behind organization from below, is, of course, that when you stand together and act in a coordinated way, your struggle against coercion becomes more effective. In other words, what we are talking about is counter-organization. However, there are several possible diversionary manoeuvres that may be used by those in power when they confront a tendency towards counter-organization among the expelled.

One diversionary manoeuvre may be found in the idea of 'individual treatment'. 'Individual treatment' – handling of the individual through individual rewards and punishments – was earlier (and still is) one of the answers of the factory owners to tendencies towards organization among the workers. Such individual handling – ruling through division – is of course also part of the strategy employed by the prison governor, the head-doctor, and the supervisor of the old people's home against tendencies towards counter-organization among the prisoners, the sick, and the old. But these wielders of power have something more to add. What is particularly important in connection with the handling of the expelled is that the 'individual treatment' may be elevated to a distinct ideology. The medical-psychiatric treatment ideology, with its stress on individual treatment according to need, provides an ideological foundation for counteracting any tendency towards counter-organization. Such counteraction may take place on the grounds that the individual needs 'individual treatment' from his own individual point of view.

The model is taken from somatic medicine – the broken leg calls for a different treatment from that of an appendicitis – and via psychiatry it is transferred to the fields discussed here. In this way, the philosophy of medical/psychiatric individual treatment becomes the servant of social control.

The philosophy of individual treatment constitutes a firmly established part of the general view that the expelled are in need of care. However, this philosophy does not reign alone. Gradually, modern ideas of 'group treatment' and 'therapeutic community' have also become important. In connection with so-called group treatment, however, the stress on the 'principle of the small group' is striking.

It is also strikingly clear that a model of co-operation is underlying such activities. Counter-organization – organization representing the bottom in its real conflict of interests with the top – has little place in the therapeutic community. In this way, the idea of the therapeutic community may become a new way of diverting any tendency towards counter-organization, The idea takes the group as its point of departure, something which counter-organization also does, but it channels matters of conflict away from constituting conflicts of interest to being understood as common problems. The dawning understanding of the expelled of being set aside by power is again obscured. And in reality the powerful largely continue to rule. This new way of concealing reality is strikingly effective even among those who ought to know better. The first issue of the Swedish journal 'R' was devoted to the topic of 'democracy in institutions' (Prisma Publishers, fall 1970). The following could be read on the back cover of the journal: 'POWER TO THE CLIENTS; THE RIGHT TO SHARE IN DECISIONMAKING; INSTITUTIONAL DEMOCRACY; THERAPEUTIC SOCIETY – these are some of the slogans in the last few years' discussion of treatment issues. The inmates in, for example, institutions for alcoholics, mental hospitals, and prisons are now claiming an increased influence over their treatment'. The mixing of different concepts which this sentence gives an inkling of stands out with great clarity within the journal itself, for example in *Kerstin Vinterhed's* article, in Swedish, 'Power to the Clients or Therapeutic Community – a Sham Fight?' (Vinterhed 1970, p. 142). The author tries to show that the difference between a 'political' and a 'therapeutic' approach is to a large extent a purely terminological one: '. . . Regardless of the point of departure and regardless of whether Maxwell Jones or Marx is the master, group activity, open discussions, and communication mean that democracy is breaking through', she writes on p. 145.

The difference is not just a *terminological one*. The therapeutic approach is based on the notion of common interests between therapist and patient. The counter-organization is based on a conflict of interests between top and bottom. In many respects, the idea of the therapeutic community may be a new form of diversion against a developing counter-organization, absorbing the counter-forces. For example, one gets a strong feeling that the idea has this function in the prison system, and that in this context it is directly dangerous to the expelled. Entering into an experiment in 'therapeutic com- munity' must be an extremely doubtful move from the point of view of the prisoners if it is done on the basis of the notion that the activities may later be changed to those of a counter-organization. The counterforces are absorbed – 'treated' – during the experiment.

I have here discussed 'individual treatment' and 'therapeutic community' as two diversionary ideologies. In more general terms, some very general features of the sick person's role itself have such a diversionary function.

Many years ago *Talcott Persons* summarized some of the main features of the sick person's role, seen from the sociologist's point of view (*The Social System*, Free Press, 1951, p. 436). Probably, this summary is over-simplified and partially wrong when seen in relation to the intentions of advanced therapists. However, it is probably not so far-fetched as an ideal-typical summary of a wide-spread lay-man's view of the role, and the layman's view is influential. In the first place, Par-sons wrote, the 'sick' person is exempt from normal social role responsibilities. Secondly, he is not expected to get well just by 'pulling himself, together', and he is therefore in a condition that must 'be taken care of'. In the third place, he is expected to view his state of being ill as itself undesirable. Fourthly, he is morally obliged to seek competent help (a doctor) and to co-operate with him.

The sick and the politically conscious have it in common that they are both expected to view their situation as undesirable. But at this point the similarity ends; the other main features of the sick person's role constitute – as Parsons has described them – an almost ideal-type description of the *unpolitical* individual. The unpolitical as well as the sick person stands outside, and is not engaged in, the role responsibilities of everyday life. Like the sick, he does not view his situation as changeable through efforts of his own, so that he too must be 'taken care of' by others. And like the sick, he cooperates with those who are over him, and he acts according to their orders. The sick and the unpolitical, then, approach the question of solving their undesirable situation in the same way.

In this way, very general features of the sick person's role itself have a concealing and disarming effect when it comes to political awareness and counter-organization among the expelled. For example, the great anxiety that afflicts a prisoner before release is regarded as 'psychological imbalance' and not as what it actually is: a real and well-grounded fear of the society which the inmate is now going to re-enter after the preparation given him by the institution. Historically we may put it this way. Originally the expelled were kept down by undisclosed coercion, for example by the divide-and-rule technique mentioned above. A basis for counter-organization was in a sense present: the power relationships were not concealed. But the balance of power was at the same time so problematical from the point of view of those at the bottom that counter-organization was quite unthinkable for this reason.

With the entry of humanism, the balance of power became somewhat less prob-lematical (though, as we shall see, the difference is hardly great), but at the same time the treatment ideologies – and the sick person's role in general- have gained a concealing and disarming function against tendencies to counter-organization. In other words, the sick person's role may not only be used as a means of control against those who are already politically engaged. In general, 'treatment thinking' is, for reasons given above, dangerous to the expelled; and the sickness terminol-ogy and the sick person's role as a means to increased social aid for the expelled are definitely a two-edged sword.

An addition is necessary. Despite what has been said here, one may under certain conditions see signs of structural similarity between psychotherapy and political maturation. In psychotherapy as in political maturation, it may be the case that one penetrates beneath the surface, viewing isolated 'symptoms' in a continually more total context. In psychotherapy as in political maturation, it may be that one starts adopting a continually more principled attitude to conflicts one is confronted with. In psychotherapy as in political maturation, it may be that one starts understanding continually more of one's own relationship to constellations of authority and power in the environment. In psychotherapy as in political maturation, one may begin engaging in a continually more active, creative relationship to power in one's environment, thereby participating in changing the environment rather than passively being changed by it. But this continually more comprehensive, principled, enlightened, and externally creative process is the exact opposite of the traditional sick person's role, and of ordinary treatment philosophies. It is therefore not expedient to employ the concept of sickness in this connection, and perhaps it is even unreasonable to employ the concept of therapy itself. What is taking place is perhaps not 'therapy', but in fact political maturation.

However, the therapeutic/political process which is outlined here is conspicuously absent in relation to the *expelled*. In relation to the expelled, ideologies and role descriptions of the kind mentioned earlier are employed. The first step for the expelled on the road towards counter-organization must, in other words, be that of seeing through, and remaining untempted by, ideological moves and role descriptions of this kind.

2. A structural feature

Imagine now that the expelled – or a group among the expelled – manage to neutralize the ideologies of treatment and the general concept of sickness. Such a neutralization would possibly have to be initiated from the outside. But even if it took place, would the organizing of the group in question immediately become a simple matter?

Obviously not. In the first place, the expelled group would be confronted by the same obstacles as the labour movement and the labour organizations have had to face. However, these will not be dealt with here – they have been analysed in detail by others. (See for example *Sverre Lysgaard: Arbeiderkollektivet* (The Workers' Collectivity), Oslo University Press 1960.). What I should like to emphasize is that, in addition to these obstacles, the situation of the expelled contains a particular and fundamental feature which makes organization among them especially difficult. I am thinking of the fact that the expelled in a fundamental sense are not contributors to the system of which they are members.

In The *Defences of the Weak* (Tavistock Publications, 1965) I described the prisoners as being non-contributors to the prison, and I referred to this as one of the main reasons for a low degree of solidarity among prisoners. To amplify, I defined 'solidarity' as a positive, expressive, and instrumental relationship among the members of a social rank, based on their membership in that rank. In this sense, prisoners are often not very solidary. I furthermore argued that the prisoners in general are not contributors to the prison system. They are not placed in such a situation that they contribute something to the prison which the prison in turn is dependent on for its continued existence. This is one of the main reasons, I wrote, for the relative lack of solidarity among the inmates. Solidarity is so to speak 'pointless' because, even as a solidary unit the inmates have no contribution which they may threaten to withdraw. Even if they were solidary, the prison would have close to total power.

In retrospect I view these statements as truths which need a certain modification. For example, when a group of prisoners in a prison engages in a hunger strike, and when this is given publicity in the press, the prisoners withdraw a 'contribution' to the prison system, namely behaviour which corresponds to the regulations of the prison. Correspondingly, the representatives of the prison may be threatened. The strike signifies that they do not manage their work in the way that society has defined, and that the prison does not function in correspondence with the model of harmony entertained by the bureaucrats. However, the point in connection with such a threat is that the group which is acting is – if its internal movement is to constitute a threatening withdrawal of a contribution – itself dependent on the reaction of the environment. The prisoners' contribution to the prison system, and thereby their ability to threaten, is not built into the prison system itself. In this respect the situation of the prisoners is very different from that of, for example, workers in a factory, who through their very work for the factory have a built-in contribution to make, and a possibility of threatening a withdrawal of that contribution.[13] Action among workers may also receive great strength through support in the mass media etc., but this is not the fundamental point here.[14]

The built-in contribution is decisive because it makes solidarity and organization possible also in 'hard times'. The organization may also survive when there is external silence concerning the matter – also when the mass media, for example, are concerned with other questions. This is hardly the situation in the typical prison. One might say that the prison is very ingeniously constructed from the point of view of maintaining the power of the authorities: the existence of the contribution of lower level participants, and thereby their ability to threaten, is dependent on friendly surroundings – such as the press – and these surroundings are often not friendly or even constantly alert.

And as we shall see, not even strong support from the press is necessarily enough.

3. The importance of the built-in contribution: an example

The discussion of the importance of the built-in contribution, and of its absence, for example in the situation of the prisoners, perhaps appears some-what abstract. Below I shall therefore make matters more concrete by discussing in detail an important example.

During the fall of 1970, an extensive wave of strikes occurred in Swedish prisons, in the form of a hunger strike lasting for six days towards the end of October. The strike was initiated in a particular prison – the prison of Österåker just outside Stockholm – a so-called central institution in one of Sweden's five geographical prison regions. (In addition, Sweden has three 'regions' which are not geographical: a security 'region', a youth 'region', and a women's 'region'.) The strike finally included several thousand prisoners in a number of penal institutions throughout the country.

The October strike had a long organizational development as a back- ground. For two years an organizational development had taken place among the prisoners at Hall security institution in Södertälje. The development included attempts at establishing inmate councils, as well as demonstrations and several rather long work and hunger strikes (see Tornklint 1971). At Hall, the prisoners' demands were to begin with of a concrete and short-term kind, but as time passed they took on a more principled and long-range character. The development at Hall in turn had an organizational back- ground partly in the activities of Swedish KRUM. KRUM had been allowed certain group discussions with the inmates, and though the discussions in fact to a large extent were 'therapeutic' rather than concerned with penal and criminal policy, they undoubtedly also gave a positive feed-back to the prisoners' notion that their demands were justified, and that the development of organized action among them was possible. Some especially politically conscious, determined prisoners with a close relationship to KRUM were the leaders of the development at Hall, and the press gave rather wide coverage to the development there. The participation of the press was important in passing on the idea of organization to other penal institutions, even if several other types of contact – for example through KRUM – were also present.

To reiterate, the great nation-wide October strike had the Österåker prison as its point of departure. The Österåker institution itself is unusual in almost every respect, and must briefly be described if we are to under- stand the spark that lit the fire. As the central institution in one of the prison regions, Österåker functioned as the mother institution for a number of other prisons. The institution constituted the reception centre for the region; from Österåker prisoners were sent to other institutions. The institution belonged to the so-called 'Kumla series': a series of large factory- prisons with ring walls, underground tunnels between the various sections and buildings, TV-surveillance, and other technical equipment. However, what characterized Österåker was that it had not been completed. The criticism against the Kumla series had from the outset been extremely intense; the authorities had finally decided to discontinue the series while awaiting alternative proposals, and the building of Österåker had been discontinued half-way through the program. Half finished, the institution was opened on 1 March 1969. In addition to the offices and a ring wall, a number of special sections were finished: the reception centre, the sick ward, a psychiatric section, a section for cases of tuberculosis, and an observational section, in addition to several sections for those considered 'difficult to handle', providing places for 195 prisoners. Regular sections for inmates, workshops, etc., had not been built. The institutional grounds were cramped and characterized by several internal walls; the institution lacked several of the things which make prison life bearable (for example regular employment facilities), and the regime was restrictive. All of this was important in creating a special need for action among the inmates in question.

At the same time, a group of staff members in the institution – the team of psychologists – supported the prisoners in their various demands for improvements. The acting psychologist in the Prison Department (*Kriminalvårdsstyrelsen*, the senior administrative unit in the prison system), a man with radical viewpoints, supervised two or three assistant psychologists in the institution. Throughout the summer of 1970 several minor strikes occurred in the institution, among other things in connection with the question of establishing an inmate council among the prisoners – which the governor at first refused, but which was permitted somewhat later by a new governor. Sometime before the outbreak of the great October strike, the acting psychologist in the Prison Department was transferred to the institution itself. The staff put the 'blame' for the unrest on the team of psychologists. Details would be superfluous here; it is only necessary to say that the psychologists sided – as I believe they ought to – with the inmates in the conflict. Thereby they probably had the function of making the inmates politically more conscious when formulating their demands and planning their activities.

As indicated already, Österåker was a central institution, and prisoners were continually sent from it to other prisons in the region. Thereby consciousness concerning the demands, and the thought of common action, spread through the region via the more politically conscious individuals. Altogether, then, the internal conditions for an effective action – a certain organizational background, justifiable local demands, a certain degree of ideological support from at least one group on the staff side, and possibilities for communication – were in fact rather well developed.

External conditions were also present: KRUM was naturally preoccupied with the situation. Everyone understood that the atmosphere was tense, and throughout the summer members of KRUM had had contact with the inmate councils at Österåker and other prisons. Though the authorities were adverse to the contact, the possibility of a strike was discussed with the council at Österåker, and the idea was transmitted to other institutions. In the Central Working Committee of the organization the question of the organization's standpoint to a hunger strike was hotly debated. For various reasons (in order not to excite conservative opinion too much, and in order to be on the safe side if the strike should turn out to be unsuccessful), the Working Committee decided merely to support a strike rather than actually to urge it. The decision, however, was made with only a very small majority in favour – a large minority wanted to urge a strike more directly, and the difference of opinion concerning this issue was considerable. But in any case important external conditions for action – careful preparation and support – were present.

The date for the beginning of the strike at Österåker was set for Monday 26 October, and KRUM was informed of the date. The uncertain factor was, of course, the question whether it would spread. The date for the strike coincided with several other activities concerning criminal policy in Stockholm, among other things a large exhibition at the State's Museum, the publication of a book produced by KRUM, and so on. Representatives of the prison authorities later claimed that the whole thing was a gigantic coordinated plan. There was coordination, but less of it than the authorities thought.

A few days before the strike at Österåker was to begin, important members of KRUM's Central Working Committee went to a conference dealing with criminal policy, arranged by Norwegian KROM far away in the Norwegian mountains. They counted on being back in Sweden at the time of the outbreak of the strike, but they were not back in time. The second and the third day of a hunger strike are the most difficult. From the fourth day on the physical symptoms decrease somewhat. For several reasons, including the aim of making the most difficult days coincide with a weekend – so that the inmates did not have to work during the most difficult period – the inmate council at Österåker decided to commence the strike a few days earlier. The strike was started on Thursday 22 October, at a time when the Swedish KRUM-leaders were virtually imprisoned in the Norwegian mountains. The conference in the mountains dealt with the right of prisoners to organize and strike, and related topics. Norwegian newspapers and authorities possibly viewed the coincidence as a gigantic Scandinavian KRUM/KROM conspiracy. We were not quite as clever as that.

At several places on the periphery of the Swedish prisons, the strike – which spread rapidly from Österåker to around 35 other penal institutions – created considerable drama.

At *Spåtind* in Norway, where the Scandinavian conference was held, we only received scant information, but the Swedish participants tried to keep informed over the telephone. The reports from Sweden became continually more optimistic, and caused increasing excitement in our mountain retreat. At *Skogkloster*, outside Stockholm, an inter-Nordic contact seminar between 'legislative authorities' and 'criminological researchers' was held immediately after the conference at Spåtind, and representatives of the prison system in the four Nordic countries were present. Here spirits were not high, but still characterized by drama. Any discussion of the strike, which at this time raged through the country, and which was widely publicized in the newspapers, was carefully and completely avoided. Towards the end of the conference a Norwegian social scientist took the floor and claimed that the strike was the very thing which ought now to be discussed. However, no discussion of it took place: on the part of the 'legislative authorities' it was informally stated that the topic 'fell outside the realm of legislation'. The essential point in this context is that the authorities at this juncture apparently felt threatened by the development.

However, in *Stockholm* itself, in the offices of KRUM, the drama was probably highest. The Stockholm section of the organization had not been well informed in advance of the coming strike, and had at first been more or less accidentally informed by some inmates in connection with a visit to an institution. This, however, did not impede their activity while the leading members of the organization were in Norway. They issued a press release which was even more radical than that issued by the Central Working Committee of the organization, in which they openly urged other inmates to go on strike in sympathy with the prisoners at

Österåker. During the whole week of the strike there was intense activity in the offices of the KRUM section in Stockholm, with hectic duplication of newsletters, continual release of telegrams, dispatching of reports to the prisons about the development of the strike, and so on. A conflict occurred between central people in the Working Committee and the Stockholm section concerning the difficulties of communication during the initial and decisive days – as we shall see, the conflict became more manifest later – but in spite of this, Swedish KRUM has never shown such an *esprit de corps* as during this week of action. Their contribution was impressive.

At the time of the strike, the mass media stated that about 2,600 prisoners finally took part in the joint effort. The Swedish prison authorities have later claimed that the figure was lower, and have stated that 1889 prisoners participated (*Kriminalvården* 1970). How they were able to specify the figure so accurately is unknown. In any case, between forty and fifty per cent of Sweden's total of 4,800 prisoners participated. If those doing short-term sentences for drunken driving – a group clearly less interested in the strike – are subtracted, the proportion of participants increases to between 60 and 70 per cent. Continually, and increasingly, the action was covered and supported by the press. Some important liberal prison officials expressed themselves in positive terms about the demands of the prisoners (two of the eight regional directors). At Österåker, the prison authorities (from the Prison Department and the institutions) gathered in order to negotiate with representatives of the Österåker prisoners (the prisoners also had a representative from KRUM on their delegation). Before the negotiations began, a long tug of war took place concerning who were to participate (for example, the inmates wanted admittance for the regional psychologist, while the authorities did not want this – the demand of the prisoners was complied with), who was to be chairman of the meeting, and so on. Participants from both sides have related how unusually dramatic the development of the negotiations turned out to be. The negotiations lasted for several days while the strike was continually spreading, and the atmosphere changed in favour of the prisoners as reports of new strikes in other prisons were received. When the strike was at its height, it became clear to the surprised authorities that the action – which was far more successful than the prisoners and KRUM themselves had expected in advance or hoped for – had to lead to compliance with the prisoners' demands.

The prisoners at Österåker set forth a number of concrete demands. They demanded that their own inmate council was really to be acknowledged and given free communication internally as well as externally; they wanted to have the duty to work abolished and to have a school program introduced as an alternative to factory work; they wanted a certain rebuilding of the institutions in order to provide for an augmented school program; they wanted greater freedom for the institution's psychologist to perform his work; they wanted to have certain inner walls torn down in order to expand the exercise yard. And last – but not least – they demanded central negotiations between representatives of all prisoners in Sweden and the authorities, with a view towards extensive reforms. The demand for central negotiations was also presented with great strength by KRUM. The Swedish prison authorities gave in to the demands, and it was decided that central negotiations should commence before the end of November.

However, the authorities maintained one reservation: the prison authorities could not introduce changes which were inconsistent with the law. The reservation was more or less forgotten during the ecstasy of victory, which was given enormous publicity in the papers. The situation was experienced as the very moment of freedom, and the reservation as a pure formality. Later on the reservation was to appear to be fatal; so was the demand for central negotiations itself.

It is important to bear clearly in mind that the prisoners in other institutions went on strike in sympathy with their fellow prisoners at Österåker.

Below I will show that the further development, after the October strike, was not a happy one from the point of view of the inmates. Here I want to emphasize clearly that this does not detract from the unusual courage shown or the great contribution made by the Swedish prisoners during these dramatic days in October. Clearly, the October revolt is by itself of nothing less than historical significance.[15]

*

November was devoted to celebration. But increasingly also to work, Preparations were being made for the coming central negotiations. In the press there was silence before the storm. Among the prisoners the level of activity was high. In somewhat varying ways, the inmates in each central institution in the eight prison regions chose one representative to take part in the central negotiations. According to the agreement made with the authorities, the inmates were allowed to include two additional outsiders of their own choosing in their delegation, thus totaling a delegation of ten. During the local negotiations at Österåker the inmates had demanded a larger number of prisoner representatives, but the authorities had opposed this and the inmates had given in. While the election of representatives was taking place, the prisoners also worked on the list of demands to be presented at the negotiations. The list was formulated by the prisoners' representatives with the aid of the two outsiders. The list, however, was not ready until just before the negotiations were to begin, on 30 November.

As 30 November approached, the sense of drama again began to be heightened. This time, however, the development took a different course.

As a whole, the criminal justice system and the bodies connected with it consist of a number of sub-systems which, through the years, have themselves adjusted mutually so that conflicts do not normally appear – at least not on the surface. The prisoners' action in October had a strongly upsetting effect on these adjustments, and led to open conflicts at a number of points.

Among the *staff* in the prison system, feelings were 'at boiling point', as one senior prison official put it. The feeling was prevalent that the prisoners were allowed to do exactly what they wanted, and that the only task remaining for the officers was that of opening doors for prisoners and senior officials when they were to negotiate. It was argued that the staff organizations, which were going to be represented at the negotiations, did not really represent staff interests. Let me add that the 'boiling point' atmosphere among the staff lasted until the whole course of events, which is to be described here, was over. Thus, the feeling of being overlooked, and of the prisoners' demands being unreasonable, was clearly expressed during meetings in the staff organizations and in the institutions before and after a series of negotiations which took place much later (January 1971), and to which I will return later.

Among the *prisoners*, a fear of being to some degree manipulated from the outside was apparently to some extent present, though leading members of various inmate councils, who had close contact with KRUM, refuted this view in very clear terms (see *Olofsson* 1970, p. 2). In addition a certain dissension probably developed between the few leading and active prisoners and the large, passive prison population.

In *KRUM*, latent conflicts broke out into the open at the annual meeting of the organization, during the weekend before the negotiations were to begin at Österåker. A certain generation gap between older liberal members and younger and more radical participants stood out clearly. The structure of the organization was discussed; some advocated abolishing the more controlling and coordinating 'national KRUM', wanting to rely purely on independent local chapters – a proposal which did not receive majority support. From several quarters it was argued that the conflict was related to a lack of communication, for example in connection with the outbreak of the October strike (see above). There was agreement on the importance of trying to remedy this defect.

In other words, in all these contexts the prisoners' initiative still had upsetting effects on traditional adjustments, especially far into the ranks of the staff.

During KRUM's annual meeting, however, the first signs of relative powerlessness on the prisoners' side could also be seen, a powerlessness which later was to increase and become crucial.

While the annual meeting took place, the representatives of the prisoners from the country as a whole arrived at Österåker, where the negotiations were to take place. At the annual meeting a report was received saying that two persons from KRUM had been elected for the two outside roles on the delegation. The two were – upon discussions and suggestions from KRUM- not lawyers or other professional experts, because people in KRUM felt – probably rightly – that if 'experts' were chosen, the fear of being manipulated would be pronounced among many inmates. For this reason, the two outside participants were ex-inmates. However, the representatives of the prisoners presented three demands to the authorities before the negotiations started: to have contact with an advisory group consisting of three lawyers and an author (all of them from KRUM) before the commencement of negotiations; to be allowed a press conference in connection with the opening of the negotiations: and to be allowed telephone contact with the inmate councils in their respective institutions. On the afternoon of the second day of KRUM's annual meeting, a dramatic message was received, saying that the prison authorities had refused to comply with these demands. The representatives of the prisoners insisted on their demands, and from the outside it could appear as if the prisoners' side felt that their position was strong. In KRUM, however, people were now greatly preoccupied with the question of getting the negotiations started, probably in part because of a growing fear that a new strike now might not be so successful. Late that day (Sunday 29 November 1970) the prisoners and the authorities agreed on a compromise: the prisoners renounced the press conference, but were permitted telephone contact with their inmate councils. A member of KRUM was in contact with both parties by telephone as the compromise was being arrived at.

However, the question of contact with the advisory group had not been solved. As emphasized in an editorial in *Dagens Nyheter* on 30 November – the first day of the negotiations – the danger of a breakdown in the negotiations was great. The paper pointed out that the authorities had now begun to take up a stiffer attitude than they had done in October, and urged them to give the advisory group admittance. The issue of contact with the advisory group became the first question at the negotiations, and only after they had clearly threatened to break off the negotiations were the prisoners allowed contact with the group. This was given extensive publicity in *Dagens Nyheter* on 1 December, under the headlines 'Ultimatum to the New Prison Director' (a new director of prisons had taken office on 30 November). The presentation gave the impression that the prisoners wielded some power to back their demands, and that the parties were in a way equals. The fact that the threat of breaking off the negotiations had an effect indicates that the inmates still did have some power in the eyes of the other party, but the further fact that such a reasonable demand was nearly rejected, shows that no real equality subsisted at this point. It is hardly doubtful that the authorities had now begun to understand, and to use, their actual power, and actively to press on in order to isolate the prisoners from competent aid from the outside.

The authorities, on their side, had all available expertise at their disposal. In outside society it is difficult to imagine similar behaviour from one of the parties involved in negotiations.

Thus, the advisory group first established contact with the delegates around 2 p.m. on the first day of the negotiations. At this late hour the group could only give sparse and fragmentary advice concerning the technical aspects of negotiations, and it was far too late to give advice concerning the formulation of the prisoners' demand. It is not unlikely that the authorities were conscious of this when they finally gave the advisory group admittance. An additional problem for the advisory group was the fact that when its members finally arrived at Österåker, the prisoners were – owing to all the introductory difficulties – in an extremely excited state of mind. This also made it very difficult to give sensible advice. Among other things, the prisoners were outraged at the fact that the psychologist at Österåker had not received permission from the authorities to participate in the negotiations. As mentioned earlier, this psychologist strongly supported the prisoners' demands. Almost the whole first meeting between the advisory group and the prisoners was spent in discussing this question, in spite of the fact that it would have been rational also to concentrate on other questions concerning the technical aspects of the negotiations. Undoubtedly it would have been easier to concentrate on such matters if the advisory group had been able to meet the prisoners well in advance – before all the problems connected with the negotiations had in fact appeared. Concerning the question of the psychologist's participation in the negotiations, it should be added that the authorities this time got the last word: he was never allowed to participate.

The formulation of the prisoners' demands was ready only just before the negotiations were to start. As far as is known, the prisoners' delegation had had three days at their disposal (together) for preparing the list of demands. The list had sixteen main points and a number of sub-points. The list read as follows (the main points in italics):

Recognition of FFCO – Forenede Fångars Central Organisation (United Prisoners' Central Organization, established by the eight representatives of the prisoners while KRUM's annual meeting was taking place, with the eight representatives as an interim board); *clearly specified rights for the inmate councils* (uncensored communication with the mass media, KRUM, other organizations and individuals, as well as between prisons; freedom to act inside the prison; a right to be heard when relevant new laws are introduced; an equalizing of work as inmate representative with participation in the school program etc., and payment according to a minimum standard – see below); *abolition of censorship* (no censorship of mail; telephone booths in all institutions; free access to the telephone booths); *more liberal rules concerning visits* (identical visiting regulations for all institutions; a right to at least six hours of individual visiting per week; a right to have visits in the cell; a right to receive visits from anyone, without restriction); *a considerable expansion of the furlough system* (regular furloughs to be granted after 1/8 of the sentence served; remand of over four weeks included in this; furloughs to be given at intervals of one month; 'visiting furloughs'[16] to be given at least once a month if the prisoner has a right to regular furloughs; inmates without the right to furloughs to be given forty-eight hours of continual visiting time inside the walls, once a month); *immediate review of the system of leaves[17]; increased wages* (a general wage increase, equal for all inmates; a minimum wage of 1.25 Swedish kroner (twenty cents) per hour until negotiations concerning wages could be commenced between the Prison Department and the Swedish Association for Institutional Labourers – established a while earlier; 1.25 kroner to be paid to all inmates, also to those studying or for other reasons not placed in regular work; 80 per cent of the wage to be paid in cash, the rest to be saved; canteens to be installed in all institutions); *an equalizing of labour with other activities* (abolition of the duty to work; studies and therapy equalized in economic terms with work; sessions with the treatment staff to take place during working time and without a reduction in wages; all prisoners to be offered a primary school education program, free of charge, *without* being kept in separate educational prisons; later lock-up time at night); *a new library system* (according to the same principle as at Hall security institution); *improved working conditions for the psychologists* (assumed to be presented by a representative of the Psychological Association); *increased reliance on probation with an improvement of the economic resources of that system; abolishment of all special restrictions for foreigners in the prisons; similar regulations for female and male prisoners; abolishment of the youth prison system in its present form; a right for all inmates to receive gifts; abolishment of all types of involuntary isolation.*

An impressive list of important demands which, taken together, would mean a shattering of the prison system in its present form, even if the inmates from a practical point of view, had, of course, taken a reasonable margin between asking and selling price into consideration. A list which gave an outward appearance of strength, as *Dagens Nyheter* stated it on 1 December: 'The Prisoners Demand Radical Changes in the Prison Society'. But a feeling of weakness as regards the bargaining position had begun to spread. As already stated, at KRUM's annual meeting the participants had been concerned with getting the negotiations started, and with avoiding a breakdown. The same had been the concern of the advisory group. There was a widespread feeling that the prisoners' side could not sustain a breakdown in the negotiations.

As we have already seen, the negotiations did get started, Representatives of the Royal Prison Department, the eight regional directors, representatives of the staff organizations, and the inmates' representatives met on Monday 30 November. The advisory group was not at any time given access to the meeting room, but was – after the permission mentioned above had been given – periodically admitted to an adjoining room, where they could confer with the prisoners' representatives when the prisoners asked for it. The advisers at all times felt it important not to give the prisoners a feeling of being manipulated. They viewed it as their task partly to formulate in words the demands put forward by the prisoners, and in part to inform the prisoners of the legal conditions for the carrying out of their demands. As far as is known, the prisoners viewed it as important to emphasize that these were the prisoners' negotiations. This, however, implied that the prisoners actually were even more isolated, against adversaries who were very shrewd negotiators.

Representatives of the prison authorities were at the outset worried that the negotiations might break down due to 'questions of procedure'. They did not want a new strike, either. But by now their worry was not great enough to prevent them from pressing through their points of view on procedure. The crucial point in connection with procedure was the fact that the prison authorities from the very beginning viewed the negotiations as 'talks' *(överlegningar)* – that is, as unbinding discussions or conversations – rather than as negotiations leading to actual decisions. The more well-informed[18] viewed the whole matter as a kind of 'group therapy' session, and as an attempt to establish continual 'contact' between the various levels within the system. The less well-informed simply stressed that decisions should certainly not be made – if anything, prison problems should only be discussed. The authorities, they argued, certainly could not participate in negotiations, because only one of the parties involved – the authorities – were to make decisions.

This crucial issue – the characterization of the meeting as 'talks' rather than 'negotiations' – became the most important topic for discussion at the meeting. In fact, this was just about as far as one got. The authorities strongly maintained that many of the demands of the inmates (but in fact far from all of them) necessitated *legal* changes which were beyond the jurisdiction of the prison authorities (and which the authorities apparently could not even recommend), and that over and above this one actually found it in general difficult to make decisions at such a meeting. Some of the points on the inmates' list of demands were discussed without the authorities professing to be capable of making any decisions whatsoever. They wished to 'discuss matters', and meet again later in order to 'continue discussions'. The representatives of the prisoners felt they were being outmanoeuvred, but gave more and more ground until they finally took a stand on the view that a decision at least had to be made concerning some sub-point or other from the long list, so that they had something, in the form of results, to bring back to their institutions, They emphasized that if no decisions whatsoever could be made, they could not guarantee order in the institutions. Despite this, the representatives of the Prison Department were unable to decide anything, and in addition viewed themselves as unable to continue the talks beyond the two days that had been set aside for them. The authorities instead wanted to appoint a small working committee with representatives from both sides, having the task of analysing the prisoners' 'proposals', and to have the large delegations meet again for further 'talks' at a much later date – on Monday 11 January 1971.[19]

The representatives of the prisoners were under serious pressure, and were naturally concerned that their own status as well as that of the prisoners' action would be seriously reduced in the eyes of the other inmates if they returned to their institutions without a single result. Such a return might mean a serious threat to the solidarity of the prisoners, and to the whole idea of a prisoners' organization. Thus, from the point of view of the prisoners' representatives it was absolutely essential to 'do something', simply in order that the prisoners' movement might survive. Late at night on the second and closing day of the 'negotiations', when the announcement had been made that the authorities were completely unable to make any decisions, the eight inmates decided to commence a new hunger strike. They emphasized to the prison authorities that this did not imply an appeal to other inmates to do the same.

In KRUM this development was viewed as rather disquieting, On the next morning – 2 December – KRUM members were preoccupied in part with explaining the development to the mass media, in order to make the new move by the prisoners' representatives understood and accepted, and in part with finding something that could make the 'negotiations' start anew in a way that was acceptable to the prisoners. It was feared that if the strike spread to the prisons themselves, a 'third' strike could this time be expected in addition to the hunger strike – and refusal to drink may be fatal within a few days.

At the same time KRUM naturally felt obliged to support the inmates. But this time there was no discussion whether one ought to urge the strike or just to support it. No one seriously wanted to urge a thirst strike – if anything, just the contrary.

Under huge front-page headlines, *Dagens Nyheter* that morning carried the news that a new strike was near at hand in all the prisons throughout the country. The announcement that the strike had in fact spread from the eight inmates at Österåker to the institutions first came over the radio. In the institutions, the decision to strike was in many cases made by secret ballot at plenary meetings. As the new major strike was spreading, diverging rumours sprang up regarding the number of participating institutions and prisoners. The exact number of participating prisoners has never been ascertained; the prison authorities claimed that at its height about 900 inmates took part in the strike, while KRUM maintained that the figure was about 1,500. In any case, the number of participants was dearly smaller than during the first strike.

The stand taken by the authorities to the December strike differed from their attitude in October – and was rather in line with their unwillingness to give admittance to the advisory group, and with their refusal to take part in real negotiations. This time the authorities were prepared, and acted as if they understood their own power. On the morning after the breakdown of 'negotiations', the prisoners' delegates were denied contact with the press, external communications were obstructed in other ways as well, and all inmates on strike were given solitary confinement in order to preclude communication within the institutions. Later, doubts were raised as to whether any order concerning solitary confinement had actually been given by the central authorities – the Prison Department maintained that it was up to the individual prison governor to make the decision. This created tension among several prison governors. The legal basis for imposing solitary confinement for refusal to eat was unclear, and the governors felt left alone with the responsibility. In any case, it is an established fact that fasting inmates were locked up in almost all the institutions. This probably contributed considerably to diminishing the extent of the strike. At the same time, it probably contributed to provoking the thirst strike, which commenced after the locking up had taken place. As far as is known, about fifty inmates in various institutions participated in this strike. At Hall security institution, it was reported that 30 prisoners took part.

The youth organizations of the Social Democratic Party and the Liberal Party supported the strike. But their support was not given wide publicity (*Dagens Nyheter*, 4 December). To be sure, the papers – and especially *Dagens Nyheter* – gave extensive coverage to the strike this time as well.

However, one sensed that this time the strike was viewed as an unhappy incident which no one actually wanted. The situation seemed precarious, with the authorities having the upper hand. *Dagens Nyheter*, which supported the prisoners, emphasized how the struggle had been intensified, and how 'the stronger party uses its strongest weapon'. The new Director of Prisons, who had taken office on the first day of the negotiations, was urged in an editorial to 'unlock the inmates'.

However, this he did not do. In Swedish KRUM people saw that this strike was not as successful as the first one, in the very important sense that *the authorities managed to stop the strike and partly to repel it with power.* A fact which earlier had only been vaguely understood was now for the first time seen quite clearly: even with the strike as a weapon, the prisoners actually had little power which they could place behind their demands.

This discovery was reflected in KRUM's further activity. There was now no question of urging the inmates to strike, even if KRUM's section in Stockholm did have some plans – which were never carried out – of demonstrations and other activities outside one of the prisons in the Stockholm region. Rather, KRUM worked with increasing intensity to settle the conflict, and was thus placed in the paradoxical situation of working for the same goal as the prison authorities. On the first day of the strike – Wednesday 2 December – several tense meetings were held in KRUM. On the strike's second day one managed to arrange a meeting with the Minister of Justice. From KRUM's side the two KRUM representatives in the prisoners' delegation participated, together with three members of the advisory group. The parties met during the afternoon, first for only half an hour, and during the first meeting the two parties expressed in general terms their opinion of the situation. KRUM's people emphasized, inter alia, the dangers connected with a thirst strike. The discussions continued somewhat later that evening. KRUM's people stressed that the negotiations had stranded owing to a lack of willingness to compromise on the part of the authorities, that the prisoners had modified their demands more and more, that there were no formal obstacles to a reopening of the negotiations, and that this ought to be done within two weeks. The KRUM representatives had hoped for an actual agreement on certain issues – for example the issue of visiting arrangements – and they asked the Minister of Justice to intervene, He did not do so – an intervention on his part could actually not be expected in the light of Swedish administrative tradition – and no agreement was made concerning concrete issues. The KRUM representatives later explained that the other party had seemed interested in renewed 'negotiations', that the Minister had to some degree shown an open and attentive attitude, but that the authorities had not seemed ready to compromise in any respect – as if they preferred a continuation of the strike to a compromise – and that little could be gained in the direction of an actual agreement. Without promising anything, the Minister of Justice let the group understand that the members of the prisoners' delegation might be brought together again (they had been sent back to their individual prisons after having issued a press release in which they said, inter alia, that they were 'tired and disappointed' with the attitude of the authorities). He recommended discussions with the Director of Prisons, indicating that the Director was interested in a solution.

During the night following the meeting, KRUM's representatives prepared a proposal for a minimum agreement with the prison authorities. Their proposal read as follows:

1   Immediate release (of the isolated inmates).
2   Permission for all inmate councils to communicate freely with

    a   fellow prisoners in the prison,
    b   other inmate councils,
    c   the two outside members of the prisoners' delegation,
    d   the advisory group.

3   A gathering of the prisoners' delegation [as a whole; my addition] at Österåker on Monday 7 December 1970. There they are to be given the opportunity for unlimited contact with all inmate councils as well as with their advisory group, which may be expanded.

4   An immediate declaration of principle from the PD [Prison Department], as follows: Immediate abolition of the censorship of mail and the introduction of visits in the cell every Sunday are connected with certain practical problems. However, our attitude to these reforms is positive and on 11 January 1971 we will present a plan concerning how these questions are to be solved in the various prisons in the country.

5   Negotiations between the main delegations will be resumed on 11 January 1971.

6   At these negotiations, the PD shall, in a positive spirit, try to make decisions concerning questions falling within their sphere of competence.

7   Two working committees, each consisting of four prisoners, two representatives of the PD, and two representatives of the staff organizations, are to begin their work on 14 December.

The reference to working committees in section 7 was included because the authorities had earlier stated that they first wanted the prisoners' demands examined and discussed in a small work group. The reference to a resumption of negotiations on 11 January was included because the authorities had wanted general contact to be renewed on that date. Yet, KRUM's proposal for a compromise was a rather strong one, with important built-in rights for the prisoners: *the whole* delegation was to meet on 7 December, *the whole* delegation was to participate in the ensuing (admittedly divided) group work, *negotiations* were to be taken up on 11 January 1971, at the negotiations the Prison Department was to propose a *concrete plan* for the abolition of censorship and for the introduction of visits in the cells, and the Prison Department was to be prepared for *an attempt to make decisions*. The stress on continual participation of the *whole* prisoner delegation in the group work phase constituted an attempt to counteract the danger of becoming absorbed and co-opted by prolonged group work.

On the morning of the next day, the two KRUM members of the prisoners' delegation met the Director of Prisons. The Prison Department could not accept KRUM's proposal. (It is actually unclear whether the proposal was presented in its entirety.) KRUM's representatives, on the other hand, were now really short of time: owing to the locking-up of the inmates, the strike was now in the process of dissolving in a number of institutions. It was feared that the main strike would be over within a short period of time, and that only pockets of hard-headed inmates on a thirst strike – in mortal danger – would be left. It was necessary to reach a result while the bargaining position at least gave the outward appearance of being reasonably strong. The KRUM people therefore accepted the following proposal for an agreement by the Prison Department:

Talks [note: not 'negotiations': my addition] between two smaller delegations from the Prison Department and representatives of the inmates will take place at Österåker on Monday 7 December 1970 at 10 a.m. The issues which are presented there will be examined in detail. Particular attention will be given to the questions which appear most urgent from the point of view of the inmates. Among other things, the question of visiting arrangements in the institutions will be discussed with a view to finding practicable solutions. In this connection the possibilities of introducing visits in the rooms or in other special quarters on a trial basis in certain institutions will be considered. Before the Prison Department takes its stand, opinions from the administration and the staff in the institutions concerned will be obtained.

After the discussions between the smaller delegations on 7 December, the prisoners' demands were to be treated in a still smaller work group consisting of three prisoners and three representatives of the authorities – the latter coming from the Prison Department, prison administration, and the staff organizations. It was agreed that the work group was to present a memorandum before 11 January 1971, and that talks (note: not negotiations) between the large delegations were then to be resumed on the basis of the memorandum. With the exception of the one-day talks between two smaller delegations on 7 December, this was in complete agreement with what the Prison Department had wanted after the breakdown of 'negotiations' (see above).

Later in the morning of the same day, the two KRUM representatives returned exhausted to KRUM's office. From the office they called the eight prisoner representatives, reporting the result and advising the prisoners to accept it. Acceptance from the inmate councils was communicated to KRUM during the afternoon, and a press conference concerning the agreement was given early in the evening. At the press conference the Director of Prisons was interviewed together with a representative of KRUM. The Director of Prisons referred to the agreement as a 'compromise'. He emphasized (on television) that in these matters quick decisions could not be expected, but that trial arrangements concerning certain issues in connection with the system of visits might perhaps be expected, KRUM's representative also had to say that quick decisions could not actually be expected.

As the evening went by, the disappointment began to be quite manifest in KRUM circles. There was particular concern over the fact that it had been necessary to accept such a substantial reduction in the number of inmates participating at the meeting on 7 December and in the following group work. People were also worried that the prisoners, because of this, would not be able to withstand the pressure from the authorities towards being co-opted, There was also concern over the fact that no real decisions were to be made at the meetings, and that the meetings – even on 11 January – were in other words to be 'talks' and not 'negotiations'. Late that evening one of the lawyers in the inmates' advisory group summarized the situation in this way:

> It's the question of time. This shows that we stand on loose sand. We have nothing to threaten with, We actually have no power. There is only an

extremely weak threat in this business of a hunger strike, because the authorities can just prolong the whole thing.

Later people simply began to wonder what the 'compromise' with the authorities actually had consisted of. Apart from the brief one-day meeting on 7 December, had not the authorities got everything they wanted? It must be added that the prisoners had had maximum support from the press. Even with such support, then, it had not been possible to obtain a better result when the prison system turned its power on. And what was worse: worse was to follow.

*

On Monday 7 December, the two smaller delegations (four from the Prison Department and four prisoners, together with the two outside participants on the prisoners' delegation) met as planned for a one-day meeting. The advisory group was not summoned, but had produced a report to the prisoners' delegation on the legal aspects of the demands – concentrating particularly on the question of the need for legal changes. The advisory group argued that the authorities exaggerated the need for complicated legal changes. After the one-day meeting, the work group mentioned above began its discussions.

The one-day meeting, which lasted till midnight, was summarized in the evening of the same day at a general meeting in KRUM. The person giving the report – one of the outside representatives on the prisoners' delegation – gave a vivid description of the meeting. He claimed that it had taken place in a 'positive spirit', and that it had been useful in this respect, but that it also had actually consisted simply of 'idle talk'. He related how seriously the authorities viewed the question of drugs in the institutions. They had brought the issue up, and had stressed the importance of the prisoners' participation in having the problem reduced. The prisoners' list had been discussed, naturally without any decisions being made, though the report from the advisory group on legal matters had been useful to the prisoners because it had given them some cards to play when the other party presented legal arguments. In all, however, the parties had not made any progress concerning concrete reforms – they had 'exchanged opinions'.

Interestingly, one important point had not been discussed in detail at the one-day meeting. This concerned an incident which will be briefly related here. Late in the evening on the day when the strike following the break-down in negotiations had been called off (4 December), six prisoners were taken away by the police from the security institution at Gävle, apparently to the austere isolation section in the Norrköping prison. On the preceding day, the inmates at Gavle had among other things seized a section for leisure time activities. They had continued their hunger strike (apparently some were also on a thirst strike). On 4 December, despite the fact that the strike in general had been discontinued, the police had been called in to take the leaders away. They were carried screaming into the night – according to newspaper articles and pictures in a very brutal way. It seemed rather unreasonable to crack down on the striking inmates in such a way, even though the strike fell outside the agreement. (In addition, it is unclear whether the Gävle prisoners had been informed of the calling-off of the strike in a way which appeared credible to them. KRUM was denied communication with the prisoners in the Gävle prison – see *Dagens Nyheter* 6 December 1970 – and if the message concerning the calling-off of the strike came from the prison staff only, the prisoners might not have believed them.) Some members of KRUM wanted the incident thoroughly discussed at the one-day meeting on 7 December, more or less with a demand to the effect that the six inmates should be brought back to Gävle. Others, however, claimed that an ultimatum ought not to be presented – the authorities would certainly not agree to sending the prisoners back, and it was important to avoid pursuing considerations of prestige, since this might result in the 'negotiations' breaking down once more. It is unclear whether the question was brought up at all at the meeting, but at any rate it did not constitute a central point, and no ultimatum was presented. The inmates' bargaining position was far from strong enough for that.

During the discussion at the general meeting in KRUM, the disappointment at the current development became very clear. It was emphasized that the prisoners' delegates had done all they could, but that the prisoners actually had nothing to threaten with; and that owing to the co-operation of the inmate members, the coming discussion in the small work group constituted a very dangerous link in the process. It was stressed that KRUM had to stop making 'demands' when actually no power could be placed behind the 'demands'; and that the reforms which were to come would at best be of a very short-term and minor character. The prisons, it was claimed, would certainly remain standing; 'the tearing down of the prisons from the inside', as the ideology stated it, was impossible in view of a fundamental lack of power.

At another general meeting a few days later, some members protested against this view. They claimed that during the time to come, the prisoners would to an increasing extent 'demand more', and that they would in this way participate actively from the inside in 'tearing down the prisons'. But from the 'critical side' – which at this meeting too was in a clear majority among those who took the floor – it was claimed that, except for a hunger strike, the prisoners had little or nothing to place behind their 'demands', and just now – after the element of surprise present in October had disappeared – the method of a hunger strike had proved to be too weak.

Approximately at the same time, the small work group consisting of prisoners and representatives of the authorities began their discussions. Detailed interviews with participants from both sides, as well as examination of certain diary notes, have given me the clear impression that the group developed in a so-called 'positive spirit'. Stated differently, the conflict model was abandoned, and the participants passed on to a model of co-operation in their work. *The possibility of co-optation had become a reality.*

To be sure, KRUM's advisory group did from time to time meet the three inmate representatives in the work group (special permission had to be given for each meeting). The first meeting between the advisors and the prisoners took place on the day before the work group was to begin its discussions, and it lasted for about three hours. In addition to giving advice of a legal kind, the advisory group now and later stressed that during the coming 'negotiations', the prisoners were not to feel obligated by the results from the small work group, that they could later very well take independent standpoints, that the three prisoners themselves ought to formulate something in writing while the work group was in process – if they did, they would have a stronger point of departure later -, and that they ought to keep in close contact with their respective inmate councils. In all, then, the advisors warned against being 'absorbed' by the work group, and against forgetting that the three inmates in the work group still were *representatives of the prisoners.*

The three inmates – three competent and politically conscious men – certainly listened to this advice, – it is clear that whenever it seemed possible for them, they maintained independent standpoints, However, it was close to useless. They were now at the Österåker prison, and with the exception of the Christmas 'vacation', two of the three inmates were physically isolated from their inmate councils: they were only allowed contact by letter and telephone (and the telephone contact was far from easy). At the same time, of course, they had very regular contact with the representatives of the authorities. It seemed that the latter placed a very strong pressure for co-operation on the inmates. Though their attitudes varied somewhat, the representatives of the authorities in general viewed KRUM's advisory group as nothing but a disturbing and diversionary element in a co-operative relationship. Understanding of the inmates' need for having advisors of their own was certainly not conspicuous among the representatives of the authorities; the latter argued that the authorities themselves could give any necessary advice. This view was also very prevalent during the later main talks, after the work group had finished its task. Furthermore, the representatives of the authorities in the work group were themselves under strong pressure from the outside – that is, from the staff organizations, which two of the three participants were representing. Both of them had agitated meetings in their organizations, and the reactions from the staff to the prisoners' demands were in part extremely negative. In this way, the representatives in the work group came in a way to view themselves as 'the advocates' of the inmates – an experience which undoubtedly was communicated to the inmates in the work group, and which could be used as a reminder when conflicts with the inmates appeared. This put great pressure on the inmates in the direction of yielding to the views of the authorities. In brief, then, the three inmates were isolated and had little to put behind their demands. Because the representatives of the authorities appeared as the prisoners' 'advocates' in relation to the staff and others, the pressure towards complete co-optation became very great, The fear KRUM had had when being forced to accept the Prison Department's proposal for an agreement after the breakdown in 'negotiations', had come true.

We shall return to the significance of the reactions and the pressure from the rank and file of the staff. At a critical moment in the later sequence of events, its significance reappeared in full strength. Here I shall only mention in passing that the inmates were thus confronted by two adversaries – the staff and the central prison administration – and that since the central administration did have to give in to their claims, the staff was not infrequently the stronger of the two (even if the staff perhaps did not always recognize this).[20]

The memorandum of the work group was ready three days before 'the negotiations' – meaning 'talks' – were to begin. It was as a whole written by one of the representatives of the authorities. In the memorandum the group examined all the main points which the prisoners had taken up before the break in the 'negotiations'. However, the group concentrated on what was called the four 'main questions' *('tunga frågor')*: the work of the inmate councils, the regulations on censorship, the visiting arrangements, and the furlough system. Consequently, for the sake of brevity I will also concentrate on these issues.

With regard to the work of the *inmate councils*, the group stated that the councils ought to be allowed to communicate – by letter and telephone – with mass media, organizations, and individuals, as well as with the inmate councils in other institutions – and in this connection enjoy freedom from censorship – 'all according to the principles covering inmates in general'. The same was to be the case for visits. The significance of these proposals – according to which the contacts of the inmate councils were, in other words, to be limited in exactly the same way as the contacts of individual, 'private' inmates – will be discussed later. Within the institution, the inmate council was to be able to meet regularly 'to the extent required' – at least two hours a week during working time. To the meetings it should be permissible to summon one inmate representative from each regular section in the prison, and – if the authorities in the institutions viewed it as permissible – similar summoning should be allowed from special units. Notice of the meeting was to be given in the way agreed upon between the inmate council and the administration of the institution. The inmate representatives were to be given the opportunity to keep in contact with each other between meetings as well: inmate representatives in closed collective sections were to be allowed to visit each other, and representatives of open sections were to be allowed to visit representatives in closed collective sections. In special cases council members were also to be allowed to visit other inmates – however, visits with the council members or with other inmates in a special section, were only to take place upon special permission from the administration of the institution. Schedules for the contacts were to be prepared by the administration of each institution in co-operation with the inmate council. To the extent that working time was spent at council activities, the inmates were to be given wages corresponding to two hours of studies per week. The inmate councils ought to be given the opportunity to express their opinion concerning new regulations of a general kind – to the extent that the regulations in question were to be subject to general hearing.

In brief: certain rights for the inmate councils are proposed, but a large number of vital limitations are also included. As we shall see later, the end result was such that the rights were entirely dropped and the limitations were *increased*.

Concerning the question of *censorship* (control of the written content of a letter) the group had no objection to examination (in contrast to censorship) of incoming mail. However, according to the opinion of the group, censorship constituted a serious interference with the inmate's private life. To be sure, 'the work group [was] aware of the fact that censorship may be motivated by reasons of security in certain situations'. But all in all the group magnanimously maintained that 'censorship of the inmates' mail ought in principle to be abolished and substituted by spot checks'. But – at the same time, however, the work group was 'aware of the fact that at the present time it is not legally possible to abolish the censorship of mail in general': Section 34 in the 'Treatment Act' states that exemption from censorship of mail may only be given to inmates who have 'shown dependability'. Therefore, the work group could 'not go further than recommending that . . . [the J regulation in the Treatment Act concerning exemption from censorship is interpreted in as liberal a way as possible'. The work group provided certain 'lines of guidance' for such an interpretation. It was felt that inmates in open institutions ought to be viewed as having fulfilled the demand for dependability concerning non-censored correspondence; 65–70 per cent of Sweden's approximately 5,250 prison places are, however, in closed sections or institutions. Inmates in closed institutions ought, according to the opinion of the group, to be able to correspond – as previously – without censorship and examination with certain specified authorities. In addition, inmates in closed institutions ought to be allowed non-censored correspondence with family members and other persons close to them. The work group presupposed that 'the concept of being close to is given a liberal interpretation'. Concerning persons other than family members and 'close' individuals, a more individualized examination of the inmate's 'dependability' had to be performed in closed institutions. It was therefore 'not possible . . . in general to give all inmates in closed institutions freedom to write to and receive letters from persons outside the group specified above . . .' An arrangement at Österåker, with examination rather than censorship of letters, was pointed out as a praiseworthy example.

In connection with the question of censorship, the work group also dealt with the question of telephone booths. The installation of telephone booths was recommended for outgoing calls in open institutions, and as a parallel it was recommended that inmates there ought to be able to use the telephone without restrictions, on the condition that they were permitted to carry cash. It was presupposed 'that such an arrangement [with cash] will be introduced in the near future in all institutions in the country'. The wage level was not discussed in this connection. (It was taken up later from another point of view, but only in a very cursory and non-committal way.) With regard to closed institutions, the group reckoned that permission to use the telephone still had to be examined 'in each individual case'. 'To the extent that reasons of security do not demand anything else, the inmate who has received permission to use the telephone, shall be permitted to talk without being listened in on'. Telephone *booths* might perhaps also be attempted on a trial basis in some closed institutions as well.

With regard to the question of *visits*, it was pointed out that present conditions in many respects left much to be desired. Reforms in this area were viewed as very important. However, it was clear that existing defects 'to a large extent are caused by practical conditions connected with the technical and architectural design of the institutions, and that in so far as this is the case the defects cannot always be improved immediately'.

The work group was also 'familiar with the fact' that another work group had been appointed in the Prison Department in September 1970, with the task of reviewing visiting arrangements. The work group considered it necessary to await the results of the other work group. The group were, however, anxious to submit certain proposals and certain statements of principle which might 'serve as guidelines for the continued work of the above-mentioned special work group'. The statements of principle concerned a liberal interpretation of the regulations as far as the circle of visitors was concerned. But at the same time it was 'needless to say' necessary to 'take into consideration organizational conditions in the institution, schedules and resources, which may to some degree lead to a granting of visits according to need . . .'. One did, however, want to fix as a minimum for visits in all institutions, that the inmates were to have the right to receive visits at least twice a month, two hours per visit. (The inmates had originally demanded six hours per week.)

Visits by persons 'close to' the inmate were to take place under surveillance only when 'special reasons' ('reasons of security' or 'special risk for the smuggling of narcotics etc.') prompted it. Neither were visits by others to be supervised 'if it is not necessary'. A visit by an attorney 'should as a rule take place without surveillance'. What has been said here concerning surveillance was to be practised in closed institutions – containing 65–70 per cent of the total number of prison places. With regard to open institutions, the work group magnanimously maintained that a 'motive for the surveillance of visits [can] almost never be demonstrated'. But at the same time it was stated that technical and architectural changes ought to be made, and also that since 'very costly changes' were necessary, provisional arrangements ought to be employed during a period of transition. As a compensation for the poor visiting arrangements, 'visiting furloughs' were recommended to be used extensively instead.

The work group returned to the regulations for 'visiting furloughs' in their section on *furloughs*. By way of introduction, a series of pretty statements were made concerning the importance of furloughs. Furloughs might remedy lots of things. But of course, it was necessary to observe the existing legal provision, stating that furloughs are only to be given when 'danger of abuse cannot be considered to be present'. It was maintained that an inmate who has received and observed the rules of his first regular furlough ought then to be eligible for 'visiting furlough' once a month – provided that the 'personnel resources' of the institution 'permit it'. And what, then, were the conditions for receiving one's first regular furlough? The work group proposed a certain liberalization of the regulations concerning this question, and spelled out a new complicated network of rules. In open institutions, furloughs ought to be permissible at the earliest after 4 (previously after 6) months, However, if the punishment exceeded one and a half years but not four years, furloughs ought not to be given before 6 months had passed (previously 8 months). According to the opinion of the work group, furloughs in closed institutions ought to be given at the earliest after 7 (previously after 10) months, provided the punishment did not exceed four years. In open as well as closed institutions, furloughs to persons with a punishment exceeding 4 years ought not to be given before the inmate had served 1/6 (previously 1/4) of the sentence. An inmate on a life sentence should normally not be given furlough before at least 2 (earlier 3) years had passed. Certain special regulations, in a slightly more liberal direction, were suggested for those sentenced to youth prison and to security measures. At the same time, the group was again 'aware of the fact' that the changes might presuppose staff reinforcements. In addition, the inmates were of course themselves obliged to pay the expenses connected with their furloughs. And among other things because of the new 'class difference' between the wealthier and the less wealthy inmates which might then fellow, the group was 'aware of the fact' that the change which had been suggested could perhaps not be carried into practice straight away. During the short time at the disposal of the work group, it had not been possible to calculate costs with any degree of certainty.

These were the main proposals for reform which the work group had agreed on suggesting. On a couple of points, disagreement could be discerned between the inmate and non-inmate members of the group. The inmate members proposed that prisoners who had received especially long sentences, and who could not count on furloughs in the foreseeable future, ought to be allowed a 48-hour continual visit within the institution once a month. In its memorandum, the work group comments as follows on this proposal: 'The work group believes (!) that attention should of course, be paid to the proposal, but has in the short time at the disposal of the group been unable to examine more carefully whether the conditions are present for a full or partial carrying-out of the proposal'. This work group proposed, however, that the other work group concerned with the examination of the question of visits should be asked to carry out an investigation in the central institutions, in order to find out 'whether and to what extent resources in terms of space and personnel permit the introduction of forms of visits of the type referred to here'.

The inmates in the work group had view-points of their own on the question of visits in the cells. The inmates placed great emphasis on such visits. Visits in the cells also constituted an important element in the inmates' original list of demands, as well as in KRUM's proposal for a compromise in connection with the second strike (see above p. 143). It had even been mentioned in the proposal for a compromise presented by the Prison Department – and agreed upon by the parties involved – in connection with the second strike, There it had been stated that 'the possibilities of introducing visits in the rooms or in other special quarters on a trial basis in certain institutions will be considered'. The conditions in the closed institutions were here of primary importance. The paragraphs in the memorandum concerning visits of this kind opened with the following words: 'The work group has also discussed the question whether and to what extent visits may be granted in the living rooms ['*boligrommene*'; a euphemistic term for 'cells']'. One felt that in open institutions such visits ought to be permitted, but not if other inmates in the same section definitely objected to it without having other quarters where they could stay during the visiting hours. With regard to closed institutions 'the representatives of the prison authorities in the work group [were], on the other hand, aware of the fact that visits in the living rooms can hardly be permitted for reasons of anonymity and security (above all because of the difficulty involved in preventing the smuggling of narcotics)'. One had, however, 'in itself no objections to' the introduction of an experiment with such visits in suitable institutions, but maintained at the same time that such an experiment would have a very limited value. As we shall see later, this conclusion was even more diluted in its final form.

To reiterate, this was the main content of the memorandum. The form was glib, polished, and characterized by an official terminology showing that the authorities had drafted the document, and giving an impression – so typical of official documents – of alienation towards the prisoners' real problems. The few reforms which are suggested are extremely cautious. They are characterized by the authorities' preferences concerning solutions; at times they give the impression of a certain radicalism while actually being highly reserved. The last point may be seen in connection with the proposal concerning regulations for communication between inmate councils and the outside world. Here the same rules were applied as for inmates in general – rules which were only to a very small degree changed later in the memorandum. The point may also be seen in connection with the magnanimous proposal concerning visiting furloughs: everything is taken back by a maintenance of restrictive conditions concerning the granting of the first regular furlough.

The general impression is not improved by the fact that even the classical way out, that of referring matters to another working committee, was utilized.

The representatives of the authorities in the work group were very enthusiastic about their product. Indeed, this is precisely what it was: their product. Several of them felt they had come a long way towards significant reforms. As has been stated, they viewed themselves as a kind of defenders of the inmates: this would 'go over fine', they felt; this would be agreed to by the authorities during the coming talks.

*

The distance between the memorandum and the inmates' original demands was very great. After the final central (national) talks, which took place at Österåker 11–12 January 1971, the distance became even greater. Six representatives came from the Prison Department, together with the eight regional directors. The staff organizations (there were four of them) were represented by altogether ten representatives. The prisoners were also represented by ten: eight inmates and the two ex-inmates from KRUM. The prisoners' advisory group was not admitted to the negotiating room itself, and were only allowed access to the institution when the prisoners asked for their advice. In this way, the advisors could take no initiative in giving advice. The contrast between the two main sides, in terms of sheer numbers as well as negotiating expertise, was glaring. At this stage, the prisoners had to accept all of this.

The very opening of the meeting underscored the difference in position between the parties. Together with the regional directors, the representatives of the Prison Department – who had been transported to the institution in special cars – first enjoyed a cup of coffee together in an adjoining room, whereupon they graciously moved on to the 'negotiating' room. They were formally dressed in suits and wearing ties. The representatives of the staff organizations proceeded to the negotiating room through another door, also formally dressed. Then – when the rulers had found it suitable to appear – the representatives of the prisoners were shown in through a third door, in a long row and ten in number, informally dressed, many of them with long hair and several with hippie-like jewellery, running the gauntlet to their places. Such must have been the meeting between the whites and the representatives of the American Indians when the Indians tried to negotiate land rights of their own. We all know that the land rights which they were promised were rapidly eroded. So were the prisoners' claims, in spite of an almost heroic effort on the part of some of the prisoner representatives.

For the last time the prisoners' 'demands' were examined. The talks lasted for two days, until about 2 o'clock in the morning of 13 January. With only a few exceptions – towards the end of the last day – the results of the work group's memorandum were presented to the conference by one of the representatives of the authorities in the work group – almost as if it were his sole product. (In addition to the memorandum of the work group, some points brought up by the staff were also discussed: escapes etc. and the general atmosphere in the institutions. The staff had also wanted to discuss the question of the inmate councils' participation in disclosing the smuggling of narcotics by inmates, but the prisoners' representatives had managed to refuse discussing this, on the grounds that it would place the inmate council in an impossible position.)

Despite the fact that the memorandum of the work group consisted of proposals, and not decisions, and in spite of the fact that the advisors of the prisoners had emphasized this to the prisoner delegates, the prisoners actually were strongly pressed to agree to the formulations of the memorandum, or to the changes of them made by the *authorities* – this despite the fact that they not infrequently had divergent views. Thus, on a number of occasions the prisoners' representatives from the work group were more or less directly reminded of what they had 'committed themselves to' (the expression was not used) through the memorandum. The reminders, which were presented with increasing strength, undoubtedly influenced the prisoners' attitudes to other questions as well. The most important reminders will be described here in some detail: they illustrate not only how committed you generally become by group work preceding 'negotiations', but – in the light of the prisoners' strong tendency to yield to the authorities, as well as the unusual tone which the authorities allowed themselves to adopt – also how unusually committed you become if you have no *power* with which to back up your claims.

The first reminder came early on the first day, and concerned the question of substituting the word 'and' for the word 'or' at one place in the memorandum's proposal concerning furloughs. One of the representatives of the authorities in the work group quickly answered that '. . . we shall read this memorandum as it is written, and if there are any words which have been carefully chosen here, it's words like "ought" and "shall", because we have really been over those words. When it says "ought", it means "ought", and "shall" when it says "shall"!'

This was simply the *first and the last time* this type of question concerning wording was taken up by the prisoners. It is obvious that such questions may be very significant.

The second reminder, a little later on the same day, concerned the question of telephone booths. One of the representatives of the prisoners in the work group was now – afterwards – dissatisfied with the statement in the memorandum that 'in closed institutions one must still count on assessing the granting of permission for the inmates to use the telephone in each individual case'. He felt that a more general permission ought to be given. One of the representatives of the authorities answered bluntly that the prisoner in question had agreed with the others in the group. This precluded any further discussion of this question, despite its great importance. The third occasion also concerned the question of telephone booths in closed institutions, In the memorandum of the work group it was further stated that: 'It will be suitable to try out telephone booths . . . on an experimental basis in a few larger closed institutions with a cash system within each region'. In this connection the chairman (the Director of Prisons) declared that the matter had been considered in the Department of Prisons, and that the department had concluded that telephone booths ought to be tried out in a few smaller closed institutions. No mention was made of trying them out within each region. One of the representatives of the prisoners in the work group doubted whether it would be possible to draw conclusions on the basis of such a limited experiment. After a discussion the chairman made it clear that what had been said now was the proposal of the Prison Department. In other words, this was all. The inmates interpreted this – quite correctly – as a curtailment in relation to the memorandum, and argued against the proposal. At this point one of the representatives of the authorities from the work group broke in, emphasizing that he viewed the proposal of the Prison Department as satisfactory. 'I certainly do not feel squashed', he said, 'because here it's quite on the contrary the Prison Department which has gone further in the closed institutions than proposed by the work group'. How he could draw this conclusion is very unclear indeed. The prisoners' representative from the work group answered back by quoting the above-mentioned sentence from the memorandum. The representative of the authorities replied angrily: 'I think you should stand by what you have signed!' The prisoner answered in a despairing voice: 'But that's exactly what I'm trying to do . . .' After a few further statements concerning among other things the difference between 'open' and 'closed' sections and institutions, the discussion concerning this issue was simply terminated.

The Fourth occasion concerned a detail to which the authorities reacted in a similar fashion. The fifth occasion, however, concerned an important issue: the position of the psychologists in the institutions. This was a delicate topic, because the psychologists – as mentioned earlier – had in many ways supported the actions of the prisoners. By way of introduction the chairman now said that only the prisoners had expressed an opinion concerning this topic in the memorandum. This was a correct description on the part of the chairman. However, before any prisoner was permitted to speak, one of the representatives of the authorities from the work group cut in, emphasizing that at first the work group had agreed on not taking up this topic. Disapprovingly he explained that the topic had been taken up for the first time by the prisoners a few days before the talks were to begin; in addition he felt that this was a purely professional question, and a matter for the psychologists themselves. The discussion which then followed became very general and vague. Possibilities of altering the position of the psychologists were not seriously debated.

The sixth and the last occasion in this enumeration concerned non- institutional treatment of offenders (*kriminalomsorgen i frihet*). One of the inmates from the work group referred to a report on non-institutional treatment which the inmates in the work group had mentioned and agreed to in the memorandum, but which they now – after having reviewed it more closely – found unsatisfactory. The chairman asked if it was not the case that they had agreed in the work group. The prisoner answered that they had in fact agreed, but that he had now come to a different conclusion. He was supported by another prisoner from the work group, who said that they had referred to the report in question as 'a last straw', 'in a feeling of panic' over the fact that there was such a lack of sensible plans in this area. One of the representatives of the authorities from the work group this time defended the prisoners by pointing out how difficult it is in general even to sketch a good program for non-institutional treatment. After a few further statements, however, another representative of the authorities from the work group was given the floor, and he maintained in an acid tone: 'Well, these discussions have now lasted quite long . . . The statement about this particular point is the inmates' state-ment' (which was true – and the inmates had later come to regard it differently). *'You have had experts at your disposal,* you have had the representatives out there [the advisory group]. *There has been continual contact,* so you could have formu-lated a more detailed statement . . . It seems absurd when you sit around for weeks spelling out what you want to say, and then afterwards appear to be dissatisfied!' (It should be mentioned that the issue concerned the question of deleting four lines in the memorandum.) A prisoner reiterated that in the memorandum they had grasped at such straws as could be found; this was the reason why this particular report had been mentioned. Another prisoner defended his group by saying that also the inmates in the work group had concentrated on the four 'weighty' ques-tions; this was the reason why the conclusion was not thought out more carefully. A third prisoner pointed out, in an irritated tone, that the authorities again wanted to rely exactly on what the memorandum said. He pointed out that there were many more prisoners in the room than just the three from the work group. A fourth prisoner asked the representative of the authorities whether he believed that all of his people (the staff) would support everything he had said in the memorandum. The representative in question concluded: 'I don't know, because I haven't talked with all of my colleagues . . . but every day we have given [the advisory group] facilities for making contact with [the delegation]; the group has had facilities for talking with its advisory group and in part to discuss matters there . . . and now you are at the same time sitting there quarrelling when we come here . . . It was the inmates' representatives who kept on wanting to present this at all costs!' After a few further comments the debate concerning this issue was simply over.

Let me repeat, I have included these details in order to show how extraordinarily bound you are to the formulations and/or points of departure of those in power when you have no power yourself.

Concerning a few other important issues, however, the prisoners continued to offer some objections. I shall specifically mention two issues which will be important in later parts of this presentation. In the first place, the prisoners again emphasized the importance of experimenting with visits in the cells, also in closed institutions. This point of view received no support (the reasons given by the authorities are recapitulated in the summary of the memorandum given above). Secondly, one of the prisoners emphasized the importance of having specific rules for the communications of the inmate councils. In other words, he emphasized that the suggestion of the work group – proposing that the (restrictive) rules concerning individuals were also to be applied to inmate councils – should not be followed up. The treatment of this question will be rendered in some detail, because it illustrates how completely outsmarted you may be in a 'negotiating relationship' when you have only arguments, and no power, to rely on. Let me add that even if a general lack of training in the tactics of negotiations may also have played a part, the prisoner in question was an exceptionally intelligent, articulate, and alert person, who had conferred with the advisory group concerning the legal aspects of the issue (the advisory group had brought the issue up first). Lack of training – which undoubtedly played a part in other contexts and which the authorities most likely were aware of in the light of their negative attitude to admittance of the advisory group – was thus hardly the crucial dimension here. (I add, however, that the importance of 'lack of training' may also be related to differences in power – as we shall see later.)

The issue of how the communications of the inmate councils were to be regulated – the question whether other rules might be needed for the councils than for the inmates as individuals – was presented in a long and well-formulated statement, and it created a certain interest among the lawyers from the Prison Department. They looked up from their papers: the idea of regarding the inmate council as an independent 'legal person' (the expression was not used) was apparently viewed as a sophisticated point. One of the representatives of the Prison Department nodded with interest. After the important statement (or better: speech) by the prisoners' representative, however, one of the representatives of the authorities from the work group took the floor, saying that this was certainly interesting, but that it had never been discussed in the work group. The chairman intervened, saying that the wording of the work group actually took the prisoner's point into account. The said representative then immediately changed his argumentation, and agreed with this: this was precisely what the wording did, he stated. In fact, the wording did nothing of the sort. Concerning this issue, the wording of the memorandum went as follows:

> The work group believes that the inmate councils ought to be allowed communication by letter and telephone with the mass media, organizations, and individuals, as well as with the inmate councils in other institutions, and in this connection enjoy freedom from censorship, all according to the principles applying to inmates in general . . .
>
> Also concerning the right of inmate councils and their representatives in this capacity to receive visits from the outside, the same principles are to apply as for visits with inmates in general . . .

Following an unclear contribution from a representative of the staff organizations, a representative of the Prison Department took the floor, giving the prisoner-delegate a certain measure of support. As the only one from the other side to do so, he expressed the view that there was a need for general rules concerning the inmate councils. The prisoner-delegate answered that they were searching precisely for such general guidelines concerning the councils in particular. He felt that since such rules had not been included in the memorandum of the work group, the memorandum contained a fundamental error. The above-mentioned representative of the authorities from the work group, however, now quickly intervened again, once again changing his argumentation by saying that 'I have a feeling that N.N. [the prisoner] is banging on open doors . . . We have explicitly stated that we in this matter think you ought to be allowed to communicate; . . . It's too bad that we did not have this present discussion in the work group, . . . but I don't really believe – in view of our discussions there – that it would have made any difference'. His tone of voice was irritated. The representative of the prisoners answered calmly that the rules included in the memorandum aimed at the treatment of the individual, and that such rules could not without more ado be made to apply to the inmate councils. He felt that even if everything were certain to work out well in practice, the rules also had to be right on the formal level. He then read aloud the excerpts from the memorandum quoted above. The chairman now returned to his view that the point made by the prisoner had been taken care of in the memorandum. Thereby, this interpretation was established as the main argument of the authorities. In more detail, the chairman answered that the sentences following the excerpts quoted above showed that the authors of the memorandum had meant to take the prisoner-delegate's objection into account. The 'following sentences' went like this:

> (Following the first passage quoted above). This implies that letters coming into or going out from inmate councils are in principle not to be censored, but that random tests may be made, and that envelopes and packages may

be examined in order to ensure that they do not contain forbidden objects of various sorts.

(Following the second passage quoted above). From this it follows that permission should in principle be given to receive visits which may not for special reasons be assumed to injure the inmate or others. As in connection with visits in general, due allowance must obviously be made for conditions concerning institutional organization, resources, and schedules.

Later on in the memorandum, however, these formulations were intended as *general and agreeable preliminary regulations for the treatment of the individual inmate.* And as far as the treatment of the individual inmate went, the memorandum later made a *series of important exceptions from the preliminary regulations,* as explained above. The view that the sentences were meant to take the prisoner-delegate's objection into account must therefore be characterized as at best grossly misleading.

And what happened then? No further support for his view, or for his feeling of having been tricked with regard to the implications of the memorandum, was given to the prisoner-delegate. And faced by all this 'legal expertise' the prisoner-delegate began to waver. 'Well then,' he said, 'our intentions are probably the same. Well – I think I'll wait a little.'

And with this, the debate concerning this topic was over. It was 11.45 a.m. on the second day of the talks. This part of the discussion gives an (however extreme) example of how the arguments of the prisoners were met.

After this battle, the participation of the prisoners for a long time seemed more half-hearted. Then came the last series of dying spasms.

*

Towards the end of the second day the prisoners and their advisors made a last attempt to have some concrete and precise results specified, and this termination of the talks deserves closer description.

Towards the end of the first day, a representative of the prisoners had raised the question whether one ought not to formulate in writing some of the points which the parties had agreed on earlier that day. This was given a flat refusal by the chairman, who hinted that one would return to the question of a final communiqué at the close of the second day. The prisoner, however, brought the question up again on the morning of the second day – the advisory group had emphasized the importance of having some of the conclusions that had been reached concretely specified. The chairman replied that first each point on the agenda ought to be discussed, and then – if an agreement was reached – a common communiqué ought to be formulated as a conclusion. The inmates found this to be sensible and reasonable. Against this background – and on the basis of the view that your position is stronger if you have formulated something in writing yourself – the prisoners and their advisors began during the lunch break to plan the formulation of their proposal for a final communiqué, and during the afternoon, the advisory group in the adjoining room began the last hectic writing-out of the proposal.

The prisoner-delegates, untrained as they were, were now beginning to feel very tired, a fact which impeded communication with the advisors, and which – during the intermissions which remained – prevented careful discussion of tactics. But this consequence of lack of training was also related to the prisoners' lack of power in the situation – through the agreement which the authorities had secured earlier, the advisors had no access to the conference room. The authorities must have known that such access would have improved communications, and to some degree eased the tactical planning of the inmates.

Nevertheless, the advisory group formulated a draft of a final communiqué, on the basis of information from the prisoners and with their interests in mind. Just before 4 p.m. they had their last reasonably thorough discussion with the inmates in the adjoining room, discussing and correcting the proposal. At about 4 p.m. the proposal was handed over by the prisoners to the representatives of the Prison Department.

The proposal contained a substantial number of concrete suggestions for decisions – what the inmate side feared was a final communiqué of a vague kind, not even guaranteeing the implications of the memorandum. As examples of how the advisory group tried to formulate proposals for concrete decisions, I shall recount what they wrote concerning visits in the cells (a main theme running through these proceedings as a whole) and concerning the communications of the inmate councils.

> *Visits in the rooms:* With regard to visits there is a difference of opinion between the prisoners and the Prison Department together with the representatives of the staff, concerning the principles involved. The prisoners believe that visits in the cells should gradually be introduced in the institutions. The representatives of the Prison Department, on the other hand, propose an expansion of the facilities for visits by equipping special visiting sections or pavilions. It is the view of the department that it is not possible to introduce visits in the cells on an experimental basis.

This proposal for an agreement in other words specifies not only the prisoners' principal view, but also an alternative standpoint in principle on the part of the authorities in the direction of enlarged visiting facilities through a special visiting section. The authorities stressed this alternative view as one of two possibilities in their own (adopted) proposal for a compromise after the preceding breakdown in 'negotiations'. The same alternative view was built into the memorandum of the work group in so far as it stressed the great need for improvements of an architectural kind, and it was a view which representatives of the authorities had explicitly advanced. In addition, the proposal contained suggestions for seven specific improvements of the visiting system.

> Concerning the *communications* of the inmates councils (item 2 from a list of 9 items concerning inmate councils): Inmate councils have the right to communicate by letter and by telephone with mass media, organizations, and

individuals, as well as with inmate councils in other institutions. Correspondence must not be read and telephone conversations must not be tapped, but
random tests may be made in the presence of representatives of the inmate
council, in order to ascertain that mail does not contain forbidden objects.

This item – specific rules for the communications of the inmate councils – was
included because it was of very great importance in principle, and because the
authorities, as mentioned earlier, had shown an 'interest' in this question.

Over and above the items concerning visits and inmate councils, the proposal
for an agreement contained five specified items concerning censorship (including telephone conversations), a recapitulation of the work group's specifications
concerning furloughs (with two small additions), and a proposal for a decision
concerning the system of leaves. Below we shall concentrate particularly on the
question of visits in the cells (an issue which we have already seen diluted) and
the communications of the inmate councils.

As already stated, the prisoners' proposal for an agreement was handed over
to the Prison Department at about 4 p.m. on the second day of the talks. It was
never presented by the chairman to the plenary meeting, a fact which must be said
to constitute a remarkable practice on the part of a chairman of a meeting. By 10
p.m. the meeting had gone through all of the items in the original memorandum
(with the exception of the question concerning the use of isolation cells, which
the prisoners proposed to postpone – partly because they wanted to be certain
that the meeting would arrive at a concrete final communiqué), with no mention
whatsoever of the proposal for a communiqué which had been handed in by the
prisoners.

At 10 p.m. the intention was to take a short break, but the break proved to be
a long one. During coffee it became known that the prisoners had handed in a
proposal for a final communiqué containing 'a number of biases'. The prisoners' representatives were rudely and very loudly rebuked for this by one of the
regional directors (who had not seen the proposal) – his main expression was
'a *damned* summary containing a series of biases'. On the authorities' side a certain excitement could be observed, but by and large no anxiety. The prisoners
actually said little or nothing. One of them stated, in a sullen tone of voice, that
if he could just get hold of a type-writer he could quickly rewrite this proposal
which was criticized so severely.

The meeting was not called to order before 10.50 p.m., after the Prison Department's representatives had conferred among themselves, and apparently with one
of the prisoners. The chairman opened the discussion by saying that the meeting
had now reached the question of the *communiqué*.

He told the audience that a summary had been received from the prisoners, but
that it contained 'biases' compared with 'what we had agreed on'. (Why he had a
monopoly of deciding what the meeting had agreed on was not mentioned.) The
chairman further stated that it was necessary to arrive at a relatively brief communiqué. 'And', he said, 'we have prepared a proposal for a brief communiqué

which gives a rather clear picture of what the meeting has agreed on.' By 'we' he meant the representatives of the Prison Department. The proposal was then read aloud. It went like this:

The participants in the talks at Österåker on the 11 and 12 January 1971 have agreed on the following statement:

> At the talks the following questions have been dealt with: furloughs; censorship of mail; the activities of the inmate councils; visiting conditions in the institutions; escapes and disappearances; the general atmosphere in the institutions; telephone booths; the system of leaves; payment for work and studies; work, studies, and other equivalent activities; the operation of the libraries; the occupational task of the psychologists; non-institutional treatment; the problems of the foreigners; the youth prison system; the women's prisons; and gift packages.
>
> A memorandum prepared by a special work group has provided the basis for the talks.
>
> With regard to the sections on furloughs, censorship of mail, and the activities of the inmate councils, agreements have been reached concerning the material content of the proposals which the [work] group has unanimously presented.
>
> With regard to the visiting conditions, agreement has been reached concerning the need to improve these according to the guidelines and presuppositions which the group has recommended, with the exception of the proposal concerning experimentation with visits in the rooms in closed institutions.
>
> With regard to the remaining sections of the memorandum, it has been possible to ascertain a large measure of agreement.
>
> In regard to the sections where agreement has been reached, the Prison Department intends as soon as possible to make the decisions and to draw up the provisions which the talks provide a basis for. To the extent that the talks, in connection with the remaining sections, call for special regulations, these will also be drawn up by the Prison Department.

Polished and very unspecified. The vague expression 'agreement concerning the material content' did not even provide a guarantee that the conclusions of the memorandum would be carried out. On one issue, however, the proposal was clear: visits in the rooms on an experimental basis in closed institutions, one of the few independent points really emphasized by the prisoners, were not to be permitted. And no alternative in the direction suggested by the prisoners' advisors was provided.

After the proposal had been read aloud, two prisoner-delegates mentioned that this certainly sounded just as sensible as everything else from the Prison Department, but that the prisoners would perhaps like to take a look at the proposal. Here, however, one of the representatives of the most important staff organization broke in. Clear and concise reservations were necessary in this communiqué, he said. Reservations had to be made concerning the staff situation, he forcefully reiterated. The chairman did not immediately understand – this clearly came as a surprise. The representative of the staff organization in question repeated harshly: '. . . We cannot accept that the inmate councils are to communicate as they want, we have said this before and we will insist on it now . . . And more staff is needed – it's simply the cold facts which tell you that . . . we must have guarantees that we get more staff'. The chairman replied that a break was necessary.

And a break was taken, from 11.15 p.m. to 00.15 a.m. During the break the representatives of the Prison Department conferred with the people from the staff organizations, and to some degree with the prisoners. The others walked back and forth in the corridors and waited. To some degree the people from the Prison Department seemed excited. At 00.15 the meeting was again called to order, and photostat copies of a proposal for a final communiqué had now been made. The proposal was also read by the chairman. The proposal was identical with the one suggested earlier, with the exception of two crucial reservations – precisely the two reservations wanted by the staff organizations. In the fourth passage the following had been added:

> With regard to the activities of the inmate councils this [that is, the agreement mentioned in the first sentence of the passage] implies, as far as the use of the telephone from closed institutions is concerned, that the requirements concerning permission relevant to the inmates individually are also to be applied to inmate councils.
>
> Preceding the final passage a new passage had been inserted:
> The carrying-out of the proposals is to take place to the extent permitted by economic and staff resources.

Through the first addition, the communiqué had become still more reserved. Through the second addition it had become almost completely diluted. The staff organizations had managed to get exactly what they wanted.

The inmates responded to this that even though they knew the hour was late, they would like to have a ten minutes' conversation about it. At 00.20 a.m. there was a new break. This break also lasted for almost an hour.

As usual the prisoners left the conference room and moved to their own adjoining room. Earlier the atmosphere in the adjoining room had always been lively and rather jocular. Now it was serious and actually depressed.

And at this moment, at half past twelve that night, the prisoners saw quite clearly their own fundamental powerlessness in the situation, even considering the strike 'weapon' and the 'negotiating' delegation. For the first time, these eight prisoners saw with complete clarity that they had no way of fundamentally threatening the adversary. One of them repeated three times in a row, loudly and in despair: 'We have no threat!', throwing his pencil on the table. A second inmate expressed it this way: 'They have complete power. They can do what they like'.

Someone asked what they were to do, and a third inmate replied with resignation 'I don't think it makes any difference what we do'.

At first the advisory group did not have much to say, either. They suggested publicizing in the press the proposal for a final communiqué which the prisoners had handed in, and which had never been presented to the meeting – in order to show how the prisoners had understood what the meeting had agreed on. The suggestion to do so was received positively but hardly with enthusiasm. At 1 a.m. a guard looked in and asked if they would soon be ready. The reply was that it would only take another 15 minutes or so. During these last 15 minutes, the advisory group made a final attempt to save a little of the inmates' cause. One of them made a short and forceful statement, in which he stressed how the last series of events had shown how little the authorities could be trusted. Then he proposed a few changes in the existing proposal for a final communiqué: deletion of the two conditions of the staff organizations concerning the communications of the inmate council and the economic and staff resources; introduction of the term 'concrete content' instead of 'material content' in connection with the agreements made on the basis of the original memorandum; an addition to the effect that the new regulations concerning furloughs which the parties had agreed on were to become effective on 15 March at the latest (this date had been mentioned as a possibility by the Prison Department); and an addition stating that the representatives of the inmates, if not the others, felt that visits in the cells ought gradually to be introduced in the institutions. With these suggestions for changes, the inmates returned to the conference room at 1.15 a.m., after an hour's break, entering the very last phase of the meeting.

The last phase was short but dramatic. The chairman opened by asking whether the parties accepted the proposal of the Prison Department. One of the representatives of the staff organizations answered that the proposal of the Prison Department was accepted. The fact that this proposal was actually sprinkled with reservations from the staff organizations was not mentioned.

The chairman looked inquiringly towards the inmates, and one of them said: 'Yes, we have also accepted the wording which the Prison Department has proposed, but on the other hand not the additions which N.N. [the representative of the staff organizations] has provided'. He then briefly recapitulated the changes which the prisoners wished to have introduced.

At this point the atmosphere in the room became restless. The chairman said that he found it difficult to understand what the inmates wanted to guard themselves against – everything was already there in the original memorandum. One of the inmates replied: 'This fear is based on decenniums of distrust . . . and what we feel is that not all issues raise the question of staff and economic resources . . . I personally do believe that it will turn out all right, but I can't speak only on my own behalf here, I can only speak for about 600 on security [inmates in the security region], and I know the attitudes of most of the boys . . .' From the staff side it was maintained that there was to be no delay. A prisoner replied that the staff could then just as well make their reservations known to the press, and not introduce them in a common communiqué.

The chairman now stated: 'I might consider adding what you wanted to have added concerning visits in the rooms, if you will defer to N.N. [the representative of the staff organizations] concerning the other items'. This change, however, was entirely unimportant from the point of view of the prisoners: it only expressed the view of the prisoners concerning visits, and nothing about agreement on alternative reforms between the parties. The prisoners answered that they might let the general reservation as regards necessary resources remain, but not the reservation concerning the inmate council's use of the telephone. They said that if the staff wanted this reservation as well, they had to state it as their own item, and not as an agreement. The spokesman of the staff organizations answered that this reservation also had to be maintained, because the members of the staff organizations wanted it. His words were: 'You are to accept this . . . We think that the communiqué is to look this way, which we have now agreed to on the part of the Prison Department and the staff organizations'. One prisoner could not understand why just this partial question was to be maintained in a so-called general communiqué. The chairman replied that a communiqué of this kind is a compromise, that the prisoners had now had their formulations improved, and that the staff also had to receive something comparable.

A brief discussion took place concerning the concepts of 'concrete content' and 'material content'. The prisoners could not understand the meaning of 'material', and the chairman stated that 'the work group has prepared a proposal for a legal text; the danger for us, of course, is that if we write "concrete" we will be bound by the wording . . . When you are talking about "concrete" proposals, do you mean that we in all details are to be bound by that text in regard to changes in the prison regulations mentioned by the work group? If so, our views on this are completely different'. A representative of the authorities could not understand why the difference between 'concrete' and 'material' was so important; a prisoner asked why the word 'concrete' was so dangerous then; a representative of the Prison Department answered that he, for his part, could not allow himself to be bound by details; the same prisoner then said that what they wanted to ensure was the time for the carrying into effect of the reforms (15 March), and since the authorities were willing to keep this date, one might perhaps just as well use the word 'material'. Another prisoner murmured apologetically: 'Well, then, I have in other words probably misunderstood the word "material".' A regional director answered bluntly and half aloud: 'I have certainly heard the word "material" before.'

Then came the finale, which – like all the quotes given above – is reproduced verbatim from the tape recording of the meeting and own notes:

A REGIONAL DIRECTOR (breaks in agitatedly): 'This is simply to make fools of us all, since we are sitting here, a number of grown-up people who know what we have stated and promised. This is just to jeer at us, when you're now trying to get in such changes. Personally I agree with everything in this communiqué!' (Gets up and walks towards the door. A number of others, especially regional directors and representatives of the staff organizations, also get up; the prisoners and the representatives of the Prison Department remain seated.)

THE CHAIRMAN: 'The only change, then, will be this on page 2 concerning visits in the rooms. There we'll include the reservation you wanted . . . We cannot agree to the other changes'.

A REGIONAL DIRECTOR (half aloud): 'It's those fools out there [the prisoners' advisory group] who have created all of this'.

A PRISONER: 'But we have not intended to make fools of you. The reason why we question this business about concrete and material is that we are so damned uneducated . . . You must try to help us, and make it so that you do not leave the table before it is ready . . .'

THE CHAIRMAN: '. . . We were supposed to wait here for ten minutes, and we had to wait for an hour [the corresponding and equally long deliberations of the staff organizations are not mentioned]. Then it must be understood more or less as if you're making fools of us, when you're bringing up such subtle nuances'.

SAME PRISONER: 'That's probably the risk you have to take when you're negotiating with people of our category'.

THE CHAIRMAN: 'Our offer, in any case, is to change this concerning visits in the rooms, and to let you include your reservation on that point. The remaining changes cannot be introduced in this communiqué'.

A PRISONER: 'Are you prepared for this limit of 15 March with regard to purring the regulations concerning furloughs into effect?'

A REPRESENTATIVE OF THE PRISON DEPARTMENT: '. . . That might be possible, but we cannot say for sure. We have a work load today which you are perhaps not quite aware of . . . We can't in any way give any guarantees'.

(Movement in the room; all of those who have risen walk towards the doors.)

A PRISONER: 'Can't you make it if you give priority to it?'

ANOTHER PRISONER: 'We can, of course, give the Prison Department a chance . . . ?'

THE CHAIRMAN: 'The promises which we have made are recorded by the tape recorder. But we can't specify a date which we may not be able to keep'.

THE FIRST PRISONER (in a resigned tone of voice): 'Can't we accept this?'

(A murmuring of 'yes' from the prisoners.)

THE FIRST PRISONER: 'But at any rate we want the protocols [from the tape recording] from the meeting'.

THE CHAIRMAN: 'You shall of course have those.'[21]

(Many stand waiting impatiently by the doors. Everybody is clearly expecting the meeting to be adjourned.)

THE CHAIRMAN: 'There is one other little thing which I think we should do before we depart: There is one man who has pulled a very heavy load here, namely N.N. [a representative of the authorities from the work group, a regional director who during the discussion had been almost alone in presenting the memorandum of the work group]. And he is 50 years old today. *I suggest we give him a round of applause!*'

(General applause for the representative of the authorities in the work group; he is congratulated as the room is emptied.)

*

It must be added that in February, March, and April, new circulars were issued concerning the furlough system, the inmate councils, and the visiting and censorship systems respectively.

In the circular concerning inmate councils (which simultaneously provides guidelines for 'joint councils', which are to include inmates *and* staff), a number of vague stipulations may be found limiting the councils' freedom of action.

Thus, as a point of departure it is stated that 'with regard to the councils' ways of operating, it is up to the governor – after having heard the joint council – to specify more detailed guidelines for this'. Furthermore, the principles guiding the councils' forms of operation are specified as follows: 'In order for an inmate council to be regarded as representative in relation to the prison system, it is *imperative* that the representatives are elected by secret ballot, *controlled by the institution*' (my italics); 'the activity of the inmate councils must be regarded as resting, among other things, on the assumption that matters concerning the individual staff member or inmate are not to be discussed in a way that is insulting to the individual, or that can end in improper collective actions' (what are discussions 'insulting to the individual', and what are 'improper collective actions'?); 'just as it is important for the administration of the institution and the staff to support and encourage well-functioning inmate councils, so is it urgent that the administration intervenes against inmate councils which break adopted regulations' (what are the consequences of this for possible collective actions?); 'it is the duty of the governor to see to it that the activity of the inmate councils does not take place in such a way that order and security in the institution are at stake, or that the treatment program over and above this is damaged' (what is meant by the 'treatment program' being 'damaged'?).

Furthermore, the governor is given a wide power of controlling the inmate councils' opportunities of meeting, In this connection, it is stated that 'inmate councils are to be given an opportunity to meet regularly in the institution to the necessary extent [and] in the way decided by the governor . . .'; 'to meetings at which special issues are dealt with, inmate councils are to be able to call in special inmates staying in regular sections, and, if it is considered appropriate by the administration of the institution, also from special sections – announcement of meetings are to take place in the way decided on by the administration of the institution;' 'representatives of the inmate council are to be given facilities for keeping in contact with each other between meetings as well, subject to the governor's permission . . .'

In the light of the debate at the so-called 'negotiations', the further stipulations concerning the inmate councils' facilities for external communication are of special interest. Under the heading 'contacts with mass media, etc.' it is stated: 'The inmate council or its representatives may communicate with mass media, organizations, and individuals according to the same principles as are in force for the individual inmate, and which are prescribed in the prison regulations. The circumstance that the inmate represents the inmate council does not in and of itself give occasion for any exception from existing regulations concerning examination of letters and telephone contact'. It appears that the prisoners' view at the 'negotiations' is explicitly taken into account – in the sense of being explicitly excluded. Here, no mention is made of the view that an independent regulation of the communications of the inmate council was 'taken care of' in the memorandum of the work group. Concerning 'contacts with other inmate councils' it is stated, inter alia, that in connection with the examination of letters, the rules for individual inmates are to take effect, and – as if to rub it in – the following is said by way of conclusion concerning the representatives' visiting facilities: 'With regard to the question of the right of a representative of an inmate council to receive visits in the capacity of representative, the same principle as is in force for visits to the individual in general is to be adopted'.

This is all the circular says specifically about the inmate councils. The authorities have secured themselves against everything.

The new guidelines for the application of the regulations concerning visits follow the very vague lines which were drawn up in the memorandum of the work group (see above). Of course, nothing is said here concerning experimentation with visits in the cells in closed institutions. More interesting, however, is the fact that nothing is said concerning visits in the cells in open institutions – despite the fact that the work group, as indicated earlier, proposed this on certain conditions. The interpretation of the agreement concerning 'the material content' is, in other words, wide. Furthermore, it is of interest to note that concerning the one item where the work group was precise – it emphasized the right to receive visits twice a month, two hours at a time, as a minimum standard for all institutions – the new guidelines have become imprecise. Following a vague formulation to the effect that 'the length of visits must naturally be determined as dependent above all on the supply of staff and the number of visiting rooms', the circular states: 'One should, however, endeavour to stretch the visiting time as far as possible, with the aim in mind that the inmate should have the right to receive visits at least twice a month, two hours at a time'. To sum up, the prisoners' original demand emphasized the desirability of having six hours of visiting per week. In the work group, this was reduced to four hours per month. In the guidelines the number of hours is reduced to a vague goal.

The new *guidelines for the application of the regulations concerning censorship* also follow the vague dues from the memorandum of the work group (see above). I should like to emphasize what this means to the great majority of inmates – those in *closed institutions*. While freedom from censorship (not freedom from 'examination' of the contents of the envelope) '*ought . . .* to be the rule' [my italics] with regard to written correspondence with family and other close persons, an individual test of 'dependability' must take place before other correspondence is freed from censorship.

To be sure, the guidelines emphasize general freedom from censorship on the part of inmates in *open institutions*. But liberal censorship in open institutions was already an established principle in the prison regulations, so that little new is added by this.

Finally, in *the new regulations concerning furloughs*, the new time intervals etc., proposed by the work group in its memorandum are by and large repeated: time intervals which only imply a very small improvement. This improvement in the regulations concerning furloughs is the only change of actual regulations introduced through the whole process (the other changes are merely new guidelines for the interpretation of existing regulations), and it is as far as I can see the only observable positive result of it all. The guidelines for inmate councils are almost completely restrictive, and the new guidelines for the application of regulations concerning visits and censorship are in part very vague, and in part still very restrictive.

With regard to the improvements in the regulations concerning furloughs, it must be added that many feel these would have come in any case at about this time.[22]

For this, then, the prisoners had struck and 'negotiated'. Many promises have been broken, and the prisons remain just as solid.

*

As an epilogue it must be mentioned that a new hunger strike broke out in Swedish prisons in the beginning of June 1971. About 700 prisoners in about 13 institutions went on strike in sympathy with three inmates who were sitting – and had long been sitting – in the isolation section in Norrköping. The new strike, however, could also be interpreted as reflecting dissatisfaction with the outcome of the 'negotiations'.

The strike, however, attracted little attention in the mass media. Other news was more important, and prison strikes had apparently become more commonplace. Even *Dagens Nyheter* - which again faithfully supported the prisoners – by and large carried brief reports far inside the newspaper. Besides, it was summer, and in outside society the strike was only like a rather distant rumbling – as a kind of signal from far away indicating that something was wrong in society.

This time, the prison authorities did not have to rush to the institution on which the strike was focused. Now they simply said that suspension of the isolation of the three inmates was out of the question. On the radio the Director of Prisons stated that the three inmates were not isolated – they were being given treatment in individual rooms. To the fact that the head psychiatrist of the security region had called the isolation 'human torment', the Director stated that they had other doctors to look after the inmates. When asked whether this meant that he doubted the qualifications of the regional head psychiatrist, he simply answered that he would not make any statements concerning the qualifications of the regional head psychiatrist. This time no soft tone was necessary. The strike was no surprise.

The end of it all was that after nine days of hunger strike, representatives of the Prison Department condescended to initiate talks with the inmate council at Hall security institution – the central institution in the region concerned. It is unclear why they went there when the initial point of the strike was Norrkoping, and the content of the talks is unknown. However, it was announced that talks would be initiated with the inmate council in Norrköping – and with the three isolated inmates – after two more days; that is, after 11 days of hunger strike. Thus, on Friday 11 June, representatives of the Prison Department arrived for talks at Norrköping. At this point the strike was naturally receding rapidly, and later that day it was called off. The isolation of the three inmates was not suspended. One of the three was an important narcotics dealer; the conservative newspaper *Svenska Dagbladet* had severely criticized the strike in view of this, and the inmate council at Hall had stated that they could understand the view of the authorities with regard to one of the three inmates. But the three were given certain material reliefs.

Moreover, the prisoners were promised new talks in the fall of 1971. It was emphasized that the talks were not to constitute negotiations . . .[23]

*

The prisoners have no built-in possibility of threatening the prison system. They do not contribute to the system, and therefore have nothing permanent which they may threaten to withdraw. Here lies the main basis for the development in connection with the Swedish prison strike.[24]

For the sake of accuracy, I should emphasize that by this I do not mean that a prison strike and 'negotiations' such as those we have witnessed in Sweden are ineffective in general terms: such actions may give the participants a feeling of solidarity and a common cause, and when the mass media cooperate they can show at least some receptive outsiders that the expelled are human beings with abilities for action and democratic decision-making. Such effects may be regarded as important. However, here the question of the consequences of the actions as regards the structure of the prisons constitutes my criterion of 'effect'.

Let me, moreover, add that also in relation to this criterion of 'effect', prisoners' actions may be effective – under general conditions very different from those present in the Swedish situation. I will return to this below.

The situation which has been described here in relation to the prisoners concerns the expelled in general. In the first place, it concerns the vagrants, the mentally ill, the old, the handicapped, and so on, in their respective institutions. But in the second place, it concerns these groups in a broader societal sense: through the way in which the expelled are related to the larger society. In our society, the expelled are expelled from society precisely because they – according to the way in which 'contribution' is defined in our society – *do not contribute to it:* precisely because they are not 'productive', precisely because they do not 'render anything' to the capitalistic – or state-capitalistic – system. This may be seen most clearly in connection with the vagrants, who 'bum around' and wander 'aimlessly' about, according to the government and the public. It may also be seen clearly in connection with the criminals, who – by and large – have stolen from others and thereby shown how they are 'parasites' rather than contributors. For all of these groups, the basis for being expelled by society is precisely that they are not contributors to society. Again I am using this term in the more narrow sense of their not being providers of a contribution which is built into the social system, and I am thinking of 'contribution' as it is defined in our society. They are not positively productive.

And thereby an important necessary condition for organization among the expelled in general is lacking. Because it follows that such an organization cannot effectively threaten with the withdrawal of anything. If such an organization tried to threaten with a withdrawal of something, it would in a sense just be held up to ridicule, unless very powerful forces in the environment provided it with support. As we have seen, even massive press support is often not enough. And in addition, the powerful forces in the environment often fail to appear.

I have here placed little emphasis on the difference between joint councils, etc., on the one hand, and separate independent inmate councils on the other. Despite the fact that this difference is continually stressed in political discussions, and despite the fact that it has been strongly emphasized by the defenders of the expelled, I am of the opinion that it is relatively uninteresting and not very fundamental. It is obvious that any counter-organization from the bottom must be based on independent councils etc., rather than on pleasant cooperative bodies. My point in this section is that even if the point of departure is such an independent fight for one's interests, the expelled in a structural and fundamental way lack a basis for organization.

*

From the above analysis it follows that one must go about it much more radically. A necessary condition for organization among the expelled is to alter the basic condition governing their existence, which is to alter the very grounds for their being expelled: *their lack of contribution.*

Such a change may go in one of two 'directions': 'upwards' or 'sideways'. The difference is crucial. I will discuss them both, in the above-mentioned order.

4. The positive organization

By an 'upwards' change in the basic condition governing the existence of the expelled is meant that the groups in question become contributors in relation to the coercive system (unit, institution, total society) which at one time expelled them, or which is responsible for executing their expulsion. I do not know how this is to occur in practice on a very large scale, but it is conceivable within smaller units. For example, it is conceivable that the prisoners begin to 'contribute' economically to the prison, through work in modern factories in the institution. (The fact that to some degree they do so today may be seen from the budgets for the modern factory prisons. See the budget of the Norwegian Ministry of justice for 1971.) And it is conceivable in a more subtle way: in countries which introduce 'negotiations' of the kind described for Sweden, the authorities may over a period of time develop a certain dependence on the prisoners' contribution to a pseudo-democratic process. For example, internationally 'negotiations' with prisoners are likely to cause a sensation as something advanced. Through this the authorities – who also seek an international reputation – will in a somewhat paradoxical way become dependent on the contribution of the prisoners – the contribution to the maintenance of pseudo-democracy. In their hopelessly difficult situation, the prisoners may in fact contribute.

The notion that the development in the Swedish prison system may be used in gaining an aura of legitimacy from good publicity internationally is actually more than a loose hypothesis. As early as in April 1971 the Swedish Director of Prisons issued a lengthy press release in English – intended for foreign countries – concerning the 'negotiations' etc. in the prison system. (*Bo Martinsson:* 'Prison Democracy in Sweden', Viewpoint, Swedish Information Service, 16 April 1971). The Swedish development is here presented as an interesting and progressive experiment in democratization. Concerning the 'negotiations', the director proudly states, inter alia:

> According to those who are learned in law, the negotiations which started November 30 1970, at Österåker prison are unique in history. They placed on an equal footing the delegates of the country's 5000 prisoners on one side and representatives of the correctional authorities and the personnel organizations on the other . . .

Thus, to a limited degree it is conceivable that expelled groups may become contributors 'upwards'. However, let us for a moment imagine that the limitations on this are taken away: that the prisoners, and other expelled groups, really do become contributors to their respective systems of control. In this event, the point of principle which I should like to get at in this section stands out in bolder relief. A natural result of the contribution would be that the group in question would, through the transition to organization on this basis, at the same time cease to be a counter-organization, and to a large extent become a positive organization supporting the system which originally was to be fought. As real contributors to the prison, the prisoners would have something on which to build their organization, because they would have something which they could threaten to withdraw in 'quiet periods' as well. At the same time, however, they would positively support the prison, and – if not directly build it up – at least participate in keeping it going as society's solution to a social problem. To reiterate, they would contribute to it. Similarly as contributors to the social welfare system (if this is conceivable) the handicapped – or the 'retarded' – would have something on which to build an organization, again because they would have something which they could threaten to withdraw. But again, these groups too would participate in supporting and building up the existing – degrading and stigmatizing – welfare system. Contact groups established by and for clients would, for example, easily be characterized by this. Generally, this is the problem of benevolent organizations in relation to the welfare system.

In this way, then, there is a built-in fundamental ambiguity in the process of becoming a contributor 'upwards'. You establish a basis for opposing the larger system, because the larger system becomes dependent on you (here we probably find the deeper reason why prison guards are taught to avoid 'dependency relationships' with inmates, etc.), but at the same time you are incorporated as a positive supportive organization within the larger system. You do not negate the fundamental premises of the system; you become – in the most real sense of the word – a positivist.

This is not the case only for those who are at present expelled. I used the word 'positivist', and what I have said here obviously concerns contributing scientists. And the parallel to the situation of the workers' organizations is clear. The great *rapprochement* between the workers' organizations and the capitalists, together with the fact that we – despite the whole development of the labour movement in our country – still have a capitalistic system, shows the positivism of the workers' organizations in relation to those who were to be the adversary. The basis of their positivism lies in, among other things, the ambiguity discussed here.

I believe the analysis may be carried yet another step. As contributors you may organize: the main system is dependent on you. At the same time you yourself in a new way become dependent on the main system. To be sure, as expelled you were dependent on the main system – you were dependent on the mercy of the system and the crumbs from the master's table. As organized contributors you are dependent in a new way. You cannot have a *prisoners'* organization without a prison. You cannot have a workers' organization without employers. The prisoners' organization presupposes the prison, as the workers' organization presupposes capitalism. The dissolution of the main systems would lead to the dissolution of the organizations. The organization should, in my opinion, work for the dissolution of the main system – and thereby for the dissolution of the organization itself. This is not only psychologically extremely difficult. The prisoners' organization and the workers' organization underline the existence of the prisoners and of the workers, and thereby of the main systems themselves. Through 'negotiations', the main systems also receive their share, in a 'legitimate' way and through consensus, and thereby they are strengthened. 'Negotiations' support the main system, even if both parties have a reasonable bargaining position; even if those at the lower level in the organization have something to place behind their demands. The employers have discovered this. It must be essential to avoid the same development in the prison context.

5. The negative organization

By a 'sideways' change in the basic condition governing the situation of the expelled is meant that the group becomes a contributor in relation to social units other than the system responsible for expelling the group or executing its expulsion. If the other social unit in question is itself in protest and has at least some power in relation to the system that expels, it is conceivable that organization among the expelled will remain negative; will remain untransformed to a positive organization supporting the expulsive system.

The 'sideways' contribution of the expelled – their contribution to other social units – what might it consist of? When powerful forces are the defenders of the weak, the powerful are given new legitimacy. When powerful forces are the defenders of the weak, this may give them a certain ideological renewal. When powerful forces, are the defenders of the weak, this may activate problem solutions which otherwise might be overlooked. And above all, when outside forces look for material unmasking how society really operates, the prisoners are among the groups who can really tell. More than anyone, prisoners and other expelled groups can provide information telling how our social structure actually operates. In general, we have not used much imagination or time in seeking ways in which the expelled may contribute to social units outside the local system of coercion, and resources should be devoted to this, because otherwise the expelled easily become only an appendix to the powerful – at the bottom of their list of priorities. Examples of this may be found – thus, the cursory treatment of penal policy among the (existing) political parties constitutes a clear example. The traditional political parties – at least the more established ones – are probably too dependent on other large groups – the electorate, which is in opposition to the expelled – to make it possible for the expelled to become contributors, Another way of saying this is perhaps that the political parties have entered into a relationship with the electorate, and 'public opinion', which makes them no longer interested in changing 'public opinion'.

From this it follows that the traditional political parties are far from necessarily the right type of social unit. At the same time, the outside social units in question must be political – in the general sense of having it as their goal to influence social structure and its system of power. Among other things, this is a necessary – but not sufficient – condition for having power themselves, and thus for being able to work effectively for the expelled. In other words, the work for the expelled must be politicized.

Now, which outside political units with power might identify sufficiently with the expelled to make the expelled contributors in the relationship? In the United States, the movements inside the prisons are to a large extent tied to broad racial groupings and conflicts in the outside society. For the present, it is difficult to trace similar points of contact in the Scandinavian countries, a fact which makes the task more difficult. A general point of view may, however, be presented. Such external units must probably have a high ranking on some dimensions of power and a low ranking on others – the latter in order to provide a basis of identification with the expelled. Possibly, radical political youth organizations might constitute examples. The most important of them have a certain influence while at the same time – owing to the age level – being in part outside and nearer to the expelled. From the occupational sector, large groups such as the social workers perhaps constitute a corresponding example. But it must be admitted that examples of such units are not easily found. Groups and organizations tend to be consistent – either they have power on several dimensions or on none.

Possibly, one should therefore rather seek groups not yet in power, but on the road towards power -law students, social work students, etc. (To some degree political youth organizations constitute examples of this as well.) In relation to these groups, the expelled may – through material exposing the power system – provide a particularly important contribution to awakening the groups in question before they begin to take part in the shaping of society.

But in the last analysis, the outside force must be the radical part of the working class – the class to which the prisoners belong, and with which the prisoners have concrete interests in common. The activation of the other groups mentioned above may be steps towards such a future relationship.

Thus, there are latent possibilities in interaction with external protesting political units, Through this interaction, it is possible for the expelled to avoid the misfortune of the positive organization. *And here the expelled – however indirectly – become the most serious threat to the coercive system.*

In Norway we have seen a development which perhaps constitutes the first, slight, beginning of this. On a day in May 1971, 120 of the 150 prisoners at Ullersmo National Prison near Kløfta ceased work. The work strike lasted for about ten days, and KROM gave it full support. The concrete demands concerned higher wages (the average wage was 80 øre – 13 cents per hour) and an arrangement for having an independent inmate council. The demands were not met; the prison authorities rejected them, referring to budgetary considerations and to a committee appointed by the Prison Department with the aim of examining the question of democratization in the prison. The same committee was also referred to during several later inmate attempts to organize (see below), thus having a postponing and suppressive effect on the inmates' independent attempts. No sham negotiations were entered into between prisoners and authorities; the strike was handled in a tough way by the latter (for example, all striking prisoners were immediately isolated), so that the Swedish development was in fact avoided (even if this, then, was due more to the attitude of the authorities than to that of the prisoners). The authorities handled the situation in a rather unskillful way. To an important Oslo evening paper the Minister of justice, a social democrat, stated bluntly that 'a continual process aiming at a humanization of the prison system is taking place. The inmates in Norwegian prisons have nothing to complain about, nor with regard to adjustment to society'. The statement was presented under the five-column title 'The Minister of Justice: THE PRISONERS HAVE NOTHING TO COMPLAIN ABOUT.' The Minister also refused to let the press interview the prisoners' representatives: 'We cannot let just anybody into the institutions, that would create disorder. There must be order in the institutions'. Simultaneously, a certain articulate opinion, positive to the demands of the prisoners, developed in various political circles outside. The most significant result of the strike was the fact that two important political youth organizations, several important politicians, a number of social work students, as well as others, openly supported the action and/or the demands of the prisoners. More specifically, to some degree they gave the impression that they might go ahead with these matters independently – outside the prison – and the evening paper quoted above could conclude, in a political commentary: 'The Minister of Justice without Support in the Ullersmo Case – Pihl, Kielland and Haugland [social democrats of radical inclination, MPs] Support the Prisoners' Demands'. It appears that this central point was much more threatening to the prison authorities than the strike itself. The prisons do not become insolvent even if a part of their income is lost, and the prisoners' action was calm and quiet, in the sense that the internal security was hardly threatened by the action in and of itself. The prison governor stated to a newspaper that 'the worst that could happen was that the prisoners got the feeling that forces outside backed them up'. This, he said, could 'make the crisis acute'. Considerable evidence indicates that this was not the real fear; statements of sympathy, etc., which were stopped by the prison, nevertheless got in through the newspapers without the action becoming any more 'acute' in the intern al system. To be sure, this was the first serious Norwegian prison strike – comparable to the October strike in Sweden – so that the element of surprise was probably still present. The real fear of the authorities nevertheless seemed to be the flash of interest which more powerful outside political forces seemed to take in the matter, against the coercive system. Such outside resistance is dangerous to the coercive system, because the forces in question may go over and round, thus getting power without entering into a positive contributive relationship to the coercive system itself.

I do not think it is nationalistic reasons that make me view the development of the first Norwegian prison strike in more positive terms than the Swedish action. To be sure, the above-mentioned interest among the more powerful forces in the environment of the Norwegian prisons on this occasion proved to be short-lived. During the following summer, in 1972, a new wave of prison strikes occurred, in connection with the founding of a prisoners' organization – The Norwegian Prisoners' Trade Union. The organization spread to several prisons, and actions occurred among the prisoners in at least 6 major prisons. The authorities were extremely adverse to the development, the press gave extensive – and largely negative – coverage to it, and few or no politically important individuals or groups outside dared to support the prisoners. (Norwegian KROM, of course, supported the prisoners strongly.) In other words, the road ahead is very long and thorny. Among other things, the road is probably dependent on the general economic situation in outside society: in periods of depression, outside political life is likely to be less preoccupied with prison issues, and less attentive to signals from the prisoners. Such periods may be trying. Yet, the Ullersmo strike of 1971 may be viewed as a not entirely insignificant gain – as a very first beginning. The support of the press is important, but the power of the press is largely limited to the period of publication, and fades when the news again disappears from the headlines. The power of actual political organizations is more solid and long-term, though it may be stimulated through the mass media.

Simultaneously, it will be important to warn Norwegian prisoners against converting the prison issues into internal matters, through 'negotiations' etc. – thus following the development in Sweden. Perhaps it will be difficult to warn them effectively against this, because there are so many pressing, short-term questions of reform which to-day can only be solved through the favours of the authorities, and because the Norwegian prisoners themselves have demanded negotiations (in connection with the establishment of the Prisoners' Trade Union in 1972). So far the Norwegian authorities have not understood what they might gain through 'negotiations', and they have therefore flatly refused them. If this changes, it is possible that the Norwegian development of strikes will follow in the Swedish track. Therefore, warning the prisoners is important. The end result of the Swedish process has clearly shown that even short-term questions of reform are not solved as internal matters.[25]

Thus, the possibility of a future, continual interaction between more powerful political organizations and the expelled gives hope, even if this is an ideal and even if it is conceivable only through a very long-term process. The main goal of the expelled must, to begin with, be that of attracting the attention of outside organizations, as the first Ullersmo strike to some degree did.

And the task must then not only be that of finding external support for the internal battle. A main part of the battle itself, against the coercive system, will have to be waged outside the ranks of the expelled. The outsiders will be able to use the large quantity of illustrative material, exposing the system, which the expelled may bring forth through their own actions inside the coercive system. Not the least illustrative, and therefore useful, material for organizations outside is the unmasking of the real authoritarian character of the coercive system which internal activity may bring about. Everything, from co-operation concerning complaints on matters of principle to larger collective actions, may here be relevant. The authoritarian refusal of the prison system to the demands of wage increase etc. on the part of the Ullersmo prisoners in 1971 (and also in 1972), the prison's refusal to give the inmates contact with the press, its stepping of statements of sympathy from the outside, etc. had such an illustrative or unmasking character, which 'negotiations' inside the system would only have remasked. In this way, the expelled themselves are given a very important role in the struggle. Through their 'practice' they will prevent the outsiders from becoming nothing but sterile 'theoreticians'. But for the expelled, the main bat-tle itself must – as I hope the preceding paragraphs have shown – nevertheless be indirect. Thereby, the expelled will in other words be less independent than we optimistically might hope for, and the original Swedish belief that the 'walls can be torn down from the inside' becomes an illusion. I am sorry to say I believe this to be realistic.

The fear – in itself quite understandable – of being 'manipulated' from the outside, which was present in the Swedish situation, is a fear which in fact must be overcome; restraint only implies that the system 'manipulates'. But even this, then, is not enough. The outsiders must themselves fight, from the outside.

*

Now, the further question is how such external political organizations may con-cretely be activated into joining in a struggle together with and for the expelled. Below I shall discuss some aspects of this tactical-strategic problem. One possi-bility is the establishing of direct contact between the expelled in the institutions and the external organizations. Such direct contact, however, implies a danger – at least if it constitutes the first contact between the expelled and their external partners. To begin with, the external partners will be poorly trained for the han-dling of the task and the struggle. In terms of knowledge and political know-how, political organizations will not be particularly well prepared for tasks within the field of penal and correctional policy – even if they are previously identified with the cause of the prisoners. If a (gradual) training in the situation and issues of the expelled does not take place, radical political youth organizations may, for exam-ple, possibly support 'negotiations' between the prisoners and the authorities. They may do 50 on the basis of an oversimplified comparison with the situation of contributing groups in outside society, and by trusting – again in an oversimpli-fied way – the insight of the authorities.

In other words, it will be essential to introduce a connecting link between the expelled and the other organizations, a connecting link intensely trained in the politics of the expelled, a connecting link which may function as the 'party' of the expelled. This connecting link must exist outside the coercive system repressing the expelled (but may very well consist of people who have earlier been under that system), because only then will they be sufficiently free to act. In the Swedish situation analysed above, KRUM in part operated as such a con-necting organization; yet the organization viewed the internal awakening of the prisoners as their primary task. Such a perspective would have been correct if the prisoners had been a group with independent potential power. Such, however, is not the situation of the prisoners, and what I am stressing here is a connecting organization which sees communication both ways as its task, and which is par-ticularly geared towards extracting and interpreting to outsiders the large quantity of exposing material coming from the expelled inside the coercive system; an organization which is geared towards bringing the material out to the right – and more powerful- organizations.

Let me add that in relation to this external connecting organization, it makes sense for the expelled to have their 'representatives'. To amplify, earlier I mentioned that even with independent inmate councils – in contrast to joint councils – the expelled will in a structural and fundamental way lack a basis for organization, and that the difference between joint councils and separate inmate councils thereby is rather uninteresting. When saying this, I had in mind joint councils/inmate councils seen in relation to the coercive system which the expelled are exposed to. This, however, does not mean that bodies representative of the expelled are unimportant in relation to the external connecting organization. On the contrary, in this relationship such arrangements may, under certain conditions, contribute to making the channelling of the material from the expelled more effective. Thus, it is essential for the prisoners, when electing representatives, to view their representatives as participants in this relationship, and not primarily in the relationship to the prison and its organs.

*

I have suggested that contact between the prisoners and an outside, externally orientated, connecting organization is something which the coercive system above all has reason to fear – because it may constitute the most effective type of connection with outside and powerful organizations. Now, are there any examples showing that the representatives of the coercive system do in fact fear such contact with a connecting organization, examples showing that it constitutes a weak spot in the armour of the coercive system?

There are numerous examples which at least may very reasonably be interpreted in this direction. For example, Norwegian KROM has tried to function as an externally orientated connecting link to the outside world. From the many legal and illegal attempts on the part of the system to break the connection between the prisoners and KROM, it appears that such externally orientated activity seems threatening to the prison system. Below I shall briefly recapitulate some of the attempts.

The first example was referred to in Part II of this book, but may be mentioned here in a different context. During the fall of 1968, just after the establishment of KROM, the Norwegian Prison Department – the highest authority in the prison system – decided to deny KROM an opportunity of sending a brief and neutral mimeographed account of the organization to the prisoners. The account simply called attention to the existence of the organization, and had an attached form which could be filled out and returned by those who wished to become members. In their answer to the application from the association, in which the association emphasized, inter alia, the importance of *co-operation between the organization and the prisoners*, the Prison Department wrote: 'In this connection the Prison Department wishes to state: One generally does not oppose inmates' seeking and maintaining membership in associations or organizations . . . With regard to co-operation of the kind you are mentioning, the Prison Department doubts whether this may be reconciled with the principles and rules covering the carrying-out of penal measures in a prison institution, and therefore finds that the prison system or its staff members should not aid in such a distribution of letters to inmates as you are asking for'. In *Dagbladet* on 22 October that year the Director of Prisons expanded on this in a way suggesting that the externally orientated informational activity which the association had begun to emphasize was viewed with uneasiness. The Director expressed himself in the following way: 'What the Prison Department feels is that you are demanding a little too much if we are being asked to co-operate concerning an association whose goal is to create lack of confidence in the prison system and its staff members'.

There are clearer examples. During the winter of 1968–69 Botsfengslet – at that time the main prison in the country – tried to stop a correspondence between the organization and some prisoners concerning manuscripts for a book. Correspondence not dealing with such externally orientated interpretation of the prison situation was not similarly stopped. In more detail, the prison stopped letters from the association to two prisoners, in which the association asked for permission to reprint articles which the prisoners had earlier published in the internal prison newspaper. The letter from the prison to the representative of the association clearly shows how the prison viewed externally orientated informational contact from the prisoners via the association to the external world. The prison governor wrote, inter alia:

> In this connection it is opportune to remind you that some time ago you took up with me over the telephone the question whether inmates might be allowed to write about their experience of imprisonment, and to send it out with a view towards publication in book form. I took a negative view towards this, and I understood you over the telephone to mean that you would respect this standpoint. This must apparently have been a misunderstanding on my part.
>
> It is still my firm conviction that the existence of the ABC-mail [the prison newspaper] rests on the condition that it is to be an entirely internal local paper, written by inmates for inmates.

The representative of the association had found the articles in the University Library' s copy of the paper. The articles were entirely innocent expressions of opinions concerning prison life, falling clearly inside the limits permitted by the prison regulations concerning the sending out of manuscripts. The prison governor nevertheless went on like this:

> I am . . . astonished that you have taken advantage of the University Library to obtain the material which you must know Botsfengslet does not want published . . . In order to avoid that the ABC-mail is discontinued at the present time, I have to-day written to the University Library and asked that the copies of the local paper which the library has received and receives, be kept under sea! for up to 50 years pursuant to § 3 in the Act Concerning the Duty to Deliver Printed Matter to Public Libraries . . .

In a letter addressed directly to the association the governor amplified his point of view in the following way:

> We regard the ABC-mail as being published on the responsibility of the prison, and we presume that 'borrowing' any of this material for publication without the consent of the prison is not permitted. In our opinion, this must also be the case if the inmate himself has given his consent.

In addition, he puts forward the following threat:

> If earlier contributions to the ABC-mail, contrary to our presumption, nevertheless be published, we will regard this as a very serious matter and take the necessary steps in this connection. In this connection it may become relevant to discontinue the paper. We presume that this will be regretted also from your point of view.

KROM complained to the Prison Department about the prison's holding back of the letters from the organization to the prisoners, but the complaint was not supported. The organization then took the case to the Ombudsman, and there received clear support to the effect that the holding back of the letters was illegal. The Ombudsman concluded in the following words:

> Thus, in my opinion, it would have been correct to let the two inmates receive the inquiries. If they consented to the use of the articles, a concrete evaluation of the articles should have taken place in relation to § 64.7 [in the prison regulations] and the consent ought to have been permitted to be sent out if this provision would not have been an obstacle to the sending out of the article as a manuscript.

To the contention of the prison that no material from the local paper could be used without the consent of the prison, the Ombudsman made the following comment, among others: 'It seems clear that such an independent right on the part of the prison cannot be based on the provisions of the Copyright Act'.

The outcome of the case attracted considerable attention in the press and other mass media. However, the battle was not over. In the light of the Ombudsman's statement, KROM again sent letters to the two prisoners, asking them if they would consent to having their articles reprinted in a later book. This time the prison had to let the letters pass, in accordance with the Ombudsman's ruling. Instead, however, a reply was prevented from going out. To amplify, one of the prisoners did not wish to have his article reprinted, and his answer was promptly forwarded by the prison to the association. However, the other prisoner's answer was positive, and this was stopped, with the justification by the acting governor of the prison that 'the content of the article is . . . of such a character that I am unable to consent to its further publication'. KROM once again complained to the Prison Department, which this time reversed the decision of the prison, so that the article – finally – could be published with the consent of the prisoner (see *KROM- NYTT*, No. 3, 1970). However, the reversal of the decision was half-hearted, and clearly forced by the great likelihood of new and strong criticism by the Ombudsman. That is, the Department avoided taking a stand on the question of the legal basis for withholding the letter, by writing, inter alia: '. . . regardless of whether the article mentioned could have been held back on the basis of the prison regula-tions . . . there is no ground for seeking to have it confiscated'. A photostat copy of the article, from the University Library in Oslo, was already in the possession of the association, and the Department in other words found no basis for 'seeking to have' this photostat copy 'confiscated'! Concerning the letter from the prisoner, containing the prisoner's consent to the reprinting of the article, the Department stated: 'Furthermore, there was agreement to the effect that the consent which has been held back could be sent to the addressee, since he is already aware of the fact that the author of the article has given his consent to publication'.

*

During the winter 1970–71 the prison authorities took great trouble to obstruct contact between a group of liberal/radical criminologists (members of KROM) and the prisoners in the Ila institution – the country's security institution for so-called abnormal but not insane offenders. A prisoner who participated in a politi-cal study group in the institution had established contact with some of KROM's board members. The prisoners' study group, which had started out by emphasiz-ing general political topics and later focused increasingly on penal and correc-tional policy, had received visits from a representative of the Prison Department and two representatives of Norges Vernesamband – the central office of the proba-tion service.[26] Now the inmates wanted to hear the 'counter-expertise'. KROM's board transmitted a list of seven experts who were all very interested in meeting the prisoners, not least in order themselves to learn: two University professors of sociology of law and criminology respectively, one associate professor of social medicine, two assistant professors in jurisprudence, a consultant in the Ministry of justice, and a research director – the latter being also chairman of KROM. The prisoners presented the list to the governor's secretary – for tactical reasons KROM's chairman was at this stage deleted from the list – and the list was sub-mitted to the governor. The governor answered (in writing) that this 'was not relevant'. In *Dagbladet* on 2 February 1971 he enlarged on this as follows: 'No refusal has been given at all . . . The point is that we have received an offer from an outsider which it was not relevant to accept'. How the governor in any reason-able way could maintain that a 'refusal' had not been given, was not explained. The question was taken up in Parliament, and the Minister of justice supported the governor. His answer included the statement that 'the authorities in the institution found that lectures concerning topics of this kind were outside the field which the group were to cover, namely that of giving the participants in the group a general political orientation', Therefore, it 'would not be relevant to call in the persons mentioned'. Why representatives of the Prison Department and Norges Vernesamband had then been called in to discuss penal and correctional policy was not explained.

However, as an answer to an additional question from the questioner, the Minister of Justice also said that:

> [I suppose] that in principle one ought not immediately to take a negative stand to the notion of giving the inmates an orientation concerning questions in penal and correctional policy, provided this can take place through professionally competent people. Also, in my view the institutional authorities ought to have control over any prospective program, in consultation with the Prison Department, in order, inter alia, to try to secure a certain balance and to avoid possible attempts at one-sided indoctrination.

Now, it was among other things precisely in order to include 'professionally competent people' and in order to 'try to secure a certain balance' that the prisoners had proposed to call in the experts in question. All the same, in the light of this part of the Minister's statement, the study groups persevered. The prisoners presented a new proposal to the governor, in which they referred to the Minister's statement, and in which they proposed three meetings on penal and correctional policy with the experts in question and representatives of the prosecuting authorities, the prison system, and the probation and parole agency. This time, the governor's inscription – in red ink – on the prisoners' application went like this: 'At this time of the year group activity will not be started'. The spring of 1971 had arrived and, according to common practice, outdoor activities were to begin.

The decision was given very negative newspaper reviews, for example under the editorial title 'Spring at Ila'. The refusal was transmitted to KROM, together with a request from 22 prisoners (including the study group itself), asking the organization to take action. KROM complained to the Prison Department. Over two months later – when the interest in the proposed meetings was no longer so great – the Prison Department answered by supporting the governor. The Prison Department stated, inter alia, that:

> The discussion meetings which are proposed, must be supposed to be of limited value in so far as their goal be that of giving the inmates information concerning reforms in penal and correctional policy which it is relevant to introduce today. Such information may in that case be given to the inmates in other ways.
>
> One should not disregard the fact that the inmates may be exposed to an influence which may make it more difficult for them to accept the incarceration, and induce in them a negative orientation towards the treatment efforts of the institution.

It appears, then, that the Department was worried about the internal effect (influence) of the meetings, on the prisoners (see the last paragraph). The prisoners might wake up and begin to act politically. However, it also appears rather probable that the first paragraph in the excerpt quoted above reflects a fear – actually a rational fear – concerning what the outsiders in turn might learn from this and publish to the external world.

*

In the fall of 1970 the prisoners at Ullersmo National Prison – at present Norway's main prison – elected an inmate council, which they called 'the working committee'. The working committee presented, inter alia, a proposal for statutes concerning inmate representatives, which were discussed locally with the institutional authorities. Typically, no decisions whatsoever were made concerning statutes. However, the working committee also functioned as a catalyst for the 1971 work strike described above. After the 1971 strike, the working committee wanted to establish a closer contact with KROM. The committee approached the organization by letter, asking for legal aid in organizational questions. In a forwarding letter the prison governor emphasized:

> In this connection I want to stress that the question of the establishment of inmate councils, including the question of whether, and in which forms, such councils will be able to contact individuals, organizations, and the press, is at present being examined in the Ministry of Justice. The sending out of the enclosed letter therefore does not imply any recognition on my part of the working committee as an inmate council *or of the type of external contact which is being sought* [my italics].

In other words, external contact was feared. The examination in the Ministry of justice, referred to in the letter, was actually based on a report from a committee which had consisted only of representatives of the prison system – a slightly unusual 'democratization committee' – and upon request KROM as well as the press had earlier been denied access to the report. The Ministry had referred to the report as an 'internal working document' – by law exempt from public inspection. At a much later date it was finally made public, in the form of a proposal for establishing 'joint councils' in some prisons. I shall return to this later.

On the basis of the inmate working committee's request for legal aid, KROM now applied to the prison for permission to visit representatives of the committee. The association wrote, inter alia: 'In the light of the second paragraph in your letter to us [quoted above], we mention, for the record, that the visit we asked for will not later be referred to by us as a precedent'. The prison governor's reply went like this:

> Referring to your letter . . . I am regrettably obliged to state that on the basis of N.N.'s letter of 9th July of this year and my letter of the 13th of the same month

[quoted above], I do not for the present find it possible to consent to giving representatives of the Norwegian Association for Penal Reform permission to participate in meetings with the inmates in Ullersmo National Prison.

The refusal had an aftermath. Instead of the visit, KROM's Legal Committee sent a lengthy written account to the working committee concerning various aspects of organizational law. In the account, the Legal Committee pointed out that as a point of departure the prisoners had a right to organize, and that even if the prison was not obliged to recognize such an organization, for example as a counterpart in negotiations, the prison had no right to declare the organization illegal or non-existent – as long as the organization kept to legal means. A newspaper contacted the prison in order to find out whether the letter had been allowed in to the working committee. The letter was clearly inside the limits concerning correspondence permitted by the prison regulations, and it had in fact been allowed in – but with a special justification. On the envelope of the letter the association had written the name of a particular inmate, who at the time was the chairman of the working committee. In other words, the letter was addressed to 'The working committee, c/o N.N.'. The governor told the newspaper that he did not accept the working committee, which, according to his view, did not exist, and that 'KROM's letter to the committee was taken into the institution because the name of an inmate was also written on it'.

The justification was untenable: holding back of the letter would under all circumstances have been illegal as long as the governor knew who the committee consisted of, so that he was able to forward the letter. But the sequence of events as a whole, and the justification, says something about the attempts of the institution to break contact between organizational trends among the prisoners and an external connecting organization.

*

In February 1971 a prisoner at Ullersmo sent a letter to KROM. The prisoner was a rather active and politically conscious member of KROM, and the letter contained some critical remarks concerning the prison. Shortly afterwards, the prisoner was called in to the assistant governor, and as the prisoner understood it, the letter was then stopped by the prison censorship. The prisoner complained to the Prison Department concerning the holding back of the letter, and KROM supported his complaint in a separate letter. Another letter from the prisoner, in which he briefly summarized the contents of the first letter, was also stopped – again as the prisoner understood it – and the complaint also covered this letter. Exactly two months after the prisoner's complaint, the Prison Department answered as follows:

According to the governor of Ullersmo National Prison, no decision has been made concerning seizure of the letter referred to. The issue of assessing the question of seizure has not been relevant, since the convict himself has withdrawn the letters.

This, then, two months after the *prisoner himself had complained.* In the light of the fact that the prisoner himself had complained, the Prison Department must have understood that the prisoner had not 'withdrawn the letters' voluntarily. On behalf of the prisoner, KROM complained to the Ombudsman concerning the handling of the case as well as the withholding of the letters. In June – four months after the prisoner's first attempt to send a letter to KROM – the prisoner could not stand the waiting any longer, and sent the main letter illegally to KROM. The letter proved to be a harmless – however critical – expression of opinion concerning the mail delivery (!) and the management of the workshops in the prison, which clearly could not be affected by the provisions concerning withholding of letters in the prison regulations. KROM sent the letter to the Ombudsman, explaining how it had been received (the prisoner had given KROM his permission to use the letter as the organization saw fit), and emphasizing how unreasonable the withholding of it had been. The Ombudsman, however, returned the letter to KROM, writing, inter alia, that 'I do not find it correct to review the case on the basis of a letter which is sent from the institution without having passed the regular control. The sender may at any time legally send it here'. He also stated that he had asked for the treatment of the case to be expedited, and for the Prison Department to produce the two letters in question. The main letter, however, was now in KROM's hands – after being returned by the Ombudsman. Triumphantly the Prison Department could therefore assert that they could not produce the letter, because it had been 'sent out of the institution, in conflict with the rules concerning the sending of letters'.

KROM now had to act quickly. We sent a photostat copy of the letter in again to the prisoner (through the regular control), asking him to send the photostat copy *out again* to the Ombudsman – as had already indirectly been suggested by the Ombudsman. The prisoner sent the photostat copy out to the Ombudsman. The Ombudsman could now review the case, and sent the photostat copy in again to the Prison Department, asking the prison governor 'as soon as possible' to make a decision concerning the question of withholding the letter.

There is probably a kind of implicit comedy in the Prison Department's contention that the prisoner – after having complained – had voluntarily 'withdrawn the letters', as well as in the subsequent sequence of events. To the prisoner, however, none of this was particularly comical. The development of the case is quite revealing as regards the ineffectiveness of complaints as a safeguard of the prisoners and the Kafka-like feeling which the 'system' must elicit. It is part of the story that the Ombudsman's decision in the case was further delayed owing to a long delay in the Prison Department. The Ombudsman's reply came 9 – nine – months after the main letter in question had been written. The Ombudsman criticized the prison authorities for their handling of the case. The case shows how anxiously the prison authorities attempt to stop communication from the prisoners to the connecting organizations.

*

The case material given above reveals a series of different justifications given by the authorities for barring contact between the prisoners and KROM. (*1*) *KROM's co-operation with the prisoners is presumed to be at variance with 'the principles and rules covering the carrying-out of penal measures'; (2) material published by prisoners in institution newspapers is barred from further publication because it is 'published on the responsibility of the prison'; (3) the same material is, upon criticism from the Ombudsman, again barred from further publication because of the 'character' of its content; (4) experts in criminology and criminal policy are denied contact with prisoners because a visit from them is 'not relevant'; (5) the same contact is denied again because of the 'time of the year'; (6) the denial is further justified by the view that information concerning criminal policy may 'be given to the inmates in other ways'; (7) the denial is also justified by the view that the contact may 'induce in [the inmates] a negative orientation towards the treatment . . .'; (8) personal contact concerning legal matters is denied on the grounds that the question of inmate councils 'is at present being examined in the Ministry of Justice'; (9) a critical letter from an inmate is not delivered because 'the convict himself has withdrawn it'.* To this list of justifications, a few more may be added in connection with several attempts made by the inmates in the Norwegian *youth prison* to establish organized contact with KROM.

(10) A request in the form of an article is not sufficient. In the fall of 1971 the prisoners in the youth prison's open unit wrote an open letter to KROM in an Oslo newspaper. They wondered why KROM did not come to them: 'Can't you rather come to us and discuss this together with us, because it concerns us and our problems'. KROM at once applied to the governor for a meeting between representatives of KROM and the prisoners. The governor refused with the following justification: 'KROM's application comes as a reaction to an article in *Verdens Gang* from the inmates at the Berg unit. The inmates have not requested any meeting with a view to discussing the youth prison measure with KROM, and I do not find sufficient grounds for complying with the request in your letter'. In their newspaper article, the prisoners clearly asked us to come, but a request from them in the form of an article was apparently not sufficient.

(11) Printed matter is enough for the prisoners. In February 1972, 14 prisoners in one of the youth prison's closed units (accommodating about 30 inmates) sent a letter to KROM. They asked the organization to send a representative to the unit to inform them about the work of the organization. The prisoners considered becoming members, but were in doubt as to what the organization stood for. Once again KROM applied to the governor for an informational meeting with the prisoners. This time the governor answered as follows: 'I refuse the request, in 50 far as I assume that the inmates who consider membership in KROM, and who wish to be informed about the objectives of the association may be sent printed informational material'. Printed matter was enough for the prisoners.

(12) The organization KROM has not convinced the governor. In the light of the governor's reply, KROM sent some printed material to the fourteen prisoners. At the same time, we wrote that if this was not sufficient, we would straight away apply to the governor again. The inmates now replied (at the suggestion of a teacher working in the prison) that the printed material which they had received was not sufficient, and that the most important matter for them was to meet someone from the association, so that they could ask questions and participate in a real discussion.

Again KROM applied to the governor. Again he refused, referring to the printed material, which he still assumed to be sufficient. However, to a newspaper which gave an account of the refusal, the governor gave a rather different justification: 'To *Dagbladet*', the paper wrote, 'governor B. justifies his refusal to KROM by the view that the attitude of the association has not convinced him during the past year'. 'The reason is', the governor said, 'especially the fighting signals from KROM about compromising the prisons from the inside' (see pp. 000–000 above).

(13) The closed unit of the youth prison is difficult. The governor also gave other justifications to the paper. Visits, he stated, may only take place 'when compatible with order and security in the institution. We have had many difficulties at the Oslo unit [the closed unit] last fall, and it is impossible to say what effects a visits from KROM would have'. The paper here reminded the governor of the fact that he had also rejected a request from the open unit. The paper wanted to know: were the difficulties in the closed unit also relevant for the open unit? This the governor denied: 'The Berg unit [the open unit] is a stable unit'.

(14) Various unstated reasons. To this statement about the stable open Berg unit, the governor added a sentence: 'But it is my opinion that our relationship to KROM for the present does not give occasion for any visit from the association'. In other words, one justification was given for one unit, and another for the other. The latter justification, used in connection with the open unit, could allude to the fact that KROM had not convinced the governor (justification No. 12 above). However, the formulation was sufficiently general to include other, unstated, reasons. The fact that various unstated reasons were included, appeared from still another statement in the same interview. Confronted with the fact that with regard to the open unit he had given one justification to KROM and another to the paper, the governor replied secretively: 'Here there are many reasons. In a brief letter to KROM I have given the reason which I find most relevant. I do not see any contradiction in giving *Dagbladet* also *one of the other reasons* [my italics].

In short: The closed unit in the youth prison is viewed as 'difficult'. But the open unit is not regarded as difficult even by the prison authorities. The organization KROM has not convinced the governor. But an entirely different justification is given to the organization itself. Requests in article form are not sufficient. But direct requests from the prisoners are not complied with either. And so on. Should we laugh or should we cry? We should certainly not laugh. The authorities' change from one justification to another, their pronounced tendency to find new justifications as the old ones are exhausted – until refuge may only be found in the category 'various unstated reasons', conceals what is common to all of the refusals. Political contact between the prisoners and an outside connecting organization must at all costs be strangled.

*

A final set of examples will be given.

The various justifications discussed above may be viewed as a series of strategies used by the authorities. The strategies all imply very flat refusals of 'sideways' political contact. The final series of examples illustrates a strategy of a more subtle kind: that of 'offering' the inmates a limited measure of international 'co-operation' as an alternative to external co-operation with KROM.

As mentioned earlier, during the summer of 1972 the prisoners in several Norwegian penal institutions founded a Prisoners' Trade Union, and went (in some institutions) on an orderly one-day work strike to manifest their demands. The founding of the union was the result of a long development, including KROM's outside political activities from 1968 to 1972 (see Part II above), the series of Swedish prison strikes in 1970–71 (transmitted through the mass media), and the long series of rather revealing refusals of external contact discussed in the preceding pages. The union's statement of objectives read as follows:

1   The organization has as its goal to look after [ivareta] the members' interest, trade questions, questions concerning wages, general well-being, and work, in addition to acting as negotiator and advisor. The organization will set forth demands towards the authorities, on behalf of the members, concerning reforms in the treatment of prisoners.
2   Advance demands concerning:

  a   Abolition of the present work system. Instead to introduce wages for the work performed by the prisoners.
  b   No controls on the use of wages.
  c   To be recognized as an equal of the other labour organizations, and to develop the same rights and duties.

3   To become a spokesman for all persons to be found in Norwegian prisons.

On the outside, KROM strongly supported the new movement, through newspaper interviews, numerous articles, press releases, etc. At its peak, six major prisons were involved in the movement (through brief strikes, signed statements of sympathy with the initiators, etc.). In three of the prisons, local chapters were founded. At Ullersmo prison – where the movement started – the prisoners demanded somewhat higher wages (kr. 2.50 – 40 cents – per hour), three weeks' vacation per year inside the walls (from the tiresome and partly heavy industrial work in the prison), occasion to determine the use of their wages without controls from the institution, and a new control system in connection with visits (the prisoners have to strip, submit to a body search, and change underwear after unsupervised visits; the prisoners wanted these controls to be undertaken only as spot checks). The demands were flatly refused by the authorities; at Ullersmo the prisoners who went on strike were resolutely isolated for long periods of time (some of them up to three weeks for the one-day strike); the prisoners there were only let back to work after having signed a mimeographed document concerning their duty to work (KROM asked to see a copy of the document, but was refused access to it with the justification that the document was 'an entirely internal working document', thus presumably exempt from the regulations in the Public Information

Act); and their organization was largely suppressed. A statement to a newspaper by the Minister of Justice – a social democrat – gives an indication of the reaction and tone of the authorities:

> From the Ministry's side we had planned an arrangement for co-operation between inmates and prison authorities. . . . This they [the prisoners] have not agreed to. Instead I have to my great surprise been informed that they have founded a prisoners' 'trade organization'. Despite the seriousness of the situation, it is not without comical aspects. What kind of a trade is it they represent?

The prisoners at Ullersmo had called their organization a 'trade' union because work in the prison is largely of an industrial kind, carried out in large, modern workshops. The social democratic Minister's scornful statement was carried in 24 other papers, under headings like 'The prisoners' "trade demands" not accepted without further ado – Serious case with comical aspects'; 'Are the prisoners "craftsmen"?'; 'The Minister of justice is surprised at new "trade union"'; 'Comical with prisoners in LO [the National Labour Organization]'. The authorities' alternative to the prisoners' union, alluded to by the Minister, was 'joint councils' in the institutions. Such councils were to include staff members as well as inmates, their authority was to be very limited (for example, none of the demands set forth by the Prisoners' Trade Union – see above – could be discussed in a joint council), and the prisoners had refused to participate in: the light of a warning from KROM. We had argued that the joint councils – like the negotiations in Sweden – would co-opt the inmates in an internal prison arrangement, and to the prisoners we had rather stressed 'sideways' co-operation with outside – more powerful – organizations. The authorities viewed our warning and our advice with considerable anxiety, and very actively tried to stop our contact with the prisoners.

   In the first place, a letter of congratulation to the Prisoners' Trade Union at Ullersmo prison, sent in July 1972, was stopped by the Prison Department. The Prison Department withheld the letter – in which we expressed our support of the Prisoners' Trade Union as well as our looking forward to contact and co-operation with the new organization – on the grounds that:

> the activity which the organization PTU plans to carry out, clearly falls outside the arrangement for co-operation with inmates which is stipulated in existing regulations [i.e., joint councils].

This time the Ombudsman supported the authorities. His reasoning shows how much he, as an institution, is actually a part of the administrative system which he is to supervise. Referring to the regulations on censorship of letters, which state that letters to the inmate may be 'refused delivery when there is reason to believe that the letter may have an unfortunate effect on his treatment, or when other special reasons indicate that it should not be delivered to him', the Ombudsman wrote, inter alia:

> This regulation gives the prison authorities a basis on which to withhold any letter to an inmate or groups of inmates when there is reason to believe that the letter may have an unfortunate effect on the treatment, or when other special reasons indicate that it is not to be delivered. Such a special reason must, for example, be that the letter is assumed to counteract a co-operative arrangement which the Prison authorities wish to introduce, or in other ways to have an unfortunate effect on conditions in the institution . . .
>
> The question of whether a letter may have an unfortunate effect on the treatment, or of whether other special reasons indicate that it should be kept back, must rest on an evaluation. . . . I do not find sufficient grounds for objections from this office to the Prison Department's evaluation of the letter to the Prisoners' Trade Union.

The fear against contact with KROM is apparently great. In October 1972 the prison authorities followed up by stepping a mimeographed letter to all KROM members in the prisons. The letter contained a two-page review of a meeting on the topic of the Prisoners' Trade Union, held in the law students' association in Oslo, with one speaker from the prison authorities and two speakers from KROM. The meeting had earlier been reviewed in the newspapers, which the inmates get. The letter also contained a brief commentary on a radio program on prison issues. The commentary had previously been published in a newspaper. The Prison Department justified their decision by saying that the letter 'contains statements which one must assume may stimulate inmates to oppose the measures of activation of and co-operation with the inmates which the prison authorities have stipulated through circulars'. Again, the Prison Department's decision was supported by the Ombudsman.

Finally, in November 1972 the prison authorities stopped a new mimeographed letter to all KROM members in the prisons. The letter simply stated that the previous mimeographed letter had been stopped by the Prison Department, that the withholding of the letter had been taken to the Ombudsman (his ruling had not yet been received), and that the association would keep its members informed. In addition, the letter contained photostat copies of *three newspaper reviews* of a KROM meeting which had partly dealt with the issue of the Prisoners' Trade Union. The newspaper reviews were also stopped. To a newspaper, a representative of the Prison Department first explained that the 'last letter referred to the first refusal, and because this case is under review, a current case, the Prison Department decided that the last letter should also be stopped'. The legal basis for this justification was doubtful to say the least. In their formal justification, however, the department changed their reasoning, focusing on the newspaper clippings:

> According to the opinion of the Prison Department, it would be hazardous if inmates are from special quarters furnished with one-sidedly selected

newspaper material, the content of which is liable to stimulate the inmates to reject the institution's offer of co-operation to the inmates, The Prison Department has found that the association's 'message' [*melding*] may counteract the system for co-operation which the prison authorities wish to carry out, and that it over and above this may have an unfortunate effect on conditions within the institution.

Again the Ombudsman supported the department, Newspaper clippings may be refused delivery when there is ' "reason to believe that [they] may have an unfortunate effect on the treatment" of the inmate or when other special reasons indicate that [they] should not be delivered to him':

> The newspapers from which the clippings are taken [two large Oslo newspapers] have . . . been accessible to the inmates, so that the clippings in and of themselves did not contain information other than what the inmates had access to previously. However, I agree with the Prison Department that this cannot be unequivocally decisive. Articles on questions concerning prisons and penal and correctional policy are only a very small part of the material carried by the newspapers, and such material may have a different effect when it is collected and sent to the inmate under separate cover . . .

*

The examples mentioned here of the prison authorities' interest in arresting the contact between the prisoners and KROM as a connecting organization are part of a much longer series of similar legal and illegal attempts. As indicated above, the concern of the prison authorities is probably in part that such contact may have an awakening influence on the inmates inside the prison. However, the excerpts from letters, statements, etc. also indicate a preoccupation in obstructing the connecting organization in its transmission of material from the prisoners who have – through the contact – become politically awakened. Such transmitting is dangerous to the coercive system. Yet, what the prison authorities cannot obstruct is the fact that their obstruction of cross-wise communication may in itself be transmitted as typical of, and exposing, their system. Thus, KROM systematically gathers and publishes information about the obstructions. To this new level of warfare, the authorities react with a new series of strategies. They react with arguments at public meeting, in newspapers, etc., presenting KROM as an organization essentially working at cross-purposes with, and against, the interests of the inmates.

KROM is presented as having developed from a sensible, reformist starting point to a senseless, revolutionary present. The fact that the authorities viewed KROM as senseless and dangerous from the very beginning is set aside. KROM is presented as a group of abstract theoreticians, entirely unfamiliar with the realities of prison life. The fact that the organization includes ex-inmates and other practitioners in its ranks is forgotten. KROM is presented as an extremist political organization, merely using the inmates as pawns in a general political struggle.

And KROM is presented as a divided organization, containing deep conflicts of opinion concerning means as well as goals.

Of course, KROM has developed since 1968 (see Part II above), KROM includes 'theoreticians', KROM is fairly radical, and KROM at times debates means as well as goals. These grains of truth, however, are enlarged out of proportion by the authorities, and emphasized as decisive features of the organization.

Through this emphasis, and in view of the lack of regular communication, the prisoners inside the walls are easily estranged from KROM. This is part of the reason why the arguments are presented. They isolate, and insulate, the prisoners from KROM. (Another part of the reason is that they throw doubts on our exposure of the system.) However, slowly but surely the systematic presentation of the authorities' obstruction of cross-wise communication – for example, systematic presentation of letters and memoranda such as those quoted above – seems to have a positive effect on the prisoner population. Today a certain number of Norwegian prisoners seem alert to the importance of engaging in brief collective actions with a 'signalling' effect to the outside world (rather than in long strikes intended to exhaust the adversary), they seem increasingly aware of the significance of trying such actions to concrete issues in the prisons with which the outside public may identify (such as in the most recent action at Ullersmo prison, in May 1973, when the prisoners went on a two-day work strike in sympathy with a sick prisoner who had died without adequate treatment), and they seem more alert to the extreme importance of getting revealing information about prison life out to the connecting organization, if necessary through illicit means. These are important tactical improvements.

But it must be reiterated that the road ahead is long and thorny. 'Politics', Max Weber wrote, in his Politics as a Calling, 'is a strong and slow boring of hard boards'.[27]

6. On organizing

Counter-organization among the expelled thus first encounters diversionary treatment ideologies and ideas about illness. If you manage to unmask their pacifying function and to get them out of the way – which is not easy – such an organization encounters a fundamental structural difficulty linked to the situation of the expelled: the very basis for being expelled – their lack of contribution – which is the fundamental condition for their existence. And if you managed to change this fundamental condition so that the expelled also became contributors 'upwards', you would to a large extent get a positive, system-supporting organization. The last point is a general one. It is relevant not only for the expelled of today, but also, for example, for the organization of the labour movement. In a flash we perhaps see the deep tragedy of this. A main basis for effective protest and struggle is that you contribute – and are inside and positive. But then an important main ground for the protest is simultaneously taken away. What you ought to wish to protest against is precisely the fact that the ones who do not contribute, are resolutely expelled. What you ought to wish to protest against, then, is the very basis of our type of society. But the main basis of our type of society is such that protest easily becomes effective only if it takes place on this basis. And thereby it is no longer really a protest.

For the expelled, however, the hope and the possibilities – however long term – lie in becoming contributors 'sideways' – to more important political counter-organizations and movements, The hope and the possibilities lie in an interaction between political organizations and the expelled, and in having a main battle waged outside the ranks of the expelled. Representatives of the coercive systems often cry out when political points of view are presented in connection with discussions of the expelled. Immediately it is maintained that you are no longer 'client orientated', that you are 'using' the expelled for your own political ends, and so on. Suddenly the representatives of the coercive systems become the 'defenders of the clients'. The representatives of the coercive systems have undoubtedly perceived the threat against themselves which is implied in an alliance between political organizations and the expelled. It is in their interest to break attempts at such alliances, and to keep the expelled politically unconscious.

*

But here the question arises: How far, in their turn, do the external organizations bring us? To the extent that they are powerful, they can change the existing coercive systems. But even if their power means that they can go around and over the coercive system, thus receiving authority in relation to it, their power also means that they are involved in a contributive relationship to other, still more superior, systems. In relation to these other, superior, systems, organizations with power thus simultaneously are or become supportive organizations, because their power is based on the contributing relationship. In other words, on a new level we are again confronted with the ambiguity of the contribution: it gives power, but at the same time it becomes a 'positive' relationship, a binding link. The binding results in the superior system not being fought, in the same way as the coercive system is not fought by a contributing, 'positive' prisoner group. It may be maintained that this new problem is so far away that it need not preoccupy us now. It may be maintained that this problem must be tackled only when the coercive systems which we are trying to change now are beaten, which is itself a distant prospect. The question is, however, whether you actually – in the long run – beat the coercive systems in this way. The question is whether new coercive systems are not developed under new names. Even if the problem is a distant one, even if the immediate risk is that of removing aspects of the present-day solid coercive systems, I must say a few words about the more long-term issue before closing this essay. Hidden coercion, in new systems, is perhaps more dangerous than to-day's open coercion. I have, however, no solution to the problem. What I have to say is *ad hoc.*

As we have seen, the old system is not fundamentally threatened by an incorporated 'counter'-organization. But the old system is threatened by any *transition* to counter-organization, that is, by any counter-organizing, any counter-organization in the making.

This is the transition *from* being non-contributing *to* becoming a contributor. In the first place, then, this is the moment at which the character of being a non-contributor is abolished. Its abolition is the condition for the organizing. Simultaneously, the group is not yet incorporated in a positive contributing relationship: the established contributor-relation does not yet exist. You have in this way – in the sociological sense of the word – no role. No normative expectations define your behaviour, and neither can predictions be advanced concerning it. You cannot be placed. For example, you can neither be placed as 'sick' nor as 'normal'. Thereby, the adversary does not know where you are heading. The only thing he knows is that you are heading somewhere, because you are organizing. At this moment the power of the system is threatened, because you are yourself neither powerless nor incorporated in a fully developed positive contributing relationship.

May such organizing take place *inside* the present-day coercive systems, for example in the prison system? Organizing tendencies in such systems have had a clear tendency to remain as tendencies, that is, to remain in a stage prior to the intermediate organizing phase described here. The reasons for this have been discussed in earlier sections of this essay: splintering and coopting ideologies of treatment and illness, together with the prisoners' fundamental character of being non-contributors, have had an impeding effect. Therefore the people in prison have, as indicated already, to a fairly large extent been characterized by lack of solidarity (Mathiesen 1965/2012; Street *et al.*1966). Yet, as mentioned earlier, a neutralization of the treatment ideologies and a building-up of a contributing relationship is conceivable – the latter at least on a smaller scale – and organizing is therefore possible. The first phase of the Swedish prison strike was perhaps such an organizing phase. Temporarily it clearly threatened the power of the system by revealing the inability of the system through the mass media. Many Norwegian prisoners are currently, I believe, in an organizing phase. The difficulty, however, is that a coercive system like a prison or a prison system is built in such an integrated and monolithic fashion – is so characterized by being *one* hierarchical structure – that its subjects actually get only one chance to organize. When that chance is used up, when the authorities have opened the way for and legalized organized activity[28] and the organizing merges into organization – with the unfortunate integrating process that then follows – there are actually no more chances.

A continually budding organizing, in which new organizing begins as the old organizing merges into organization, presupposes a more disintegrated, complicated system with a larger number of lines of conflict, so that organizing may begin anew 'in another place'. This constitutes an additional reason why a main part of the struggle of the expelled must, in my view, be fought outside, in the more complex and less surveyable larger society, through an organizing process there. But let me reiterate, in order not to be misunderstood, that the outside struggle can only be successful if it takes place on the basis of material which the expelled may bring forth from the coercive systems. Thus, the role of the expelled is crucial – the point is that its importance is indirect.

Even on the outside the organizing process, and the struggle, are difficult enough. The perspective which is presented here places great demands on the connecting organizations of the expelled – among other things the demand of dissolving and renewing, and of tying oneself to continually new and more radical groupings in society. This is very difficult. The problem is general. In order to be successful in a struggle, a certain measure of stability in organization is needed. At the same time, such an organization may become an impediment to the budding process of organizing. Illustrations of the conflict may be found by studying the development of the labour movement.

*

Are there any empirical examples suggesting that anyone has managed to maintain a really thorough-going budding organizing? There are, but the question must be made more precise: Are there any examples showing that anyone has managed to maintain such a budding counter-organizing? There are certainly examples of organizing in the service of the old system – e.g. in commercial life. With regard to budding counter-organizing, I am more uncertain. If they do not exist, the future is gloomy. But perhaps the new China (and Albania) constitute approximate examples. When you read about the internal criticism during the cultural revolution, about the merging of – and the reciprocal learning process between – intellectuals and others, and so on, you get the feeling that here is a people actively trying to 'make counter-organizing permanent', seeking the ever-present counter-process.

When I have talked about making the counter-organizing permanent, into a thorough-going counter-process, this actually also implies that there is always something to counter or be against – a system you want to develop away from and abolish. As I tried to show in the essay on 'The Unfinished', I believe it will be like this, and that the 'alternative' lies in the growing unfinished counter-process, If I am right in this, what are then the fundamental conditions for the maintenance of such a counter-process or budding organizing? In slightly different words, this was the problem with which I concluded the essay on 'The Unfinished'. There I felt I did not manage to provide an adequate analysis of the question. Perhaps we may here get a slight step further.

It is conceivable that the solution to the problem presupposes – as a necessary but hardly sufficient condition – a new relationship between 'theory' and 'action'. In the essay 'On Action Research', I discussed the importance of continually developing out of and abolishing the bindings following from withdrawal as well as from action. In our society, a peculiar wall exists between withdrawal and action: either you withdraw, or you act; either you are a theoretician, an educated researcher, or you are a practitioner, an experienced politician. Research and action are separated, The continual oscillation or movement between theory and action which was suggested in the essay 'On Action Research', the continual oscillation involving that you develop out of *whatever theoretical or practical field you are involved in at any time*, is perhaps a condition for a budding organizing; for continually new organizing. If so, there is a connection between what I am saying here and what I said earlier.

In the way I have stated it here, the connection perhaps seems a little abstract and artificial. Let me try to view it in a somewhat different way: perhaps continually new organizing is, or presupposes, a continual, ever present process of totalizing: a process through which the small individual case, the small question, is placed within a continually wider context of causal relationships, which then in turn is attacked. You discover that what you are attacking is not 'the real thing', and you proceed further, to new organizing, to more encompassing attacks in continually wider circles. This presupposes a continual oscillation between action and theory: a continually new understanding of action in the light of theory, a revision of theory in the light of this, a re-evaluation of the action in this light, and so on. And furthermore, since the point here is 'development' in this negating sense of unfolding or evolving from something, rather than in the usual positivistic sense of building up, since the point actually is to counter-act positive contribution, we get a glimpse of a connection to the abolishing viewpoint which was so central in the essay on 'The Unfinished'. The process then consists of developing out of or abolishing (abolishing the stress on) what you are doing at any time, and to proceed further to uncovered and more encompassing relationships. *In other words, the stress on abolition is here turned against your own activity, but through its relationships with the environment, also against the environment, and it may thereby become the basis of a more persistent counter-organizing.* (We are reminded of the therapeutic/political process suggested earlier in this essay.)

And this in turn requires its own presuppositions, which I am unable to discern here. It should be stressed, however, that, seen in this light, a part of the struggle itself is to abolish the boundary between theory and action.

VII

On the negative

In the essay on 'The Unfinished', I emphasized how psychologically difficult it is to work for short-range reforms introducing improvements into a system, and simultaneously maintain the long-range objective of abolishing that system. Furthermore, I stressed that over and above these purely psychological difficulties, reforms of an improving kind may, by their very adjustment of, and re-legitimation of, the prevailing order, actually lessen the possibilities for a long-term abolition.

In other words, what we were discussing there, were 'positive' reforms. 'Positive' reforms are *changes which improve or 'build up' the system so that it functions more effectively* - whereby the system is strengthened and its abolition made more difficult. The increase in effectiveness – and thereby the strengthening – takes place in several ways, but most important is the renewed legitimacy which an improvement bestows on the system. The fact that a positive reform is followed by renewed legitimacy is related to the positivistic value system of our society, a value system which in turn may probably be traced to fundamental relationships of power. I shall return to this later. At this point I want to stress that renewed legitimacy means that the general public interprets the system as more reasonable, better , more correct, more rational, etc.

Later on in the essay on 'The Unfinished', I discussed reforms of an 'abolishing' kind, and the significance of the persistent contradiction between abolishing forces and forces constructive to the system. I emphasized that the psychological difficulties linked to a traditional policy of improving reform need not appear here. Furthermore, I suggested that such reforms of an 'abolishing' kind do not postpone a more long-term abolition, because they do not re-adjust and re-legitimize the prevailing order.

In other words, what we were discussing there, were the 'negative' reforms. *'Negative' reforms are changes which abolish or remove greater or smaller parts on which the system in general is more or less dependent.* A negative reform may soften public criticism, and thereby in a way improve the system's basis of legitimacy. For example, the abolition of forced labour in Norway probably had such a consequence. But the negative, abolishing reform does not provide the system with a new, positive addition of legitimacy. After the abolition of forced labour, no one said that the prison system in general had thereby been improved. An abolishing reform may reduce the debit side of legitimacy, but it adds nothing to the credit side. This makes it easier to return to new abolishing reforms.

The abolishing of forced labour, then, constituted an example of a 'negative' reform. An increase of the treatment staff in penal institutions may be mentioned as an example of a 'positive' reform. What does such a 'treatment orientation' imply for the prison and the prisoners? An increase of the treatment staff confers added legitimacy on the prison as a solution to crime as an inter-human problem. The rationality of the treatment idea is ascribed to the prison. We have seen a series of examples of this throughout the more recent history of criminal law administration (*strafferettspleie*). In Norway the transition to forced labour, Borstal, etc. had precisely the function of bestowing increased legitimacy on the prison system at times when its legitimacy appeared to be at a critically low level. And when a 'type of treatment goes out of fashion, or is criticized too strongly because of its lack of effectiveness, a transition to another 'type of treatment' takes place. Thus, the idea of individual psychiatric treatment is to a large extent abandoned today; instead the fashion is 'group treatment' and 'milieu therapy' in the prisons, and thus a new legitimacy is created. At the same time, we know that the 'treatment reforms' in actual practice are absorbed by the prison system in such a way that the prisoner benefits little or nothing from them. Altogether, the struggle for the reform becomes, to say the least, of very doubtful value.

*

In view of what has been said here, and in view of a more long-term abolishing objective in relation to a given system, it is correct to work for the negative – and not the positive – reforms on a short-term basis as well. Only if this is done consistently, will the otherwise hopeless dilemma between 'short-term' and 'long-term' objectives be abolished.

*

Above I have chosen examples of positive reforms through which the groups of clients in question do not even enjoy short-term benefits. Let me emphasize, however, that the dangers linked to positive reforms are present even if the group of clients should receive short-term benefits from the reforms. When this happens, you are confronted with a moral dilemma. When faced with this dilemma, it may well be that you choose to work for the positive reforms. If so, you ought to be fully aware of the further consequences of that choice. In practice, however, the dilemma very often does not present itself. For example, it usually does not present itself in the prison system, in which very many short-term positive reforms are actually of little or no real help to the inmates.

Below I assume that the choice of working for negative reforms has initially been taken. Furthermore, I assume that the discussion of method from the preceding essay, in which I stressed an externally orientated, exposing activity on the part of the prisoners in relation to more powerful external organizations, is known, and with respect to the prison I add that such a 'horizontal' principle of action concerns progressive staff as well as prisoners. Let me at the same time emphasize that progressive prison staff members may combine such externally orientated, exposing work with attempts at making life more livable for the prisoners. As long as the externally orientated unmasking activity 'makes up for' the internal positivism, it may be said that the activity as a whole does not consolidate the system. The maintenance of such a balance is far from simple. Some of the difficulties involved will be dealt with below, where I will discuss some of the complicating practical types of difficulty which it is necessary to be aware of in work of a negating kind.

1. External pressure

In the first place – and if you are not conscious of the problem – it is easy to be subject to pressure which forces you out of the negative track over into the positive one. Such pressure may be exerted from at least three sides.

First, the groups which the positive reforms are said to help are not infrequently deceived by the glitter of reforms. This is indeed one of the functions of positive reforms: they give 'hope' to groups in difficulty, by which the system receives new legitimacy even in their eyes, and the groups in difficulty – dependent as they are on the system – may thereby come to be defenders of the system. Only after a long time may understanding spread of the fact that the reforms nevertheless did not help fundamentally, and perhaps not even in the short run. In the meantime, the system has acquired a new gloss. The concrete practical-political task becomes that of creating an awareness among groups in difficulty of the deceptiveness of positive reforms.

Secondly, the adversary himself – the representatives of the system exerts great pressure on you in the direction of 'being positive'. The governor of Trondheim Local Prison stated in an interview (*Adresseavisen* 12 June 1971), as a comment on the organization KROM: 'If I am going to answer that [the question from the interviewer concerning KROM] briefly, it must be this: it is easy to criticize, anyone can do that. What is wanting are constructive and realistic counter-proposals'. The governor of Trondheim Local Prison is wrong. It is not easy to be consistently critical; it is not easy radically to maintain the line of negative reforms.

Our social structure as a whole is based on the positivistic philosophy; a philosophy with a value system putting a premium on the positive, constructive effort – that which 'stands out' and may be observed as a layer covering the preceding one – rather than the negating and abolishing effort – that which peels off and exposes layers which otherwise would have remained hidden. The positivistic philosophy, and the positivistic value system, are probably a philosophy and a value system which are produced by those in power. In any case, the philosophy and the values are supported by those in power, because they are a successful means of covering up and 'forgetting' past errors; they provide new legitimation – the legitimation fostered by improvement and 'progress' – when the former basis of legitimacy has become too weak. Thereby the system of power is also maintained and strengthened, and the adversary – the representatives of the system – will exert strong pressure to obtain this.

On the 'basis of the same philosophy, and the same value system, an enormous pressure is placed on the negating actionist not only from groups he is trying to help and from the adversary, but also from the greater or smaller category of 'third parties'. (It is, incidentally, the support given by this latter category to the main adversary that makes it so difficult to withstand this adversary's pressure.) Here also – as in connection with the groups in actual difficulty – the concrete practical/political task becomes (in addition to avoiding the positive sidetrap) that of creating an awareness of the deceptiveness of positive reforms. I shall not here discuss this practical-political task in detail. It has been dealt with earlier, in connection with the relationship between 'theory' and 'practice'. Here I only refer to the significance of continually developing out of, or unfolding from, theory towards practice, and from practice towards theory. I believe that in this oscillation lies the function of creating such an awareness.

2. Seeming negation

I have now discussed pressures from various sides which make the maintenance of the line of abolition difficult. In connection with the question of practical difficulties linked to this line, I also have to mention the danger, which may be present, that a seemingly negative form is just specious or false.

An example may be found in connection with the building of modern prisons. Through certain architectural changes, these prisons in fact abolish certain limitations on freedom of movement. Seen in isolation we have here a negative reform. It is a question of an alteration which – *if it stood alone* – would weaken the system by abolishing something on which the system in general depends. However, together with this change, and as a compound neutralizing the effect of the negative reform, TV-surveillance, new types of concrete walls, etc. are simultaneously introduced, i.e. technically improved, positive reforms. The gain is lost in the getting.

Still more intimate neutralizing combinations exist, and the danger is particularly great when the critic loses sight of the positive neutralizing reforms because of the effective propaganda from the system for the (neutralized) negative reform. Eagerness and direct initiative on the part of the system to carry the negating reform into effect may generally be taken as a sign that a neutralizing positive reform is hidden behind the negating reform. Representatives of the system rarely show such eagerness and initiative without having a compensating positive reform, an 'alternative', to put in its place.

This is a general and serious problem. Often systems do not give in to negating pressure without having secured (in a more or less consciously planned way) another arrangement which – with greater legitimacy – takes over the function of the arrangement just abolished. This is to say – as was said in the essay on 'The

Unfinished' – that when boundaries which you want abolished are abolished, the field is also thrown open to influences from other systems of an undesired character, When a certain system is abolished, there is a danger that other systems with the same function arise, or invade the now open field. What was a negative reform results in a positive change.

As suggested in the essay on 'The Unfinished', the concrete practical political task is therefore that of insisting on the abolishing line also in relation to the new, invading systems, *in a continually greater circumference.* From the essay 'On Action Research' I repeat that this takes place through the oscillation between – development from and to – theory and action. The two give rest to and understanding of each other; the separation between them is the abandonment of the line of abolition, because theory and practice respectively are no longer being abolished, and are thereby no longer remaining unfinished and in process.

3. Unstrategic negation

But it is not enough programmatically to insist on the abolishing line in a continually larger circumference. At the same time, it is essential to avoid using up your strength on unstrategic negation – that is, on negative reforms directed at points which are more or less ineffective in relation to the system in general. 'Points' in the system will of course vary greatly in this respect. The ability to find consequential points is dependent on how good your theory about the system is; how well the theory analyses the functional relationships of the points to other parts of the system.

A possible external sign indicating that you have hit a strategic point may be the expression of fear on the part of the system's representatives for negative reforms. When the fear is great, there is reason to believe that you have hit a consequential point. The strong fear within the prison system aroused by the abolition of the prisoners' political unawareness is thus perhaps a sign indicating that a crucial point has been hit – all the time assuming that neutralizing positive reforms are avoided. However, we also saw that it is important to 'guide' such an abolition in 'the right direction'. While the political awakening in the prisons may provide exposing material to outside and more powerful groups, the structure is not such that the prisoners themselves have power to 'tear down the prisons from the inside'. It is, in other words, essential not to use the 'alarm' of the system's representatives as a blind criterion, but to interpret it in a theoretical context, as I tried to do in the essay on 'Organization Among the Expelled'.

What I have said here concerning negative reforms within the prison system also holds good within more encompassing sectors of society – for example in connection with the relationship of the prison system as a whole to the more encompassing policy of coercion and control towards the expelled. That is, it may be asked whether a negative reform such as the abolition of the prison system in general actually is strategic in relation to the more encompassing policy of control, and – if the long-range objective is still more general – whether the abolition of this policy of control in turn is strategic in relation to fundamental and unequal power relationships in our society. It is often maintained that the prisons are mere 'symptoms' of the general policy of control in relation to the expelled, that the policy of control is a mere 'symptom' of the fundamental power relationships, and that if you also have a more encompassing objective, the attack on the penal and control policy is unstrategic. Is this true?

I believe it is wrong to regard the prison system – and still more the encompassing policy of control in relation to the expelled – in this way. To be sure, these systems are 'symptoms' in the sense of being effects of more fundamental power relationships, but at the same time they in turn have important consequences for the maintenance of these power relationships. We gained some understanding of the latter consequences through the analysis of the situation of the expelled given above. Those who do not contribute to the positive society are expelled and later kept out of very disturbing circulation precisely through the penal policy and the policy of control. This process of isolation and separation seems to be increasing rather strongly in our society. And not only that, the process also seems to be much more systematic in the modern capitalistic and state-capitalistic societies. The groups having the best reason to protest increasingly appear to be placed in such a way that they do not contribute, and thereby in such a way that their protest becomes powerless. This process may be viewed as the core of the policy of the modem welfare state. Seen from this perspective, the penal and control policies become an extremely important dimension in society, and not just a passive 'symptom' of the application of power elsewhere. Abolition of the measures implicit in our policy of control would produce very important changes in our 'positive', productive life. For one thing, the expelled would concretely be pressing over old boundaries, and through their integration in and 'sanding' of the ultra-effective productive society, they would take part in altering that society, and thereby in changing fundamental power relationships. For another, the abolition of the measures following from our policy of control would show to the world what kind of policy our type of society presupposes in relation to the expelled, thereby increasing public understanding of the need for a protest against this type of society. Stated differently, some reformists maintain that prisons and similar arrangements of control are not necessary in our society, that society could manage just as well without them. This is their main argument for a general abolition of imprisonment and similar arrangements of control. I believe this analysis is wrong. By maintaining as expelled those who do not contribute, the prison system – and even more so, the general control system – is necessary for the maintenance of the effective, productive society, which in turn is important in maintaining fundamental relationships of power in society. Thereby, it makes more general political sense to work for the abolition of a system of control like the prison system. But let me reiterate, the struggle is useless if the expelled protest alone. The main struggle must take place outside the ranks of the expelled, using crucial material supplied by the expelled.

As suggested already, this means at the same time working for the line of abolition 'in a continually wider circumference', as mentioned above – a task which is necessary if the abolition of a limited 'point' or system – e.g. the prison system – is not just to be specious or false. In order for the abolition in a *limited* field to remain real, the abolition *around* the limited field must continue in a continually wider circumference; if not, the liberated field is invaded by systems having the old function. This means that the wider political perspective which is taken here is in the interest of the expelled themselves. And it means that new fighting organizations, with wider objectives, must be established when a given objective is achieved, in order also to retain the result which has been obtained. The limited and the wider objectives join.[29]

In this way we perhaps understand more fully why it is impossible to visualize any final goal or state at which the policy of abolition simply ends. As mentioned earlier, the very existence of 'society' in itself seems to be (restructuring in a limiting way. The point, therefore, must be precisely that of not letting the policy of abolition end. In the abolition itself – in a continually wider circumference – lies the alternative, the unfinished.

*

In the preceding paragraphs I have talked in very general terms, The praxis of negating political work is necessarily much more concrete, yet all the time one must keep in mind that the difference between negative and positive reforms is decisive in the long run. Now, how can we describe the 'core' in the policy of negating reforms? It may be traced through several steps.

A negating reform – in which you work for abolition also on a short-term basis – concretely means abolition of whatever gave or gives legitimacy to a system you regard as wrong. Thereby you unmask the attempts of the system to mask its true nature; you unveil whatever the system veils. The system dresses itself up; you undress the system. What shows itself behind the negation is thereby not a 'nothing', but a 'something' – a reality which the system has tried to hide. Through the abolition of forced labour – the undermining of the last remnant of legitimacy on the part of this system – a reality showed itself which the system had hidden: poverty in Norway – or at least a 'new' important aspect of poverty in Norway. Forced labour was a way of keeping the expelled paupers out of circulation and out of sight.

The negating reforms unmask the system's attempts to mask its true nature. In other words: the negating reform abolishes (aspects of) the concealment, so that a reality (the paupers at Oppstad) becomes unconcealed. To keep something concealed when someone inquires is 'untruthfulness'; 'unconcealment' when someone inquires is 'truthfulness'. Through the uncovering of reality the negating, abolishing reform thereby makes the world *more truthful.*

Truth is a value in and of itself, but this is not the reason why I stress its importance. The abolishing reform uncovers the concealed reality, brings forth the unconcealed and thereby the truth, and this uncovered truth is a *necessary* – not sufficient – *condition for giving the counterforces long-range freedom of action.* Concretely, the counterforces may be very different social groups and organizations; some of them have been mentioned earlier – in the essay on 'Organization Among the Expelled'. The point here is that the counterforces must be liberated from the ties to the positive and masking aspect which conceals. The issue is that of liberation from having your attention distracted from what you actually have to act against: where the enemy actually is. But the issue also concerns being liberated from an inhibition having to do with 'conscience' – the inhibition of conscience following from the false belief that the system, or its representative, is 'morally good'. The question, then, is that of liberation from cognitive as well as moral ties.

Working for negative reform, in other words, means working for one of the conditions necessary for a liberation to become a more long-range counterforce. The uncovering of truth leads to the liberation of this force. In this way we can, in other words, see a connection between 'truth' and 'freedom'.

Innumerable trivial and simple everyday events confirm this connection. The feeling of being 'liberated', which follows from having 'spoken out', is a simple little example. Another everyday example may be found in the released inmate who said that he had to tell 'everything as it was' to potential employers, etc. – if he did, 'he would be free'. He was right in this: no one could *later* again get power over him; later there would be nothing more 'to hold over him', and thereby nothing more to press him with. Let me mention in passing that the very pledge of professional 'secrecy' which the prison system invokes in relation to its prisoners – names are not to be mentioned, background should be kept hidden – draws a veil over reality and thereby creates a lack of freedom. It inhibits the prisoners' political freedom of action to protest against the prison system. It prevents them from standing forth and from bringing material unmasking the system to those in the external world who want to fight as their allies – a process which is, as we have argued above, essential for them.

The process leading from the unmasking of the concealed to the unconcealed and thereby the truth, and in turn from this to freedom of action, is perhaps a part of what *Martin Heidegger* was thinking of when he wrote that 'the essence of truth is freedom'.

4. The politics of abolition

Some threads may now be collected.

With regard to the question of maintaining a policy of abolition, I have in these essays mainly treated the difficulties connected with this as they appear in a policy in relation to a system which you are working to abolish on a long-term basis. In such a policy, the relationship between short-term and long-term objectives presents itself as a pervasive problem. In slightly oversimplified terms it may be said that the literature generally refers to one of two solutions to the problem. On the one hand, some maintain – often hoping that the maximizing of a crisis may lead to final abolition – that you must not in any way enter on work for short-term reforms, because such activity inevitably leads to corruption or quenching of the work for the long-term goal of abolition. Against this, others maintain that such a policy is in practice impossible to follow and paralysing to action, and that you therefore have to enter on work for short-term reforms – while maintaining the long-term abolishing objective. The conception underlying these essays is that both general views contain some truth, but that neither of them is entirely valid. Completely to avoid any work for short-term reforms is often politically impossible as well as paralysing to action, while short-term reforms often have a corrupting effect on the long-term work. The question is whether there is any solution. I have emphasized – at least as a tentative view of the problem – that the short-term reforms which you work for – have to work for – as a road to the long-term goal of abolition must be of a very specific type: they must also consistently be of an abolishing kind. Only then – by a stubborn insistence on abolition also in what is close at hand – do you have a chance to solve the conflict between short-term and long-term objectives. The fact that such stubborn insistence is no simple matter should appear from the preceding discussion of method.

Let me mention that the type of short-term changes which I have stressed do not correspond to the reforms which an author like *André Gorz* finds it possible to combine with a long-term abolishing objective (Gorz 1964, Norwegian ed. 1967). *André Gorz* represents the view that complete dissociation from short-term reforms is paralysing to a protest movement. He therefore believes that you have to enter on a reform policy. However, he distinguishes between 'reformist' and 'non-reformist' reforms and emphasizes the importance of stressing the latter type. 'Reformist' reforms have goals which are subordinated to the facilities and the presuppositions of a system and a policy presented by the adversary. A 'non-reformist' reform, however, is not geared to whatever is possible within the framework of a given system, but to that which 'should be realizable' in view of human demands and needs. A 'non-reformist' reform, in other words, goes beyond the facilities and presuppositions presented by the adversary's system. Pure wage demands constitute *Gorz's* main example of a 'reformist' reform. Demands concerning the right to decide over working conditions constitute an example of the opposite. According to *Gorz*, in their work for the 'non-reformist' reforms, the labourers must enter into negotiations and compromises with the capitalists. 'This', *Gorz* says, 'can only be shocking to maximalists, whom even Lenin turned against when he maintained that there are good and bad compromises' (p. 51 Norwegian edition). Thus, with *Gorz* the struggle is terminated by a partial victory, but during the struggle the awareness of the labourers has developed, so that one is prepared for new struggles. Thereby, one does not give up one's goals through a compromise, but 'on the contrary . . . approach the goals' (p. 51 Norwegian edition).

Gorz's distinction between 'reformist' and 'non-reformist' reforms is theoretically interesting. However, none of his examples of 'non-reformist' reforms are guaranteed against being absorbed by and consolidating the main system (a fact which *Gorz* incidentally admits, at least on one occasion – see the Norwegian edition p. 36). And they are, in fact, at the same time examples of what I have here called 'positive' reforms. Another way of stating this is to say that in order to be what *Gorz* calls 'non-reformist' – in order to break with the presuppositions of the main system – a reform must be of *the abolishing kind.*

*

But in these essays I have not only discussed the maintenance of a policy of abolition in relation to a system that you are working to abolish on a long-term basis. From time to time I have also touched on the question of the maintenance of what you have abolished after the long-term goal of abolition in fact has been attained: after the prison system is abolished, or after a revolution has taken place. A fundamental assumption in this work is that a differentiation here between two levels is false. As suggested in 'The Unfinished' as well as later, there is no reason to expect any terminated condition of final abolition; for example, no country can count on attaining a terminated condition of final revolution; a retrospective 'consolidation' of the abolition which has been attained – for example a revolution in a country – is the same as finishing the abolition and in large measure returning to the old. The maintenance of an abolition implies that there is constantly more to abolish, that one looks ahead towards a new and still more long-term objective of abolition, that one constantly moves in a wider circle to new fields for abolition. Thus, if a country after its revolution does not manage to maintain this perspective, the revolution dies. Stated differently, not only is it necessary, in order to attain a long-term goal of abolition, that you stubbornly insist on abolitions on a short-term basis and in the immediate present; conversely it is just as important, in order to insist on abolitions in the immediate present, that you have a more long-term goal of abolition to work for.

Finally, it may be asked: Has anyone ever managed to insist on such a perspective in the most encompassing unit – in a country as a whole, after a revolution? Perhaps not. All the same, it is again tempting to turn to places like China and Albania – this time with a certain, cautious expectation. In these countries one works for a more encompassing revolution, outside the physical borders of the countries. As long as one in fact works for this, one can probably manage to avoid finishing the revolution at home. We know, however, that the thought of a more encompassing revolution has died in other societies, after other revolutions, and that China and Albania are in part confronted with rather consolidated societies which they are in fact themselves dependent on. In order to preclude the process of finishing, it is therefore probably imperative for these countries to find methods inside their physical borders, with new internal goals of abolition. With the reservation that the environment outside the physical borders is present all the time as a limiting and threatening condition, it may be possible that the peoples of these countries have found methods which, with great difficulty, make it possible for them to prevent the process of finishing, or at least to prevent the finishing from taking place so fast. We touched on this possibility earlier, in connection with the notion of 'organizing', and it may be expanded on here. It seems that, for example, the Albanians are busily engaged in, and struggling with, keeping their society and their revolution uncompleted by working for continually new goals of abolition. The stress on a foreign and an only suggested road further on, past the partial goals, is prominent; the techniques to prevent bureaucratization – among which physical labour for the cadres is only one – are stressed; the conscious search for, or at least use of, new 'turning points' (the break with Yugoslavia, the break with the Soviet Union) – which counteracts consolidation – is conspicuous; the emphasis on a continual and thorough-going 'revolutionizing' is noticeable.

But we certainly know that all of this is difficult and uncertain.

Postscript: on an attempt at breaking out

I have to add a few words on an attempt to break out of a prison. To a considerable extent, the attempt was successful, and I will therefore recommend other prisoners to follow the example.

The attempt took place at the prison of Kumla in Sweden, at about 3 p.m. on 23 November 1971. Eight prisoners took part in the attempt.

I have described the background of the attempt in Chapter VI above. There I analysed among other things the development of prison strikes and 'negotiations' in the Swedish prison system. In this connection I mentioned that after the hunger strike in June 1971, still another round of talks between prisoners and authorities was announced. These talks took place in November 1971, and the attempt at breaking out took place in connection with them.

*

The story is actually brief. In each of Sweden's eight prison regions the prisoners again elected a representative for the talks, and the eight met for preparatory deliberations on 1–5 November 1971. This time the prisoners had also elected substitute representatives – two from each region – and originally they asked to have all 24 representatives participate in the preparatory deliberations. Permission for this was not given. After a discussion, the eight nevertheless decided to meet the authorities as planned, on 23–26 November 1971, at Kumla.

This time the Prison Department had invited the representatives to discussions. Furthermore the Department had – apparently with enthusiasm said yes to a television program about the talks. As earlier, the staff organizations had had reservations concerning the talks, but this time they had agreed as well. The interest in new talks on the part of the Prison Department was probably related to several factors. Most likely, talks were in part seen as a way in which to integrate the various parties in the prison system, and as a way in which to hear more directly the prisoners' views. The extent to which the authorities understood how distant prisoner representatives may be from their group is not known. Neither do we know whether the authorities were aware of how little information people actually transmit through such formalized structures as the nation-wide 'talks'. But in addition, the authorities had clearly discovered that talks are entirely unthreatening to the system, and that they are in fact an *important way of supplying the system with new – and badly needed – legitimacy.* To amplify, as mentioned in Chapter VI, the Prison Department had long ago begun to advertize abroad the 'democratization' of the prison system, and representatives of the authorities had publicly referred to how unusual in international terms the Swedish experiment in democracy was.

During the preparations between 1 and 5 November, the prisoners were given the opportunity to consult with an advisory group three hours per day (on the last day, the time was extended somewhat). The advisory group consisted of an associate professor in penal law, a psychologist who had earlier worked at the Kumla institution, an ex-prisoner who had taken part in the Österåker-talks in January 1971, and a sociologist (the present author). To fill the two open places in the prisoners' delegation itself, the prisoners this time chose a lawyer from KRUM and a psychologist who had earlier worked at the Österåker prison. The two were chosen against the advice of the advisory group (and they were also reluctant themselves). The advisory group thought that the best thing would be to have the open places in the delegation filled by ex-prisoners, and the members of the advisory group were themselves unwilling to take a direct part in the 'negotiations'.

This time too the authorities apparently viewed the advisory group as a difficult and interfering element from outside the prison system. Thus, a detailed memorandum had been issued concerning how the advisors were to be treated during the preparatory meetings. Among other things, the staff at Kumla were especially to ensure that the members of the group did not arrive at the institution in an intoxicated state. The representatives of the prisoners were carefully searched (stripped) after each visit by the advisory group. The advisory group was denied the use of the telephone in the institution: the group had to make use of a public telephone by the entrance to the institution – a fact which complicated the necessary and difficult long distance calls which the advisors had to make from time to time. One of the advisors (the present author) once by mistake entered the office of a trainee to make an *internal* telephone call to a social worker working in the institution. The advisor was sharply rebuked by an assistant, and more or less thrown out of the office.

The advisors asked the Prison Department for permission this time to listen to the actual 'negotiations' through loud speakers – in order to be able to give better advice. This was refused, one of the justifications being that if this were arranged, permission to listen would also have to be given to other advisory groups (the staff organizations this time brought along advisors). The plea that the prisoners' bargaining position and bargaining experience were especially weak did not lead anywhere.

Several of the members of the advisory group were beforehand very sceptical about the new talks. They felt that the result would be a repetition of the talks at Österåker, where little or nothing was gained except added legitimacy, or publicity, for the prison system, and they viewed it as their duty to communicate this view to the representatives of the prisoners. The prisoners had, however, decided to try the method of discussions. Seven of the eight representatives had not earlier participated in talks of this kind, and since the promise of new talks actually was the end result of their last strike, they felt that they had very little freedom of choice. At the same time they also hoped and believed that something positive would come out of the discussions. Without saying so directly, they probably felt that the prison authorities were the only ones who might be able to improve the prisoners' situation. What can prisoners do under such conditions, except to approach these authorities and ask for their mercy? What can prisoners do except grow conservative and timid in their views on prison?

In the light of this choice on the part of the prisoners, the advisors concentrated during the further preparations on giving legal advice and advice concerning the technical aspects of negotiations – relevant to the concrete demands which the prisoners wished to present at the talks. To some extent, the advisors also gave advice concerning the content of the demands. However, during the fourth of the five preparatory meetings an important change of plans took place. During this meeting one of the advisors – the ex-prisoner who had participated as a representative at the Österåker talks – *was alone with the inmates' representatives*. With his own bitter experiences from Österåker as a background, the ex-prisoner during this meeting gave a strong warning against entering into talks with the authorities without having received guarantees to the effect that concrete decisions were to be made.

When the other advisors returned to the last preparatory meeting, the prisoners had decided to *demand* that actual decisions were this time to be made during the talks. The demand was later formulated as follows: 'FFCO demands that the composition of the representatives from the Prison Department and the staff organizations is such that decisions may be made, and that decisions are made at the negotiations concerning the points to which existing law may be applied.' The advisors were later accused by the representatives of the prison system of having 'influenced' the prisoners in the direction of stressing such a condition, and thereby in effect making the talks impossible. If any 'influence' was exerted at this point, it came from an *ex-inmate* who had himself been exposed to the discussions at Österåker. The other advisors were unprepared for the development mentioned here when they came back to the last preparatory meeting, That they viewed the development as a political maturation, and that they supported it later on, is a different matter.

The prisoners also presented a series of other demands – which received their final formulation during a hectic afternoon on the last day of preparations. But we were aware of the fact that the authorities would hardly agree to Point 1 on the list – the demand for actual decisions. Therefore, a strike action was prepared – partly a work strike, partly a hunger strike which were to be the prisoners' reaction if the authorities only wanted noncommittal talks. The prisoners were permitted to give a press conference after the five preparatory days – but the press was not heavily represented. As mentioned in Chapter VI, prisoners' 'negotiations' were no longer news, a fact which weakened still further the prisoners' bargaining position in connection with their concrete demands. However, the press conference was hectic for the inmates, who for a while seemed to forget their decision to break off 'negotiations' if the authorities refused to make decisions. The temptation to 'negotiate' and 'co-operate' was in other words still present, perhaps particularly because the bargaining position was weak.

On 23 November, the opening day of the discussions, the Swedish flag flew over Kumla prison. The authorities arrived – as on the previous occasion in their black sedans, smilingly shaking hands as they proceeded to the 'negotiation' room. The prisoners – as on the previous occasion – were the last to be admitted.

But there was a difference. This time the prisoners had – together with their advisors – planned a certain strategy. In connection with the introductory demand that decisions now had to be made, the prisoners' side had decided to argue that this time decisions were to be made jointly by the parties. In other words, real *negotiations* were to take place. However, the prisoners' side calculated that the prison authorities would refer to Swedish law, which states that only the Prison Department is to make decisions on questions concerning the prison system. The prisoners' side had therefore also prepared an additional question to the authorities, namely whether the *Prison Department* would then be willing to make decisions *at the table*, after hearing the views of the inmates, This was prepared as a question and not as a demand, because the prisoners would thereby be more independent when evaluating the answer of the authorities, This two-step tactic was suggested by the advisors, and accepted by the prisoners after a lengthy discussion.

The verbatim protocol from the talks, which this time was issued only a few weeks after the meeting, shows that the authorities, as expected, quickly made it clear that joint decisions could not be made. The Director of Prisons, who – judging from the protocol – seemed interested in getting the talks on their way, wisely played the ball to the representatives of the staff organizations. The latter made it clear that they were unwilling and unable to make any decisions at the table.

Next, in answer to the question from the prisoners whether the Prison Department's representatives were then willing to make decisions alone, it was stated, inter alia, that many of the demands of the prisoners presupposed legal changes and economic grants which were outside the competence of the Prison Department. Decisions could therefore not be made concerning every point. Replying to a question whether the authorities would at least indicate their opinion concerning matters outside the competence of the Prison Department, the Prison Department answered in the negative. The standard procedure of hearings had to be followed ('in other words, you mean that the Prison Department, here at this table, is to make statements concerning questions which might be sent to us as a part of a hearing one or two years from now . . . ?'), existing agreements were referred to ('we have . . . no knowledge of how the staff organization will view that agreement'), and so on. With regard to the question of making decisions concerning issues within the competence of the Prison Department, a vague answer was given to the effect that first it was necessary to begin to talk about the various points, and wait and see. Possibly one might fetch the two section chiefs whose presence would be necessary to enable the Prison Department 'to make decisions in questions not to be submitted to the Prison Department with its laymen representatives' (the Prison Department in Sweden is a board which also includes laymen representatives). It was necessary to talk through the various demands on the list, and wait and see.

The prisoners were, however, prepared for such a vague answer. In advance the prisoners and their advisors had acted out the various possible moves of the Prison Department – among others, the vague reply mentioned here – and they had decided not to give in to such a move, but either to break off the 'negotiations' or withdraw to discuss the situation. The prisoners now knew that a vague answer on the part of the Prison Department would not contain any significant guarantee; and that the Prison Department would not under any circumstances make any significant decisions at the table. Protocol No. 4/71, from the National Meeting of Employees in the Prison System of 20 September 1971, had fallen into the hands of the prisoners. In § 5 in the protocol it was stated:

> The chairman [the Director of Prisons] gave an account of the renewed talks between the Prison Department and the inmates, planned to take place at the Kumla institution during week 43 . . . Inspector N. N. emphasized the importance of clarifying from the beginning the character of the negotiations as non-decision-making discussions, in order to avoid misunderstandings on the part of the inmates. The chairman was of the opinion that this had been stated also before the previous round of talks. One should, however, this time remember to *stress even harder that the issue at hand is talks [at det dreier seg om overlegninger], and that all decisions must be made in standard administrative order [my italics]*.

This was quite unequivocal. One could in other words not expect that the vague statement from the Prison Department would lead to results of any significance. If decisions were to be made at all, they would be made in insignificant questions. This, in fact, was also admitted at the meeting itself. A representative of the Prison Department stated that important questions involving matters of principle must be decided by the laymen's board of the Prison Department. 'Then the question is in each case to decide whether the issue is of this kind, and I should think that a good deal of what we will arrive at here will be of this nature', It did not help the prisoners that the Prison Department had perhaps actually wanted to be more accommodating to the prisoners, and that they were actually hampered and. bound by the decision-making structure as well as by pressure from the staff organizations. To the prisoners' representatives – and their advisors -this only showed still more clearly how meaningless such 'top level talks' actually are.

The protocol from the employees' meeting quoted above (which had fallen into the hands of the prisoners after their preparatory meetings at the beginning of November) was discussed by at least one inmate council before the talks began on 23 November. The advisors learnt about the protocol on the day before the talks were to begin.

After the Prison Department had made their vague statement (in which some representatives of the authorities more or less implored the prisoners to stay), the prisoners withdrew to discuss the situation (they had also had several breaks earlier). The advisors were of the opinion that the prisoners now ought to break off the 'negotiations', and not enter into non-committal talks about the concrete demands, because in such talks the prisoners would – on the background of what was now known from Österåker – be in a very weak position, One of the advisors, however, urged the prisoners individually to state their personal view of the situation. The prisoners did so, round the table and in some detail, and it was unanimously decided that the 'negotiations' could not be continued on the present basis. The question was discussed whether the result of the statements, and the final vote, were to be presented by the chairman of the prisoners' delegation, or by each delegate individually. The latter procedure was chosen, and in the conference room each prisoner individually stated his view. At 3 p.m. on 23 November, the breaking off was in other words a fact.

The reaction of the authorities to the breaking off was spontaneously negative. A message arrived at the prisoners' separate conference room stating that the press conference which had been planned following the discussions was now cancelled. Most likely because the press and other mass media had already arrived, this decision was reversed (more concretely: a new message arrived at the prisoners' conference room, stating that the press conference was to be held after all). The prisoners and their advisors prepared a press release – based among other things on an earlier proposal for a press release from one of the prisoners – stressing that the prisoners could not take part in what they understood to be a 'P.R.-show' on the part of the authorities. I have earlier mentioned that the prisoners were in my view right in believing that talks – and actually also real negotiations – would only strengthen the legitimacy of the prison system itself. At about 4 p.m. the prisoners marched into the magnificent lobby of the Kumla prison – where prisoners rarely if ever set foot – and the prisoners' chairman read out the press release in front of TV cameras and photographers. Afterwards, the prisoners were interviewed individually by the journalists. We who were on the prisoners' side experienced this as a moment of freedom. The attempt to co-opt the prisoners' organization had, at least for the present, been avoided. The representatives of the authorities, however, followed the press conference with grim faces from the gallery of the lobby. This was not what they had expected as a conclusion. Some of them more or less furiously addressed the advisors, stating that this was their work. A regional director loudly scolded the prisoner representative from his region, maintaining that he had no authority to break off discussions in this way. The Director of Prisons did not wish to meet the press – the Prison Department and the staff organizations simply handed out each its mimeographed communiqué. The disappointment of the authorities was obvious and great.

*

What is the more general significance of the breaking off of the talks at Kumla?

I view the breaking off at Kumla as an attempt on the part of the prisoners to break out: an attempt to break out of the 'circle' surrounding prison authorities and prisoners, making the prisoners so powerless when acting inside it. As mentioned in Chapter VI, through 'negotiations', the conditions in the prison system become 'internal issues' – issues between the prison authorities and the prisoners. In this relationship, the prisoners are powerless and therefore without a bargaining position. Their powerlessness is related to a fundamental structural feature of the prison, the prisoners' position as non-contributors to the system. As non-contributors, the prisoners have nothing they can threaten with. In contrast to the workers in a factory, they cannot threaten with withdrawing a contribution to the system. (The description is ideal-typical, but the empirical facts are not far from the ideal type.) This one-sided dependence on those in power easily leads the prisoners into a coalition – however ambivalent – with those in power, in which the prisoners have no way of purring pressure behind their demands. During the first preparatory consultations preceding the talks at Kumla, the prisoners' representatives were willing to move further into this coalition. After consultations with the ex-inmate from the Österåker discussions, however, an alternative view gradually matured: co-operation would only take place on certain clear conditions, and a breakdown would occur if these conditions were not fulfilled. Among several there was probably an underlying feeling that it was necessary to extricate oneself from the role as the powerless party in a coalition, and that a way of doing so was to insist on the condition of concrete decisions. By breaking off when the condition was not fulfilled, the prisoners' representatives seriously tried to get out of the system *in which their position is so weak*, out of the structure which is such that the prisoners are powerless in relation to their counterpart. Instead of continuing 'negotiations' along the 'vertical' axis of the system, they began to move 'horizon tally' – in the direction away from the system (see Chapter VI). In my view, this was very courageous of the prisoners, because the counter-pressure was great. The disappointment of the authorities over the development indicates, in my opinion, that the prisoners chose the right road: their more externally orientated movement is at least to some extent threatening to the system.

*

But of course, it is difficult to say whether the prisoners' breaking out is permanent, and whether the prisoners will more concretely manage to establish permanent 'horizontal' relationships with outside organizations of the kind mentioned in Chapter VI. Two circumstances must be mentioned which may indicate that this will not be easy.

In the first place, immediately after the breaking off at Kumla, a new prison strike took place in Sweden. It was a work and hunger strike, with an admixture of occasional thirst strikers. The number of participants has never been ascertained, but a fair number of institutions were included. However, it was only to a small extent covered by the press *(Dagens Nyheter* again constituted a faithful exception). To KRUM – which again tried to coordinate the strike as best as possible – it soon became clear that the strike ought not 'just to fizzle out': it ought to have a conclusion which the prisoners might be reasonably satisfied with as a 'result'. Where do you find conclusions of this kind? KRUM first sought a way 'out' of the system of penal and correctional policy. We tried to find independent politicians who might support the prisoners' demands; by sending out mimeographed press releases an attempt was made to mobilize political youth organizations in support of the prisoners, etc. This, however, led to nothing, and as time began to be short, KRUM – as earlier – had to revert back 'into' the system. The penal system controls most short-term, realistic values important to the prisoners, and a satisfactory 'result' could finally only be found there. More concretely, upon approval from the six prisoner representatives we were now able to establish contact with (the authorities had again turned on their means of power, including instructions concerning isolation of the inmate councils from the mass media and from KRUM, isolation of prisoners on work strike, etc.), the lawyer from KRUM who had filled one of the open places at the 'negotiation' table contacted the Minister of Justice, and proposed a meeting between the Minister and the eight prisoner representatives. It was thought that at such a meeting, the prisoners might be able to present their view on the talks as well as on issues in penal and correctional policy, and at the same time hear the Minister's views. It was felt that this would constitute a fair result from the point of view of the prison population, and it did imply the bringing of the issues in penal policy further up, to a political level. The Minister of justice seemed positive to the proposal, but had first to discuss the matter with the Director of Prisons. When the Minister later called back, the strike was rapidly decreasing. Reports came in stating that various prisons were in the process of ending their strike. The Minister of justice now said that he only wished to meet the lawyer from KRUM – possibly with a view to a later meeting with the prisoners' representatives. At this time KRUM had no bargaining position, and could do nothing but accept the Minister's offer. The alternative could have been a strike without any 'result' at all. Those of us who sat listening to the telephone conversation between the Minister and KRUM's man while the reports from the prisons came pouring in, had probably never before experienced so intensely where the power lies. In short, the control of the authorities over values relating to the prisoners brutally forced us back into their system. Let me add that the meeting between the Minister and KRUM's lawyer took place during the following week. The Minister found it difficult to meet the prisoners' representatives because it meant disregarding the prison authorities, but an agreement was finally made concerning a meeting between the prisoners' representatives and a recently appointed parliamentary committee for the review of penal and correctional policy. This meeting – which was very brief, and which only comprised a few of the prisoners' representatives, took place four months later.

In the second place, among the masses of prisoners as well as in the general public, the attitude towards the break at Kumla is hardly only positive. From the prisoners, criticism of the break has been presented, and at least one inmate coun-cil proposed during the strike itself that arbitration between the parties ought to take place, so that the 'negotiations' could start anew. In the newspapers the break was in part experienced as unwanted, and when the plan concerning a meeting between the Minister of Justice and KRUM's lawyer was made public, *Göte-borgstidningen*, for example, presented it as if KRUM's man was now working intensely to have the talks resumed. The political maturation, and the understand-ing of the structure of the system and the prisoners' position within it, which the prisoners' representatives at Kumla gradually attained, has not yet penetrated into the consciousness of the prisoner population and the broader public. A breakdown in 'negotiations' is experienced as a conflict which immediately demands a 'solu-tion' in the form of new 'negotiations'.

In line with this, the development in the Swedish prison system *after* the break at Kumla has vacillated between the 'line of negotiations' and the 'line of external action'. In May 1972, a considerable number of Swedish prisoners (between 900 and 1,450) went on a hunger strike in sympathy with some inmates in the isolation section at Kumla. The strike led to activity among persons outside the prison sys-tem. They criticized the conditions at the isolation section. In July/August 1972 some prisoners (400–500) again went on strike, now caused by the conditions at Österåker prison. This time, certain talks were initiated between the Österåker prisoners and the authorities, the prisoners' demands were largely turned down, and the Österåker inmates dissolved their inmate council in protest against the kind of 'co-operation' which the council was now being involved in. (The inmates in some other prisons did the same.) Informal meetings were the result of a brief and more dramatic action at Kumla (a number of prisoners barricaded themselves on the roof – under extensive press coverage) in November 1972 directed against the repressive conditions in the institution. A relatively small-scale work strike in May 1973, on the other hand, was geared towards stimulating a discussion of penal policy in outside society rather than 'negotiations'. But some inmates are certainly hoping for negotiations – perhaps especially after a widely publicized bank robbery in August 1973. The robbery, which involved the taking of four hos-tages, was extensively covered as a great sensation by the mass media throughout Northern Europe, and the law-and-order movement in Sweden – at present grow-ing in a period of unemployment – gained at least temporary momentum.

Therefore the future is uncertain, and it may well be that new talks will come about. To those who have seen through the prisoners' bargaining position within the prison structure, the political task becomes two-fold: in the first place, to transmit the recently won understanding of the structure and of the alternative possibilities to the broad masses of the prisoner population, and in the second place to transmit the same understanding to the public. The former may take place through critical and thorough discussions of the 'negotiation line' at ground level in the institution, in which it is necessary to stress that even in negotiations at which actual decisions are made, the prisoners' position will be extremely weak. The latter is probably a question of a very long-term influencing of public opinion, by which it is necessary to make external political organizations – with which the prisoners, in a long-term perspective, may ally themselves – conscious of the prisoners' cause.

The tasks are far from simple. With regard to both, the break at Kumla will be a road sign.

Bibliography: *The Politics of Abolition* (1974)

Bill No. 54, 1968/69.

Bill No. 1, 1970.

Christie, Nils (1962): 'Noen kriminalpolitiske særforholdsreglers sosiologi' (The Sociology of Some Specialized Legal Reactions), *Tidsskrift for samfunnsforskning,* Vol. 3 No. 1 pp. 28–48.

Edling, Stig and Göran Elwin (1972): *Autopsy of a Dead Committee Report* (probably an unregistered Report).

Eriksson, Jörgen (1970): *Revolt I huvet* (Revolt in the Head). Albert Bonnier.

Gorz, André (1964/1967): *Stratègie ouvriére et nèocapitalisme.* Editions du Seuil/Norwegian Edition.

Kriminalvården (The Prison Department) (1970).

KROM-nytt (KROM-news) (No. 3 1970).

Lysgaard, Sverre (1960): *Arbeiderkollektivet.* Universitetsforlaget.

Martinson, Bo (16 April 1971): 'Prison Democracy in Sweden'. *Viewpoint. Swedish Information Service.*

Mathiesen, Thomas (1965/2012): *The Defences of the Weak. A Sociological Study of a Norwegian Correctional Institution.* Tavistock Publications/Routledge Revival.

Mathiesen, Thomas (1971): *Det uferdige* (the Unfinished). Pax Publishers.

Mathiesen, Thomas (1973): *Pressgruppe og samfunnsstruktur* (Pressure Group and Social Structure). Pax Publishers.

Mathiesen, Thomas (1975): *Løsgjengerkrigen* (The Vagrancy War). Sosionomen Publishers.

Olofsen, Clark (1970): *Rapport från Österåker* (Report from Österåker). Kumla Prison, December 20.

Parsons, Talcott (1951): *The Social System.* Free Press.

Street, David et al. (1966): *Organization for Treatment.* Free Press.

Tornklint, Hjalmar (1971): *Förtroende för fånger* (Confidence in Prisoners). Bonniers Publishers.

Vinterhed, Kerstin (1970): 'Makt åt klienterna eller terapeutiskt samhälle – en skendebatt?' (Power to the Clients or Therapeutic Community – A Sham Fight?) *Pockettidningen R* s. 142–145.

Weber, Max (1919/first published 1921, 1958): "Politik als Beruf" (Politics as a Calling), *Gesammelte Politische Schriften,* Duncker & Humbot.

Wittgenstein, Ludwig (1922): *Tractatus: Logico Philosophicus.* Harcourt, Brace and Company.

Notes

1. The details concerning this Act will be discussed at length later. The paragraphs regulating criminalization of being intoxicated in public and regulation of forced labour were repealed after an intense struggle in 1970, and the Act as a whole, including begging, was repealed during 2006. The repeal of the paragraph against begging was later

criticised because the number of beggars from Eastern Europe increased considerably. This note was added in 2013.

2. The concepts of 'criminal policy' and 'penal and correctional policy' are used interchangeably, denoting society's policy towards those who have committed acts in contravention of the society's laws. The concepts are unfortunate: they imply an acceptance of the established society's frame of reference and delimitation of fields of political action. As shown in Chapter 1, the rulers in part rule through language. The concepts are used because a competing language is lacking. The development of such a language is an important political task.

3. Today, in 2013, the organisation has about 200 members who have e-mail and are coupled to the Internet; there is an estimate of less than 50 members who are inmates (and who do not have e-mail). Today over 30 % of the prisoners are foreign nationals. The population of prisoners increased from 44 per 100,000 in 1970 to 73 per 100,000 in 2010. See the Introduction to this book. This note was added in 2013.

4. The developments further on showed that our struggle in the protracted initial phase in the final analysis led to an important victory. Probably drafted in the 1990s, but decided 16 May 2002, the following two items of a statement were introduced in the Regulation concerning the Norwegian 'Law Concerning the Carrying Out of Punishment' ('Straffegjennomføringsloven'), on 'Furloughs for particular purposes' (my translation):
    'Inmates who actively participate at the yearly KROM conferences as speakers, panel participants, moderators, and the like, may be granted furloughs to the conference outside the ordinary quota of furloughs, provided the other conditions for furloughs are present. Inmates may, furthermore, be granted up to 12 short term furloughs per year outside the ordinary furlough quota for participation at board meetings in KROM, provided the other conditions for granting short term furloughs are present.' The note was added in 2013.

5. The idea was realized after the completion of the 1974 edition of this book, and for the last decades SON, the Norwegian Association of Punished People, has lived a precarious life outside KROM, but also definitely in co-operation with KROM. See the Introduction to this edition of the book.

6. Abbreviated EEC, a Treaty signed in Rome in 1957, bringing together a number of European countries whose aim was to achieve integration via trade with a view towards economic expansion. After the Treaty of Maastricht (1992) the EEC became the European Community, with political powers, eventually the EU. National referendums were held In Norway twice over membership in the EEC/EU (1972 and 1994). Both times Norway voted no. This note was added in 2013.

7. After the completion of this book, the Advisory Council on the Penal System has finally proposed to have the youth prison system abolished. The Council has also proposed limitations on the use of security, while KROM's goal again is full abolition.

8. A further, postponed, report on the need for a closed institution was issued after the completion of this book (spring 1973). A majority of the committee advised against the building of a closed institution on a country-wide basis. The same majority also suggested a seeming limitation of the means of coercion given in the so-called 'Temperance Act'. However, the present provisions in the 'Temperance Act' are sufficiently hard to make them rather useless in practice. The proposed limitation may therefore simply mean that the means of coercion may be used more easily, a fact which was pointed out by KROM in a lengthy paper, and in various articles in the fall of 1973. Thus, the subtleties of coercion, and of defensive work, are very great.

9. The work of the action group has continued after the completion of this book. A continued stress on defensive work has been pronounced. In connection with a debate in the Municipal Council of Oslo, in the spring of 1973, where a council member raised the question of the 'environmental disturbance' in the city (thus implicitly suggesting the need for new measures of coercion), a delegation of vagrants met a group of council

members and presented their views and needs. At a later meeting in the Municipal Council, the group increased and 30 to 100 vagrants were present in the gallery, in several rounds of discussion, and under extensive press coverage. These activities probably gave the debate in the Council far less of a 'coercive' slant. And were part of what may be called a 'defensive victory'. See my *Løsgjengerkrigen* (The Vagrancy War). Sosionomen Publishers 1975. This note was reworked in 2013.

10. In general it is important to remember that several of the events which are here described as isolated from each other, actually took place simultaneously.
11. Today all inmates receive educational possibilities, and some also receive higher education. See Torfinn Langelid and Terje Manger (eds.): *Læring bak murene. Fengselsundervisningen I Norge* (Learning behind the Walls. The Prison Education in Norway. Fogbokforlaget Publishers 2005). But conflicts are frequent and neutralization due to security precautions, rapid movements of prisoners to other prisons, etc. make educational possibilities difficult. This note was added in 2013.
12. See, however, above.
13. The description of the situation in the factory is ideal-typical. A number of factors – for example unemployment with consequent competition on the labour market also weaken the workers' position.
14. In modem factory prisons the institution is to a limited degree dependent on the economic contribution of the prisoners. I shall return to this exception later.
15. After the publication of this book in Norwegian, nation-wide prison strikes have occurred in other countries as well, notably in England, Norway and Denmark. The Norwegian strikes will be referred to below. However, none of these strikes were anywhere near the Swedish October strike in terms of coverage of the prison population.
16. 'Visiting furlough': the inmate is given a few hours' leave of absence with a visitor, in the neighbourhood of the institution.
17. A leave: permission to leave the institution during the daytime, for example to work or to go to school, with the obligation to return to the institution at night. Leaves are rarely used and the inmates wanted their use extended (later on, through the 1990s and early 2000s, leaves in Norway were somewhat extended, though strictly regulated; added to the note in 2013).
18. And the most dangerous to the inmates? See section I above.
19. The prisoners had also wanted to discuss the role and democratization of the staff. This was sharply rejected by representatives of the staff – this was a matter to be dealt with by the staff alone.
20. As already indicated, the governing idea in this work is that the prisoners lack a bargaining position in so far as they do not contribute to the system of which they are members. However, the staff does have a bargaining position through their very clear-cut contributions. Considerable evidence indicates that the authorities were particularly concerned with the reactions of the staff – for example, the authorities were greatly worried at the fact that fifty employees in one institution at one point during the conflict threatened to resign. They advertised in the press for new employment.
21. The prisoners received the protocols over ten months later – in December 1971 – and only after some staff-inmate talks which took place at Kumla prison in November 1971. See the postscript to this part of the book.
22. The actual prison regulations concerning visits have later been changed. The changes, however, have been of negligible importance. Furthermore, after the publication of this book in Norwegian, new regulations of a restrictive kind concerning furloughs were introduced for long-term prisoners. For those with sentences of over 2 years, applications for furloughs are now to be reviewed by the Prison Department rather than by the institutions, and the practice is apparently very restrictive. It should be added that a new Prison Act is being prepared. It is expected to be in force by 1974.

23. See the postscript to this book.

24. And here probably lies the main basis for the development in connection with the negotiations between prisoners and authorities in the Attica prison in the United States, September 1971. The main result of the Attica affair seems clear: even in a situation where the prisoners resort to the most extreme means – that of taking a large number of guards as hostages – the authorities have power to break off the negotiations and crush the revolt completely. As is well known, in Attica this happened with military aid and at the cost of many lives.

25. After the termination of the first Norwegian prison strike (1971), certain discussions were entered into between the prison administration and the inmates. As far as is known, however, the discussions were limited to the wage question and certain minor matters.

   In connection with a suicide which took place later that summer, in the same institution, the prisoners sent out an account of the incident to an important newspaper, and simultaneously carried out a new brief sympathy strike (work strike). The prisoners demanded public investigation of the suicide, and were thus in an excellent way externally orientated in their action, probably again partly because the attitude of the prison authorities was strongly negative. The action led to a rather strong political reaction outside (and to a court investigation of the suicide case). The essential – and difficult – thing is to *keep* to the external orientation even if permanent inmate councils are established and the prison authorities change tactics.

26. At the time of writing, a private organization. Taken over by the state in 1980. This note was added in 2013.

27. Weber 1919, printed 1921, 1958. One of the most difficult tasks is that of transmitting hard-won experience concerning tactics to new groups. In July 1973, after the completion of this book, the prisoners in a number of Danish prisons went on a work strike, largely on the basis of wage claims. A Danish Prisoners' Union had been formed a few months earlier, following Sweden and Norway in the third Scandinavian organizational attempt of this kind. The prisoners' strike became very protracted, the initial press interest waned after a while, and the strike finally ended in a wage 'compromise' through which the prisoners gained very little. At the time of writing, the Danish Union is demanding central negotiations.

28. The question of the legality of prisoners' organizations is currently hotly debated in Norway. KROM has maintained that the legality of such organizations is clear, and that the illegality of work strikes is unclear. The authorities have claimed that the legality of the organizations is dubious and the illegality of work strikes perfectly clear.

29. Compare *Trotskij's* concept of 'the permanent revolution'.

Book III

Scholars and prisoners on prisons

Thomas Mathiesen

Activism as an exercise of public intellect

Vincenzo Ruggiero

The republication of a book produced in 1974 should not be seen as a mere nostalgic drawback to the formidable, turbulent years of conflict with which one may associate the 1970s. In order to deserve republication, books have to display what I would term a double substantive originality: first within the context in which they first appeared, and second amid concerns prevailing at the time they are reissued. When it first appeared, the book was highly original in that it supplanted orthodox Marxism, which was a mainstream of thinking at the time, with a far more modern Marxist approach. Today its originality consists in the way it problematizes today's so-called public criminology, stressing for example collective action that can bring change from below. In what follows I will attempt to highlight the double originality I read in *The Politics of Abolition*.

Superfluous humanity

When the book first appeared, Marxism as a system of thought was predominant, and thinkers or activists could hardly display their own intellectual originality, unless they were prepared to distance themselves from the prevailing orthodoxy, namely from a static and dogmatic reading of Marxism. This is what Mathiesen did, wittingly or otherwise. Of course, there are scattered elements of Marxism in his early work, for example in his analysis of the law, which, we are told, is shaped and reshaped by changes of, and changes in, material structures in society. If materiality, in the last instance, takes precedence, the legal rules created by structures feed back on the material structures themselves, perpetuating them while producing legitimacy and consensus. In the Marxist tradition too, the notion that the law is divorced from its economic basis is regarded as an illusion: the civil law, for example, is said to have developed simultaneously with private property out of the disintegration of the natural community. As for the general apparatus that constitutes the repository of the law: 'the state is the form in which the individuals of a ruling class assert their common interests; the state mediates in the formation of all common institutions and thus the institutions receive a political form' (Marx, 1974: 80). The law is a symptom, an expression of other social relationships on which state power lies.

Mathiesen (1980), after reiterating in his own way this materialist analysis, proceeds with the examination of law as 'totality'. In other words, he crosses the boundaries of the legal sphere into other systems of ideas such as religion, art and science. 'The law is viewed in relation to these other systems of ideas', before addressing a crucial problem, 'that of how systems of ideas, in more general terms, relate to material structures in society' (ibid.: 10). Finally, he moves on to exploring the possibilities of what he describes as 'boundary-transcending political action'. His contention is that most sociologists, Habermas among them, unwittingly paralyse action, because they limit themselves to the description of existing conditions rather than 'discussing the conditions for the abolition of existing conditions' (ibid.: 6). In brief, after leaving the legal sphere behind, Mathiesen probes the validity of other systems of ideas, namely ideas that may accompany a type of political action which is boundary-transcending or revolutionary in relation to the material structure.

There is, however, a more important aspect that distances Mathiesen's work from orthodox Marxism, and this pertains to the very subjects which form the heart of his conceptualisations and organisational efforts for action. Orthodox Marxism focuses on working class organisations and struggles, confining the excluded to the amorphous army of vagabonds who have no particular historical mission to accomplish. At the beginning of the manufacture system, this surplus population could not be turned into disciplined labour, if not through the most extreme necessity. Henry VIII of England had seventy-two thousand of these vagabonds hanged, thus proving how disposable they were, economically as well as politically (Marx, 1974: 73–74). When describing the conditions of the English working class, Engels (1973) is forced to also consider the conditions of the non-working surplus population, and to focus on conventional crime as one of the anti-social expressions of such population. Contesting Malthus' argument that there are too many people in the world, Engels suggests that there are as many as are sufficient to depreciate labour. This superfluous humanity swells during the periodical industrial crises, when charity organisations are put under siege and starvation spreads. Crime as one of the effects of such crises is described by Engels as open warfare against the rich who wage a covert warfare against the poor. But there is nothing heroic in this: when crowds run amok, robbing, stealing and killing, they do express disdain towards the social order, but they also testify to their 'corruption', as they manifest the blind fight of each person against the rest.

There is a paradoxical aspect in Marxist analysis of marginalisation, one that comes vividly to light in some powerful pages of *Theories of Surplus Value*. The argument sets off with the observation that crime takes a part of the superfluous population away from the labour market, thus reducing competition among labourers and preventing wages from falling below the minimum. The struggle against crime, in its turn, absorbs another part of this population. The argument continues with the famous observation about the 'productive' nature of crime and criminals:

> Thus the criminal comes in as one of those natural 'counterweights' which bring about a correct balance and open up a whole perspective of 'useful'

occupations . . . The criminal . . . produces the whole of the police and of criminal justice, constables, judges, hangman, juries, etc.: and all these different lines of business, which form equally many categories of the social division of labour, develop different capacities of the human spirit, create new needs and new ways of satisfying them. Torture alone has given rise to the most ingenious mechanical inventions, and employed many honourable craftsmen in the production of its instruments.

(Marx, 1964: 375)

If we followed Marxist analysis literally we would be tempted to argue that it is in the interest of the working class to press for more laws and criminalisation, because by constantly removing part of the population from the labour market wages for the employed will be kept high. In sum, there are ambivalent aspects in the way Marxist analysis addresses the marginalised, particularly when it focuses on their political behaviour, their passivity or even their moral putrefaction (Marx, 1965).

Mathiesen's distance from this analytical tradition is evident, in that it is exactly what Marxism regards as the surplus population which is the objective of his work as a sociologist and activist. An example is provided in the following fictional account (Mathiesen, 1974). Quoting from a novel by Jörgen Eriksson (1970), Mathiesen describes a gathering of people from juvenile correctional institutions, youth hostels and hostels for vagrants, condemned houses and slums, mental hospitals and institutions for alcoholics and ghettoes for gypsies and immigrants. And when the handicapped are threatened by the police, a staggering crowd of vagrants launch an attack with injection needles and beer bottles. The street whores pull out large knives, while the gypsies sneak around stealing horses from under the police officers. The mental patients scuttle back and forth and confuse the law enforcers, spitting, scratching, tearing and biting. This is an eponymous revolt of those who, even within radical politics, are denied an emancipatory role.

> Some versions of Marxism identify one particular sector of society as the leading force bringing social change, discarding other sectors which may oppose or hamper the revolutionary process. The marginalised, in an orthodox perspective, are unreliable as they easily shift their allegiance according to the contingent moment. In Marxist teleology, moreover, the problem of crime cannot be resolved before the revolutionary process is complete.
>
> (Ruggiero, 2010: 138)

An endless process

As an implicit critique of this teleology, Mathiesen (1983) not only focuses on social movements which orthodox Marxists would not deem relevant for the 'revolutionary process', but also elaborates and practices a strategy of action revolving around the idea of 'the unfinished', which provides an alternative to millenarian postponement of change.

The unfinished is the sketch, the embryo of what is not yet in full existence. Mathiesen's (1974: 13) premise is that 'any attempt to change the existing order into something completely finished, a fully formed entity, is destined to fail'. The process of finishing, in other words, will lead back to the social order one wants to change. Oracles are given as examples as they provide sketches, not fully-formed answers. The first problem, therefore, is how a sketch can take shape and how it should be mobilised. If the existing social order changes while assuming a new structure, the second problem is how the sketch can be maintained as such or how, at least, its life can be prolonged. 'An enormous political pressure exists in the direction of completing the sketch into a finished drawing, and thereby ending the growth of the product. How can this be avoided, or at least postponed?' (ibid.) The solution to these problems is the core concern of penal abolition.

In order to clarify his argument, Mathiesen considers love as an unfinished relationship that is a boundless rapport leading to unpredictable developments. When is love going to stop? Love stops when boundaries are determined and precisely drawn, producing either resigned loneliness or routinized marriage. Treatment experiments are also unfinished while they are carried out. They have no boundaries with respect to outcomes, and offer potential alternatives to the state of things, for example, in hospitals or prisons. As the pioneering aspects of the experiments are incorporated into the structure in which they take place, and as the outcomes are precisely inscribed in that structure, they are appropriated by the establishment. Finally, the notion of the unfinished can be applied to the building of alternative societies. Such societies, presumably, contradict and compete with the societies they intend to replace. Their being alternative, however, lies in the never-ending process through which they attempt to establish themselves, in the constant experimenting with new features and values, rather than in their bringing change to completion.

'Completion, or the process of finishing, implies full take-over, and thereby there is no longer any contradiction. Neither is there competition' (ibid.: 17).

In this sense, abolitionism must inform each immediate objective, concretely linked to the long-term goal. The concepts of positive and negative reforms may help strengthen this point. The former contribute to the perpetuation of established control systems, whereas the latter to their constant erosion. In order for the long-term abolitionist goal not to be set aside, short-term reforms should therefore be of the negative type. 'That is, when working for short-term improvements in the prison, one should in principle work for reforms negating the basic prison structure, thus helping – at least a little bit – in tearing that structure down rather than consolidating it' (Mathiesen, 1986: 82). Reforms of an 'abolishing type' contain the long-term strategy while dealing with short-term issues. Abolitionism implies that 'there is constantly more to abolish, that one looks ahead towards a new and still more long-term objective of abolition, that one constantly moves in a wider circle to new fields of abolition' (ibid.: 212). Readers will find of interest how in the introduction to this new edition of the book Mathiesen updates these concepts.

Olympian observers and activists

Mathiesen's originality today becomes apparent when we locate his 'abolitionist stance' within the debate around public criminology. Advocates of public criminology stress that, historically, the discipline has been the domain of reformist intellectuals prepared to engage in discussions of social problems and interact with equally sensitive groups and individuals. Criminological knowledge, in this perspective, is deemed suitable for forging views, insinuating doubt, rejecting face-value assumptions about crime and control and promoting fairer justice policies (Loader and Sparks, 2010; 2011). The search for 'windows of opportunity' through which knowledge can pass to receptive groups and individuals is, therefore, instigated, as if criminologists, 'respectable, kind and useful', were there, permanently pursuing any opportunity to help our societies (Christie, 2011: 709). The calm, limited, engagement proposed by Loader and Sparks (2010), on the other hand, is interpreted as a message implying that 'criminology might serve the public and the polity best by doing pretty much what it is already doing' (Currie, 2011: 711).

The notion that such alternative knowledge and better policies may be appreciated and met with the consent of the authorities, however, hides an unrealistic view of the political arena, where 'crime policy, like other realms of social policy in our time, has been a battle waged by groups with often starkly opposing interests, wielding very different degrees of political power' (Currie, 2011: 712). The elite, it is argued, is contemptuous of democracy, of 'better policies' and, for that matter, of knowledge itself. Contemporary 'democratic politics' is, in fact, the problem, a core factor 'in the degradation of political institutions and in the perversion of the law and order debate' (Sim, 2011: 724). How can a 'public criminologist' engage with a political process 'steeped as it is in the turgid mire of such hypocritical cynicism – cynicism that is underpinned by the generalised pathology of chronic mendacity that prevails in modern capitalist culture?' (ibid.: 725).

Criminologists, public or not, like Olympian observers, believe they can see the whole picture. 'The excuse for occupying such a bird's eye view is usually that scientists are doing reflexively what the informants are doing unwittingly' (Latour, 2005: 33). As Bauman (2011: 163) has contended, our objects of study are not dumb by nature, but in order to retain our status 'and to secure the sovereign authority of our pronouncements, the objects to which our pronouncements refer need first to be made dumb'.

Public criminologists do not dispel the impression that their study of marginalized communities is inspired by a missionary zeal and a honeyed paternalism that derive from traditional philanthropy. Mathiesen, on the contrary, expresses a genuine public stance, for example when he addresses collective actors and social movements. Mathiesen spends as much time with students as he does with prisoners, and his sociology, in brief, prioritizes specific actors and their collective action that can bring change from below.

Abolitionism does not address the powerful with 'pleas to be nice', because such pleas would give them a clear monopoly over the power to pardon (Ruggiero, 2012). As this power solidifies, disadvantaged actors might grow accustomed to interpreting their deeds as exclusive outcomes of their individual decisions, rather than the result of collective, social, conditions. They might even get accustomed to the notion that, while being pardoned, they themselves are required to pardon the groups and the mechanisms responsible for the conditions in which they live.

Public criminology as practised by Mathiesen posits academic work as intellectual activism, as a form of cultural work engaged in a social conflict. His abolitionism is not scared away from the notion of conflict; in fact, like other radical thinkers he believes that conflict is a precious resource and has to be nurtured and cherished. In this way, he echoes Georg Simmel (1971), for whom conflict is a fundamental experience leading to socialisation. As for knowledge, Mathiesen would argue that it is not only a question of 'windows of opportunity' through which it is transmitted to receptive groups. It is also constituted by a number of tools, experiences and repertoires of action that help people engaged in conflict. The research-action advocated by Thomas Mathiesen is an example: his involvement with groups of prisoners aims to produce knowledge that can be of use in their struggles for reform.

In conclusion, the reluctance of academics to 'go along the action chain', namely to join a social movement, may be tempered through the recognition that mainstream academics are themselves well connected in this chain and engaged in a social movement. In this respect, it is useful to adopt the following concise definition: a social movement consists of an informal network of groups and individuals engaged in conflict which produces and is produced by collective identity. Are we sure that 'scientific' inquiry itself is so neutral, that it is not involved in a social movement? Surely, mainstream criminology is constituted by an informal network of groups and individuals engaged in a conflict against the powerless for the perpetuation of the status quo and the exacerbation of social injustice, a conflict which produces and is produced by a specific, dominant, sectarian, collective identity. Mathiesen and his book *The Politics of Abolitionism*, after forty years from its original publication, are still able to throw light on these vexed issues.

References

Bauman, Z. (2011), *Collateral Damage: Social Inequalities in a Global Age*, Cambridge: Polity.

Christie, N. (2011), 'Reflections from the Periphery', *British Journal of Criminology*, 51: 707–710.

Currie, E. (2011), 'Thinking about Criminology', *British Journal of Criminology*, 51: 710–713.

Engels, F. (1973), *The Condition of the Working Class in England,* Moscow: Progress Publishers.

Eriksson, J. (1970), 'Revolt I huvet', quoted in Mathiesen, T. (1974), *The Politics of Abolition: Essays in Political Action Theory,* London: Martin Robertson.

Latour, B. (2005), *Reassembling the Social: An Introduction to Actor-Network-Theory,* Oxford: Oxford University Press.

Loader, I. and Sparks, R. (2010), *Public Criminology?,* London: Routledge.

Loader, I. and Sparks, R. (2011), 'Criminology and Democratic Politics: A Reply to Critics', *British Journal of Criminology,* 51: 734–737.

Marx, K. (1964), *Theories of Surplus Value,* London: Lawrence & Wishart.

Marx, K. (1965), *Class Struggles in France: 1848–1850,* Moscow: Progress Publishers.

Marx, K. (1974), *The German Ideology,* London: Lawrence & Wishart.

Mathiesen, T. (1974), *The Politics of Abolition: Essays in Political Action Theory,* London: Martin Robertson.

Mathiesen, T. (1980), *Law, Society and Political Action,* London: Academic Press.

Mathiesen, T. (1983), 'Civil Disobedience at 70° North', *Contemporary Crises,* 7: 1–11.

Mathiesen, T. (1986), 'The Arguments Against Prison Construction', in Bianchi, H. and van Swaaningen, R. (eds.), *Abolitionism: Towards a Non-Repressive Approach to Crime,* Amsterdam: Free University Press.

Ruggiero, V. (2010), *Penal Abolitionism,* Oxford: Oxford University Press.

Ruggiero, V. (2012), 'How Public is Public Criminology?', *Crime, Media, Culture,* 8 (2): 151–160.

Sim, J. (2011), 'Who Needs Criminology to Know Which Way the Wind Blows?', *British Journal of Criminology,* 51: 723–727.

Simmel, G. (1971), *On Individuality and Social Forms,* Chicago: The University of Chicago Press.

The politics of abolition

Effects on the criminal sociology
and criminal policy debate in West
Germany

Knut Papendorf

When *The Politics of Abolition* was published in 1974, it finally made accessible
a strategy for action on prisons that looked beyond the usual demands for reform,
based on criticism of the treatment of inmates. The book fundamentally called into
question imprisonment itself, and ultimately demanded its abolition. Five years
later, in 1979, there followed a German version – *Überwindet die Mauern!* – that
facilitated the reception and discussion of the Scandinavian prison movement's
abolitionist strategy in West Germany. This book drew on the original Norwegian
texts, like *The Politics of Abolition*,[1] though with a slightly different emphasis. An
introduction to *Überwindet die Mauern!*, written by Karl F. Schumann, served as
proof that Mathiesen's suggested strategy for the work of political fringe groups
and prisoners could have some impact in West Germany.

There can be no doubt that *The Politics of Abolition* and its German counterpart stimulated discussion of criminal sociology and criminal policy in West
Germany. Programmatic book titles such as *Vom Ende des Strafvollzuges* (On the
end of imprisonment) (Schumann, Steinert, Voss 1988), *Gesellschaft ohne Gitter*
(Society without bars) (Papendorf 1985) and *Freiheit statt Strafe* (Freedom not
sentences) (Ortner (ed.) 1981) demonstrate the influence of Mathiesen's theories.
In this essay I will attempt to shed light on some West German abolitionist activities that can be viewed as attempts to transfer the experience of the Scandinavian
prisoners' movements into a German setting (1). One of these activities is an academic project, the aim of which is to steer the discussion of juvenile detention
reform in an abolitionist direction (2). Finally, I will end this short piece with
an attempt to point out parallel discussions and connections to abolitionist perspectives, arising in the context of the Scandinavian theories' reception in West
Germany (3).

The criminal policy working group – KRAK[2]

In its heyday, up to the mid-1980s, KRAK[3] was probably the most ambitious
attempt to put the Nordic fringe groups' experience to work on West German criminal policy. The starting point for the organisation was AG SPAK,[4] an umbrella
organisation for fringe groups, which offered an organisational platform for a

whole range of related initiatives and individual campaigns. Voluntary "prison work" was then, as it is now, faced with the danger of being permanently axed for taking up a position that was critical of prisons, or, at the other end of the spectrum, becoming bogged down in providing charitable aid for individual cases. In this phase, when work with and for prisoners lacked orientation and was searching for new perspectives, the abolitionist perspective of the Scandinavian prisoners' movement offered an alternative view.

The conference at which KRAK came into being took place in autumn 1980. It was dominated by four central themes: the planned building of a juvenile detention centre in Neumünster; the Weiterstadt remand centre; the attempt by inmates to create an independent prisoners' union within prisons; and finally the issues around drugs. The Weiterstadt complex in particular gave rise to intense strategic discussions, with the aim of preventing or postponing these building works. The conference coined the slogan "Spargelbau statt Mauerbau!" (Grow asparagus, don't build walls!). The idea was to use a "young entrepreneur" to lease or buy a parcel of the land that had been proposed for the prison site, in order to delay the building project. This first campaign idea electrified the delegates, creating the ideal impetus for the establishment of KRAK, and the first objective for its work.

At its height, KRAK represented a truly impressive cross-section of the discussions and activities around prisons in West Germany. Some of the criminal policy initiatives and groups that regularly gathered under the KRAK umbrella are remembered here with a certain sense of wistfulness: Arbeitskreis kritischer Strafvollzug (AKS) in Darmstadt, Initiative für eine bessere Kriminalpolitik (IbK), Forschungsgruppe Jugendstrafvollzug in Bremen,[5] Das Andere Transparent (DAT), Knotenpunkt and Gefangeneninitiative (GI) in Dortmund, Gittersäge, Verein für Kriminalreform, Bürger beobachten die Polizei, Arbeitsgruppe Knast/ Justiz der Alternativen Liste (AL) in Berlin, Fachgruppe Knast und Justiz der Grün Alternativen Liste (GAL) in Hamburg, initiatives around the Judos in Baden-Württemberg and others.

The big issues that primarily motivated KRAK over the course of its existence were planned prison expansions – particularly in the state of Hesse, but also in other West German states such as Berlin, Baden-Württemberg and Schleswig-Holstein. A wealth of materials, including occupancy statistics, was put together on these issues; the regional initiatives held meetings, and various regional branches of the Green Party engaged in collaborative work. Another emphasis was support for the thinking on prisoners' unions. Indications that this effort was gaining momentum included the entry of prisoners' representation groups into the register of associations. Attempts were also made to promote the flow of information to and between prisoners' associations. Discussions took place with the Komitee für Grundrechte (the German committee for civil rights) on individual problem areas in the penal system, from the perspective of civil rights abuses. The issues around juvenile detention formed one of KRAK's most important areas of discussion, at least in its initial phase. And there were attempts to address other topics, including forensic commitment, detention awaiting trial and juvenile detention.

There is a legitimate question to be asked about why KRAK was so short-lived, in spite of the plethora of initiatives referenced here. Several factors seem important to me in this context – the first of which is that KRAK never really grew beyond its role as a simple presentation platform for the activities of its various groups and initiatives. It was no coincidence that the "Reports from the Groups" took on a central significance to the organisation. On the one hand, KRAK functioned as a pool of information about nationwide criminal policy activity; and on the other, it took on a kind of control function over this very praxis, in a way that meant questions were asked about its abolitionist substance. This was a problem that would dog KRAK over the course of its existence: namely, the inability to see the organisation as an independent medium, and to use it for the West German discussion. KRAK was always overly theoretical. From the outset, it was disadvantaged by the fact that, unlike the Scandinavian prisoners' movement, it had not extrapolated its original strategic and theoretical focus from its own praxis.

In this context – with all due sympathy for the basic democratic model of KRAK – the question must also be raised of whether addressing criminal and legal policy is even possible without a minimum of organisational structure, and the intention of becoming a permanent entity. The example of KROM proves that any intervention that is intended to be more than an isolated action requires some staying power.

Finally – and here I see the principal reason for the early decline of KRAK – the Green political movement, whose ideology at the time was similar to that of KRAK, offered the group an enormously attractive political stage. However, this political arena absorbed too much strength from the newly established criminal policy working group, meaning that it began to neglect its own basic work.

Pressure-group politics against the expansion of state control

This was the title of a piece of academic research[6] that asked whether and to what extent an action research project could influence the course of a legislative process for a juvenile detention law. This project's criminal policy – or to be more precise abolitionist – perspective was oriented towards reversing the state's exclusionist policy. The project essentially concentrated on *creating expert opinions* that contradicted the ideas of the youth detention commission[7] and the Ministry of Justice, and on *mobilising an active public.*[8] For reasons of space, I cannot go into the various project initiatives here.[9] But the evidence shows that our interventions defied an unwritten rule of legislative processes, namely the avoidance of public criticism of ministry drafts – documents which the legislative bureaucracy viewed as internal, since they were circulated for consultation and agreement only within the Ministry of Justice and other established organisations.

It was therefore possible to break through this apparent attempt by the ministerial bureaucracy to make draft laws "watertight" by having them pre-agreed, and the criticism may have contributed to the moratorium that was then placed on this legislative process.

The second and most important theme of the project aimed to mobilise an active public into exerting influence as advocates,[10] and beyond this, aimed to create the ability to deal with conflict through "institutional converters".[11] Our primary concern here was to work with the media to popularise an abolitionist perspective that was critical of traditional youth crime law, and thereby set in motion an articulation of interests through advocates. A large number of media initiatives were targeted at a narrower audience of experts on criminal sociology and criminal policy. Others were targeted at the rather left-leaning, liberal (academic) public, and a third category focused on areas of discussion around social work and social pedagogy.[12] Alongside these various individual interventions, another focal point for the project was helping to initiate the criminal political working group KRAK, with the aim of creating a criminal policy network acting on a national scale.

Theoretical connection points to abolitionism

As already indicated, *Überwindet die Mauern!* was published with an emphasis on the book's potential usefulness for criminal policy strategy. This was accompanied by a clear reticence regarding the academic sociological classification of the abolitionist "perspective".[13] This was some time before clarifying suggestions were put forward by Scheerer and Steinert, who positioned abolitionism as a "sensitising theory" (Scheerer 1984, p. 97) or as a "heuristic, theory-led perspective" (Steinert 1988, p. 10f.).

In his substantiation of this view, Steinert argues that we must keep "the remarkable, absurd quality, and the danger of this state arrangement in view. And take this insight seriously enough so that we can at least imagine a society without prisons" (Steinert 1986, p. 2). In this context, he goes on to consider the question of "freedom from domination (or at least – from poverty)" (ibid., p. 6).

Smaus widens abolitionism even further to include the wider goal of "abolishing penal law" (Smaus 1986, p. 2). The relationship of abolitionism to a labelling-theory approach, and materialist and anarchist approaches, has also given rise to intense discussion. Schumann in particular has considered the relationship between a labelling approach and abolitionism (1985, p. 19ff.). An 'epistemological potential of the same status as labelling theory', which has its foundations in symbolic interactionism, is not shared by abolitionism.

With regard to the significance of abolitionism for criminal policy, clear convergences can be seen: Schur's book *Radical Non-Intervention* (1973) indicates, at least from its title, the criminal policy aims of a labelling approach. From the standpoint of abolitionism, the epistemological interest of labelling theory is an elementary part of substantiating abolition policy. In the first instance, a labelling approach suggests conducting a survey of the control praxis of certain authorities, from the inside perspective of everyone involved, to create an "eth-nography of social control". Only on the basis of such findings can it be assessed whether cases in which control has apparently been given up are not in fact cases of simple modification, where functional equivalents have been found (Schumann 1985, p. 24ff.).

In the discussion of the social model in the abolitionist movement, Smaus sees the point of departure of Mathiesen's conception as "materialist" in the class relations of a society. To underpin her theory, Smaus draws in particular on *Law, Society and Political Action* (Mathiesen 1980). Here, Mathiesen puts forward his ideas on the possibilities of a change in late capitalism that would transcend the system, under the auspice of a stabilization of systemic logic.[14] Steinert (1987, p. 131ff.) also works explicitly from the assumption of a strong affinity between abolitionism and the Marxist theoretical tradition in criminal sociology. This assessment is derived in particular from the category of "liberation" – generally in the spirit of the "withering away of the state", and specifically in the sense of a (total) loss of power for control agencies like prisons, the police and penal law (ibid., p. 131ff.). Having made a sceptical assessment of the ideal of justice, Steinert elaborates on the relationship between Marxist analysis and abolitionism at the end of his essay. The judicial agencies responsible for the production of justice "were not like private oppressors; they systematised the present form of authoritarian power and perfected their hold on it [. . .] [I]nstead of campaigning for 'justice' from the authorities, we could campaign with the same vigour for less domination by the authorities" (Steinert 1987, p. 152ff.).

It is at least doubtful to what extent Mathiesen can justifiably be labelled a "materialist" theorist. The concept of things remaining "unfinished", which he advanced in *The Politics of Abolition,* in fact suggests an explicit dissociation from a system of ideas founded in materialism. The principle of "unfinishedness" has to dissociate itself from a neatly formulated concept of revolutionary policy, in order to remain competitive. On the other hand, in his chapter on "The strategy of negation", Mathiesen takes his considerations on the relationship between reform and revolution from the armoury of materialist strategic thought. He also uses Trotsky's "permanent revolution" as a cipher. Finally, Mathiesen's *Law, Society and Political Action* (1980), is without doubt a study founded on materialist principles. In later years, Mathiesen admittedly gives us more nuanced versions of his earlier positions. This is particularly the case for a strategy of negation: "Thirdly, to my mind our work to rid ourselves of the prison solution must still be carried out with 'negative' reforms in mind. But the term needs to be specified in a different way than I did fifteen years ago. The importance of improving conditions of life for prisoners (as far as it is possible within the structure of the prison) should certainly not be underestimated. The dismal character of the prison makes any other policy cynical to say the least" (Mathiesen 1986, p. 86).

However, for Mathiesen this means placing even more emphasis on the visionary nature of the unfinished: "We need visions of how society should be alternatively structured. [. . .] We need ideas of how human relationships might be alternatively organized so that conflicts are resolved in new and socially acceptable ways. In short, we need images of society or of structures within society, formulated as ideologies in a positive sense of that word, to work *for*" (ibid.).

Notes

1. Thomas Mathiesen, *Det uferdige* (1971) and Thomas Mathiesen, *Pressgruppe og samfunnsstruktur* (1973).
2. Here I am essentially following reflections that I set out in a previous publication (Papendorf 1993 b, p. 76ff.).
3. The naming of this organisation makes clear its affinity to the Scandinavian models KRIM (Denmark, Finland), KROM (Norway) and KRUM (Sweden).
4. Arbeitsgemeinschaft Sozialpolitischer Arbeitskreise, a consortium of social policy working groups.
5. This project is presented in the following section.
6. Led by Karl F. Schumann and carried out by Knut Papendorf and Michael Voss.
7. These ideas were available to us from the start of 1980, in the form of a final report.
8. For various reasons, the planned "dialogue" with the juvenile detention commission did not take place.
9. For further details, see Papendorf 1993 b, p. 69ff.
10. In the absence of interest organisations capable of organising and dealing with conflict, self-declared "advocates" can step in, to take over these functions (at least in part) on behalf of the people affected.
11. "Institutional converters" are people, or groups, with privileged access to decision-makers.
12. On the details of these initiatives, see Papendorf 1993 b, p. 73ff.
13. Terms like position, line, campaign, policy and approach were used in relation to the word "abolitionist", which suggest a degree of uncertainty regarding the theoretical positioning of abolitionism.
14. In this context, systemic logic is understood to mean that both sides, contractors and workers, are subject to the same system rationality (in the sense of "imperatives" of the economic structure), from which they can no longer escape as individuals (Mathiesen 1980, p. 216ff.).

References

Mathiesen, T. (1971): *Det uferdige*. Pax Forlag: Oslo.
Mathiesen, T. (1973): *Pressgruppe og samfunnsstruktur.* Pax Forlag: Oslo.
Mathiesen, T. (1974): *The Politics of Abolition: Essays in Political Action.* Martin Robertson: London.
Mathiesen, T. (1979): *Überwindet die Mauern!* Luchterhand Verlag: Neuwied and Darmstadt.
Mathiesen, T. (1980): *Law, Society and Political Action.* Academic Press: London.
Mathiesen, T. (1986): The Politics of Abolition. In: *Contemporary Crisis,* 10, p. 81ff.
Ortner, H. (ed.) (1981): *Freiheit statt Strafe.* Fischer Taschenbuch Verlag: Frankfurt/Main.
Papendorf, K. (1985): *Gesellschaft ohne Gitter.* AG SPAK Bücher: München.
Papendorf, K. (1993 a): Zur Rezeptionsgeschichte dieses Buches und was macht KROM heute? In: Mathiesen, *Überwindet die Mauern!* AJZ: Bielefeld, p. 195ff.

Papendorf, K. (1993 b): Ausgrabungen aus der bundesrepublikanischen aboli(tioni) stischen Frühzeit. In: Papendorf/Schumann (Hrsg.), *Kein schärfer Schwert, denn das für Freiheit streitet!* AJZ: Bielefeld, p. 65ff.

Scheerer, S. (1984): Die abolitionistische Perspektive. In: *KrimJ*, p. 99ff.

Schumann, K. F. (1985): Labeling approach und Abolitionismus. In: *KrimJ*, p. 19ff.

Schumann, K. F./Steinert, H./Voss, M. (Hrsg.) (1988): *Vom Ende des Strafvollzugs.* AJZ: Bielefeld.

Schur E. M. (1973): *Radical Non–Intervention.* Prentice Hall: Englewood Cliffs.

Smaus, G. (1986): Gesellschaftsmodelle in der abolitionistischen Bewegung. In: *KrimJ*, p. 1ff.

Steinert, H. (1986): Abolitionismus: Die harte Wirklichkeit unde der Möglichkeitssinn. In: Christie N. *Grenzen des leids*: AIZ Verlag, Bieledfeld, pp. 1–13.

Steinert, H. (1987): Marxsche Theorie und Abolitionismus. In: *Kriminalsoziologische Bibliografie*, p. 131ff.

Steinert, H. (1988): Sicherlich ist Zweifel am Sinn der Strafe, von Freiheitsstrafe erlaubt. In: Schumann/Steinert/Voss (Hrsg.), *Vom Ende des Strafvollzugs*, AJZ: Bielefeld, p. 1ff.

Abolition in the times of pre-crime

A view from Germany

Johannes Feest

"The post-crime orientation of criminal justice is increasingly overshadowed by the pre-crime logic of security" (Zedner 2007: 262). This pre-crime logic was aptly depicted by Philip K. Dick in his famous science fiction story "Minority Report" (1956): "in our society we have no major crimes . . . but we do have a detention camp full of would-be criminals" (Dick 2002: 3). In Germany, this finds fitting expression in the expansion and the growing importance of security facilities. There are similar developments in other countries.[1] It seems about time for abolitionists to take these new developments into consideration.

Re-reading "The politics of abolition"

Most German readers have read the German, not the English, version of Mathiesen's book. The book had enormous importance in the 1970s in spreading the message of abolitionism in Germany. On closer inspection, the two versions are far from identical. The German book is an independent translation from the Norwegian original and not based on the English version. The comparison gives rise to a number of comments.

KRIM, KROM, KRUM

The German version (Mathiesen 1979) is called *Überwindet die Mauren* (Overcome the walls) and it carries an additional subtitle, in which the Scandinavian prisoners' movement is seen as a model for political work with fringe groups. The reference to *Randgruppen* (marginal groups, fringe groups, groups of disadvantaged people) is not by chance. They were, in the 1970s in Germany, a favourite subject of sociological analysis and leftist strategy. It is therefore not surprising that the book's structure has also changed in the German version. It starts with what was originally Part II, "Pressure Group and Social Structure", bringing the topic of political action to the fore. At the same time, the long chapter VI on the "organization of the expelled" is completely missing. It is replaced by a chapter on "strategies of the opponent", i.e. the methods with which the prison administration tried to frustrate the contact between KROM and the prisoners. Probably, the rich details about the Norwegian prisoners' movement were seen as not directly relevant to the German scene. An analysis of the Norwegian prison administration's strategies, on the other hand, was probably seen as more applicable to what happened in Germany at the time. I am thinking of the successful suppression of the only major book that came out of the collaboration between prisoners and their outside supporters: a "Guidebook for prisoners with medical and legal tips" (Ratgeber 1981; for the story of this conflict see Feest 1991: 253–264).

Today, it is only a few older people who still remember KRIM, KROM and KRUM, maybe because of their funny sounding names. There is not much *Randgruppenarbeit* left in Germany and there is no prisoners' movement to speak of.

The abolitionist perspective

The more theoretical elements of the English version form the second part of the German book. But the wonderful essay on "the unfinished", with which the English version starts, ends up sandwiched between a discussion of the social functions of imprisonment and considerations about the strategy of negation. How did these ideas fare in Germany?

The philosophy of "the unfinished" made a lasting impression on some people in Germany (including me), even though or because it remained somewhat mysterious. But I have not seen any reception in the German literature (including my own writings). Mathiesen's discussion of the social functions of imprisonment (briefly repeated in Mathiesen 1987 and 1989) is only rarely mentioned in the current German criminological literature. Mathiesen's discussion of positive and negative reforms did, however, in the 1980s, inspire lively discussions in prison reform groups. Karl F. Schumann, in his introduction to the German edition, used this distinction to criticize a campaign (in which he himself had participated) in favour of the introduction of regular wages in prisons as "a good example for positive reforms". In the following years, Schumann, Papendorf and others were involved in at least one true negative reform, the closing of the one and only "Jugendarrest" facility in Bremen, an institution for short-sharp-shock imprisonment. The facility has never been reopened. But today, there are very few people who use the positive/negative terminology in reform discussions any more.

Abolitionism as such had its heyday in Germany in the late 1970s and early 1980s. There were numerous publications in *Kriminologisches Journal*, the journal of critical criminologists.[2] This did have the effect that "abolitionism" is still mentioned routinely as a "theory" in textbooks of criminology and in handbooks on prisons. But, despite of the fact that a second edition of *Überwindet die Mauern* was published in the early 1990s, with a new afterword on the reception of the book in Germany (Papendorf 1993), the idea that prisons could and should be abolished receded into the background. Apart from very small anarchist groups, there are hardly organizations left that rally around this concept.

A brief note on translation

Another thing that occurred to me while comparing the English and German versions of *The Politics of Abolition* may seem pedantic. I am talking about the fact that "prison" (*Gefängnis*) is in most cases translated as *Strafvollzug*. There is not much wrong with that, since most German speakers would use the terms interchangeably. But if one translates *Strafvollzug* back into English, it means "the implementation of punishment in prisons". The institutions in which this takes place are called *Strafvollzugsanstalten* (serving prisons, penitentiaries). Clearly, Thomas Mathiesen is talking about prisons in a much broader sense, including youth prisons, security detention, work houses and remand facilities; as a matter of fact, one of his early empirical studies was conducted in a security detention facility (Mathiesen 1965). This is lost, at least terminologically, in the German version. In what follows, we will see that this makes a difference with respect to prison statistics as well as with respect to prison abolition.

Germany as a "deviant case" with respect to prisons

In his discussion of prison growth, Thomas Mathiesen (1987: 11) has called Germany a "deviant case", because of a noticeable drop in the prison population. And in his new preface (above), he notes that Germany is a possible exception in that it "shows relative stability over the years". Actually, Germany can indeed be characterized as a deviant case in more than one way.

Imprisonment rates

The prison population in West Germany[3] had its ups and downs (Weber/Feest 1998). But it is fair to say that these ups and downs average out into a state of relative stability. For the last ten years, the German prison statistics even show a marked decline. As of August 2013 the imprisonment rate was 77, down from 88 in 2010 and from 98 in 2004.

However: the German prison statistics include only those prisons run by the justice administration (remand prisons and serving prisons). In order to get the full picture, one would have to add those prisons organised by the Ministries of the Interior (police cells, facilities for immigration detention)[4] and the Ministries for Health (hospitals for the criminally insane, alcohol and drug clinics). While Germany has not experienced a growth in the penitentiary population and even a decrease with respect to remand prisoners, the forensic prison population has seen a spectacular growth. These statistics are published by the health administration, not by the justice administration. Figures for forensic prisoners in West Germany[5] show a constant increase from 3,746 patients (in 1987) to 10,423 (in 2011). If one could add the East German forensic prison population, the German imprisonment rate would be up to nearly 100. This would still mean relative stability, albeit on a much higher level.

Excursion: measures of betterment and security

The reason for these misleading German prison statistics goes back to the creation of a second track within the German criminal justice system. *Maßregeln der Sicherung und Besserung* (measures of security and betterment) were introduced in 1933 as one of the first legislative actions of the Nazi regime. This was, however, in line with long-standing demands by the social defence movement, and similar changes occurred in a number of other European countries. In Germany, the classical school of criminal law had long been opposed to these "modern" innovations, for fear that they would undermine the time-honoured principles of criminal law. It took the Nazi government to overcome this blockade. From now on, criminal courts were authorized to detain "dangerous habitual offenders" for indeterminate periods in "alcohol clinics", "security detention facilities" and in workhouses or, if they were pronounced mentally ill or of diminished mental capacity, in forensic clinics. In 1935, when the renowned International Penal and Penitentiary Committee held its congress in Berlin, the Nazis were not criticized but applauded for this seemingly progressive legislation (van der Aa 1936).[6] After the Second World War and the end of the Nazi regime, the two-track system was kept on, while most other European states abandoned it. Only the word order was changed: "measures of security and care" became "measures of betterment and security". While workhouses were abolished in 1968, security detention was preserved.

The case of security detention

Offenders sentenced to imprisonment can be additionally sentenced to the indeterminate measure of *Sicherungsverwahrung* (security detention[7]), to be served after the end of the prison sentence. During the Nazi era, the security detainees were in the thousands. After the Second World War, their number declined. This trend was reinforced by legislation, which, inter alia, created an upper limit of ten years for first time security detention. By the year 1997, the total number of security detainees had become almost insignificant, since only 200 of them were left, all accommodated in regular prisons.

But in 1998, new legislation[8] revived this almost extinct institution. Mass media and not a few politicians saw it as the solution to the moral panic caused by a few highly publicized cases of child sexual abuse and murder. In 1998, the ten-year cap for first time security detention was lifted, with retroactive effect. In 2002, a new category of "conditional security detention" was created, in order to give the courts the possibility to postpone a final decision on security detention until the end of the prison term. The real breakthrough came, however, in 2004, when the new category of "retrospective security detention"[9] was added to the existing institutions. It made it possible to separate the decision about security detention completely from the criminal trial; from now on it was possible to make that decision at the end of the prison sentence, based on additional information gained during imprisonment. In 2008, retrospective security detention was extended to juvenile criminal law. All of these new measures went beyond the Nazi original. All of them were subsequently approved by the German Constitutional Court. By 2010, the number of detainees had almost tripled in less than ten years. And other countries, like France, followed this model and started to introduce versions of retrospective measures.

In 2009, these developments were interrupted by a decision of the European Court of Human Rights. It held that most of these new measures were in violation of Article 7 of the European Convention of Human Rights (prohibition of retroactivity in criminal law).[10] The German government had argued that this principle applied only to punishment in a strict and narrow sense and not to mere "measures of betterment and security". But the ECtHR reserved for itself the right to define autonomously the concept of "penalty" in Article 7 ECHR. It pointed out that security detention in Germany was, for all practical purposes, indistinguishable from imprisonment as punishment: the "measure" is imposed by a criminal court, it is implemented in regular prisons, its execution is determined by the courts responsible for the execution of sentences and it "appears to be among the most severe – if not the most severe" measures of German criminal law. Therefore, it has to conform to the relevant principles enshrined in the convention for those sentenced to punishment.

As a result, security prisoners who were held under the new statutes had to be released. Their number is still not clear, but estimates range between 100 and 150. However, not all were in fact released, because some German courts felt not directly bound by the Strasbourg decision. Many politicians railed against the Strasbourg ruling and vowed to oppose it. Mass media painted a picture of dangerous criminals roaming the streets. Consequently, those detainees who were released, found themselves confronted by angry mobs of "concerned citizens". In some cases they had to change their places of residence several times. In other cases, they were put under 24-hour police supervision, with groups of police officers following their every step. Critics are calling this procedure "mobile prisons".

Abolishing pre-crime imprisonment?

Imprisonment used to be and still is largely post-crime. It presupposes that a crime has been committed or at least suspected. But predictions of future crime or dangerousness have become ever more important. This is evident in decisions about release on parole, even with determinate sentences. But it is all the more evident with indeterminate sentences, e.g. placement in forensic clinic/prisons and security detention, where release is almost exclusively based on expert opinion. So far, the clearest case of pre-crime imprisonment constitutes retrospective security detention. Even though it still requires at least one prior offence, its imposition depends exclusively on predictions of the future. There is only a small step left to pure pre-crime imprisonment, without any prior offence.

It is somewhat ironical that originally Germany resisted the introduction of pre-crime measures and it was the Nazi regime that introduced them, after other European states had already done so. Today, on the other hand, Germany leads the world in the expansion of such programs. What about the resistance against these developments in Germany?

Abolishing forensic prisons?

The introduction of measures of betterment and security has strengthened the system of sanctions. These measures need to be seen, to use KROM's term,[11] as masked forms of punishment. The European Court of Human Rights has started to unmask their punitive character in its decisions about retroactive and retrospective security detention in Germany. But the ECtHR has stopped short of forensic prisons. Placement there is still seen exclusively in terms of treatment and not of punishment. This kind of detention can still be legitimised by Article 5 paragraph 1 e ECHR, which lists among those that can be deprived of their liberty "*the lawful detention of persons for the prevention of the spreading of infectious diseases, of persons of unsound mind, alcoholics or drug addicts or vagrants*".

This clause, with its strange mixture of marginal groups, harks back to the worst incapacitative ideas of the social defence movement. As long as this clause is not removed, not much can be expected from the ECtHR with respect to a further unmasking of "penal measures".

In Germany, the distinction between penal sanctions and mere penal measures is still regarded as a progress in criminal justice. Such measures are seen as a more rational and even a more humane way of dealing with "dangerous" offenders, as something that is different from and "better than criminal law", to quote a revered legal philosopher (Radbruch 1956: 269). While some scholars have written about a "crises of the system of measures" (Kaiser 1990) and urged to make all of these measures less indeterminate, the system has remained largely unchanged. Especially the placement in forensic hospitals by criminal courts does not face any serious threat of being abolished, because psychiatrists are in charge and not prison directors. Recent cases[12] have, however, led to plans to move away from the indeterminate character of the detention in psychiatric prisons.

Abolishing security detention?

The situation is somewhat different for security detention. There are a number of good reasons to demand abolition of this institution, e.g.:

- its origin in one of the first legislative acts of the Nazi regime in 1933
- the presumed violation of a number of constitutional principles (e.g. human dignity, double jeopardy, disproportionality)
- the high number of false positives found through empirical research

- the factual lack of rehabilitation offers both during the time served in prison and in the detention institutions itself
- the ensuing difficulty for the detainees to prove that a release could be legitimized

The unconstitutionality of security detention was argued in a number of academic articles over the years. But the Federal constitutional court has for a long time rejected all attempts to invalidate the institution as such. When the same court finally did invalidate all norms governing security detention in 2011,[13] the decision was not based on any one of these arguments. It was only to force the legislative bodies to clarify the difference between imprisonment as punishment and as security detention and thereby demonstrate to the European Court of Human Rights that the measure does not constitute retrospective punishment. When both the Federal legislature (with respect to the measure itself) and the state legislatures (with respect to prison conditions) passed new statutes in 2012, security detention got a new lease of life.

Many people working in the field of criminal justice were not satisfied with the new legislation. They criticized both the process and the outcome. Early in 2013, a few of us formed a small working group, which consists of academics and criminal justice practitioners of different professional backgrounds. Over its first year, the group has met four times in different locations to discuss policy options, with a view to organize a larger conference in 2014. Some of us have earlier demanded the abolition of security detention,[14] but it soon became apparent that we could not agree on a strictly abolitionist platform. Some of us put their hopes into alternatives like social therapy as a new measure of treatment. Others reject this approach as being a new kind of anti-abolitionist positive reform. However, we continue our discussions in order to find ways to at least stop the expansion and as far as possible reduce the scope of security detention.

Against the expansion of security detention

The only kind of security detention that seemed effectively banned for the future by the ECtHR is the retrospective variant. This fact is, however, seen by both big political parties in Germany as a security problem, which they have vowed to fix. The new Federal government that came into office at the end of 2013 has pledged to reintroduce retrospective security detention under the new name of "retrospective therapy placement" (*nachträgliche Therapieunterbringung*). In this way, the government tries to find a new basis in the European Convention of Human Rights, namely in Article 5 paragraph 1 e, where deprivation of liberty is allowed in case of persons "of unsound mind". This represents an obvious attempt to find a substitute for the illegalized retrospective security detention.

This created a broad consensus in our working group. We agreed to denounce such an attempt and to formulate an Open Letter to the new Federal Minister of Justice. In this letter, we give ten reasons why this plan should not be implemented and demand a "thorough revision of the system of measures, oriented on the principle of proportionality and to abstain from an extension of security detention under the guise of "therapy". The letter[15] has been signed by 18 relevant organizations and more than 150 persons (including attorneys, judges, psychiatrists, social workers, professors and even some prisoners and detainees). Their demands constitute anything but straightforward abolitionism. But they are at least in line with what Thomas Mathiesen has called a defensive policy with respect to a further expansion of prisons.

What about mobile prisons?

Electronic fetters are increasingly seen as an "alternative" to imprisonment. Again Germany was late in joining other countries to allow this instrument to be used in the criminal justice context. There were some model experiments with electronically supervised house arrest. The scientific evaluations seemed less than promising. The breakthrough came after the release of some of the security detainees as a consequence of the Strasbourg decisions. Without further evaluations, a completely new technology (GPS tracking) was introduced and legalized as a way to supervise released security detainees. The practice is criticized by the police as not helpful and by abolitionists as a form of "mobile prison". The number of cases is still small, but can be expected to increase fast.

Some concluding remarks

Pre-crime imprisonment is on the rise in many parts of the world. Abolitionism will have to face these new developments, which are based on a theory of incapacitation. Thomas Mathiesen (2000: 85 sequ.) has suggested that the two basic critical issues with respect to incapacitation are accuracy and principles. But true pre-crime measures sidestep the question of criminal law principles, because they claim to be non-punitive, focussing exclusively on future security risks.

That seems to leave abolitionists only with the issue of accurate predictions ("false positives"). Fortunately, the recent German developments have also permitted new empirical research. At least three independent studies, based on the subsequent lives of released detainees, have confirmed that only a very small number of those released from security detention was reconvicted for serious crimes (Alex, 2013; Kinzig, 2010, Müller and Stolpmann, 2012). Incidentally, all of these studies were conducted before the police organized "mobile prisons".

But also principles need to be reconsidered. As we have seen, the European Court for Human Rights has started to apply principles of criminal law to cases of pre-crime. This needs to be expanded to all cases where "the detention is punitive in substance, irrespective of whether it is also preventive in purpose" (Ashworth et al., 2014: 167). In addition, we should push for new principles to deal specifically with the pre-crime logic.[16]

Notes

1. Cf. papers from a workshop that took place at the International Institute for the Sociology of Law in Onati in May 2012, e.g. John Pratt, Risk and Fall and Rise of Preventive Detention; Kent Roach, The Pervasive Use of Preventive Detention in Canada and the Limited Restraining Effects of Human Rights and Proportionality.
2. Cf. the references in *Kriminologisches Journal* 2008, p. 5
3. No annual statistics are available for the German Democratic Republic.
4. No statistics are available.
5. No annual statistics are available for the German Democratic Republic, nor are they available for East Germany until the present day.
6. See especially the speech given by the infamous Roland Freisler, in which he mentioned the special importance of security detention and stressed that it is by its very nature "not susceptible to previous limitations as regards duration" (p. 437). The report notes "loud applause" from his international audience.
7. This is the literal translation. The usual translation "preventive detention" is too broad, since it covers all kinds of preventive arrangements (remand, clinics, even isolation wards for patients with infectious diseases).
8. For a comprehensive discussion see: Drenkhahn et al. 2012.
9. This is how the ECtHR translates *nachträgliche Sicherungsverwahrung*, but maybe "post-hoc" or "subsequent" would be less confusing.
10. ECtHR, M. v. Germany, 17.12.2009. The Court also saw a violation of Art. 5 para 1a ECHR. It has confirmed this line in a number of decisions since and extended it to cases of retrospective security detention.
11. Quoted by Mathiesen 1979: 99.
12. See especially the case of Gustl Mollath (http://en.wikipedia.org/wiki/Gustl_Mollath).
13. BVerfG, decision of May 4, 2011, NJW 2011, 1931 (also available online www.bun desverfassungsgericht.de).
14. Asprion, 2012; Katholische Arbeitsgemeinschaft, 2002.
15. Open Letter: www.strafvollzugsarchiv.de/index.php?action=archiv_beitrag&thema_id= 4&beitrag_id=667&gelesen=667
16. Cf. the list of "restraining principles applicable to coercive prevention endeavours by the state" in: Ashworth et al., 2014: 168–169.

References

Alex, Michael (2013) *Nachträgliche Sicherungsverwahrung – ein rechtsstaatliches und kriminalpolitisches Debakel*. 2. Aufl., Holzkirchen.

Ashworth, Andrew/Zedner, Lucia/Tomlin, Patrick, (eds.) (2014) *Prevention and the Limits of the Criminal Law*. Oxford University Press, 167.

Asprion, Peter (2012) *Gefährliche Freiheit. Das Ende der Sicherungsverwahrung*. Freiburg: Herder.

Dick, Philip K. (2002) *Minority Report*. London: Gollancz.

Drenkhahn, Kirstin/Morgenstern, Christine/van Zyl Smit, Dirk (2012) "What Is in a Name? Preventive Detention in Germany in the Shadow of European Human Rights Law", *Criminal Law Review*, Issue 3, 167–187.

Feest, Johannes (1991) "Über den Umgang der Justiz mit Kritik. Am Beispiel von juristischen Ratgebern für Gefangene", *Kritische Justiz*, 253–264.

Kaiser, Günther (1990) *Befinden sich die kriminalrechtlichen Maßregeln in der Krise?* Karlsruhe.

Katholische Bundesarbeitsgemeinschaft Straffälligenhilfe *et al.* (2003) *Gegen Menschen-verwahrung! Ein Plädoyer zur Abschaffung der Sicherungsverwahrung.* Freiburg, Schwerin, Berlin.

Kinzig, Jörg (2010) *Die Legalbewährung gefährlicher Rückfalltäter.* 2. Aufl., Freiburg.

Mathiesen, Thomas (1965) The *Defences of the Weak. A Sociological Study of a Norwegian Correctional Institution.* London: Tavistock Publications.

Mathiesen, Thomas (1979) *Überwindet die Mauern!. Die skandinavische Gefangenenbe-wegung als Modell politischer Randgruppenarbeit.* (Translated by Knut Papendorf). Neuwied: Luchterhand.

Mathiesen, Thomas (1987) *Prison on Trial.* Second English edition published by Waterside Press in 2000.

Mathiesen, Thomas (1989) *Gefängnislogik.* 1989.Müller, Jürgen L. and Stolpmann, Georg (2012) "Untersuchung der nicht angeordneten Sicherungsverwahrung – Implikationen für die Neuregelung der Sicherungsverwahrung". In: Jürgen L. Müller/Norbert Nedo-pil/Nahlah Saimeh/Elmar Habermeyer/Peter Falkai (eds.), *Sicherungsverwahrung – wissenschaftliche Basis und Positionsbestimmung.* Berlin, 111–128.

Papendorf, Knut (1993) "Zur Rezeptionsgeschichte dieses Buches und was macht KROM heute?" In: Thomas Mathiesen. *Überwindet die Mauern!.* 2nd ed., Bielefeld, 195–212.

Radbruch, Gustav (1956) *Rechtsphilosophie,* 5th ed., Stuttgart: K.F. Köhler.

Ratgeber für Gefangene mit medizinischen und juristischen Hinweisen (1981) Hamburg: Libertäre Assoziation.

Schumann, Karl (1979) "Politische Randgruppenarbeit nach Mathiesen und Foucault". In: *Überwindet die Mauern! Die skandinavische Gefangenenbewegung als Modell politischer Randgruppenarbeit.* Neuwied: Luchterhand, 1–23.

van der Aa, Simon, (ed.) (1936) *The Transactions of the International Penal and Peniten-tiary Congress in Berlin,* vol. 3, Bern.

Weber, Hartmut and Feest, Johannes (1998) "Germany: Ups and Downs in the Resort to Imprisonment – Strategic or Unplanned Outcomes?" In: Robert P. Weiss/Nigel South (eds.) *Comparing Prison Systems. Toward a Comparative and International Penology.* Amsterdam: OPA, 233–262.

Zedner, Lucia (2007) "Pre-crime and post-criminology", *Theoretical Criminology* 11 (2), 2, 261–281.

4

Prisoners speak out

Monrad, prisoner number 162/90
and prisoner number 03/43

Fifteen years for violence

Excerpts from Monrad, Botsfengselet 1969

How does a person sentenced to 15 years for violence manage to get out of prison? The location is Botsfengselet, "The Penance Prison", built on the basis of the Philadelphia model and opened in 1851 as Norway's major prison at the time. It still stands and was used until 1970. In fact, it is also now in use, after rehabilitation, as a section of Oslo Prison. The essay was published in 1969.

Image 3.1 The picture of Botsfengselet in Christiania (now Oslo), a Philadelphia prison opened in 1851, taking at the time about 240 prisoners. Botsfengsel literally means 'prison of penance'. It was Norway's central prison until 1970. In 1975 and after rehabilitation it became a section of Oslo Prison. Photo: Turid Eikvam

[. . .]I first sat in the "tank", in the basement. It is a cell which is placed inside another cell, where one blue bulb lights up the room slightly and around the clock, and where the edges in the cell are rounded. I would view it as an architecturally devilish design which after a few hours gives the prisoner the sense that the walls press themselves in on him, and that he is choked. I think that precisely this sense, further strengthened by a total quiet, prevents almost anybody from managing this kind of isolation for more than a short while. The fear of such isolation lies there and is undoubtedly latent, and just as undoubtedly it becomes as vivid as fire once the door is locked behind the person. It may be compared with what a small child may feel, when the mother for a little while closes the child in a dark closet – even as a grownup it is difficult to re-live what a person as a child in this way would have experienced. The furniture of the cell consists of a matrass and a couple of blankets. That's all. The blankets have an unstated mission, in so far as the prisoner by pulling them over his head may escape into his own world. A world where rounded corners no longer make him remember the hours of fright which he experienced, once in a time far removed in the past.

The day passed, and they came. All of them came, the warden, the doctor, all of the dignitaries who designate an institution.

"How long do you plan to be sitting here in the basement?" There was irritation in the question, and I understood that the vice-warden, second in command, was expecting a concrete answer. I gave that to him.

"Until release takes place."

"You will not gain anything by this isolation."

"I have, sir, no illusions about the isolation shortening the length of punishment. Botsfengselet has nothing to give me, and I prefer the basement."

After a while I exchanged the "tank" for the "cage", where the difference consisted of the "cage" having two walls with vertical bars from floor to ceiling. A reader who has visited the Zoological Gardens may compare this with the cage of a gorilla – the only difference being that a gorilla gets bananas. I didn't receive any bananas.

The days came, and the weeks passed. The weeks became months. The officers were made responsible for the meals, and thereby I had contact with the world around me three times per 24 hours.

"Have a good dinner!"

The food was served in cardboard mugs, eaten with a wooden spoon. It would have been less troublesome if they had given me bananas; I would have been able to peal the fruit myself, and gloomy men with golden braids would have been spared carrying the wooden spoon up and down. They were certainly irritated by this change of the prison routine.

The days were long, and I felt undressed, naked. . . . I sought warmth for the body. This took place in the form of an application where I asked the mighty Council to have a pair of trousers [not just 'the striped underware' . . .] The application was granted. [. . .] I was informed by one of the prison's staff people that the mighty Council had laughed most heartily over the application from where the excerpt is taken. They probably saw the sick humour in the situation, and in a seizure of bureaucratic splendour they could indulge in a laugh which broke the tension, hopefully softening a conscience which already was shaky [. . .].

The Chief Doctor was the only one who never urged me to break the isolation. As a psychiatrist he understood at an early point in time that for me this was a principle, and that I would never deviate from this principle. Through various channels I understood that he, after all, had to admire my strong will, whereas others saw the attitude as mere defiance. However, the Chief Doctor warned me against the harmful effects of isolation. Physically harmful due to where the basement was situated: stone floor etc., and health-wise not designed as a permanent place of residence. The Chief Doctor warned specifically against the harmful psychological effects, insofar he made it clear that even if I could not register the harmful effect from day to day, a deep-seated mental damage would take place in a longer perspective. The Chief Doctor also maintained that vis-a-vis the Prison Board and as a doctor he would renounce any responsibility. The Prison Board did nothing.

Also early on during the isolation he asked me if I would be willing to go to a psychiatric clinic or an asylum, if this could be arranged. I agreed to this. It would be in line with the forensic conclusions in the case – in so far as the medical experts in court had recommended curative psychiatric treatment – which, by the way, the Intermediate Court and later the Supreme Court agreed to, too. With my intimate knowledge of Norwegian legal practice I was aware of the fact that this view on the part of the courts would constitute an illusion and just a way of throwing dust in the jury's eyes, in view of the fact that the Prison Bureau has final authority and is not bound by views on the part of the courts and in practice takes no notice of such decisions. As a prisoner I was fully conscious of the fact that upon entry my identity would be exchanged with a Number in the protocols of the prison, so that I, myself, would have to provoke a situation – a situation which literally speaking *forced* the prison authorities to arrange a break with the sleepwalker-like practice which is an aspect of the ways of bureaucracy. The isolation appeared to bear fruit.

The nights were long, too.

I often stayed awake, and recited long monologs . . . I thought of all the defeats in the life of a human being. How many defeats can a human being tolerate? At times, the quiet was strange, as if the earth was barren and I myself was the only survivor. The loneliness is perhaps not so related to the external things – it lives in the very mind of the human being. A recidivist is rarely capable of feeling any spontaneous joy when release comes. It is strange. It is a tragic thing that when the gates of the prison finally open, *fear* will, with a crushing knock-out kill all expectations, all dreams about the future, which the prisoner through months and years has lived on and believed was a reality.[. . .]

During my stay in the basement I never had any thought or conscious wish to move upstairs to a regular cell in the prison. . . . When would the grey mass prisoners as a unit march down to the basement in a silent protest against such a system? [Their lack of action] can only be caused by a servile attitude on behalf of the prisoners and the threat of reprisals. The system in the prisons is based on the principle of *informing*, which in turn makes it unnecessary for the authorities to fear the threat from a collective prisoners' opinion. I wonder what a purely scientific analysis of this would show in terms of results concerning the prisoners' constant and limitless feeling of *lack of power*.

A stay in prison is in itself a paradox. How can you expect a prisoner at release to able to adjust to the normal conditions of society when he has lived for months and years in the prison under highly deviant conditions? [. . .]

[. . .]My God, I prefer the isolation!

I shouted it out loud, you should think it had to be heard and give an echo far up through the corridors of the prison. I want to be alone! ALONE!

I mentioned this in a talk with the officer in charge of education. "I begin to hear voices; it seems as if the voice comes from a place under the roof, on the right hand side. Tell me, do you think this is a bad sign?"

The officer in charge of education looked at me through the bars. I noticed a faint smile, as if he tried to interpret this as a usual result of my grim humour. "No", he responded, "it doesn't have to be that. – It depends on *what* the voice says!"

Afterwards I thought that the voice came from the bottom of my own sexual life. [. . .]

[After this, many further paradoxes met Monrad in his life at Botsfengselet. A few times he visited the yard for exercises, he learned to know extremely few people, after his many months of complete isolation the prison finally let him have a bed in the nursery ward of the prison, the nursery ward applied for a stay in a psychiatric hospital, it was denied but finely granted. In the psychiatric hospital he was allowed to walk around, he wondered whether a sick woman he met there was more or less as sick as the prisoners back in Botsfengselet. This way, through all of these obstacles, he finally won his battle with the administration of the prison. The last words of his story from Botsfengselet were the end of a whole "speech" on forensic psychiatry which he gave to a nurse who offered him coffee. I include the end of the "speech" here, ed.:]

MONRAD: "According to professor Gabriel Langfeldt [a professor of psychiatry] the condition 'lasting weakness of mental faculties' does not have to be everlasting. Following this it seems that 'danger of repetition of punishable acts' should be a conclusion following right before release; the opposite would be a clear denial of the prison's significance as an educational institution – which I, in parenthesis, can understand very well, even if it is irrelevant under these conditions. Many arguments may be employed against the use of security as it is used, and even if the term 'weakness of mental faculties' is language-wise misleading with unknown consequences for those who are struck by it."

NURSE: "But what does the concept mean?"

MONRAD: "A lack of ability to adapt in a social sense, which again is a relative concept".

NURSE: [Not understanding much of what he talked about] she smiled, "A cup of coffee?"

Translation by Thomas Mathiesen.

Desks and modern treatment of prisoners

Prisoner number 162/90, inmate in Ullersmo
National Prison 1992

How does an inmate tackle the rigid bureaucracy of a modern prison? One way among several is a kind of irritated or even desperate humor. The location is Ullersmo National Prison, which was opened in 1970 and which took the role of Botsfengselet (see the above essay) as Norway's central prison. This essay was written in 1992.

Complaint concerning new regulations of the placement of desks, and complaints concerning confiscation of television set, radio, and cassette player following "denial of orders" in relation to this.

The undersigned serves a sentence of 10 years for breaking § 162 of the Criminal Act. So far I have served the first three years of the sentence, the last 21 months at Ullersmo National Prison.

By way of introduction I would like briefly to point out some of the background for this complaint. During the almost two years I have served here at Ullersmo, I have been confronted by an endless number of ludicrous regulations. I have constantly been presented by new burlesque "measures of security" which almost without exception lack any shred of reasonable logic.

Largely I have tried not to let new ignorant regulations provoke me so much that it has gone contrary to the daily "satisfaction of doing time". However, sometimes

Image 3.2 A prison cell anywhere in Europe. Photo: Per Jørgen Ystehede

it has exceeded my jackboots so much that I have felt an urge to point out the lack of judgment on the part of the management. Especially after NN's appointment as acting inspector, it has from time to time been like Texas out here. I hope his engagement is only temporary, and that the Prison Board now for once cuts through and stops this circus.

The Regulation I wish to complain to the Prison Board about, is inspector NN's last stroke of genius, and that concerns something as prosaic as the placement of desks in the cells. It is probably not possible to come closer to a soup pot of a Council than this.

On my way back to my cell at the end of the day yesterday (7 July 1992) I was able to enjoy the following humourous note from the Inspectorate: "The desk is supposed to be placed under the window! This will be checked tomorrow."

There is nothing special about this note, because we are, as is well known, exposed to continuous and ever-present cell controls. It does not make any *great* difference between cells if the desk stands north-wise or east-wise. I will not argue about that. But the placement of the desk under the shelf instead of under the window gives important free space of about one meter between the bed and the desk. By placing the desk under the shelf, that is, facing north or facing south, you had the possibility of "taking a walk" back and forth between the door and the window, which has its limitations when the desk fills all of the East- or the West wall. To the bureaucrat in the Prison Board this can probably seem like å luxury problem. Anyway the fact is such "back and forth trampling" may be of great significance during sleepless nights and long hours of confinement in your cell.

I shall refrain from pointing out further solid reasons for the choice of placement of the desks, but hope that the responsible official now understands that the complaint has very real and partly pressing motives.

In any case – on the background of the above I chose to let the desk sit in its old place, despite the inspectoral note of "change of address". Usually we do not take these inspectoral notes so seriously, because they usually they do not show anything other than an expression of the individual officer's wish to show a measure of childish self-assertion. As is well known, many of the blue-shirts choose their occupation from precisely such motives. Something which is particularly expressed through the above mentioned cell stressing.

I was therefore slightly surprised to be summoned to "Post 2" now to day (7 July 1992). It turned out, however, that a "large action" was carried out upon the order of the inspector, with a view to "co-ordinate the placement of desks in the institution". It followed that I was interrogated as to why I had not already turned my desk around, and was ordered to the unit to do this immediately.

I went through the points which I have mentioned above, and elaborated them in a reasonable and impartial way. Furthermore, I clarified *whether* there were simple and reasonable reasons for me to turn the desk around. If so, I would of course do so right away. However, no such reason was presented.

The officer could only refer to a rather sweeping regulation that "this was the usual way", and to the importance of the blue-shirts to find their way to the bed in case of fire.

The fact that they in this case have managed to produce a fire-technical argument, is of course additionally humorous. Especially on the background that the prisoners for many years have pointed to the need for fire alarms, without having seen or heard anything in this direction. In view of this, I was able to amplify vis-a-vis the officer that that the arguments counted only in "my" favor, certainly when considering the fact that a north-south placement of the desk opens the passage to the window.

The guards' argument to the effect of that they in a dark and smoke-filled cell would have to know where the bed was placed, is so unreasonable as to cancel itself out. In the first place, the question here concerns the placement of the desk – and the desk does not have any effect on the placement of the bed (which, by the way, is bolted to the wall). Secondly, because even a blue-shirt who is on the average disoriented, must be able to orient himself in an area or 6 square meters, regardless of the placement of furniture.

The fire-technical point (or the lack of such a point) is of course only a substitute argument when lacking an objective reason for finding new methods to stress large parts of the prison population. The officers have understood that some prisoners try to create a certain amount "atmosphere", or the best possible practical context to their barely six meters of space, and wish to sabotage it. The argument of "fire security" has, then, been added after the regulation in question.

I would like to add that the officer who interrogated me, in all respects was obliging, understanding the absurdity of the situation. In any case I was presented with the possibility of various reprimands, without at any point in time viewing them as relevant. I felt there would obviously be limits as to how much prestige would be placed in the placement of a desk. Even for inspectors.

I would like also to emphasize that when seen isolated this turmoil over a desk is not *that* important to me. Furthermore I think it is rather paradoxical that grown-up people (read: inspectors at the institution) in fact used time and resources to lower themselves to a level such as this.

What, however, *is* important to me, is how one follows entirely one's own interpretation of things in here, without understanding the deeper consequences of this kind of shaky treatment of laws and regulations, as well as with no understanding of the consequences which a lack an ordinary view and ordinary fairness may have in a longer perspective.

People who are in prison are most often incarcerated due to a lack of ability to follow laws and rules. When the institutional management systematically makes people continue to live on with a view that laws and rules have no other practical function than being an irrational provocation, they only contribute to making people even less prepared for the day when the sentence is finally served.

After the conversation with the officer I went back to my studies, where I stayed during the rest of the day. Coming back to the cell, I found that my desk had been turned around the rather funny 90 degrees. The Inspector's note "Move the desk!" was probably meant to emphasize the humor of the situation. What was not so humorous was the note to the effect that the television, the radio and the cassette player had been confiscated, due to ". . . denial to follow orders".

Now, it is not a particularly great problem for me to be without a television and a radio, despite of the fact that I this way, I am sorry to say, lose the rather important teaching programs which are adapted to the basic university program I follow (history). The crux of the matter is, however, not the television (even though several guards I have been in contact with through the day in fact think the confiscation is contrary to the rules). The crux of the matter is simply how the management *again* have chosen to rely on means of power right after a "problem" has come up. Again they right away chose to bite. Personally I am not serving a sentence for violence, neither have I had particularly great problems with my temper or mastering reasonably objective arguments. Nevertheless, many at the institution are *precisely* in this situation. How do they expect that these individuals are to relate to others on the day they are released, and when they are confronted by a conflict situation?

A human being who is taught that all conflict situations are solved by means of power, will use means of power in similar situations. This way the prison functions as a direct stimulator of continued violence, precisely the contrary of the whole intention of the system.

And that's why I am sitting here formulating this with my face to the east rather than the usual north. Of course I have now a better view of what is happening in the yard and in the guards' tower, but since the blue-shirts largely are preoccupied with their usual hobbies like playing cards and reading comics, it doesn't give particularly good compensation for the earlier solution.

Otherwise, I wish the bureaucrats a pleasant summer.

Translation by Thomas Mathiesen.

Norwegian prisoners' struggle for privacy: an illustrating tale of system change from below

Prisoner number 03/43, inmate in Ila Prison and Preventive Detention Institution 2011

How does an inmate tackle the ultra-modern aspects of our society, heavily dependent as we are on the Internet and digital equipment of all kinds? Prisoner number 03/43 discovered that something very serious was going on in the prison. He dug into it, and finally won.

The prison has a varied history. Construction originally began in 1937 as a prison for women, during World War II it was used as a concentration camp for Norwegian resistance people, after the war it was used for Norwegians who had been collaborators with the occupants during the war (and staffed by the Norwegian military coming across the border from neutral Sweden), from 1951 it was a medium security supervision institution (see Jane Dullum's article in this volume) and now, after 2002, a high security prison and preventive detention institution.

The European Convention on Human Rights (article 8) protects individuals' private life. An individual's right to privacy – a personal sphere wherein he or she can act freely without coercion or interference from the state or other individuals – is imperative in a democracy. In a broader sense, the right to privacy also includes the right to control information regarding oneself. In Norway, restrictions on collection, processing, storage and disclosure of personal data have been emphasized as important aspects of individuals' right to privacy (Schartum & Bygrave, 2011). The purpose of the Norwegian Personal Data Act is "to protect natural persons from violation of their right to privacy through the processing of personal data" (section 1). Furthermore, the act emphasizes that personal data must be "processed in accordance with fundamental respect for the right to privacy, including the need to protect personal integrity and private life and ensure that personal data are of adequate quality" (section 1).

In many respects, a prison sentence comprises a curtailment of fundamental rights and needs. Prisoners are subjected to legitimate coercion and forced exclusion. Being imprisoned entails being "forcibly removed from community and placed in a total environment from which there is no immediate escape" (Cohen and Taylor, 1972, p. 53). Prisoners are placed in a total institution, with omnipresent barriers against social interaction with the outside world (Goffman, 1961), and the prison institution collects, produces and stores personal data regarding its prisoners.

Norwegian prisoners are not legally deprived of their right to privacy. Like other Norwegian citizens, prisoners are protected by the Personal Data Act. One may actually argue that the right to privacy becomes particularly important when individuals are deprived of their freedom through a prison sentence.

Pre-scandal conditions

Our story begins in the early 2000s in Ila prison, a middle-sized Norwegian prison, primarily housing long-term prisoners. Among prisoners, this prison was notorious for its extensive gathering and use of personal data about its captives, aimed at producing clinical and actuarial risk analyses and predictions. Every prisoner's behavior, statements, social interactions, social networks and health conditions were thoroughly recorded on standardized forms by the guards, and prisoners were routinely subjected to psychological tests by the prison's psychologists. The prison's evaluations, based on this massive complex of personal information, constituted the foundation for the institution's decisions of whether a prisoner was to be released on parole, whether he was to be forcibly placed in solitary confinement, whether he was to be granted a leave from the prison, and so on.

Over time, prisoners observed that documents containing their sensitive personal data were stored in offices in which every prison guard in the prison had access and that electronic information was accessible to every prison guard in the country. Neither were the prisoners informed about the extent to which the information was restricted to outside disclosure. Some guards even admitted to reading the prisoners' personal files for entertainment purposes only, as a result of some of the inmates being nationally known through the media. A few long-term prisoners began to investigate more thoroughly. They found that prisoners' right to privacy was heavily under-communicated and repeatedly experienced prison guards claiming that the Personal Data Act did not apply to individuals in captivity, or that guards were not aware of the act's existence at all.

The research period

The prisoners sat down and decided they had to do something about the current situation. This was not a question of personal privileges or individual benefits, it was a matter that applied to every prisoner in the country. They wanted to learn more about the relevant legislation and requested the prison to provide them with a copy of the Personal Data Act. The prison refused to do so, claiming that this act was not relevant to their status as prisoners. Instead, the prisoners received a copy from a legal aid clinic in Oslo. They studied the legislation and inquired further through phone calls and letters to government agencies. Their activities were subjected to thorough surveillance by the prison, even though prisoners' phone calls and correspondence with government agencies should not be monitored, pursuant to the Norwegian Execution of Sentences Act.

The first attempt

In 2005, the prisoners presented their concerns to the prison management through their established cooperative forum. They claimed that the prison's routines were not in line with the Personal Data Act and requested the prison management to ensure that personal information about the prisoners were restricted to those employees who in fact were in need of that information. The prison inspector blatantly rejected the prisoners concerns and stated that every single guard had to have access to sensitive personal information about every single prisoner. The inspector continued: "It may be that a prisoner has hemorrhoids. Every guard must be aware of that so that no one commands him to sit in a chair". The prisoners were, not surprisingly, unsatisfied with such an explanation. They kept asking questions until they were told "this is a situation you better stop inquiring about".

The data protection authority enters

The prisoners soon realized that attempts to solve the problem in co-operation with the prison management would bring them nowhere. Instead, in 2006, they filed a formal complaint to the Norwegian Data Protection Authority. The data authority accepted the complaint and started investigating. The Norwegian Ministry of Justice and the Police was confronted with the prisoners' claims and required to respond. The ministry upheld, based on information they had received from the management at Ila prison, that treatment of Norwegian prisoners was conducted in line with the Personal Data Act. The prisoners were now faced with a colossal opponent, a team of government-employed lawyers, who kept denying that anything was wrong. However, the prisoners kept trying to prove that this was in fact not the case.

In 2007, the Data Protection Authority decided to physically send two representatives to Ila prison. Prison staff was interrogated, but still they rejected the prisoners' claims. The authority representatives then inspected the prison's personal data filing systems and discovered that the prisoners' claims were both correct and accurate.

Scandalous findings

In a public report from 2008 (Datatilsynet, 2008), the Data Protection Authority emphasized that Norwegian prisons systematically and seriously violated several provisions stated in the Personal Data Act. The data authority concluded that prisons' processing of prisoners' sensitive personal data did not in any way meet the basic statutory requirements for protecting individuals' personal integrity. In the report, the data authority emphasized that prison staff and officials had intentionally misled the authority by rejecting the prisoners' claims with false and inaccurate information. The data authority demanded far-reaching system changes to be employed.

The scandal at Ila prison received great public attention. Newspapers as well as radio and television channels reported extensively on the situation and some of the involved prisoners were even interviewed. The Minister of Justice had to account for the Ila case in the Parliament, and the Ila situation was presented as part of the curriculum for law students at the university.

Great challenges in a difficult landscape

Despite the prison authorities' ambitions of prisoner rehabilitation (see e.g., Norwegian Ministry of Justice and the Police, 2007–2008), the purpose of imprisonment is to inflict pain on the prisoner. The execution of punishment involves inflicting pain on a human being with the intention of creating a harmful experience (Schaanning, 2009). In prison, one group of people (guards) is given the task of making sure that another group of people (prisoners) remain unfree and in captivity. Hostile relationships tend to develop between prisoners and guards (Goffman, 1961), probably as a result of the prisoners' life and activities being subjected to social control and sanctioning at the hands of the totalitarian prison regime and its guards. The prison landscape, being a polarized and hostile institution primarily designed to punish, does not constitute a good point of departure for co-operation between prisoners and guards. Hence, it is not surprising that the Ila prisoners were unable to solve their problems in co-operation with the prison management.

Moreover, each individual prisoner is very vulnerable in captivity due to the current prison ideology. The prison is not ideologically isolated from its surrounding society. In Western, individualistic cultures, individualism dominates with its emphasis on personal achievements (Nafstad, Blakar, Carlquist, Phelps & Rand-Henriksen, 2007). Based on individualism, the foundation of the modern correctional system is a prison structure in which the individual prisoner, instead of being given fundamental rights, must earn privileges by behaving in a manner that converges with the prison's conception of the "model prisoner" (Giertsen, 1995; Goffman, 1961). Being labelled as "oppositional" or "difficult" by prison guards, may have consequences for whether the prisoner is granted privileges, and perhaps even for when the prisoner is released from captivity. As such, the Ila prisoners may have run a great personal risk by challenging a prison system that monitored their every move.

Changing the system is possible

Despite great challenges, the prisoners were able to produce significant system changes. Today, there is reason to believe that Norwegian prisons have been forced to safeguard prisoners' right to privacy to a much greater extent than prior to the Ila prisoners' struggle. Of course, the right to privacy is only one among many areas in which system change is called for. However, the most important lesson from the Ila story is that it is possible for prisoners to initiate and produce system change from below. Hopefully, the struggle of the Ila prisoners may inspire others by clearly showing that the system is not invincible.

References

Cohen, S., & Taylor, L. (1972). *Psychological survival. The experience of long-term imprisonment.* New York, NY: Pantheon.

Datatilsynet. (2008). *Endelig kontrollrapport etter tilsyn ved Ila fengsel* [Final control report after inspection at Ila prison]. Available from www.datatilsynet.no

Giertsen, H. (1995). Fengselsvesenets skjulte verdimønstre [The hidden value patterns of the correctional service]. *Lov og Rett. Norsk juridisk tidsskrift, 7,* 414–427.

Goffman, E. (1961). *Asylums: Essays on the social situation of mental patients and other inmates.* New York, NY: Doubleday.

Nafstad, H. E., Blakar, R. M., Carlquist, E., Phelps, J. M. & Rand-Hendriksen, K. (2007). Ideology and power: The influence of current neo-liberalism in society. *Journal of Community & Applied Social Psychology, 17*(4), 313–327. doi: 10.1002/casp.931

Norwegian Ministry of Justice and the Police. (2007–2008). *St.meld. nr. 37 (2007–2008). Straff som virker – mindre kriminalitet – tryggere samfunn* [White paper no 37 (2007–2008). Punishment that works – less crime – safer society]. Oslo, Norway: Author.

Schaanning, E. (2009). *Den tilsiktede smerten. En blindflekk i norsk kriminalpolitikk* [The intended pain. A blindspot in Norwegian criminal justice policy]. Oslo, Norway: Unipub.

Schartum, D. W., & Bygrave, L. A. (2011). *Personvern in informasjonssamfunnet: En innføring i vern av personopplysninger* [Right to privacy in the information society: An introduction to the protection of personal data] (2nd ed.). Bergen, Norway: Fagbokforlaget.

5

Abolitionism and reform: a possible combination?

Notes on a Norwegian experiment

Hedda Giertsen

It is long ago now, 40 years, since Mathiesen (1974) presented an abolitionist stance in a text on the first years of KROM, The Norwegian Association for Penal Reform. In certain respects, it seems to have been much longer ago when looking at the many reforms that have taken place in this period (more on this later). But in other respects time seems to have been standing still: the purpose of imprisonment is still to punish and to inflict pain.[1] Security is the main priority, and intimidating controls and sanctions like solitary confinement are still being used (The Penal Implementation Act (PIA) §§ 37, 39, 40; Hellevik 2001; Smith *et al.* 2014). Prison policy, with its dual aims of punishment and rehabilitation, is no less mixed and contradictory today than it was back in 1974.

Right from the beginning KROM-members were challenged by the question of abolition and reforms: how to improve prison conditions without strengthening the idea of the prison and its expanded use? One overarching answer was to divide reforms into 'positive' ones, those that seemed to support prisons, and 'negative' ones challenging the system (see the preface to the present volume). KROM-members' discussions on reforms provide a unique basis and possibility for bringing further ideas into the discussion on abolition and reforms. I will suggest a way of looking at this.

Two main groups of reforms

I suggest that the influence of reforms and whether they support or diminish prisons has less to do with the content or quality of the reforms than with their position within penal policy: are they available to all citizens, widely implemented in society and based on rights? Or are they directed exclusively toward prisoners with the intention of reducing crime? Prison authorities have implemented both groups of reforms, but others have been suggested by people from the outside, two of which have been in a KROM-setting.[2]

First I will present reforms that are widely implemented in society, based on legal rights or humane values, independent of prison policy aims, here called *independent reforms*. These may contribute to reducing the importance of prisons. The second group contains reforms that are tightly interwoven with the aim of rehabilitation with the intention of reducing crime, and which may contribute to strengthen the idea and use of prisons.

Independent reforms

Two main reforms, of education and health services, will be outlined. These are not isolated occurrences, but situated in an environment and tradition of reforms, which add to their impact. These other reforms were implemented one by one, but looking back one may notice a connecting line, which is to highlight the value of human beings and their integrity. These reforms are: *the import model* (Christie 1969) from the 1970s, which is explained later; the principle that prisoners are *deprived only of their right to move around freely* (*frihetsberøvelse*) (Vedeler 1973), later developed into *the normality principle* (White paper 2007–2008); the short sentences;[3] the position not to provide psychiatric or psychological treatment inside prisons (White paper 1977–1978), and *the guarantee of return to society* (Soria-Moria declaration 2005).

Education

Since 1969 educational authorities have had responsibility for education in prison (Langelid 2009: 87). In 2012 there were schools in all prisons in Norway, and a total of 9,600 prisoners were enrolled in school or courses.[4] Fifty percent of prisoners (N = 3,591) took part in education on a daily basis (ibid., Norwegian Correctional Services (NCS)[5] 2013: 36). The formal basis for schooling is *the law on education,* stating that every citizen has a right and an obligation to complete lower secondary school (*ungdomstrinnet*), usually in 12 years. Everyone has access to upper secondary (*vidaregåande opplæring*) and tertiary education if they meet the educational requirements. Today education in prison is encompassed by PIA §3 as one of the mandatory activities for prisoners.[6]

One argument against an expansion of the education system inside prisons could be that this will increase the number of staff and expand the prison system with additional personnel and professions. This has not happened. The teachers are brought in as extra personnel according to the import model (Christie 1969/1993) introduced in the 1970s. In this model staff providing services not connected with essential prison tasks such as security, controls, etc., are employed and paid by the administrations that employ all professionals within their sector, whether working inside or outside prison walls. The employers are usually municipal, county and state administrations, and rarely private foundations.[7]

Another argument could be that prisoners appreciate school in prison and therefore also find imprisonment acceptable and positive, opening up possibilities not found on the outside. In this way education in prison might support prisons. For some prisoners this is the case (Langelid 2009), where education inside prisons is more easily available and better adapted to their needs than outside. Prisoners' views on education in prison vary. Some display an instrumental attitude, seeing education as a means for further education or employment after release, and some find that education may improve them as a parent. Other answers point to education as positive and enjoyable in itself. Still other answers relate, in two different ways, to the prison situation itself: one is that education makes the sentence more lenient, time passes more quickly. The other describes classrooms as a different social space than prison, and for a moment they feel free, like having time off from prison (Viljugrein 2000). In such situations prisoners visit and anticipate a role that is well established and accepted in society. For a moment, they turn into ordinary citizens. Even if prisons offer education in a way that prisoners can meet, it may still not outweigh the daily pains of imprisonment (Sykes 1958).

Most important in discussions on reform and abolition is the position and tasks that education has within a prison policy context: it is not argued that this is a tool to combat, cure or reduce crime. Of course, education may have the effect of supporting a law-abiding life, but this is not the main justification for introducing education in prison. Education has its own purposes, and is evaluated by educational administrations according to their obligations and aims (Langelid 2009: 113ff.).

Prisoners who apply for education are not evaluated based on a possible future in crime or a law-abiding life, but according to their position on the educational ladder. The intentions behind recruiting pupils or students inside prisons are the usual educational ones: to improve knowledge and insight, to prepare for waged labour, and also because education is seen as a good in itself.

Prisoners have the right to education. A prison sentence deprives the convict of the right to move around freely *(frihetsberøvelse),* but not other rights as long as the sentence does not explicitly include other deprivations (Vedeler 1973). Yet formal rights are not always sufficient; practical conditions also matter. When education has been widely implemented within prisons it is partly because it has become a substantial establishment in society, encompassing a large part of the population, and seen as an important field for investment in the future. This seeps through the prison walls and creates a base for arguing for education inside prisons as almost self-evident. But somebody has to help ideas be realized, and enthusiastic leaders and teachers have promoted schools inside prisons (Langelid 2009). Even so, rights are not always fulfilled. Practical matters, or arguments framed as such, may outweigh principles and push rights to the background, left with no importance. Education in prison is dependent on its prison environment, buildings, daily routines, the qualifications and qualities of personnel and, not to forget, security considerations. Prisoners experience this when suddenly being transferred to another prison and education is interrupted, or when books are brought to the prisoner student too late in the term and so forth.

School in Norwegian prisons is based on educational traditions, ideals and values in general, and also on legal rights. Also needed is the tedious work to sort out practical solutions that require political and administrative co-operation on all levels – on employment, expenses and the professional responsibility for education behind walls. These matters are outlined and stated in policy documents and circulars (Langelid 2009). The Norwegian experience illustrates what has been possible to bring about in political and administrative contexts, within the framework that the Norwegian society provides. This is not to say that no prisoners experience obstacles, hindrances and problems when they want education in prison. So they do. And even if much has been achieved, several of the educational authorities' obligations toward prisoners are still to be met (ibid.).

Health care

The provision of health care resembles that of education in some respects: health workers do not add to prison staff; they are employed and paid by municipal or state health administrations.[8] In principle, they follow their own professional standards, laws regulating health services and policy documents on health services in prison.[9] But tasks and values relevant to penal systems are different from those informing general health services, as are the laws regulating the two. Nonetheless, it should be possible on a daily basis to handle satisfactorily both activities, with mutual respect (Directorate of Health 2013: 14). But sometimes this does not happen. Situations appear when central values protecting life and health and considerations regarding security and punishment run into conflict. The prison environment claims its rights, where prison directors have the last word and may overrule advice from a physician (ibid.). That has happened and has caused serious harm to the health of prisoners (Hammerlin 2009, Karlsen 2008, Rua 2012). Suicide and self-harm bring dilemmas of health and security to the forefront, unmasking conditions that effect the security of the individual at risk (ibid). So do discussions on sterile syringes (Ekeid 2009). Values of health and life have a standing that can challenge prison assessments.

Health authorities at the municipal, county and state levels evaluate health services according to the aims, rights and laws of these services (Directorate of Health 2013). The justification for health services for prisoners is strictly legal rights and humane values.[10]

Further imports

Opportunities like religious services and library services are organized in the same way as school and health services. So are cultural events such as plays, music and poetry workshops. Social welfare services are partly performed by social workers employed by prison authorities, partly by Norwegian Labour and Welfare Administration (NAV)[11] staff as imported services following the main principles of education and health services in prison (Schafft et al. 2013).

In our context, the significant characteristic of the services imported from the outside is that they are not integrated with prison policy and justified to serve the aim of rehabilitation; but they do not work against this either. They are independent from prison policy, based in their professional and administrative positions in society. Their results may, and most likely do, contribute to the prison policy aim of rehabilitation. This is a benefit. But this is not the primary reason for their implementation inside prisons. Thus they are not evaluated in relation to reported crime, nor brought into the setting of whether prisons function one way or the other. But other reforms have different justifications and occupy different positions.

Reforms co-opted by prison policy

This group of reforms is integrated with prison policy and tasked with curing crime. This is not a new approach. There have been several instances of efforts seen as self-evident measures to assist this task over the past hundred years or so until today.

Efforts to cure crime

Houses of correction from the 1600s on (Mathiesen 2006) absorbed a common and dominant idea at that time based on work and discipline. From 1852 solitary confinement was introduced in Norway as a self-evident measure for prisoners' personal improvement, ideas manifested in a huge brick building named the penance prison (*botsfengselet*). But complete solitary confinement did not produce the expected effects, and prisoners' work was re-introduced in an Auburn way (Eskeland 1988, Schaanning 2007).

From 1900 until the 1970s three different reforms were introduced, also with the expectation of curing crime for some groups of people. One group were alcoholic vagrants, and the measure was to criminalize drinking and public intoxication. The reactions were fines, imprisonment and, as a last resort, high security imprisonment combined with heavy farm labour for a maximum of three years. A second group were young convicts sentenced to reform school (*arbeidsskole*) for as long as education required, not according to the seriousness of the crime. A third group were convicts considered to be at risk for recidivism and being in need of psychiatric treatment.

The problem with these reforms was not their content. We find similar content among *independent* reforms: education, health services, farm work (Bastøy prison 2014). The problem was the obligation laid upon them to cure crime. This combination of services and prison policy led to other problems: the prison policy and system set the premises for the evaluation of results – which was to reduce recidivism. This was the effect asked for. But education, health care and farm work are established in society as answers to completely different situations and needs than reducing crime. Here they were given a strange and unknown task that they were not prepared to comply with – to cure crime. The three reforms did not work out: the expected results never appeared, but some unexpected ones did. Systems and professions were messed up: the prison system disregarded rules of law like the principle of proportionality. The professions adapted to the prison environment, and prisoners lost confidence in the services from the outside and the control system. They experienced the length of imprisonment as deeply unjust and lost their respect for courts, judges and the prison system, as they did not keep up with their own values and the rule of law.

1978: the end of aspirations to cure crime

In 1978 the idea to cure crime was finished as prison policy (White paper 1977–1978). The experiences led to the conclusion that treatment should not take place within prison, because it would be corrupted. Of course, there is still an aim within prison policy and among prison staff to rehabilitate and improve prisoners' situations, and to prepare them for their release, as has always been a task despite changes in ideology. But the aspiration is no longer to cure crime by education, farm work or treatment. To rehabilitate is designed as a moderate and complex aim, balanced and seen in relation to the rule of law and humane conditions (White paper 2007–2008).

Today: cures re-introduced?

But today we see some signs of reintroducing ideas of curing crime in Norwegian, and even more apparent in Nordic, prison policies (Nylander *et al.* 2012, Kolind *et al.* 2012). The protagonists are drugs. To consume, possess, store, produce, sell, buy or smuggle drugs is criminalized. Drugs are also connected to crime when their use and dealing imply stealing, burglary and other for-profit crimes. Illegal trade in narcotics often leads to violence, as does the use of some drugs. The authorities see it as a win-win situation to cure prisoners of drug use, as this is assumed to also cure other crimes (Circular KDI 10/2013). The scope seems promising, as around 50 percent of prisoners in Norway report having serious drug problems before incarceration (Friestad & Hansen 2004), and their situation in prison seems useful for a move towards a drug free life or one with the drug use under control (Giertsen 2012, Schafft *et al.* 2013). Today about 4 percent of prison places are reserved for prisoners with drug problems (Giertsen 2012).

But even if judicial and prison authorities see rehabilitation measures for drug-using prisoners as important, there are still no explicit political aspirations to cure drugs and crime in Norwegian prison policy.[12] This is not seen as the main and decisive argument for offering measures to prisoners with drug problems.

Reality nonetheless takes its own course, as in this case: measures to help prisoners with drug problems have been implemented at the same time as controls are expanding. One might have expected that control and sanctions of drugs would be traded for offers to help drug users in prison. But this does not happen. They both expand. Soft measures are not seen as being in conflict with control and sanctions, rather the opposite; they seem to support each other. This is the view of staff at all levels in the prison system (Giertsen 2012, Giertsen & Rua *forthcoming*).

The striking impression is that when services and resources are brought into prisons to support prisoners and prevent criminal recidivism, the resources are easily embraced and colonized by the system, silently subordinating the idea of punishment. The result being that the prison as idea and as a place for rehabilitation is strengthened, while the realities of punishment and pain are kept on the sidelines (Giertsen 2012). This illustrates the danger of tying up rehabilitation measures with prison policy, instead of keeping them in their own administrative and professional bases. This does not mean to give up on rehabilitation in prison.

Tuning down prisons

The point is one of who is in charge of rehabilitation. *The guarantee of return to society* (*tilbakeføringsgarantien*) (Soria-Moria declaration 2005) shows how increased rehabilitation may diminish the position of prisons. Surely, this is in line with the purpose of rehabilitating prisoners, underlining continuity between sentence and what takes place after release. This approach is far from new, but has been worked into PIA § 4, prison policy documents and implemented by prison officer liaisons and social workers for many years. But the *guarantee* makes challenges on release a more prominent political theme (Giertsen 2012).

This is not a *guarantee* in legal terms, but a statement belonging to the political sphere. Its main concern is to improve contacts between prison administrations and health and social welfare services to secure prisoners the relevant services they are entitled to.[13] Up until now this has been made concrete in circulars and law on municipal health and care (2011), but is not fully implemented.

In our context of reforms and abolitionism this guarantee is significant. It directs attention toward the health and social welfare services as the main systems that prisoners must relate to, preparing for their lives after release. NCS (fn. 10) makes this a decisive point: *prisoners do not belong to the prison system, they belong to their municipality before, during and after release* (NCS 2011).

Read into prison policy this means that the importance of the prison system in rehabilitating prisoners decreases, while the general health and social welfare services become more important. Prison policy certainly does not dismiss rehabilitation, which remains an aim to work for. But prison officials moderate their aspirations and become more realistic as to their contributions to rehabilitation. They reduce the instrumental approach a bit and bring forward values of legal rights and humanity (White paper 2007–2008). First and foremost, they place responsibility where it should be: in the ordinary public services, as it is for other citizens.

In an abolitionist context the reform of *guarantee of return to society* developed as a principle that *the prisoner belongs to the municipality*, it is a reform that tunes down the importance of prisons, in practical terms as well as in principle.

A Norwegian experiment

This experiment is based on the reforms since the 1970s (cf. above), all following an ideal of improving the position of the individual and his or her integrity, though in praxis improvements are still forthcoming.

These steps in prison policy reforms make it clear what this is all about. In a criminal law perspective, the crime is exceptional and entirely dominates the understanding of events and happenings. By using a sociological perspective on prisoners another view appears, which is about poverties. Prisoners need help to sort out dwelling, income, activities, health care and somebody to meet with for rehabilitation. If answers and solutions define the problem, then prisoners' problems clearly are poverties in all variations, as research indicates (Friestad & Hansen 2004; White paper 2007–2008).

Penal policy is policy on poverty, in some places given the form of incarceration (Wacquant 2009). In the Norwegian experiment the control apparatus picks up poor people and contains them, as elsewhere. But there is a clear intention in the Norwegian prison policy of today to hand them over to the welfare system, where they belong according to their needs and rights. By this policy, prisons will not stand out as tempting solutions to problems of poverty, drugs or crime. It will not be so easy to conjure prisons as welfare institutions.

This may be the Norwegian contribution to discussions on reforms and abolitionism: that prisons are for punishment and should be discussed as such; that reforms implying services from other institutions in society should, self-evidently, be implemented for prisoners. But when services are implemented they must never compromise, but keep their aims, professional and administrative bases intact, and never make ideas of curing crime their significant justification. Then there will be no problem to combine reforms with a clear position that prisons are for punishment and pain, and should not be used selectively against poverties as today, but as little as ever possible.

Notes

1. High Court 1977 in Hennum (2006: 10).
2. Christie introduced the import-model at the KROM-conference in 1969 (Christie 1993: 113). Vedeler introduced his principles at the KROM-conference in 1972 (Vedeler 1993: 121).
3. In 2010, 40% of all releases took place within one month (N = 12,135) and 72% within three months (SSB 2012a; 2012b). Almost all releases, a total of 87%, took place within one year, while 0.2% of the releases were made after five or more years. In 1981 twenty-one years was introduced as the maximum of imprisonment. There are no lifers in ordinary prisons, except for some in preventive detainment (*forvaring*) but these are very few.
4. County Governor of Hordaland 2013 (Fylkesmannen i Hordaland 2013).
5. *Kriminalomsorgens sentrale forvaltning*, later divided into the Department of Correctional Service and the Norwegian Directorate for Correctional Services.

6. § 3 "The convict has an obligation to take part in activity while serving the sentence. The duty may consist of work [. . .] education, programs or other measures suitable to hinder recidivism."
7. There are two main positions for people from outside the prison who work with prisoners. One is occupied by NGOs visiting prisoners for cultural, religious or sport events. The other is defined by the import model, opening up for professions outside the prison system to take on long-term, substantial work with prisoners. It is an important distinction whether employers of imported staff are public welfare services, NGOs or private enterprises (Donohue & Moore 2009), and this distribution varies across states.
8. The import model was implemented for health services in 1988 (Directorate of Health 2013: 12).
9. For an overview of this, see Directorate of Health (2013).
10. Circular KDI-10/2013, Directorate of Health (2013).
11. www.nav.no/English
12. As opposed to in Sweden and Denmark (Nylander *et al.* 2012, Kolind *et al.* 2012).
13. This is mirrored also in prisoners' situations: a large part of the preparations for release is about acquiring information and relating to administrations of prisons, health and social welfare services; learning about laws and regulations, experts and services and one's rights and possibilities (Giertsen & Rua *forthcoming* b).

References

Bastøy fengsel [Bastøy Prison] (2014). Arbeidsdrift. Landsbruksavdelingen [Work operations. The Agriculture section]. www.bastoyfengsel.no/arbeidsdrift-landbruk.html

Christie, N. (1969/1993). Models for the prison organisation. [Modeller for fengselsorganisasjonen.] T. Mathiesen & A. Heli (eds.), *Walls and people. A book from KROM on prison and penal policy.* [Murer og mennesker. En KROM-bok om fengsel og kriminalpolitikk.] Oslo: Pax Forlag.

Circular G-1/2008. *Circular on administrative co-operation between the education sector and the prison and probation services.*

Circular KDI 10/2013. *Rammebetingelser for drift av rusmestringsenheter i fengsel. Samarbeid mellom kriminalomsorgen, spesialisthelsetjenetsen og kommunehelsetjenesten* [Framework conditions for operating drug-measuring units in prison. Co-operation between the correctional services, the specialist health services and the municipal health services]. Oslo: The Ministry for Justice and Emergency & The Ministry for Health and Care.

County Governor of Hordaland [Fylkesmannen i Hordaland] (2013). *Education within correctional services 2012* [Opplæring innanfor kriminalomsorga 2012]. Bergen: County Governor of Hordaland.

Directorate of Health (2013). *Helse- og omsorgstjenester til innsatte i fengsel* [Health- and care services for inmates in prison]. Veileder [Guidelines]. Oslo: Directorate of Health.

Donohue, E. & Moore, D. (2009). When is an offender an offender? Power, the client and shifting penal subjectivities. *Punishment and Society* 11(3): 319–336.

Ekeid, Svein Erik (2009). *Tilgjengelighet i norske fengsler til sterile sprøyter og spisser for injiserende rusmiddelavhengige* [The availability in Norwegian prisons of clean syringes and needles for intravenous drug users]. Helsedirektoratet. Available online: www.helsedirektoratet.no/vp/multimedia/archive/00099/Tilgjengelighet_i_no_99349a.pdf [read 31.10.2011]

Eskeland, S. (1988). *Fangerett. En studie av rettssikkerhet ved fullbyrdelse av fengselsstraff* [Prisoners' Law. A study of rule of law while enforcing imprisonment]. Oslo: TANO.

Friestad, C. & Skog Hansen, I. L. (2004). *Levekår blant* innsatte [Living conditions among inmates]. FAFO-rapport 429. Oslo: FAFO.

Giertsen, H. (2012). Increased control, answers to poverties and looking for a life after release. *Nordic Studies on Alcohol and Drugs* 6(29): 589–604. url.: www.degruyter. com/view/j/nsad.2012.29.issue-6/v10199–012–0049–0/v10199–012–0049–0.xml

Giertsen, H. & Rua, M. (forthcoming). Møtested for straff og velferd. Rusmestringsavde-linger i fengsel [Meetingplace for punishment and welfare. Drug management units in prison]. *Nordisk tidsskrift for kriminalvidenskab*.

Giertsen, H. & Rua, M. (forthcoming b). Where punishment and welfare meet. Drug man-agement units in prisoners' perspective.

Hammerlin, Y. (2009). *Selvmord og selvmordsnærhet i norske fengsler. Selvmordsfore-byggende arbeid i fengsel* [Suicide and closeness to suicide in Norwegian prisons]. KRUS-håndbøker nr. 3/2009. KRUS handbooks nr. 3/2009. Oslo: Kriminalomsorgens utdanningssenter [Correctional Service of Norwegian Staff Academy].

Hellevik, V. (2001). *Bruk av isolasjon i norske fengsler* [Use of isolation in Norwegian prisons]. JussBuss. Department of Criminology and Sociology of Law. Stensilserien JussBuss, nr. 84. Oslo: The University of Oslo.

Hennum, R. (2006). Strafferett og straffeprosess. L. Finstad & C. Høigård (eds.). *Straff og rett* [Punishment and law]. Oslo: Pax Forlag.

Karlsen, K. (2008). Statsadvokaten banaliserer alvorlige spørsmå [The district attorney underestimates serious questions]. *KROM*, The Norwegian Association for Penal Reform, url.: www.krom.no/artikler_more.php?id=120_0_31_0_C

Kolind, T. *et al.* (2012). Prison drug treatment in Denmark: A historical outline and an anal-ysis of the political debate. *Nordic Studies on Alcohol and Drugs* 6(29): 547–560. url.: www.degruyter.com/view/j/nsad.2012.29.issue-6/v10199–012–0046–3/v10199–012–0046–3.xml?format=INT

The law on education [lov om grunnskolen og den vidaregåande opplæringa (opplæring-slova)]. LOV-1998–07–17–61.

The law on municipal health and care [lov om kommunale helse- og omsorgstjenester m.m. (helse- og omsorgstjenesteloven)] LOV-2011–06–24–30.

Langelid, T. (2009). Norway. T. Langelid *et al.* (eds.). *Nordic prison education. A lifelong learning perspective.* TemaNord 2009: 536. Copenhagen: Nordic Council of Ministers.

Mathiesen, T. (1974). *The Politics of Abolition: Essays in Political Action Theory.* London: Martin Robertson.

Mathiesen, Thomas (2006). *Prison on Trial.* 3rd ed. Winchester: Waterside Press.

NCS (2011). The guaranty of return to society. [Tilbakeføringsgarantien.] *Smått & Stort*, nr. 2, mars 2011. Kriminalomsorgen [National Correctional Services]. Oslo: Justis- og beredskapsdepartementet

Nylander, P.Å. *et al.* (2012). Drug treatment in Swedish prisons – moving towards evidence-based interventions? *Nordic Studies on Alcohol and Drugs* 6(29): 561–574. url.: www. degruyter.com/view/j/nsad.2012.29.issue-6/v10199-012-0047-2/v10199-012-0047-2. xml?format=INT

The Penal Implementation Act (PIA) (2001). [Lov om gjennomføring av straff [straffegjen-nomføringsloven] LOV-2001-05-18-21.

NSC (2013). *Kriminalomsorgens årsstatistikk 2012.* [Norwegian correctional services sta-tistics 2012]. Oslo: Norwegian Correctional Services.

Rua, M. (2012). *Hva gjør fengselsleger? En institusjonell etnografi om isolajson og helse* [What does a prison doctor do? An institutional ethnography study on isolation and health]. Bokserien Institutt for kriminologi og rettssosiologi, nr. 1/2012 [Department of Criminology and Sociology of Law]. Oslo: University of Oslo.

Schafft, A. *et al.* (2013). En *ny rolle for NAV i fengsel. Evaluering av NAV-prosjektet "Samordning av tiltak for tilbakeføring"* [A new role for NAV. Evaluation of the NAV-project "Coordination of measures for return to society"]. Arbeidsforskningsinstituttets rapportserie [The Work Research Institute's report series] AFI-report 12/2013. Oslo: The Work Research Institute.

Schaanning, E. (2007). *Menneskelaboratoriet. Botsfengslets historie* [The laboratory on human beings. The history of Botsfengslet]. Oslo: Scandinavian Academic Press.

Smith, P. S. *et al.* (2014). Isolation i skandinaviske fængsler [Isolation in Scandinavian prisons]. *Social Kritik, tidsskrift for social analyse og debatt* [Social critic, journal for analysis and debate] vol. 25 (136): 4–20.

Soria-Moria declaration (2005). *Soria-Moria-erklæringen. Plattform for regjeringssamarbeidet mellom Arbeiderpartiet, Sosialistisk venstreparti og Senterpartiet 2005* [Platform for co-operation between the Norwegian Labour Party, the Socialist Left Party of Norway and the Centre Party 2005]. 13.10.2005.

SSB (Statistics Norway) (2012a). Table 52. (Ref. 26.09.2012 Online: www.ssb.no/a_krim_tab/tab/tab-2012-03-08-52.html)

SSB (Statistics Norway) (2012b). Table 58. (Ref. 26.09.2012 Online: www.ssb.no/a_krim_tab/tab/tab-2012-03-08-58.html)

Sykes, G. (1958/1974). *The society of captives. A study of a maximum security prison.* New Jersey: Princeton.

Vedeler, G. H. (1973/1993). Frihetsstraffens innhold. *Lov og rett* [Law and justice]. In T. Mathiesen & A. Heli (eds.), *Murer og mennesker. En KROM-bok om fengsel og kriminalpolitikk* [Walls and people. A book from KROM on prison and penal policy]. Oslo: Pax Forlag.

Viljugrein, T. (2000). Skole, språk og fengsel. Undervisning av mannlige minoritetsspråklige fanger i fire norske fengsler. Evaluering av fengselsundervisninga [School, language and prison. Education for male prisoners of minority language in four Norwegian prisons. Evaluation of prison education]. Kompendium med oppsummering frå forskningsrapportane [Compendium and summaries from the research reports]. Bergen: Fylkesmannen i Hordaland, Utdanningsvadelinga.

Wacquant, L. (2009). *Punishing the poor. The neo-liberal government of social insecurity.* Durham, NC: Duke University Press.

White paper (1977–1978). *Stortingsmelding nr. 104 Om kriminalpolitikken* [On the penal policy]. Oslo: The Ministry of Police and Justice.

White paper nr. 37 (2007–2008). *Stortingsmelding nr. 37* (2007–2008) *Straff som virker – mindre kriminalitet – tryggere samfunn* [Punishment that works – less criminality – a more secure society]. Oslo: The Ministry of Justice and the Police. (Ref. 01.11.2011. Online: www.regjeringen.no/nb/dep/jd/dok/regpubl/st-meld/2007–2008/stmeld-nr-37-2007-2008-.html?id=527624&epslanguage=NO)

6

The fall and rise of preventive detention in Norway

Jane Dullum

In the preface to this book, Thomas Mathiesen maintains that an abolitionist stance may contribute to what he calls "turning points". Examples of such turning points in Norway are the abolition of forced labor for alcoholic vagrants and the youth prison system in the 1970s. The background for these abolitions was complex, but the abolitionist stance was indeed important. Another special measure – preventive supervision – was also under serious attack for decades. However, this measure was not abolished. The use of the sanction was for a period limited, but in 2002 it was replaced with the sanction preventive detention and two special measures for the mentally ill and the mentally disabled. These sanctions are today in full use.

This raises questions about recent developments in the Norwegian penal system and culture. The abolitionist stance succeeded in some penal fields, but not in others. Why was the sanction of preventive detention maintained? What are the social processes behind this? Can this tell us something about recent developments in Norwegian incarceration practices and penal culture? And to what extent are there challenges to the rule of law associated with today's schemes? These are questions that will be addressed in this article.

The situation up until the 1970s

Penal special measures were an important part of Norwegian penal law up until the 1970s. Special measures were particular initiatives instituted for offenders, initiatives going beyond the regular punishments such as fines or prison sentences. In Norway we had the special measures of forced labor for vagrants (implemented in 1907), reform school for young offenders (implemented in 1951), as well as preventive supervision for mentally deviant offenders thought to be at risk for recidivism (implemented in 1929). There was a condition for a sentence of preventive supervision that the offender had been subjected to a forensic psychiatric evaluation and diagnosis. Until 1978 the psychiatrists were also to state whether there was a risk that the accused, on the basis of the established mental state, could be expected to reoffend.

The concepts of correction and treatment were central to the special measures. The measures were indefinite, lasting as long as necessary for the resocialization of the offender. The young were to be cured through schooling, the older alcoholics by hard labor. The main purpose of preventive supervision was to protect society from abnormal offenders, but this measure was also eventually justified for its treatment purposes. The special measures thus had a special deterrent purpose; the justification for punishment dominant in Norway up until the 1970s.

The special measures were eventually subject to strong criticism.[1] The Norwegian Association for Penal Reform (KROM) was a significant voice and advocate in this criticism, which, *inter alia*, encompassed: serving an indefinite sentence was a great strain to those sentenced. The treatment ideology also led to people being locked up for much longer than they would have been with regular punishment. That the length of the incarceration did not correspond to the offence committed represented a breach of the principle of proportionality. Additionally there was very little happening to the offenders deserving the name treatment. The special measures were therefore deeply unjust.

Concerning the criticism of preventive supervision in particular, it also included that preventive supervision was applied to offenders who were more of a nuisance than actually dangerous. There were also many criminally irresponsible offenders who were incarcerated in prisons despite the fact that they should have been taken care of by the health services. A particularly important criticism concerned the participation of the forensic psychiatrists in the cases involving preventive supervision. The psychiatrists made statements on the risk of recidivism on insufficient grounds; the proportion of so-called false positives was high. This constituted a significant rule of law problem. Through their diagnostics they also gave partly stigmatizing and disparaging descriptions of the accused. It was therefore considered important to reduce the participation of psychiatrists in cases involving preventive supervision.

What happened next? Quite a bit. The abolitionist critique made an impact in several areas. Forced labor for alcoholics was abolished in 1970; reform school for young offenders was abolished in 1965. The reform school was initially replaced with youth prison, but this was also abolished in 1975. In addition, the use of preventive supervision decreased. The penal apparatus was also humanized in other areas during this period: The use of prison sentences decreased, and there was a decriminalization and reduction in the punishments for several types of crimes (Hauge in NOU 2002: 4).

New special measures for the dangerous are resurrected

But in one area there were also soon changes. During the 1980s the use of preventive supervision was again increasing. A legislative effort was also initiated to find *alternatives* to the system of preventive supervision. Several preparatory legal works were needed, but finally – in 2002 – preventive supervision was replaced with new special measures: preventive detention for criminally responsible offenders, and two special measures for the criminally irresponsible – compulsory mental health care for psychotic defendants, and compulsory care for the mentally retarded to a high degree. The measures are indefinite, lasting as long as the dangerousness persists. In principle this means that the measures can be lifelong. This is an area, then, where the abolitionist critique did not make an impact. So what are the new schemes built on? What is the basis for maintaining this type of special measures? In the following I will give a brief account of the rationale for the introduction of preventive detention and the special measures for criminally responsible offenders. Three arguments were prominent:

The need for societal protection

"There is a general agreement that there are offenders who are more dangerous than others, and that there exists a smaller group particularly dangerous to the life, health and liberty of others. This may be established as a relatively uncontroversial fact (. . .)", writes a task force that was instrumental in shaping the current special measures (NOU 1990:5, p. 105, my translation). Because of society's need for protection against these offenders the task force claimed that an indefinite measure was necessary.

So who are these dangerous offenders? For a long time offenders relapsing into property crimes were the largest group sentenced to preventive supervision. It is, however, no longer thought that this is a group which society needs protection from through an indefinite measure. Due to a general increase in prosperity, and that material destitution must be said to be a rarity in Norwegian society, there was cause for an increased tolerance toward violations of property rights. There were, however, other groups that society was thought to need to protect itself from now. These were offenders who had violated the life, person, health or liberty of fellow citizens. This would include, e.g. rape and sexual abuse of minors, arson, bodily harm (also resulting in death). These were also types of crimes that were increasing, it was argued. The number of murders was increasing from the 1980s onward, as was the registered magnitude of other serious violent crimes. It was acknowledged that an indefinite sentence was a disadvantage to the convicted, but concern for the individual had to yield to society's need for protection.

At the same time it was thought to be a *lacuna* in the penal code in regards to these offenses. Normally these crimes would qualify for what in a Norwegian context would be short to medium-long imprisonment of up to six to eight years. But an offender could be considered particularly dangerous despite this relatively brief prison sentence, it was thought. It was thus important to close this "gap" in social control (cfr. Janus 2000).

Dangerousness can be predicted

The second argument for introducing preventive detention was that it was maintained that dangerousness could be *predicted*. This justified subjecting these
groups of offenders to special penal treatment. KROM protested vigorously
against the possibility of predicting dangerousness having been improved,[2] but
in this they were not heard. The legislature agreed that dangerousness could not
be predicted with complete certainty, but here society's need for protection had
to receive precedence. Besides, there was to be a greater objectivization of the
risk assessments; the dangerousness of the offender was to be judged primarily
by objective markers such as the nature and severity of the presently and earlier
committed crimes. But an evaluation of the accused's mental state by psychiatric
experts was still desired. The contribution of court psychiatrists in cases involving
preventive detention sentences was, however, no longer to be required.

But the risk assessment at the time of sentencing was also to be supplemented
by a *continual* risk assessment of the offender. The duration of the preventive
detention was to be evaluated in relation to the convict's personality development
and risk of recidivism at any given time. This was maintained for the sake of the
offender. Such a continual risk assessment was thought to provide a sufficiently
ethical foundation for introducing preventive detention.

More treatment oriented prison conditions

The fact that preventive detention is indefinite, and that the duration is to be evaluated in relation to the convict's personality development and the degree of risk
of recidivism at any given time, should be compensated by particularly suited
conditions of imprisonment. The content of the preventive detention is thus to
be adapted to the needs of the individual convict. An interdisciplinary team of
experts was thought to best be able to lay the foundation for this.

So, in 2002, the sanction preventive detention came into force in Norwegian
penal law. The basic conditions for imposing the sanction are society's need for
protection; the defendant has to have committed a specified serious crime harming
life, health or liberty of other persons, and there must be deemed to be an imminent
risk that the offender will again commit such a crime. Before a sentence of preventive detention is pronounced, a social inquiry shall be carried out in relation to the
person charged. However, the court may instead decide that the person charged
shall be subjected to forensic psychiatric inquiry. (Penal code 1902, § 39 d).
When passing a sentence of preventive detention the court should determine a
minimum time frame not exceeding 10 years, and a maximum time frame not
exceeding 21 years. On application by the prosecuting authority the court may,
however, extend the fixed maximum by up to five years at a time. (Penal code §
39 e). In principle this means that the measure could last for life.

To sum up: in Norway, special measures for offenders judged to be dangerous
were re-introduced in 2002. In many areas the shape of the system of preventive

detention is not so different from the shape of the old system of preventive supervision. It is the protection of society that forms the basis for preventive detention, and a crucial point in relation to today's regulations is that they still rely on the possibility of predicting future dangerousness – or risk, in todays' terminology. Preventive detention is applied to a narrower selection of crimes than under the system of preventive supervision.

What is reflected by these developments?

What, then, is reflected by these changes in the abolition of some of the special measures and the maintenance of others, particularly of preventive detention? The space does not allow me to go deeply into these questions. Just a few words:

First of all this can be seen in connection with changes in how dangerousness is defined in Norwegian society. Vagrancy and property crimes are defined out of the concept of dangerousness, and are no longer seen as something which society needs to protect itself from through the use of society's most disciplinary means. Violent and sexual crimes are different. These are kept, and partially strengthened, as categories of dangerousness which society needs to protect itself from. Parallels to such a turn are also seen internationally, as described by John Pratt: "property based risks have almost disappeared from the dangerousness concept. Against this, the risks posed by those offenders who endanger the human body, but particularly the bodies of women, have been considerably magnified" (1997, p. 137).

There are likely several explanations for these turns. As concerns vagrancy and property crimes, the evolution of the welfare state is probably an important explanation for why these crimes disappear from the category of dangerousness. The introduction of welfare and social security schemes, as well as insurance schemes, has to a certain extent compensated for the material losses associated with these types of crimes. Violent and sexual crimes are different; here the harmful effects of these types of crimes to the victims are increasingly emphasized. In addition there might be a declining tolerance for bodily inflicted injuries. Protection of society has through this become relatively more important when it comes to the protection of body and life. We see this reflected in that the plurality of those sentenced to preventive detention – 48% – are sentenced for sexual crimes. Preventive detention is also imposed for murder, attempted murder, arson, robbery, assault and bodily harm.[3]

Perhaps also neoliberal developments can explain the turns described in this article. Neoliberal ideology is on the rise in Norway, and with this the invention of new forms of governing crime. These forms can be described as the re-emergence of punitive sanctions, disciplinary control and surveillance of "risky" populations. Today these risky populations are defined as persistent offenders, found guilty of violent or sexual crimes.[4] Simultaneously, these forms of governance imply a process of "defining deviance down", which means "lowering the degree to which certain behaviors are criminalized and penalized." (Garland 2001, p. 117). This process occurs at the lower end of the penal scale, and the main concern is cost-saving. Also this can explain why special measures for vagrancy and property crimes have been abolished.

Finally: as mentioned above, preventive supervision was subject to strong criticism because of the weak legal safeguards in the scheme. For the abolitionist stance it is important to ask to what extent there are challenges to the rule of law associated with today's schemes, and if so, what they consist of. As concluding remarks, I will point out some aspects that I consider important.

Contemporary challenges to the rule of law

First, in some areas it is reasonable to say that the abolitionist critique had an impact on the shaping of the system of preventive detention. There is a much stronger court regulation of the system today. Important questions that previously were decided administratively are now decided by the courts. The guarantees of the rule of law in preventive detention have thus been strengthened. However, in other areas, it is reasonable to say that this has not happened. The example below shows the statement by a forensic psychiatrist in court about a 26-year-old Somali citizen. In 2002, he was sentenced to preventive detention for three counts of attempted murder:

> The conclusion is that based on the most widely used available evaluation systems (HCR-20) for future risk of future violent behavior his scores are clearly elevated. Based on clinical expert opinion and the above considerations I have to express a considerable pessimism as concerns the prognosis. I particularly emphasize that he has a very poor basis for further development. He has no education, and no realistic plans to pursue one. His social support in family and friends seems meager, and his ability to develop safe, stable and supportive social relations seems to be rarely present. His ability to assume responsibility for his own social situation and his actions seem undeveloped, and this is stopped by a seemingly consistent trait of assigning responsibility to others and rationalizations.
>
> (Rt 2002–1667)[5]

The expert also found that the man met the criteria for the personality diagnoses dys-social personality disorder, adjustment disorder and mental illness pursuant to use of several drugs. In addition he largely fulfilled the criteria for psychopathy. The Supreme Court found that there was an imminent risk that the man would reoffend, and that a definite punishment was insufficient for the protection of society. The man was sentenced to preventive detention with a time frame of nine years and a minimum time frame of six years.

The quote illustrates a general hallmark of the preventive detention cases: the forensic psychiatrists are, as before, appointed in nearly all cases of preventive detention. And, as before, they diagnose the accused, and they make statements on the likelihood of recidivism – or more precisely: what is now termed risk. In line with legislative intentions, continual risk assessments of the convicts are also performed during the course of serving the sentence. And it is particularly in this area that there appears to be challenges to the rule of law in the practice of today's system of preventive detention. The problems associated with prediction of dangerousness and the participation of the court psychiatrists in this do not seem to have been solved. Finally, I will briefly point out some of the main challenges of contemporary assessments of dangerousness:

New risk technologies

As the quote above shows, the court psychiatric expert diagnosed the accused as having up to several types of personality diagnoses. The expert also explicitly made a statement on the risk of recidivism. The evaluation was based on the psychiatrist's clinical expert opinion, as well as an evaluation system for future violent behavior – HCR-20.

HCR-20 is a so-called third generation risk assessment tool developed to estimate and handle the risk an individual might represent. Internationally there have been developed several so-called third generation tools for measuring risk (such as LSI-R, YLS/CMI, SVR-20). These risk technologies differ from the so-called first generation evaluations of dangerousness, where predictions of dangerousness were based on clinical expert opinion, and the second generation instruments, so-called actuary risk instruments, based on criminal history data. The new risk assessment tools draw on historical, clinical and situational factors in order to evaluate risk. The quote above suggests that this is a type of knowledge technology employed in Norwegian courts.

Particularly from psychiatry it is claimed that the new risk assessment instruments have now made it possible to predict dangerousness with greater certainty than before. In Norway, it is claimed that the instruments are objective, and that they strengthen the rule of law, because they are rooted in research and trials from many countries, and because the premises for the conclusions are made visible (e.g. Rosenqvist and Rasmussen 2004). There are, however, reasons to seriously consider the criticisms directed by international research communities toward contemporary methods of predicting dangerousness – or risk – both in terms of the rule of law and ethical perspectives.

First of all, international studies show that the instruments are only moderately accurate and therefore should not be used for deciding such intrusive measures as preventive detention. In a meta-analysis of nine risk assessment instruments for prediction of violence, it was revealed that the instruments predicted relapse only "moderately well" (Yang, Wong and Coid 2010). The authors therefore emphasize that because of the instruments' "moderate level of predictive efficacy, they should not be used as the sole or primary means for clinical or criminal justice decision making that is contingent on a high level of predictive accuracy, such as preventive detention" (op. cit., 2010, p. 761).

There are also reasons to take seriously the ethical objections to the instruments. To name a few: it is asserted that the scientific claims of objective assessments disguise embedded moral/normative elements in this way of exercising punishment. The categorical scientific definitions of risk foster an illusion of objectivity. Hannah-Moffat (2005) shows that both the risk/need assessments and the prescribed interventions are predicated on the normative assumptions of the middle class, and that they are both "highly gendered and racialized" (p. 37). It is also claimed that the instruments individualize the causes of criminal behavior, thereby becoming more of a moral than a social tool (Stenson 2001). The instruments are also not aimed toward the improvement of social or structural conditions for individuals in need of help. In this respect the new risk technologies may contribute to the individualization of societal ills and to "the continued marginalization of populations at the fringes of the economic and political mainstream" (Silver and Miller 2002, p. 150).

Thus, there are reasons to claim that there are challenges related to how preventive detention is put into practice. One of these challenges relates to how risk of reoffending is measured, and the forensic psychiatrists' involvement in this prediction. These practices are therefore in need of serious attention and discussion. In such discussions the abolitionist stance will be of utmost importance.

Acknowledgements

The text is translated by Karl Boyd-Nafstad.

Notes

1. The protests against forced labor for vagrants were particularly fierce.
2. This was especially voiced in Thomas Mathiesen's article "Side et hundre og fem" ("Page one hundred and five"), 1990.
3. Personal communication, Berit Johnsen, KRUS.
4. And in Norway – drugs. But drug related crimes are not a condition for sentencing a person to preventive detention.
5. My translation. The quote is retrieved from Lovdata, an online system that includes all Supreme Court decisions from 1836, and all appellate court decisions from 1993.

References

Garland, David (2001): *The culture of control. Crime and social order in contemporary society.* Oxford: University Press.

Hannah-Moffat, Kelly (2005): "Criminogenic needs and the transformative risk subject: Hybridizations of risk/need in penality". In: *Punishment and Society,* Vol. 7 (1), pp. 29–51.

Hauge, Ragnar (2002): "Utviklingen av straffelovgivningen i det 20. århundre" [The Development of Penal Law in the 20th Century]. In: NOU 2002: 4 *Ny straffelov. Straffelovkommisjonens delutredning VII.* Oslo: Statens Forvaltningstjeneste.

Janus, Eric (2000): "Civil commitment as social control: managing the risk of sexual violence". In: Mark Brown and John Pratt (eds.), *Dangerous offenders. punishment and social order.* London and New York: Routledge.

Mathiesen, Thomas (1990): "Side et hundre og fem". In: *Hefte for kritisk juss,* nr. 3/1990.

NOU 1990: 5: "Strafferettslige utilregnelighetsregler og særreaksjoner". *Straffelovkommisjonens delutredning IV.* Oslo: Forvaltningstjenestene.

Pratt, John (1997): *Governing the dangerous. Dangerousness, law and social change.* Annandale NSW: The Federation Press.

Rosenqvist, Randi & Kirsten Rasmussen (2004): *Rettspsykiatri i praksis.* Oslo: Universitetsforlaget.

Silver, Eric and Lisa L. Miller (2002): "A cautionary note on the use of actuarial risk assessment tools for social control". In: *Crime and Delinquency,* Vol. 48 (1), pp. 138–161.

Stenson, Kevin (2001): "The new politics of crime control". In: *Crime, risk and justice: The politics of crime control in liberal democracies.* Cullompton: Willan.

Yang, Min, Stephen C. P. Wong and Jeremy Coid (2010): "The efficacy of violence prediction: A meta-analytic comparison of nine risk assessment tools". *Psychological Bulletin,* Vol. 136 (5), pp. 740–767.

7

Are we really witnessing the end of mass incarceration?

The strange politics of prisons in America

James Kilgore

> This is the beginning of the end of mass incarceration.
> – Natasha Frost, associate dean of Northeastern
> University's school of criminology and criminal justice

After more than three decades of "tough on crime," the New Jim Crow, truth in sentencing and three strikes, the law and order project looks adrift with no one rushing to bring it back on course. The bubble of prison construction is about to burst, if it hasn't already. Pretty soon it may be difficult to find anyone who admits they once advocated serial prison building and trying 14-year-olds as adults. Crime figures are down while other distress meters rise into the danger zone of unemployment, homelessness and deteriorating public education. No longer can Directors of Corrections masquerade as first responders and lay claim to unlimited funding streams. Budgetary and social justice alarm bells are ringing loud and clear. On top of this, as Soros Justice fellow Tracy Huling notes, a "newfound political will" from state governors of both parties "to close prisons and, in some cases, to reduce the overall size of their incarceration systems" has emerged. At a local level, more than 40 municipalities and counties from Kalamazoo to Jacksonville have passed Ban the Box legislation, which removes questions about criminal background from job applications. Even people with felony convictions seem to be getting a fair shake.

For those of us who have spent years of our lives in cages and for everyone who has been fighting mass incarceration, this reality is encouraging but also a little unsettling. We have perfected our mantras, honed our talking points of condemnation for everything from supermaxes to technical parole violations. Now everyone speaks like they are on our side. In a battle where the lines were once clearly drawn, the division between them and us is getting murky. After six and a half years inside federal and state prisons, I'm getting pressure to call prison guards "correctional officers," being told I must find commonality with them as "exploited workers." Such urgings push me into an uncomfortable corner. Time to take a deep breath and survey the lay of the land.

The carceral big picture

Capturing the big picture requires looking at several aspects of what some of us call the prison industrial complex.

The first is the numbers game: do we really have less people behind bars? The answer is, yes. For the past three years, the total number of people in prisons in the US has fallen for the first time since 1972, a post-2009 decrease of about 43,000 out of a prison population of more than 1.5 million (2.2. million including jails). No massive celebrations are in order, however. Some disturbing new trends are creeping into the mix – like the meteoric increase in the incarceration of women in the last few years. Besides, even with the reductions, the US still far outdistances the rest of the world in per capita incarceration rates, and states like Pennsylvania continue to promote massive prison construction projects.

Also, the numbers game isn't everything. We need to ask what happens to people who have been taken out of prison. Do they find jobs? Are substance abuse and mental health treatment programs available? Are they managing to avoid constant harassment by police? Do they really have a future or are they destined to live at the margins, in the gutters, alleys and board-ups of US cities? And most importantly, how many of them are locked up somewhere else just to keep the state prison statistics looking good? Answering these questions is difficult. That trending catch-all, "alternatives to incarceration," can become a shell game where punitive policies submerge themselves in benevolent clouds of risk assessment tools and evidence-based practices. Punishment adopts many pseudonyms.

A quick snapshot of the nation's four largest prison systems sheds considerable light on the complex dynamics involved. Let's begin with the good news in New York, where the most significant changes have occurred. Since 1999 the prison population in New York State has decreased by 24% with eleven prisons closed. Law enforcement officials have been quick to attribute these shifts to reduced crime produced by "hot spot" policing and "zero tolerance." Activists Judith Greene and Marc Mauer call the decreases the result of "a remarkable change in drug enforcement policy in 1999 that entailed an unprecedented curtailing of NYPD's 'war on drugs.'" These policy changes didn't come about through a spontaneous change of heart by police, nor did legislators simply wake up to budgetary pressures. Rather, the work of civil society groups like the NYCLU, the Correctional Association's "Drop the Rock" campaign, and the Drug Policy Alliance's Real Reform coalition exposed the bankruptcy of aggressive drug prosecutions. Eventually the public and then key officials like District Attorney Joe Hynes began to see the light.

Reforms to laws such as the removal of mandatory minimum sentences contributed to a decline in drug arrests, from 40,361 in 2008 to 29,960 in 2012. Moreover, while the stop and frisk policy has deservedly landed New York City with a New Jim Crow label, figures from the state Division of Criminal Justice Services show that black drug arrests have actually been decreasing – from 42% of the total in 2008 to 35% in 2012. More people now receive citations for minor possession. In other cases, instead of offering penitentiary time, authorities channel thousands through treatment-based diversions like drug courts. Relaxing conditions of parole is also part of the new approach, precipitating a huge reduction in returns to prison for petty transgressions like missing a meeting with a parole agent or failing to look for work. Still, even with all these changes, New York State's per capita incarceration rate remains at 425 per 100,000, well below the national average of 728 but about four times that of the United Kingdom and five times the rate in Sweden. Though New York has made great strides, forgiveness and mercy have not yet been thoroughly etched into the logo of the New York State Department of Corrections.

Looking west

California presents another version of the reform scenario: a set of administrative changes forced down the throat of the governor by a federal court decision. Despite its reputation as a blue state, California has been at the cutting edge of racialized mass incarceration. As recently as 2007, the state assembly voted 70–1 to pass AB 900 authorizing the construction of 53,000 new prison and jail "beds." But a high profile campaign by Californians United for a Responsible Budget (CURB), a coalition of more than 50 organizations and an advocacy heir of prison abolition pioneers Critical Resistance, slowed the state's capacity to roll out the construction. Then in 2009 the federal courts intervened. In a landmark move resulting from legal action by prison resident Marciano Plata, the court upheld the plaintiff's allegations that medical care in California's prisons was inadequate. The decision pointed to overcrowding, rather than lack of services, as the root problem. The court then ordered the California Department of Corrections and Rehabilitation (CDCR) to slash the population from its then 200% of capacity to 137.5% within two years. Failure to comply would mean the Feds would step in and run the system.

In response, Jerry Brown, first as state attorney general, then as governor, bought time with legal appeals while he developed his plan of "realignment." Vowing not to release people early, the governor "realigned" individuals from the state prison system by shifting them into county jails and community-based programs. AB 109, passed in 2011, was the enabling legislation, removing the cap on county jail sentences and clearing the deck for people to serve unlimited time in county lockups as long as they were "non/non/nons" – non-serious, non-violent and non-sexual. Despite disturbing results like one man being sentenced to 43 years in LA County Jail, Stanford law professor Joan Petersilia responded with typical Golden State hyperbole: "The importance of California's realignment experiment cannot be overstated . . . This is the biggest penal experiment in modern history."

This mega- "penal experiment" came with a local sweetener – extra funds for counties to accommodate the "realigned." Some sheriffs opportunistically used this money for jail construction rather than placing people in alternative programs. A few prosecutors developed their own pushback strategy: "upping" the charges to make sure a person's conviction would warrant a prison rather than a jail sentence. Despite these obstructions, the plan succeeded in moving some 25,000 people out of the state system over the next two years, but fell short of the court-mandated target. Earlier this year, the Supreme Court issued a final verdict: the state had to reduce to 137.5% of capacity by the end of 2013. Brown then added a second round of "bonuses" to local authorities for his pass-the-buck strategy – $315 million in extra funding to county sheriffs to accommodate their new immigrants from CDCR with the figure to almost treble by 2015.

On the surface, Petersilia does seem to have a point – that the importance of this "cannot be overstated." The issue is defining that importance. While Brown's counter to the Feds has bounced thousands out of state prisons, medium- and long-term impact remain in doubt. As more money drifts down to the county level, more sheriffs may opt to expand jail capacity rather than fund programs. If this occurs, the net result could be no significant reduction in the ranks of the incarcerated, but simply more people in county jails and less people in state prisons. This would be a clear-cut loss for the men and women behind bars, since nearly any state prison, even California's violent and racially segregated facilities where I spent a little over three years, offers programs and services vastly superior to those of most county jails.

On the other hand, if realignment were to succeed and keep reducing the number of people incarcerated in the Golden State, Governor Brown would have discovered a way of decarcerating by administrative fiat rather than a philosophical shift or significantly modifying draconian legislation and carceral practice.

Ultimately, the importance of Brown's initiative may actually be in realigning the CDCR with private prison providers. While California has largely avoided private prisons, with Brown under the gun to reach the 137.5% by the end of 2013, the governor signed an agreement with Corrections Corporation of America (CCA) to lease a minimum security facility in the Mojave Desert which holds 2,300 beds. While the privates generally are staunchly anti-union, the deal allegedly would staff the facility with guards from the ultra-right union, California Correctional and Parole Officers Association (CCPOA), a major backer of Brown's campaign.

In the meantime, CURB and many other groups continue to pressure against any expansion of the CDCR's capacity, consistently calling for the release of people with non-violent cases as a more meaningful alternative than Brown's administrative restructuring.

California's process demonstrates how decarceration is about far more than numbers. The recent hunger strike by men in the Security Housing Unit in Pelican Bay provides evidence that the punishment paradigm remains alive and well in California. The steadfast refusal by Brown and CDCR officials to negotiate with hunger strikers who were demanding an end to isolation cells in which some of them had remained for over four decades, revealed that little had been realigned in the minds of criminal justice authorities in the Golden State. Only continued pressure from below by organizations like CURB is likely to yield more permanent results.

Texas hold 'em

The upbeat version of recent criminal justice history in Texas characterizes the state as a poster child early adopter of prison reform. The narrative goes like this: when 2007 budget projections showed Texas would need 17,000 prison beds in the next five years at a cost of $1.6 billion, a now-retired, cherry red state legislator named Jerry Madden stepped in. A series of startling reforms ensued – including the spread of drug courts, mental health and substance abuse treatment and lower parole case loads. The resulting changes freed up some 12,000 "beds" in the state system, though Texas continued to carry out contracts with more than a dozen private prisons.

In policy terms Texas, once the beacon for the "make my day" set, did soften, especially when it came to releasing people on parole. In addition, a broad-based coalition which included the ACLU of Texas, Grassroots Leadership, the Texas Criminal Justice Coalition, AFSCME Local 3807, the Texas Inmate Families Association and several other groups successfully foiled attempts at private prison expansion. While the state managed to free up enough "bed space" to close two institutions, a look at the overall numbers is equivocal. Texas did register a decrease of almost 3,000 people in the state prison system from 2011 to 2012, but the numbers remain at 2005 levels of slightly over 152,000, still the largest state prison system in the United States. Furthermore, with an astronomical per capita incarceration rate of 923 per 100,000, Texas doesn't amount just yet to any beacon of hope. As a recent post from high profile blogger "Grits for Breakfast" asks: "If Texas justice reforms were so great, why does the state still have the nation's largest prison population?" Good question.

Where Texas has succeeded is juvenile justice. After a set of scandals involving abuse of youth in state lockups in 2007, authorities closed nine facilities and built community-based alternatives. Perhaps adult corrections officials should study their juvenile counterparts more seriously.

The federal system

Lastly, we come to the federal system – the nation's key carceral growth area. Despite the recent chest-beating by Attorney General Eric Holder about setting aside mandatory minimums, the federal Bureau of Prisons (BOP) has not succumbed even to the rhetoric of decarceration, let alone the practice. Instead, the Feds have adopted an expansion-oriented business model, partnering with private prisons to tap into the "niche market" of immigration detention and leading to an 84% rise in the number of people in immigration detention since 2005. In addition, Congress has imposed a mandatory quota of 34,000 immigration detainees – ICE cannot let the number fall below that figure, despite declines in actual "illegal" border crossings. Coupled with harsher immigration laws like Arizona's SB 1070, all this has led to a spiking of deportations, with 2012 numbers surpassing 400,000 for the first time in history. In a previous CounterPunch article, I have termed this wave of deportations "The New Operation Wetback," after an actual US government program in the 1950s which repatriated hundreds of thousands to Mexico. But nowadays deportation is not the only issue.

Under the current regime people with a prior illegal entry conviction can be sentenced to up to two years in prison before being repatriated. Those with a previous felony conviction who enter the US illegally can receive up to 10 years, 20 years if it was an "aggravated" felony. Locking up the undocumented has become the primary face of mass incarceration with the Feds leading the charge. The outcome has produced a drastic change in the demographics of those in prison. Since 2000, the number of African Americans in prison has actually fallen slightly, but the ranks of Hispanics have increased by more than 50%. This has provided a lifeline for an almost moribund private corrections sector. While the privates control only 8% of the "beds" in the system nationwide, in the immigration detention sector they own and/or operate roughly half of the "beds." Although the rate of African American incarceration remains about 50% higher than that of Hispanics, the large-scale operations of mass incarceration may increasingly be led by the troops of Immigration and Customs Enforcement (ICE) rather than drug squads or SWAT teams.

Conclusion

In New York, a popular mobilization along with politicians waking up to fiscal realities helped precipitate important changes. In Texas and California, the results have been much more uneven, with political pushback and bureaucratic manipulations like realignment stalling comprehensive shifts. While the national and state level conversation has altered, we stand at the precipice of a very complex period – the bursting of the bubble of prison construction can assume many forms. Tracy Huling points out some of her concerns in this regard: "I am worried that . . . entrenched special interests, including unions representing prison workers and for-profit private prison companies, might somehow combine to create the perfect storm."

Citing California Governor Brown's dealings with private prison kingpin CCA, Huling goes on to add, "In that kind of scenario, given the extent to which campaign contributions and other kinds of bribes already corrupt the democratic process, all rational public policy considerations about the costs and benefits of prisons might be thrown out the window." A key point which grows from Huling's analysis is that significantly changing the prison industrial complex entails wresting money and resources from corrections for programs and ultimately transformative processes that attack the problem at its core. In short, there is no stopping mass incarceration without redistribution of wealth and tax revenue, without attacking poverty and inequality.

Those who have benefited from mass incarceration will find new ways to resist change, new ways to brand and deliver their commodity. In 2010 the private prison operator GEO Group bought the nation's largest electronic monitoring firm, BI Incorporated. Clearly, GEO Group CEO George Zoley, who earned $7 million in 2010, thinks that GPS technology is part of the wave of the future. In a society where many people look for technological solutions to social problems, electronic home incarceration, especially as the surveillance capacity of GPS escalates, offers many attractive possibilities for investors and corrections power brokers. If prison and jails cells are rendered too costly, with home detention, families can shoulder the expense of room and board and the state can extract daily user fees for being monitored. Most programs already impose such user fees, typically from $5 to $17 a day.

Boutique prisons constitute a second reform which can sustain or expand incarceration. Not all forms of carceral punishment come with orange jumpsuits and electrified fences. Now we have a range of product variations designed to "humanize" the captive experience: "gender-responsive" institutions (which were part of Brown's realignment), mental health lockups (the GEO Group has also heavily invested here) and family friendly immigration detention centers where mothers and fathers do time with their children while awaiting adjudication. And lastly, in a society predicated on dividing the rich from the poor, we have the pay-to-stay facilities where folks in Beverly Hills can fork out $150 a night not to have to sleep with the riff raff. All of these "alternatives" keep the resources and the focus on detention and deprivation.

Ultimately, the reversal of mass incarceration necessitates not only designing genuine alternatives but transforming the dominant national mindset. Perhaps the biggest challenge to current thinking relates to notions of innocence and guilt. Often when I speak to people about decarceration or ending prison construction, they accuse me of advocating for the release of Charles Manson or backing drive-by shootings in inner city communities. But hundreds of thousands of people behind bars fall between the "non-non-nons" and the Mansons. They should be released long before their ridiculously long sentences have expired.

These people and their families are the major victims of mass incarceration. They carry the violent label in a legal system that has been structured to punish the violence of the poor, particularly that of poor people of color. African American youth catch a violent label for possessing an unregistered gun or get an assault on a police officer charge resulting from an aggressive stop and frisk. Latinos and poor whites earn the violent tag when they commit a robbery born out of the desperation of addiction or just plain old no food in the house and no access to food stamps because of a drug conviction. The bottom line dictates that if we change peoples' social and economic realities, we can change the way they act.

I have walked prison yards with many people I would not like to see back on the streets any time soon. But I have walked with far more people who were doing life or 30 years because they got backed into a corner where doing something destructive felt like or perhaps was the only option. To reduce US incarceration rates to the relatively sane levels of other industrialized countries, we have to decarcerate more than the non-non-nons. This will only come about when the social movement addressing mass incarceration grows stronger and begins to grapple with the complex racialized nexus of incarceration, poverty, inequality and the state.

Postscript

Let me end on an optimistic but contradictory note. For the past eighteen months I have been involved in a campaign to stop a $20 million jail project in the county where I live – Champaign, Illinois. After lots of ups and downs, just two weeks ago the county sheriff, who had been the chief inspiration behind the jail plans, stated that he had shifted in his thinking, was no longer asking for a cent for construction and was ready to experiment with policies that would keep people out of jail and avoid spending money on incarceration. At the end of the meeting, after considerable discussion, he reached out to shake my hand and I accepted. I thought about washing that hand as soon as I got home but I didn't. Still I'm not ready to call anyone a "correctional officer" just yet. Old habits die hard, and they usually hang around for a reason.

8

No data, no change

Bringing prisons out of hiding

Keramet Reiter

In *The Politics of Abolition,* now updated with a new foreword, Thomas Mathiesen analyzes decades of his own field notes from work as a prison abolitionist. Mathiesen's analysis focuses on cycles of revolution, reform, and retrenchment in Scandinavian prisons. He delineates the constant negotiation between advocacy for "non-reformist," or negative reforms, such as abolition of the system itself, and acquiescence to "reformist," or positive reforms, including refinements of the existing system. As reformists co-opt non-reformist agendas, revolutionary ideas wane, curtailing reform. In particular, Mathiesen explores the role of information gathering as a potential tool of both reformist and non-reformist advocates for change. He describes how information in the form of action research, as well as in the form of investigations of alternatives to existing policies, can be used to support either radical abolition or reformist refinement of existing systems.

Although focused on Scandinavia, Mathiesen's analysis has important implications for the U.S. prison system, especially for understanding the complicated role of information (or lack thereof) in movements for both abolishing reforms and refining reforms. The U.S. prison system often seems exceptional – exceptionally adversarial, exceptionally large, exceptionally harsh. After all, the United States is home to the world's largest prison system (housing almost 1 million *more* people in prison than China, its closest competitor). And the United States has the highest overall rate of incarceration in the world (751 prisoners per 100,000 population). U.S. prisons are exceptional for their lack of transparency, as well as for their scale and harshness.

Efforts to gather information in and about U.S. prisons have become a touchstone of debate for both positive and negative reformers. For instance, I testified at a California legislative hearing in 2013, and I argued for collection and analysis of data about the impacts of long-term solitary confinement. Other advocates countered: "no more studies are needed," because "we know solitary confinement is torture." In this essay, I will argue that the idea that "no more studies are needed" is potentially short sighted. Information gathering is a means to transparency, and transparency is a means to systemic reform. In other words, insisting upon information gathering constitutes the kind of "hard" reform Mathiesen ultimately suggests will move us towards revolution, or abolition, as the case may be, as opposed to the "soft" reform that gets co-opted as a means to maintain the status quo.

Three mechanisms of isolation render U.S. prisons invisible: geographic, political, and empirical. For each mechanism of isolation, information gathering has the potential to contribute to both transparency and systemic reform.

Geographic isolation

First, over the course of the U.S. prison-building boom, American prisons have become increasingly geographically isolated. Between 1970 and 2010, U.S. incarceration rates increased ten-fold, skyrocketing from a low of 200,000 prisoners in 1970 to a total prison population of more than 2 million in 2014. States quickly invested in building more prisons to accommodate this growing prison population. Over the course of the 1990s, one prison opened in a rural American location every fifteen days; in total, 245 new prisons opened in rural areas over this decade (Huling 2002, 2). California alone opened 23 new prisons between 1982 and 2000; the vast majority of these were located in rural areas, hundreds of miles from the nearest metro centers (Gilmore 2007). For instance, California's highest security prison, Pelican Bay, opened in 1989 in Del Norte County on the state's northernmost border with Oregon – 363 miles from San Francisco and 736 miles from Los Angeles, California's most populous city. Many states smaller than California depend on centralized, out-of-state prison facilities to accommodate growing, surplus prison populations; some states, like Hawaii, send more than half of their prisoners out of state to *private* prisons. Any given Hawaiian prisoner is likely housed 3,000 miles (or a minimum of a five-hour plane flight) away from his or her family and community (Johnson 2011). Such prisoners are not only far from home, but they are housed in private prison facilities, which are driven not by rehabilitative motives, but by profit motives. Indeed, private prison corporations regularly negotiate with state governments to set minimum occupancy requirements and bed quotas, which ensure prisons populations remain stable, or even increase (In the Public Interest 2013).

The geographic isolation (and privatization) of American prisons produces an abundance of prison management problems. Prison systems often fail to attend to the basic medical needs of prisoners, in part because of the challenges of attracting qualified healthcare providers to work in rural prisons (as revealed in the *Plata v. Brown* litigation in California, challenging healthcare problems and prison overcrowding). And prisoners housed hundreds or thousands of miles from home rarely receive family visits, thereby losing touch with their communities. This, in turn, creates in-prison disciplinary problems, increases recidivism rates, and makes re-adjusting to life outside of prison harder (see, e.g. Duwe & Clark 2013). As James Kilgore argues in a companion essay, prisoners constitute a "displaced and discarded labor force": isolated first within rural prisons, with little opportunity to contribute to the work force, and isolated later by the stigma of conviction, once they are released from prison.

Perhaps the biggest problem with the increasing geographic isolation of American prisons is that the isolation contributes to prison invisibility. U.S. citizens living in major metropolitan areas (as the majority of the population does) might never have occasion to drive past a state or federal prison. Public opportunities to actually go inside these facilities – take a tour, volunteer in education or self-help programs, or conduct research – are all severely limited, in part because of the geographic inaccessibility of so many U.S. prisons. In sum, prisons in rural locations trigger a variety of management and oversight problems.

But once prisons have been built in rural areas, physically moving them, or re-building them in urban areas, is expensive and politically unfeasible. Simply ceasing to operate any given rural prison is possible. For instance, in 2012, the state of Illinois closed one of its long-term solitary confinement facilities, which had been located in the southernmost tip of the state, 360 miles from Chicago, in a town with a population of just over 1,000 people. But many states, like California, are still expanding their prison capacity, making the closure of rural prisons less likely. But one means to overcoming the problem of the geographic isolation and invisibility of U.S. prisons is to work towards greater access: developing channels of transportation and communication to and from rural prisons. Another means is to increase transparency: gathering information to allow for public evaluation of prison policies, if not visual inspection of prison buildings. These pathways to visibility also constitute potential pathways to reform, cultivating policies that connect rural prisons more directly to urban communities.

Political isolation

Whereas the geographic isolation of U.S. prisons makes them physically invisible, the *political isolation* of U.S. prisons makes them legally invisible. By political isolation, I mean that U.S. prisons are exempt from many of the rules that govern other democratic institutions, including: constituent participation in policy-making; strict limitations prohibiting policies that infringe on fundamental rights, such as freedom of speech and due process; and judicial oversight of rights-infringing policies.

A number of policies unique to the United States distort the democratic participatory process as it relates to prisons. In all but two U.S. states (Vermont and Maine), prisoners do not have a right to vote. But most states also prohibit former prisoners – anyone with a felony conviction – from voting, for a term of years (up to life), or until the former prisoner takes some affirmative steps to re-establish the right to vote. An estimated 5 million U.S. citizens are currently disenfranchised through these kinds of restrictions (King 2008). However, these silenced prisoners exaggerate the voting rights of citizens living near prisons. In the United States, prisoners are counted as residents of the census tracts, towns, and counties in which prisons are located, meaning that disenfranchised prisoners count towards the number and allocation of votes in rural counties (Wagner *et al.* 2010).

U.S. prisons are also subject to minimal oversight from other branches of government. Whereas most state and federal agencies must provide public notice and a public hearing before making any substantial policy changes, most prison systems are exempt from these public rule-making processes. This expands the already substantial bureaucratic discretion of prison administrators (Shay 2009). Moreover, most U.S. courts have held that fundamental rights codified in the U.S. constitution have only limited application to prisoners. Rights to freedom of speech and association, rights to be free from unreasonable searches and seizures, and rights to access the courts and to have the protections of procedural due process, to name just a few, only apply to prisoners to the extent the rights do not compromise institutional safety and security (Boston and Manville 2010). And U.S. courts are extremely deferential to prison administrators. Courts reviewing prisoner claims about unconstitutional conditions rarely contradict prison administrators' assertions about safety and security needs. And courts require prisoners to prove that prison administrators actually knew and deliberately ignored any risks of abuse or harm (the "deliberate indifference" standard) (Dolovich 2012). This is a high standard of proof and a heavy evidentiary burden for prisoners to overcome. U.S. prisons function as island fiefdoms, run by wardens, with limited oversight from other branches of government.

This political isolation leads to legal invisibility. There is no "paper trail" of policies considered, prison disciplinary hearings conducted, or safety and security breaches justifying infringements of prisoners' basic civil rights. In my own work, I have detailed the absence of executive, legislative, and judicial oversight in California, as prison administrators designed and built long-term solitary confinement facilities, without documentation or systematic evaluation of the need for these kinds of facilities (Reiter 2013). Similarly, because prisoners do not have a right to a hearing, a lawyer, or an appeal in prison disciplinary hearings, public records of these disciplinary hearings are not made or maintained (as they would be for a criminal trial, for instance). And because courts defer to prison administrators when those administrators claim that safety-and-security needs justify infringing on prisoners' rights, little evidence has been collected about exactly where, when, and how safety-and-security breaches happen in prisons. Collecting exactly this kind of information – about how institutional policy decisions are established, about how decisions are made to treat and discipline individual prisoners, and about how and when violence takes place in prison, would render U.S. prisons more legally visible. And this legal visibility, in turn, would discourage deference to anecdotal claims, facilitating both evidence-based policy-making and more rigorous judicial oversight. Again, pathways to visibility might become pathways to reform.

Empirical isolation

Third and finally, U.S. prisons are empirically isolated, and invisible. As with the geographic and political isolation of prisons, this empirical invisibility is multi-faceted. At the most basic level, the United States is composed of fifty-one separate state prison systems: one in each of the fifty states plus the federal government's Bureau of Prisons. This makes comparing data and statistics across jurisdictions difficult; everything from basic terminology to legal structures varies across jurisdictions. What one state calls "disciplinary segregation" another calls "administrative segregation" and yet another calls "security housing." These kinds of labeling-and-definition challenges alone make tracking basic statistics, like how many people are in solitary confinement in the United States on any given day, virtually impossible (Naday, Freilich and Mellow 2008). Compounding these cross-jurisdictional differences, there is no single, empirical database tracking basic information about U.S. prison populations, like rates of in-prison violence, disciplinary infractions, and parole outcomes. Therefore, comparing and evaluating the effectiveness of various prison policies (or prison itself), is virtually impossible.

But data about U.S. prisons is not just hard to compare across jurisdictions; getting data at all, even for one jurisdiction, is frequently impossible. Often, individual prisons and state prison systems simply do not collect, let alone publish, available data (Reiter 2012). Even when states do collect basic data, they are often reluctant to make that data publicly available. In New York, for instance, lawyers seeking to obtain basic data about how many prisoners in the state were serving time in solitary confinement, on what basis, and for how long, resorted to filing lawsuits against the New York Department of Corrections (Kim, 2011). In the case of private prisons (one in every twenty U.S. prisons is privately run), corporations claim that responding to Freedom of Information Act requests would compromise trade secrets and profitability (Stephan 2008; Friedman and Petrella 2012). In both public and private prison contexts, media representatives are often prohibited from entering prisons, forbidden from investigating and reporting on conditions there (Ridgeway 2013).

Academic researchers face a different set of barriers in seeking to obtain data from U.S. prisons: institutional review boards (IRBs) at American universities review all research proposals and, under federal law, pay special attention to research involving prisoners, who are considered to be a vulnerable population of human research subjects. Although federal law permits prisoner participation in research about the effects of incarceration and conditions particularly affecting prisoners, many university IRBs prevent all, or most, forms of social science research involving prisoners (Zwerman & Gardner, 1986). The absence of basic information about who is in U.S. prisons and how prisoners experience their incarceration limits critiques of the system, hinders efforts at improvement, prevents administrators and reformers alike from learning from their mistakes, and thwarts the implementation and assessment of alternatives. In other words, more and better information could be used for hard and soft, positive and negative reforms. But without better information, both kinds of reform are often foreclosed.

From transparency to abolition?

The geographic, political, and empirical invisibilities, which render the U.S. prison system relatively opaque, make identifying and overcoming systemic abuses, and institutional failures, virtually impossible. Demands for greater transparency are the first steps not just to reform, but to revolutionary change. Transparency, through the systematic collection and evaluation of data about how prisons operate, will allow citizens, legislators, and judges alike to re-consider and re-evaluate existing prison policies. Unfortunately, in the United States, as Mathiesen describes in Norway in the 1970s, calls for more information and transparency are often met with radical critiques that real reform, not more and better information, is needed.

However, the recent movement against solitary confinement in the United States provides an important counterpoint to this radical critique. In 2011, some 6,000 California prisoners participated in a mass hunger strike, protesting long-term solitary confinement in the state. In 2013, in a second mass hunger strike, 30,000 California prisoners refused food over the course of one month. In response to persistent media requests for information about solitary confinement during the strike, the California prison system released data revealing that more than 500 prisoners had spent more than five years in solitary confinement in the state (Small 2011). California legislators have since held multiple hearings evaluating the state's long-term solitary confinement policies, and encouraged reductions in solitary confinement populations. California is not alone; similar, coordinated campaigns to raise awareness of the extremely harsh conditions of solitary confinement in the United States, through protests, art projects, class action litigation, and op-eds placed in national newspapers, have led to reductions in the use of solitary confinement in Colorado, Illinois, Mississippi, Maine, and New York over the past two years. And, as of 2014, Maryland, Texas, and the U.S. federal prison system were all developing systematic research evaluations of uses of solitary confinement in those jurisdictions. Of course, whether these reforms are sustainable, and whether they will lead to "hard" reforms like total abolition of solitary confinement, remains to be seen. But drastic reductions in the use of solitary confinement in some states suggest that harder reforms are at least possible. Meanwhile, raising visibility of the experiences of solitary confinement; increasing oversight of these institutions; and building mechanisms to enforce transparency through collection of data, legislative intervention, and media attention, leaves open the possibility of further evaluations, re-evaluations, and reductions in the use of solitary confinement. The movement against solitary confinement in the United States exemplifies the potentially revolutionary value of information gathering and increased transparency, where prison reform, or abolition, is concerned.

References

Boston, John and Daniel Manville. *Prisoners' Self-Help Litigation Manual*, 4th ed. (New York, NY: Oxford University Press, 2010).

Dolovich, Sharon. "Forms of Deference in Prison Law." *Federal Sentencing Reporter*, Vol. 24.4 (April 2012): 245–59.

Duwe, Grant and Valerie Clark. "Blessed Be the Social Tie That Binds: The Effects of Prison Visitation on Offender Recidivism." *Criminal Justice Policy Review*, Vol. 24.3 (May 2013): 271–96.

Friedman, A, and C. Petrella. "Press Release: Organizations Urge Reintroduction of the Private Prisons Information Act." (Brattleboro, VT: Human Rights Defense Center, Dec. 19, 2012).

Gilmore, Ruth Wilson. *Golden Gulag: Prisons, Surplus, Crisis, and Opposition in Globalizing California.* (Berkeley: University of California Press, 2007).

Huling, Tracy. "Building a Prison Economy in Rural America." In *Invisible Punishment: The Collateral Consequences of Mass Imprisonment.* Marc Mauer and Meda Chesney-Lind, eds. (New York, NY: The New Press, 2002). Available online at: www.prison policy.org/scans/building.htmll

In the Public Interest. *Criminal: How Lock-Up Quotas and "Low-Crime Taxes" Guarantee Profits for Private Prison Providers.* (Washington, D.C.: Partnership for Working Families, Sept. 2013). Available online at: www.inthepublicinterest.org/sites/default/ files/Criminal-Lockup%20Quota-Report.pdf

Johnson, David T. with Janet T. Davison and Paul Perrone. *Hawaii's Imprisonment Policy and the Performance of Parolees Who Were Incarcerated In-State and on the Mainland.* (Honolulu, HI: Department of Sociology, University of Hawaii at Manoa and Department of Attorney General, Jan. 2011). Available online at: http://ag.hawaii.gov/cpja/ files/2013/01/AH-UH-Mainland-Prison-Study-2011.pdf

Kim, S. Letter to Chad Powell, Records Access Officer, New York State Department of Corrections and Community Supervision. Dec. 9. New York, NY: New York Civil Liberties Union, 2011. Available online at: www.boxedinny.org/library/ (last accessed 29 Dec. 2012).

King, Ryan S. *Expanding the Vote: State Felony Disenfranchisement Reform, 1997–2008.* (Washington, D.C.: The Sentencing Project, Sept. 2008). Available online at: www. sentencingproject.org/doc/publications/fd_statedisenfranchisement.pdf

Naday, Alexandra, Joshua D. Freilich and Jeff Mellow. "The Elusive Data on Supermax Confinement." *The Prison Journal,* Vol. 88.1 (Mar. 2008): 69–93.

Reiter, Keramet. "Parole, Snitch, or Die: California's Supermax Prisons and Prisoners, 1987-2007." *Punishment & Society,* Vol. 14.5 (Dec. 2012): 530–63.

___ "The Origins of and Need to Control Supermax Prisons." *California Journal of Politics and Policy,* Vol. 5.2 (April 2013): 146–67.

Ridgeway, J. "Fortresses of Solitude: Even More Rare: Journalist Access to Prison Isolation Units." *Columbia Journalism Review,* Mar. 1, 2013. Available online at: www.cjr. org/cover_story/fortresses_of_solitude.php?page=all

Shay, Giovanna. "Ad-Law Incarcerated." *Berkeley Journal of Criminal Law,* Vol. 14 (2009): 329–94.

Small, Julie. "Under Scrutiny, Pelican Bay Prison Officials Say They Target Only Gang Leaders." *89.3 KPCC Southern California Public Radio,* Aug. 23, 2011.

Stephan, James J. *Census of State and Federal Correctional Facilities, 2005.* NCJ 222182 (U.S. Department of Justice: Bureau of Justice Statistics, Oct. 2008).

Wagner, Peter and Aleks Kajstura, Elena Lavarreda, Christian de Ocejo, and Sheila Vennell O'Rourke. *Fixing Prison-based Gerrymandering after the 2010 Census: A 50 State Guide.* (Northampton, MA: Prison Policy Initiative, March 2010). Available online at: http://www.prisonersofthecensus.org/50states/.

Zwerman, G. and G. Gardner. "Obstacles to Research in a State Prison: Regulated, Segregated, and Under Surveillance." *Qualitative Sociology,* Vol. 9.3 (1986): 293–300.

9

Afterword

Abolishing the architecture and alphabet of fear

Yvonne Jewkes

The history of imprisonment in the US and UK is a broadly shared history, with each country exporting penal philosophies and practices to the other, and in both nations crime and security have become the major battlegrounds on which political entrepreneurs have staked their power. Since *The Politics of Abolition* was first published in 1974, the number of prisoners in the United States has risen by 500% and the number of US prisons has more than tripled, from 600 to nearly 2,000. The UK's prison population has doubled in the same period and, despite promising a 'rehabilitation revolution', the Conservative-led, coalition government is committed to further expanding the prison estate, including closing some of the country's oldest prisons and commissioning new 'super-size' facilities.

As Thomas Mathiesen points out in this volume, societies with relatively little political participation, and low levels of trust and confidence in their political institutions and in each other, are more prone to rely on imprisonment. They are also more inclined to create 'others' of strangers and outsiders, to fear foreigners and foreign cultures, and to define offenders in relation to cultural discourses of vengeance and punitiveness. Politically advantageous discourses of crime and justice are circulated by the popular media, creating widespread acquiescence for longer and harsher prison sentences. With a very small number of exceptions, even in countries which traditionally have held relatively tenuous commitments to incarceration, a global shift has occurred in the four decades since Mathiesen first voiced his protest in print, resulting in a deepening cultural attachment to the prison (see also Drake, 2012). Moreover, prisons must pass the 'public acceptability' test including, in these economically challenging times, representing value for money, which is usually interpreted by the media as equating to the most basic living standards for prison inmates. But, as Mathiesen notes, public opinion may be fluid and has many, perhaps contradictory, components. In practice, we do not know very much about what the public regards as acceptable and unacceptable in the treatment of offenders. Nonetheless, our political leaders purport to represent our views and demand that the designers of new prisons not only pay due respect to ideas in circulation about what places of punishment should look like and feel like, but do so at a cost that will not incur the wrath of taxpayer.

So it is that the UK government is pursuing an oxymoronic policy of providing more prisoner places while saving money to the public purse. This is achieved by handing over contracts for the design, build and management of prisons to private companies such as G4S, which runs England's newest and largest prison, HMP Oakwood, which accommodates 1,600 prisoners for £13,200 per prisoner place – less than half the national average. Although costing approximately £150m to build, the imperative to save money runs through every aspect of the prison's structure. Its constructors 'future-proofed' it: although a Category C facility – officially a low to medium security facility, holding those prisoners who cannot be trusted in open conditions but who are unlikely to try to escape – the prison has been built with all the security paraphernalia of (at least) a Category B institution, accommodating prisoners for whom the potential for escape should be made very difficult. The rationale is that if, at some point in the future, it needs to be used to accommodate high security inmates, it can do so without the need for expensive retro-fitting of security. Consequently, Category C inmates, who would normally anticipate living in somewhat 'open' conditions (relatively speaking), as they are prepared for the minimum security conditions of a Category D facility and/or release into the community, are accommodated within high fences and walls with locked gates every few metres inhibiting their movement.

One life-sentence prisoner in the US has underlined the extent to which over-securitised and restrictive spatial arrangements manipulate their occupants and undermine opportunities for rehabilitation. Victor Hassine comments that many of the crises facing penal systems in the developed world – including overcrowding, violence, mental and physical illness, drug use, high levels of suicide and self-harm – are intrinsically related to the 'fear-suffused environments' created by prison architects (2010: 8). Prison designers and managers, he says, have 'developed a precise and universal alphabet of fear that is carefully assembled and arranged – bricks, steel, uniforms, colors, odors, shapes, and management style – to effectively control the conduct of whole prison populations' (ibid.). Unsurprisingly, then, to criminologists if not to politicians, Oakwood Prison has been plagued by problems since it opened in April 2012, including assaults, roof-top protests and an Inspectorate of Prisons Report, following an unannounced visit, that declared it unsafe, with high levels of violence and victimization and a passive and compliant ('almost to the point of collusion') staff culture (HMCIP, 2013: 5).

Nevertheless, the British Secretary of State for Justice persists in holding up Oakwood as a model prison and is currently planning a further facility, housing up to 2,500 inmates, in Wrexham, north Wales. To be built on the site of a former tyre and rubber factory that previously provided employment in the area, the new prison is due to open in 2017 and will house up to 2,500 inmates. When Wrexham was announced as the 'winner' of the competitive process to get the new super-prison, many local councillors treated the news as if they had won the lottery, which in a sense they had. The Welsh First Minister said the new prison will 'become a significant contributor to the Welsh economy, expected to create

1,000 jobs in the area, and bringing in £23m a year' (*BBC News*, 2013). There is now pressure on the authorities to improve transport links to the area (a somewhat remote area of north Wales) so that prisoners' families travelling from England can visit more easily. As with 'prison towns' in other parts of the world, an infrastructure will be established which will create its own micro-economy and will ensure the prison's permanence (Cherry & Kunce, 2001).

The drawings and plans of the new prison at Wrexham show that it will look virtually identical to its troubled predecessor: a large, bland façade with few, small windows, set in an uninspiring landscape with no trees (and, consequently, no birds or other wildlife) and with no views that are unobstructed by the high, yellow-painted metal fences that criss-cross the prison grounds. The external appearance of new-build prisons (not just in the UK but in most western nations, including the United States) – so nondescript that they practically disappear – might be regarded as a visual metaphor for the loss of public empathy for the excluded offender. We can turn a blind eye to the plight of those confined if we cast an invisible cloak over them and speak of them, and their confinement, in euphemisms. So, while we hyperbolize the character and status of those we confine, we simultaneously sanitize the architecture of fear. In the lexicon of new managerialism, prisons and jails become anodyne 'correctional facilities' within a portfolio of 'justice buildings'. Meanwhile, security within and without rises to a level of prominence that eclipses every other consideration, including what it means to be human (Drake, 2012).

By way of comparison, Norway's most recently opened prison, Halden fengsel, which cost a similar amount to construct as Oakwood, but which holds approximately 200 prisoners, might be regarded as an enlightened, humane experiment. A high security institution located in a forest which encroaches within the perimeter wall, Halden's exteriors are constructed not from concrete but from brick, galvanized steel and larch; the accommodation is open plan and domestic in feel, with large bar-less windows throughout; and the influence of the interior designers employed to help normalize and humanize the prison can be seen everywhere from the high-spec kitchens where inmates can cook for themselves to the photographic artwork adorning the walls of all the public spaces. But Thomas Mathiesen would be the first to caution that just because it looks humane to the outsider, does not mean that Halden is free of the problems and indignities that blight all carceral environments; indeed, experiments in flexible, aesthetically sensitive penal architecture and design might be regarded as representing a new and potentially more insidious form of control that brings its own distinctive pain, one all the more inhuman due to its apparent absence (Hancock and Jewkes, 2012). Moreover, the conditions of confinement experienced by prisoners at Halden must be viewed in relation to the general standard of living and level of public participation in the country as a whole; something that frequently gets overlooked in lofty proclamations about Nordic penal exceptionalism.

Whatever the experience for their occupants, design-conscious prison builds are certainly used by politicians as useful public relations tools. Halden is held up by the government that commissioned it as a symbolic manifestation of its penal policy and philosophy. Mathiesen might describe it as a 'showcase' facility that diverts attention from Norway's more basic and austere prisons and from other criminal justice and social control policies that have been labelled draconian by some Norwegian scholars (see also Ugelvik, 2013).

For abolitionists, then, designing more humane prisons is a thorny issue. As the prison building boom has become something of a feverish gold rush for architecture firms and construction engineers, one organisation led by San Francisco-based architect Raphael Sperry has, in Mathiesen's phrase, adopted an attitude of saying 'no'. Architects/Designers/Planners for Social Responsibility (ADPSR) has called for a boycott of all prison design, construction and renovation on the grounds that the current prison system is a devastating moral blight on society, and an overwhelming economic burden to taxpayers which has no place in society. Sperry is unequivocal, arguing that architects should be engaging in:

> making our country and our world a more sustainable, prosperous and beautiful place . . . Saying 'no' to prisons is a very important part of that. Saying we're going to make prettier prisons, it's not part of that. It's neither here nor there.
>
> (quoted in Fuss, 2006: 64)

The call by ADPSR for a boycott of prison building has generated heated debate within some of the main firms contracted to design and build correctional facilities, as well as more widely among members of the American Institute of Architects (AIA) (Fuss, 2006). Although approaching the experience of confinement from a very different professional angle to that of KROM and its sister organisations, ADPSR shares the abolitionist movement's view that prisons are inhumane and do not work, and has a similar goal in the sense that it is attempting to contribute to the creation of an alternative public space in penal policy, where rational argument and principled thinking represent the dominant values.

In the UK, a small victory would be for government to reverse the plans to build super-prisons with all the infrastructure they require and take a stance against going down the American route of using prisons for profit and making whole towns dependent on incarceration for their economic survival. Research by Liebling and Arnold (2004) in the UK, O'Donnell (2005) in Ireland and Johnsen *et al.* (2011) in Norway has found that the humanistic values central to the prison experience and to forging positive prisoner-staff relationships are greatly enhanced in small prison environments and significantly undermined in large establishments. Studies focusing on morale, trust, safety and quality of prison life all indicate that 'small is better'. Ian O'Donnell sums it up:

> Large prisons need to be highly regimented and life within them has an assembly line quality. Individual needs can quickly become lost in the drive to meet institutional priorities. These are dehumanising places where security

and order are difficult to maintain, vulnerable prisoners become isolated, and the slim chance of reform is further attenuated. To minimise the harms of confinement prisons must be modest in size.

(2005: 65)

When, in 2009, the British Ministry of Justice announced it was shelving its plans to build so-called 'Titan' prisons and promised a 'rehabilitation revolution', there was – briefly – some hope that money would be diverted instead into smaller prisons, crime prevention, healthcare initiatives and community based solutions. But now the Titan has returned by stealth and reform groups predict that shortly half of all prisoners will be warehoused in 'super-prisons' (PRT, 2013).

However, not all nations are irreversibly committed to incarceration. In the 1980s Finland recognized its high prison population (certainly high in relation to its Scandinavian neighbours and a legacy of Soviet influence on the country) as a problem and introduced a series of legal reforms explicitly designed to reduce it. These formal initiatives were backed up by a willingness on the part of the judiciary and prison authorities to use all available means to bring down prisoner numbers and by widespread public support for community service orders which were introduced in 1989 (Lappi-Seppälä 2000). As a consequence Finland has reduced its prison population from 113 prisoners per 100,000 inhabitants to 59 prisoners per 100, 000 (Mathiesen, this volume). Furthermore, while controversial electronic solutions may be among the reasons for Sweden's loosening reliance on the prison, that country is currently closing four of its prisons due to an 'out of the ordinary' decline in prisoner numbers – and this, despite no significant fall in crime rates (Orange, 2013).

In the relatively enlightened reaches of Scandinavia these changes are not entirely surprising; after all, countries with a strong commitment to welfarism may have a more tolerant news culture and little public appetite for excessive punishment. On the other hand, New Zealand, a country with media-shaped punitive attitudes similar to those that characterise the UK, is also turning the tide and aims to reduce prison numbers by 25% by 2017, having already achieved a 11.4% drop (Department of Corrections, 2013: 14). The New Zealand government has constructed a bold message about rehabilitation and recidivism that is designed to appeal to the public – essentially reminding New Zealanders that the people who serve prison sentences will in future be their neighbours, and if they succeed in reducing the number of offenders by 4,600, it means up to 18,500 fewer victims potentially (ibid.). The Department of Corrections does not explain how it arrived at these figures and it almost does not matter. They are persuasive and they allow the public to buy into the idea of smaller, more humane and rehabilitative prisons. Nonetheless, plans for a new maximum security prison to replace the dilapidated facilities at Auckland East will inevitably raise questions about the chances of success in achieving the goal of designing and building the 'right environment . . . for prisoners with the most challenging issues' (ibid.: 27).

An enduring problem for academics and other 'experts' when voicing opinions about 'improvements' in the prison system, including humanizing and rehabilitative initiatives, is that the accusation can be levied that one is simply tinkering at the edges and doing nothing of substance to challenge the institution of the prison itself. This is a dilemma familiar to prison reformists and the abolition movement. Given the upward trend in global prison population numbers, even groups such as KROM that were set up with a strong abolitionist agenda have been forced to switch their focus to reducing further expansion of the penal system and making prisons more humane. However, Mathiesen has never compromised on his desire to 'foster and develop an abolitionist stance, a constant and deeply critical attitude to prisons and penal systems as human (and inhumane) solutions' (this volume, p. x). The fact that different countries across Europe (and, for that matter, different states in the US) experience similar crime rates, yet have markedly varying incarceration rates, challenges the prevailing orthodoxy that greater use of imprisonment is unavoidable or is always desirable to the general populace. But now that the UK is following the American model of creating cut-price super-prisons for business regeneration in economically deprived communities, our deep cultural attachment to the prison as the primary form of punishment is being even more firmly embedded in the collective psyche. The challenge to abolitionists has never been greater.

References

BBC News (2013) *Firms set to cash in on Wrexham £250m super-prison,* 5 September. Available www.bbc.co.uk/news/uk-wales-north-east-wales-23965267

Cherry, T. & Kunce, M. (2001) 'Do policymakers locate prisons for economic development?', *Growth and Change,* 32(4): 533–547.

Department of Corrections New Zealand (2013) Auckland Prison PPP EOI briefing document, 1 November.

Drake, D. (2012) *Prisons, punishment and the pursuit of security,* London: Palgrave.

Fuss, T. (2006) 'Rethinking prison design: is it time to throw away the key to prison architecture?', *LA Architect,* May/June, Glendale CA: Balcony Media, pp. 62–64.

Hancock, P. and Jewkes, Y. (2012) 'Penal aesthetics and the pains of imprisonment', *Punishment & Society,* 13(5): 611–629.

Hassine, V. (2010) *Life without parole: Living and dying in prison today,* 5th ed., New York: Oxford University Press.

HM Chief Inspector of Prisons (2013) *Report on an unannounced inspection of HMP Oakwood,* 10–21 June. Available www.justice.gov.uk/downloads/publications/inspectorate-reports/hmipris/prison-and-yoi-inspections/oakwood/oakwood-2013.pdf

Johnsen, B., Granheim, P. K. and Helgesen, J. (2011) 'Exceptional prison conditions and the quality of prison life: Prison size and prison culture in Norwegian closed prisons', *European Journal of Criminology,* November, 8(6): 515–529.

Lappi-Seppälä, Tapio (2000) 'The fall of the Finnish prison population', *Journal of Scandinavian Studies in Criminology and Crime Prevention,* 1(1): 27–40.

Liebling, A. assisted by Arnold, H. (2004) *Prisons and their moral performance: A study of values, quality and prison life,* New York: Oxford University Press.

O'Donnell, I. (2005) 'Putting prison in its place', Address to the Annual Conference of the Irish Association for the Study of Delinquency, 5 November. Available www.iprt.ie/files/putting_prison_in_its_place__ian_odonnell_nov_2005.pdf

Orange, R. (2013) 'Sweden closes four prisons as number of inmates plummets', *Guardian,* 11 November. Available www.theguardian.com/world/2013/nov/11/sweden-closes-prisons-number-inmates-plummets

Prison Reform Trust (PRT) (2013) Bromley Briefings Prison Factfile, www.prisonre formtrust.org.uk/Portals/0/Documents/Factfile

Ugelvik, Thomas (2013) 'Book review: J. Pratt and A. Eriksson, Contrasts in punishment: An explanation of Anglophone excess and Nordic exceptionalism', *Theoretical Crimi-nology,* November, 17: 580–582.

Index

Printed in Great
Britain
by Amazon